Records Management

Sixth Edition

Authors:

Judith Read Smith
Instructor of Business and Office Administration
Portland Community College
Portland, Oregon

Norman F. Kallaus
Professor Emeritus
University of Iowa
Iowa City, Iowa

Contributing Authors:

Joseph E. Fosegan
Professor Emeritus
Alfred State College
Alfred, New York

Joyce P. Logan
Assistant Professor of
Administration and Supervision
University of Kentucky
Lexington, Kentucky

Karen Schneiter
Instructor, Business Department
Rochester Community College
Rochester, Minnesota

Reviewers:

Jane Connerton, CRM
Corporate Records Manager
PNC Bank
Cincinnati, Ohio

Kathleen F. Schaefer, CPS
Business Education Consultant
Colorado Springs, Colorado

Linda Studer
Associate Professor
Stark Technical College
Canton, Ohio

Sue Trakas
Instructor, Records Management
University of Cincinnati - Clermont
Cincinnati, Ohio

PSI ®
MODEL CURRICULUM
FOR OFFICE CAREERS

JOIN US ON THE INTERNET

WWW: http://www.thomson.com
EMAIL: findit@kiosk.thomson.com

A service of I(T)P®

South-Western Educational Publishing

an International Thomson Publishing company I(T)P®

Cincinnati • Albany, NY • Belmont, CA • Bonn • Boston • Detroit • Johannesburg • London • Madrid
Melbourne • Mexico City • New York • Paris • Singapore • Tokyo • Toronto • Washington

Managing Editor:	Karen Schmohe
Project Manager:	Marilyn Hornsby
Consulting Editors:	Mary Lea Ginn
	Kathleen F. Schaefer
Production Editor:	Denise Wheeler
Production:	CompuText Productions, Inc.
Cover and Internal Design:	Lamson Design
Photography Coordinator:	Devore Nixon
Marketing Manager:	Al S. Roane

Copyright © 1997

by SOUTH-WESTERN EDUCATIONAL PUBLISHING
Cincinnati, Ohio

I(T)P®

International Thomson Publishing

South-Western Educational Publishing
is a division of
International Thomson Publishing Inc.

The ITP logo is a registered trademark used herein under license
by South-Western Educational Publishing

ISBN: 0-538-71723-8

1 2 3 4 5 6 7 8 D1 02 01 00 99 98 97 96

Printed in the United States of America

Library of Congress Cataloging-in-Publication Data

Smith, Judith Read
    Records management / authors, Judith Read Smith, Norman F. Kallaus; contributing authors, Joseph E. Fosegan, Joyce P. Logan, Karen Schneiter. -- 6th ed.
      p. 432 cm.
    Includes index.
    ISBN 0-538-71723-8
    1. Filing systems. 2. Records--Management. I. Kallaus, Norman Francis. II. Title
HF5736.J6 1997
651.5'3--dc20
                                         96-9682
                                              CIP

Preface

RECORDS MANAGEMENT, Sixth Edition, continues the strong tradition of serving as an introduction to the increasingly comprehensive field of records management. As such, the Sixth Edition emphasizes principles and practices of effective records management for manual and computerized records systems. This approach offers practical information to students as well as to professionals at managerial, supervisory, and operating levels.

The authors' experiences and basic philosophies are presented clearly in this latest revision. Emphasis is placed on the need to understand the record life cycle within which information functions in the organization. Because the operations of all records systems—manual and computerized—rely on basic storage and retrieval rules, the authors offer a blended approach to the study of records management: traditional paper-based examples with current records management trends identified and discussed.

As a text for students in postsecondary institutions, RECORDS MANAGEMENT, Sixth Edition, may be used for short courses or seminars emphasizing filing systems or for longer courses such as quarter or semester plans. Basic manual systems concepts are discussed, and the concepts needed for understanding computerized records storage and retrieval methods are introduced. In addition, this edition updates other aspects of information technology such as the Internet, optical disk storage systems, image systems, and electronic mail, which are having an increased impact on the records management field.

As a reference book, this latest edition of RECORDS MANAGEMENT serves several purposes. It presents sound principles of records management that include the entire range of records—paper, image records, and electronic media used in computerized systems. Although the key management functions as they relate to records management are introduced, emphasis is placed on control for ensuring that the records system achieves its stated goals. Professionals who direct the operation of records systems will find this Sixth

Edition to be especially valuable because it includes alphabetic indexing rules that agree with the Simplified Filing Standard Rules of the Association for Records Managers and Administrators, Inc.

Organization of the Text

The text consists of 5 parts organized into 12 chapters and 2 appendixes. Part 1 introduces the student to the expanding area of records management. Following this overview, Part 2 centers on alphabetic storage and retrieval methods for manual and computerized systems. Part 3 presents a detailed description of adaptations of the alphabetic storage and retrieval method—namely, subject, numeric, and geographic storage methods.

Part 4 covers information technology, which includes a thorough update of image systems and the emerging technology that integrates the computer with other automated records systems. This part also stresses the continuing need to understand basic records management principles before delving into the complexities of computerized systems. To complete the textbook from a management perspective, Part 5 offers a comprehensive view of the role of control in records systems. In addition, it reviews many practical procedures for controlling paperwork problems in both large and small offices. Appendix A describes career and job descriptions in the records management field; Appendix B describes card and special records commonly used in many offices.

Learning objectives for the student are included at the beginning of each chapter. Important terms are printed in bold type throughout each chapter and are listed alphabetically at the end of each chapter for easy review. In the Glossary at the back of the textbook, these same terms are defined. Marginal questions that urge students to read carefully for meaning are included in each chapter. In appropriate chapters, a "Current Trends in Records Management" section presents the latest practices in records management and emphasizes the use of computers to facilitate storage and retrieval in manual, paper-based records systems. Bar coding is discussed throughout the Sixth Edition as a technology that enhances records storage and retrieval of any records media. New Review and Discussion items are provided at the end of each chapter.

The content of each application is identified by one or more icons. These symbols specify the learning intent as follows:

Critical Thinking

 Collaborative Learning

 International/Intercultural

 Template Application

 Practice Set

Practice Set

The filing practice set that accompanies RECORDS MANAGEMENT, entitled RECORDS MANAGEMENT PROJECTS, Sixth Edition, features a new business and includes a template disk for students to use with word processing, spreadsheet, or database application software programs. This set of practical learning materials consists of 12 filing jobs in which students practice card filing and correspondence filing in alphabetic, subject, consecutive numeric, terminal-digit numeric, and geographic filing systems. In addition, students will practice requisition/charge-out and transfer procedures.

Study Guide

The Study Guide, which is designed to reinforce the material covered in the textbook, includes review of important terms, sample test questions, and several practical activities to supplement the textbook exercises assigned by the instructor.

Printed Tests

The printed tests that accompany RECORDS MANAGEMENT, Sixth Edition, include a Placement Test, four Achievement Tests, and a Final Examination. Instructors receive an overprinted test key.

Computer Test Package

A flexible, easy-to-use test bank contains objective questions for each chapter. Questions can be modified, and instructor-written questions can be added.

Transparency Masters

A separate package of 120 transparency masters is available to instructors when the text is adopted. Masters for each textbook chapter and practice set solutions are included in this package.

Presentation Software

Each chapter is supported with WordPerfect Presentation® slides for use during class discussions. A Presentations disk is available when the text is adopted. Teaching suggestions for using the slides are included in each chapter of the Instructor's Manual.

Application Template

End-of-chapter applications may be solved using commercial application software and the template disk that accompanies the textbook. These applications are identified by a template icon in the textbook.

Instructor's Manual

The Instructor's Manual that accompanies RECORDS MANAGE-MENT, Sixth Edition, provides instructors with suggested methods of instruction, teaching aids, and time schedules that apply to different teaching situations. Teaching suggestions are also provided for each chapter, in addition to answers to Review and Discussion, solutions to the end-of-chapter Applications, and solutions to the Checking Your Knowledge of the Rules activities that appear in Chapters 2 and 3. An extra coding activity is included for both Chapters 2 and 3, and a test covering the ten alphabetic indexing rules is included after Chapter 3. The names in the extra coding activity are available on the template disk. Detailed solutions for all practice set jobs are also included in the Instructor's Manual, in addition to the finding tests to be used with the practice set and their solutions.

Acknowledgments

The authors are grateful to many firms and individuals who assisted in completing this extensive revision of RECORDS MANAGEMENT. Further, we appreciate the help of the filing equipment and supplies manufacturers and vendors who gave time and information to the authors in their efforts to update this edition effectively. A special thank you to the members of the Records Management Listserv, in particular to Maralyn Harmston, the host.

The authors are especially grateful to the following individuals who served as contributing authors on this edition: Dr. Joyce Logan— University of Kentucky, Lexington, Kentucky; Joseph Fosegan—State University of New York, Alfred, New York; and Karen Schneiter— Rochester Community College, Rochester, Minnesota.

Special thanks are given to the following people whose critical review provided helpful guidance to the authors: Kathy Schaefer, CPS, Colorado Springs, CO; Jane Connerton, CRM, Cincinnati, OH; Linda Studer, Stark Technical Institute, Akron, OH; Sue Trakas, Clermont College, Batavia, OH; and Karen Schneiter, Rochester Community College, Rochester, MN.

In addition, special appreciation is extended to our families, friends, co-workers, project manager, our consulting editors, and each other whose encouragement and direction have been invaluable in completing this revision. The result, we believe, is an easily understandable, instructive, up-to-date introduction to the field of records management.

Judy Read Smith
Norman F. Kallaus

Contents

Part 3   Subject, Numeric, and Geographic Storage and Retrieval

Part 4 Records Management Technology

Part 5　Records Control

Appendices

Part 1

The Field of Records Management

1 *An Overview of Records Management*

Part 1 introduces you to the field of records management and to the nature and purpose of records. Also, this first part includes a concise treatment of records management history, current trends in records management, and key legislation important to the effective operation of modern business firms. Highlights of the part are the discussion of records management as a key organizational function and careers in records management.

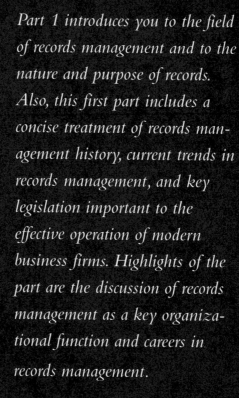

Chapter 1

An Overview of Records Management

Learning Objectives

1. Describe how records are classified and used in an office.
2. Compare early and modern records management operations.
3. Discuss relevant legislation that affects records management.
4. Describe the management functions necessary to operate a records management program effectively.
5. Identify possible careers in records management.

I n most jobs today, workers are increasing their use of information. This time in our history frequently is called the *Information Age*; this generation often is called the *Information Society*. Computers, so much a part of today's world, are called *information-processing machines* because of their key role in information systems. To survive, businesses and organizations must have up-to-date *information* in the *right form*, at the *right time*, and in the *right place* to make management decisions. In other words, information is an important and valuable business resource. Finally, most people use information minute by minute to manage their lives and to perform their jobs.

Generally information is stored on records of various types; and, in turn, records are organized into complex systems. As workers rely more and more on information and as the volume of information increases, greater numbers of records are needed. Similar to all other office "products," records must be properly managed.

In this overview chapter, you are introduced to important records management terms and concepts, to a brief history of records, to current trends in records management, and to legislation to control records. You will also learn about the content of records management programs and about careers in records management. Keep in mind that this textbook deals with records in business firms. However, the principles you learn should also help you understand how to use records efficiently in other types of organizations and in your home.

Why is this time in history called the Information Age?

Records: Classification and Use

Your study of records management includes several basic concepts: definitions of key terms, classifications of records, and reasons why records are used and will continue to be used. As you study these concepts, relate them to your personal situation as well as to your job if you are now employed. By doing so, you will learn more quickly and retain better what you will need for future work in an office.

A **record** is recorded information, regardless of media or characteristics, created or received, and used in the operation of an organization.[1] The most common records such as correspondence (letters and memorandums), reports, forms, and books usually appear on paper. An organization may receive these records through regular mail, facsimile machines (fax), special couriers, or electronically by computer networks. Correspondence, reports, and forms are often created through word processing software programs.

Other types of records to consider are *oral records* that capture the human voice and are stored on cassettes and other magnetic media. Records also are stored on films such as movies, videotapes, photographs, and microfilm. In addition, records are produced by and stored in computers and on optical disks, which are discussed in Chapter 10. Figure 1-1 shows three familiar record forms.

What is a record?

A–A record on a computer screen

Photo by Alan Brown / Photonics Graphics

B–A record on microfilm

Photo Courtesy of Eastman Kodak Co.

C–A record being scanned for computer use

Hewlett Packard

Figure 1-1   Common Record Forms

---

[1] Definitions throughout this textbook are consistent with those in the *Glossary of Records Management Terms*, ARMA International Guideline (Prairie Village, KS: ARMA International 1989); and *A Glossary for Archivists, Manuscript Curators, and Records Managers*, compiled by Lewis J. Bellardo and Lynn L. Bellardo (Chicago: The Society of American Archivists 1992).

Records are valuable property, or resources, of a firm; and, similar to all other resources, they must be managed properly. **Records management** is the systematic control of all records from their creation or receipt, through their processing, distribution, organization, storage, and retrieval, and to their ultimate disposition.

How Records Are Classified

How are records classified?

Records usually are classified in three basic ways: (1) by the type of *use,* (2) by the *place where they are used,* and (3) by the *value* of the records to the firm. Each classification is discussed in this section.

Classification by Use. Classification according to records use includes transaction documents and reference documents. A **transaction document** is a record a firm uses in its day-to-day operations. These documents consist primarily of business forms. Examples are invoices, requisitions, purchase and sales orders, bank checks, statements, contracts, shipping documents, and personnel records such as employment applications and attendance reports. A **reference document**, on the other hand, contains information a firm needs to carry on its operations over long periods of time. These records are referenced for information about previous decisions, quotations on items to purchase, statements of administrative policy, and plans for running the firm. Common reference documents, the most frequently used category of records maintained in an office, are business letters, reports, and interoffice memorandums. Other examples include catalogs, price lists, brochures, and pamphlets.

Classification by Place of Use. Classification by *place of use* of records refers to external and internal records. An **external record** is created for use outside a firm. Examples of such records are letters or faxes sent to a customer or client, to suppliers, or to the various government branches. The larger group of records classified by their place of use is internal records. An **internal record** contains information needed to operate a firm. Such a record may be created inside or outside a firm. Examples are communications between a firm and its employees (payroll records, bulletins, newsletters, and government regulations) and communications among a firm's departments (inventory control records, interoffice memorandums, purchase requisitions, and reports). Important internal records maintained by the accounting department document the presence and use of assets and liabilities and information essential for local, state, and federal tax purposes.

Classification by Value of the Record to the Firm. From an inventory and analysis of the use of each major record, a manager determines the *value of the record* to the firm. Then, on the basis of this evaluation, the manager develops a retention schedule to determine how long to keep all the firm's key records. The retention of records, an important part of a records management program, is discussed in Chapters 6 and 12.

Each record maintained by a firm falls into one of four categories that determine *how long records should be retained*. These categories are (1) vital, (2) important, (3) useful, and (4) nonessential.

Vital records must be kept permanently because they are needed for continuing the firm's operations and are usually not replaceable. Legal papers such as articles of incorporation and titles to property that a firm owns are vital records. Reports to shareholders and minutes of important board meetings are considered vital records because they are the official records of decisions made. **Important records** assist in performing a firm's business operations and, if destroyed, are replaceable only at great cost. Accounts receivable and sales records, financial and tax records, and selected correspondence and reports are important records. **Useful records** are helpful in conducting business operations and may, if destroyed, be replaced at slight cost. General correspondence (letters, memorandums, and faxes) and bank statements are useful records that may be destroyed after their value has passed. The least valuable records, **nonessential records**, should be destroyed after use. Examples of nonessential records are announcements and bulletins to employees, acknowledgments, and routine telephone messages.

Why Records Are Used

Records serve as the "memory" of a business. They "remember" the information needed for operating the firm. For example, management policies are developed and recorded to furnish broad guidelines for operating a business. Each department (for example, finance, marketing, accounting, and human resources) bases its entire method of

How do internal and external records differ?

What are the four categories of records that determine how long records should be retained?

What serves as the memory of a firm?

operations upon records. Records usually are used because they have one or more of the following values to a firm:

1. *Administrative value* in that records help employees perform office operations within the firm. Examples of such records include policy and procedures manuals and handbooks and organizational charts.

2. *Fiscal value* because records may be used to conduct current or future financial or fiscal business. Fiscal records can document operating funds or can serve tax audit purposes. Examples of such records include tax returns and records of financial transactions such as purchase and sales orders, invoices, balance sheets, and income statements.

3. *Legal value* because records provide evidence of business transactions. Examples of such records include contracts, financial agreements that are legally binding, deeds to property owned, and articles of incorporation.

4. *Historical value* because records furnish information about the firm's operations and major shifts of direction over the years. Minutes of meetings, corporate charters, public relations documents, and information on corporate officers all fall into this records category. In addition, the value of many records increases with the passage of time. Original copies of the Declaration of Independence and the Gettysburg Address are well-known examples, as is the original drawing of Ford's first Model T automobile.

Why do individuals keep personal records?

From a personal standpoint, why do you keep your diploma, birth certificate, title to your car, or promissory note that provided you with the money to attend college? The answer is simple: *In today's complex world, people cannot get along without records! They need records for the information they contain.*

Records Management History

Museums in the United States or in ancient civilizations such as those in Greece and Italy house many examples of early records. Examples include religious scrolls, documents proclaiming control over conquered people, and hieroglyphics describing early life styles. Carvings on cave walls in Latin America tell about the lives of early inhabitants and how they conducted their business affairs. Tours of early Native American dwellings in the western United States provide similar examples of records of early tribal life. Computerized records in a variety of formats (including written, audio, video, and magnetic records) provide information about the population and the way businesses operate in the United States. When comparing the records of earlier periods in history with those of the computer age, records and attitudes toward them have changed significantly.

Early Records

Most business records before 1600 were based on simple trade transactions that provided evidence of moneys received and spent, lists of articles bought and sold, and simple contracts. Such records and any copies were created by hand (that is, *manually*) until the printing press and later the typewriter were invented. These machines increased the speed by which records were created and processed.

What was the common form for most records until the 1950s?

Until the 1950s, when computers were first used in business, records were almost entirely paper documents. The most important emphasis during this stage in history was getting the records properly placed in the files. Emphasis on retrieval occurred later (see Figure 1-2).

Before World War II, management directed most business efforts toward the factory or plant. Usually the plant work force was large compared with the office staff. Consequently, managers gave their main attention to the factory because it produced the salable products that resulted in profits and against which expenses were charged. In such a setting, management assumed that records should be the sole responsibility of the office staff. Little importance or status was granted to records and to records management functions.

Modern Records

Since the early 1980s, over 60 percent of the gross domestic product (GDP) has been based on information services. This significant change from the 1950s industrial-based economy is evident in the volume and type of records. Business records are no longer just records of accounting transactions. Correspondence and information about customers are prevalent because these records are important resources about customers

How have records evolved since the 1950s?

who buy the services a firm sells. In addition, records are stored on magnetic media, microforms, and optical media as well as in paper form. Fast, accurate retrieval helps a firm meet customer needs as shown in Figure 1-2.

Figure 1-2   **Retrieving Records from a Computer**

The creation of records, the media on which records are stored, and the different types of records have evolved since the 1950s. Increasing use of technology in an increasingly global marketplace makes the management of records an important resource for a firm. The next section discusses current trends in records management.

Current Trends in Records Management

Even though more businesses than ever are purchasing and using electronic mail systems and producing documents electronically, paper use continues to increase in offices. "American businesses use more than 3.5 tons of cut sheet paper a year . . . Every employee sitting at a desk in the U.S. uses 250 pounds of paper per year."[2]

The proliferation of paper may be caused by increasing sales of equipment such as copiers, facsimile machines, and laser printers that use and produce volumes of paper. The use of electronic documents is expected to increase dramatically in the next ten years; however, the use

[2] Nancy Dunn Cosgrove, "The Paperless Office: Still a Myth in the Nineties," *The Office*, April 1993, p. 25.

of paper documents will double during the same period.[3] Another reason for the continued use of paper is its proven durability and permanence. Paper is also a friendly information interface; no special technology is needed to read information on paper, and it is conveniently transportable.

Consequently, records managers must deal with increasing numbers of records—both paper and electronic. What are some of the more common electronic records? Electronic records are discussed in the next section.

Why is the use of paper in offices increasing?

Electronic Records. An **electronic record** is created by an electronic device such as a computer and is stored on electronic media. Until the 1980s, computer records were mostly financial or other statistical data stored on punched cards or reels of tapes. With the development and use of word processing systems, letters, memos, and reports were created electronically; however, a paper printout was needed for a record to be usable. Thus, these word processing documents were not true electronic records. As technology has advanced, true electronic records are used today—i.e., records created, distributed, used, and stored electronically. The contents of these records are accessible only by machine.

The records manager has the challenge to ensure that each person responsible for electronic records follows the records management storage and retrieval procedures set up for the office. Consistently following a records systems procedure helps protect the firm in legal actions. The same benefits of following proper records management procedures for paper records also apply to electronic records: The information is available at the right time to help make effective decisions.

Electronic Mail. **Electronic mail (E-mail)** is a means of transmitting correspondence over telephone lines and/or computer networks or of relaying messages via satellite networks. A variety of electronic mail systems allow users to write and send messages via computers and software. Many systems allow the user to create electronic folders in which to place messages about a particular subject.

What is electronic mail?

Electronic mail systems may operate through connection to the Internet. The **Internet** is a series of connected supercomputers that allow communication among the connections. Businesses are discovering that they can communicate across their state, or the United States, or

---

[3] Keith T. Davidson, *Forbes* technology supplement white paper, May 1995.

the world to other businesses connected to the Internet. Records managers can belong to a "newsgroup" on the Internet to communicate with other records managers around the world.

Electronic mail, as with any new medium of communication, brings many questions related to records management that records managers must address. How do you maintain a record's integrity? Can you keep a record confidential? How long do you keep an electronic mail message? These are only a few of the questions that records managers must answer as more and more messages are sent and received electronically.

Electronic Data Interchange (EDI). **Electronic data interchange (EDI)** is a communication procedure between two companies that allows the exchange of standardized documents (most commonly invoices or purchase orders) through computers. If the two companies have compatible systems, the computers communicate with each other through a connection. For example, Company A sends a purchase order to Company B by EDI. When Company B ships the order to Company A, an invoice is created and sent to Company A, again through EDI. Company A can then pay Company B by transferring electronic funds via EDI. Thus, no paper documents are exchanged. Some large companies no longer do business with other firms that do not use EDI. Records managers must ensure that these electronic records are accurate, safe, and secure.

What is EDI?

Electronic File Management. **Electronic file management** is the management of records using a computer. Computers are capable of generating megabytes of data; this data can also be erased in a nanosecond. Individuals and organizations can provide many examples in which data or files have been lost. This may have happened to you! Perhaps the biggest problem with using a computer for storing information is the change in how information is stored. "We are not producing, managing, and saving physical artifacts, but rather trying to understand and preserve virtual patterns that give the electronic information its content, structure, context, and thus its meaning."[4] Records managers must help their organizations control key records and ensure that today's files are available 5, 10, or 15 years in the future. You will learn ways to keep track of electronic files in Chapter 4, and Chapter 10 gives more information on managing electronic information.

Document Imaging. **Document imaging** is an automated system for scanning, storing, retrieving, and managing paper records in an electronic

[4] Terry Cook, "It's 10 o'clock: Do You Know Where Your Data Are?" *Technology Review,* January 1995, p. 48.

format. A paper document is scanned into a computer, thus creating an electronic image of the document. Scanned files are usually large; consequently, optical disk storage (discussed in Chapters 10 and 11) is recommended. Textual data can be converted electronically using optical character recognition (OCR) software. Lists of key words are created for each scanned file, and an image and text database is developed, enabling a search by key words to find a document in a matter of seconds. Once found, the document can be sent to the requester by fax, computer-to-computer communication, or a hard (printed) copy. Chapter 10 includes a discussion of this technology.

What is document imaging?

Many companies are integrating microfilming and document imaging technology to provide faster, accurate retrieval of records. Microfilming has been used for years, and it is a proven technology in terms of integrity and archivability. The use of hybrid systems that combine computer imaging with microfilming is growing. Records managers must be aware of the need for developing standards, testing legal issues, lowering costs, and viewing imaging from an organizational strategic perspective.[5]

Records Management Legislation

With the changes in the volume of records, the type of media, and the information stored that occurred as a result of World War II, many people were concerned about managing and controlling these records. Questions about retention, who had access, and other concerns regarding privacy were raised.

The Hoover Commissions

In 1946 President Truman appointed the first Hoover Commission to study the policy and records needs of the federal government. The Commission's work was responsible for establishing the General Services Administration (GSA) to improve government practices and controls in records management. During this time a highly productive industrial system was in operation with new government regulations that required large volumes of records. The federal government recognized the need for controlling the volume of government records created both during and after World War II.

What was a major outcome of the first Hoover Commission?

[5] Carl J. Case, "Imaging Technologies: A Strategic Organizational Solution," *Journal of Systems Management,* July 1993, pp. 12-16.

A second Hoover Commission later found that many reports required of business and industry were already available in other government agencies. Also, industry submitted large numbers of records to the government, but many were never used. As a result, the second Hoover Commission in 1955 concluded that the need for management of governmental records was crucial and continuing. The GSA created a government-wide records management program to oversee the reduction of paperwork in each government agency.

The federal government's pioneer studies in records management were widely acclaimed. They provided the example and motivation needed by business, industry, and lower levels of government to study the need for records and for setting up programs for their management.

Since the earlier studies, the federal government's concern for properly using and controlling information has continued with the passage of important records legislation. Significant examples of federal legislation affecting records are presented in the next section.

Federal Laws for Controlling Records

As the number of information and records systems increases dramatically, so does the legislation to balance and protect an individual's right to privacy, the public's access to information, and the quest for national security. When individuals' rights to privacy have been violated, the public's access to information has been denied, or the national security has been breached, steps need to be taken through legislation to protect and to balance these three important rights in a democratic society. Following the Watergate scandal in the early 1970s, which stemmed in part from the lack of records control, Congress passed new legislation.

> **What three factors influence legislation for controlling records?**

Two laws, the Freedom of Information Act and the Privacy Act, have special meaning to you as an individual and as a professional. Both laws aim to protect individuals against the misuse of filed information. As the use of electronic information increases, these laws are being scrutinized to determine if they are still appropriate and viable.

The Freedom of Information Act of 1966 gives you the right to see information about yourself. You may request records kept by private and public organizations such as medical offices, hospitals, dental clinics, law offices, government agencies, counseling clinics, banks, and the human resources (personnel) departments in business firms. You may have access to such records after proper submission of requests to the organization that has this information on file.

The Privacy Act of 1974 (with later amendments) gives you the right to exclude others from seeing records with information about you, as well as the right to know who has accessed your records. Many states have passed additional legislation to protect the files of individuals.

What does the Privacy Act of 1974 ensure?

As you continue your studies in records management, you need to be aware of other legislation affecting records control. Of special relevance to this field are: (1) the Federal Records Act of 1950 and its later amendments, (2) the Copyright Act of 1976, (3) the Right to Financial Privacy Act of 1978, (4) the Paperwork Reduction Act of 1980, (5) the Video Privacy Act of 1988, and (6) the Computer Matching and Privacy Protection Act of 1988. Also, the Fair Credit Reporting Act allows credit bureau members controlled access to credit- and tenant-bureau files.

As an employee responsible for company files, you need to know the rights of people asking to see the files. You also need to maintain control over the files, such as preparing a log of the names of persons who have read the files. Some firms that maintain a high volume of confidential information develop lists of individuals who may see such files and of situations justifying access to their records. For other purposes, such files are off limits.

Records Management: A Key Organizational Function

Management is the process of using an organization's resources to achieve specific goals through the functions of planning, organizing, leading, and controlling.

What is management?

Planning involves establishing goals or objectives and the methods required to achieve them. With the firm's goals in mind, *organizing* takes place, a step that calls for arranging the tasks, people, and other resources needed to meet the goals set in the planning stage. *Leading* refers to managerial behavior (such as training, supervising, and motivating) that supports the achievement of an organization's goals. Finally, *controlling* means measuring how well an organization has met its goals.

Keep these four functions in mind when you study the management of records. Also, observe how you are a manager because you, too, perform these steps when you manage your study time, money, and social and professional life.

The Life Cycle of Records

As a manager, you must see the whole picture, which involves understanding the four management functions discussed earlier and how each relates to the other. In the same way, managing records involves clearly understanding the phases making up the life cycle of a record.

As Figure 1-3 shows, the **record life cycle** is the life span of a record that includes five functional phases that occur from the creation of

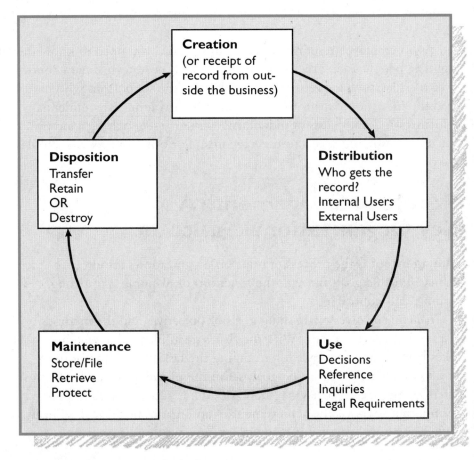

Figure 1-3   The Record Life Cycle

a record to its final disposition. Note how this cycle is carried out. Whenever a letter is produced, a form completed, a cassette tape dictated, or a pamphlet printed, a record is *created*. This record is then *distributed* (sent) to the person responsible for its *use*. Records are commonly used in decision making, for documentation or reference, in answering inquiries, or in satisfying legal requirements.

What are the phases of the record life cycle?

When a decision is made to keep the record for use at a later date, it must be stored, retrieved, and protected—three key steps in the *maintenance* of records. During this phase, the records must be *stored* (filed), which involves preparing and placing records in their proper storage place. After a record is stored, a request is made to *retrieve* (find and remove) it from storage for *use*. When the retrieved record is no longer needed for active use, it may be *re-stored* and *protected*, using appropriate equipment and environmental and human controls to ensure record security.   Also involved in the maintenance phase are such activities as updating stored information and purging or throwing away obsolete records that are no longer useful or that have been replaced by more current ones.

The last phase in the record life cycle is *disposition*. After a predetermined period of time has elapsed, records to be kept are *transferred* to less expensive storage sites within the firm or to an external storage center. At the end of the number of years indicated in the retention schedule, the records are *disposed of* either by destruction or by transfer to a permanent storage place. The facilities where records of an organization are preserved because of their continuing or historical value are called the **archives**. The records retention schedule is discussed in detail in Chapter 6.

What are archives?

The record life cycle is an important concept for you to understand. It shows, for example, that *filing is only one part of records management*. Many interrelated parts must work together for an effective records management program. Knowing the meaning and importance of each part of the *entire* record life cycle, you will be able to understand what is needed to manage all records—those on paper and those stored on other media such as microfilm or magnetic media.

Programs for Managing Records

As mentioned earlier, a records management program must be in place to manage all phases in the record life cycle. While the contents of records management programs vary, such programs generally have these features:

1. *Well-defined goals that all workers understand.* Figure 1-4 outlines six common goals of successful records management programs.

Goals of ABC Company's Records Management Program

1. To provide *accurate, timely information* whenever and wherever it is needed.

2. To provide information at the *lowest possible cost.*

3. To provide the *most efficient records systems,* including space, equipment, and procedures for creating, storing, retrieving, retaining, transferring, and disposing of records.

4. To *protect information* by designing and implementing effective measures for records control.

5. To determine *methods for evaluating* all phases of the records management program.

6. To *train company personnel* in the most effective methods of controlling and using records.

Figure 1-4   **Goals of a Records Management Program**

---

2. *A simple, sound organizational plan.* Sometimes, the records management program is *centralized* (records are physically located and controlled in one area); in other cases, it is *decentralized* (records are physically located in the departments where they are created and used). Each plan offers advantages and disadvantages that managers should consider carefully before deciding on an organizational plan. In large firms where work can be specialized, computers and other information systems, as shown in Figure 1-5, play a major role in records management.

3. *Efficient procedures for managing each of the five stages in the record life cycle.* (See Figure 1-3.) You will study these procedures in detail in Chapter 12.

4. *A well-trained staff.* See the "Careers in Records Management" section later in this chapter.

What are four common features of a records management program?

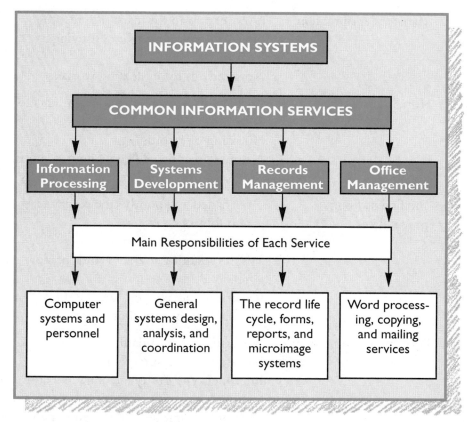

Figure 1-5   Location of Records Management in a Large Organization

Problems in Records Systems

The programs for managing records discussed earlier achieve their goals through the operation of an organization's records system. In this sense, a **records system** is a group of interrelated resources—people, equipment and supplies, space, procedures, and information—acting together according to a plan to accomplish the goals of the records management program. Anything that interferes with the operation of one or more of these resources, either individually or in combination, creates a problem in the records system and, therefore, hinders the effectiveness of the records management program.

Common problems and their typical symptoms in records systems include:

What is a records system?

1. Management problems	No overall plan for managing records
	No plan for retaining or destroying records
	No standards for evaluating workers
2. Human problems	Lack of concern about the importance of records
	Hoarding of records
	Assuming that people know how to use the files for storage and retrieval of records
3. Inefficient filing procedures	Overloaded and poorly labeled drawer and folders
	Failure to protect records
	Misfiles resulting in lost records or slow retrieval
	Records removed and placed in files without proper authorization
4. Poor use of equipment	No equipment standards
	No use of fire-resistant equipment
	Improper type of storage containers for records
	Lack of or improper use of automated systems
5. Inefficient use of space	Crowded working conditions
	Poor layout of storage area
	Inadequate use, or absence, of micro-filmed records
	Resistance to the use of magnetic media
6. Excessive records costs	Inefficiency due to the above problems

What are the six most common problems in records systems?

To resolve such problems, managers turn to various forms of information technology. Information technology has been promising the "paperless" office for many years. However, for a number of reasons, workers still use paper, and the use of paper is expected to continue to grow because of the case of producing paper copies with computers and copying machine technology.

Because most business records systems are paper-based, the paper records system is the place to begin a study of records management. The tangible nature of such records, the fact that paper records are familiar to most people, and the ease of locating such records make the study of paper records the logical introduction to the records management field. From such study, you need to understand alphabetic storage and retrieval systems discussed in Part Two, along with subject, numeric, and geographic storage and retrieval systems explained in Part Three.

Careers in Records Management

Where can you find opportunities for working in records management?

Opportunities to work with records exist in every type and size of office. In a small office with one administrative assistant and an owner/manager, working with records occupies much of the time of both people. In this setting, opportunities for records work are unlimited. The classified ads section of all daily newspapers lists many general positions in small offices.

Another potential career connected to records management is the marketing of records supplies and storage equipment. Offices need the paper, folders, file cabinets and shelves, and other supplies and equipment that are necessary for records storage and retrieval. Office supply vendors are an important resource to a records management department. A career as a marketing service representative for an office supplies company offers growth opportunities.

Larger firms with more specialized staff often employ records supervisors who direct the work of several records clerks. In major corporations or other large administrative headquarters, such as city halls in major cities, you will find three levels of records workers as shown in Figure 1-6, page 20.

1. *Managerial level*, where the top position is the records manager who is responsible for directing the entire program.

2. *Supervisory level*, which includes specialists responsible for operating the records center, supervising the design and use of business forms, and directing the creation and use of microfilm records.

3. *Operating level*, which includes those workers responsible for routine filing and retrieving tasks and for assisting with vital records and records retention work. Because this is the level of work emphasized in this textbook, we shall concentrate on the basic principles involved in storing and retrieving records.

In these days of economic downsizing, many organizations are outsourcing portions of their records management services such as archive storage. Because archive records are kept for a long period of time but may not be referenced often, archive facilities are usually located offsite in lower rent districts. Many companies offer archive services for several types of businesses. Career opportunities exist in these records management service businesses. See Appendix A for more detailed information on careers in records management, as well as job descriptions for positions in this field.

You can easily locate information on the records management profession by checking the publications of the various professional associations specializing in administrative work. The **Association of Records Managers and Administrators, Inc. (ARMA)** is the most important professional group interested in improving educational programs in schools and industry and in providing on-the-job knowledge about records management.

What is ARMA?

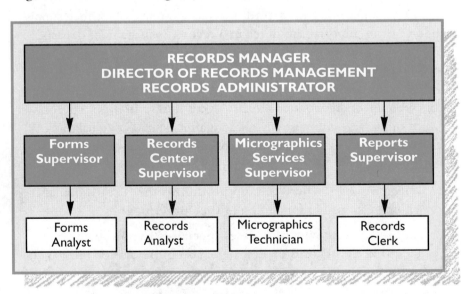

Figure 1-6   Typical Job Levels and Job Titles in Records Management

Information on records management jobs can be found in the *Dictionary of Occupational Titles* and in the *Occupational Outlook Handbook*. Other professional associations such as the Association of Information and Image Management (AIIM) and the American Health Information Management Association (AHIMA) publish periodicals that contain information about career trends in records management. You can find copies of such publications in college, university, and city libraries.

As the United States evolves more and more to a service economy based on information technology, many opportunities will appear for careers, including management positions, in information systems. Records management, a subspecialty of information systems, is evolving and changing with the impact of technology. The person who is comfortable with technology and who can apply the principles of records management can look forward to a career in this area.

Summary

A record is recorded information, regardless of its form; while records management is the systematic control of all records during their life cycle. The record life cycle includes creation, distribution, use, maintenance, and disposition. Records are classified according to their use, their place of use, or their value to a firm. Records serve as the memory of a company. Early records were physical records of simple transactions; as technology advanced, records have changed shape and form.

Records management is influenced by new technologies: electronic mail, the Internet, EDI, and document imaging. The Hoover Commissions developed regulations to reduce paperwork in government agencies and to manage government records. Computers help to manage records, but the use of computers has raised questions about an individual's right to privacy, the public's access to information, and the quest for national security, which has resulted in federal legislation to control access to individuals' records. Other federal laws affect the control of other types of records and records media. Management of records seeks to use an organization's resources to achieve specific goals through the functions of planning, organizing, leading, and controlling. Records management offers many career opportunities.

Important Terms

archives
Association of Records
  Managers and Adminis-
  trators, Inc. (ARMA)
document imaging
electronic data interchange (EDI)
electronic file management
electronic mail (E-mail)
electronic record
external record
important records
internal record

Internet
management
nonessential records
record
record life cycle
records management
records system
reference document
transaction document
useful records
vital records

Review and Discussion

1. Compare and contrast the terms *record* and *records management.* (Obj. 1)

2. What are the main classifications for records? What types of records are commonly found in each classification? (Obj. 1)

3. Compare and contrast the records operations of early offices with those of modern offices. (Obj. 2)

4. Why is more paper being used in offices despite the increasing use of automation and computers? (Obj. 2)

5. What current issues are records managers facing? (Obj. 2)

6. Compare the Freedom of Information Act and the Privacy Act. Why are these acts important to records management? (Obj. 3)

7. List the phases in the record life cycle and describe the activities that occur during each phase. What phases, if any, do you eliminate in your personal records cycle? Why? (Obj. 4)

8. What are some common problems of records systems? (Obj. 4)

9. How can you best prepare for work and advancement in records management positions? (Obj. 5)

10. Describe two benefits available for members of ARMA. (Obj. 5)

Applications (APP)

APP 1-1. Classifying Records (Obj. 1)

A. With another student in your class, visit a business and bring to class five examples of its business records. Make a chart similar to the following:

Business Record	By Use	By Place of Use	By Value to Firm

Record each business record by name, and place a check mark in the appropriate column(s). What helped you and your partner decide how to classify a record?

B. Make another chart similar to the following:

Business Record	Vital	Important	Useful	Nonessential

List the records again. Place a check mark in the appropriate column. What helped you decide how to mark a column? Compare your charts and records with another team in the class. Discuss the reasons for any differences.

C. Analyze the records from the business. Why did the business develop each record? How will each record help conduct business?

APP 1-2. Using Technology (Obj. 2)

A. Write a memorandum to your instructor identifying your goals for this class. Use electronic mail if it is available.

B. Scan a personal letter of your choice and save the image to a floppy disk if a scanner is available. Determine how many bytes your scanned file contains. If you are using a 1.44 MB floppy disk, approximately how many scanned letters could the disk hold?

C. Open the scanned image in your favorite word processing program and print the resulting document. Compare the quality of this printout to your original letter. Which is better? Do you think that scanning documents is a viable option for records management? Why or why not?

Part 2

Alphabetic Storage and Retrieval

Part 2 highlights alphabetic storage and retrieval systems. The ten alphabetic indexing rules studied in Chapters 2 and 3 are based on the ARMA Simplified Filing Rules. Chapter 4 discusses applying the rules to computer software applications. Chapter 5 presents the equipment and supplies used in manual and computer filing systems. Principles and procedures for retention, retieval, and transfer of records are discussed in Chapter 6.

Chapter 2

ALPHABETIC INDEXING RULES 1-5

Learning Objectives

1. Explain the necessity for indexing rules in alphabetic storage of names and the importance of following these rules consistently.
2. Index, code, and arrange personal and business names in indexing order of units.
3. Index, code, and arrange minor words and symbols in business names.
4. Index, code, and arrange personal and business names with punctuation and possessives.
5. Index, code, and arrange personal and business names with single letters and abbreviations.
6. Index, code, and arrange personal and business names with titles and suffixes.
7. Apply alphabetic card filing procedures.
8. Prepare and arrange cross-references for personal and business names.

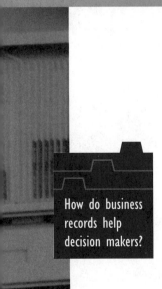

How do business records help decision makers?

Records help a business **do** business. Without an organized way of storing records, a firm would not meet the primary purpose of keeping records. Business records give the decision maker the right information at the right time at the lowest possible cost. To store records in the most efficient way possible, some type of storing or filing method must be used. A **storage method**, sometimes called a **filing method**, describes the way in which records are stored in a container. This text will present alphabetic, subject, numeric, and geographic methods of storage. Alphabetic storage is discussed in Chapters 2-6; subject storage, in Chapter 7; numeric storage, in Chapter 8; and geographic storage, in Chapter 9. The most common method of storage is alphabetic.

The **alphabetic storage method** is a method of storing records arranged according to the letters of the alphabet. Sounds simple, right? Everyone knows the alphabet! However, consistently accurate alphabetic filing isn't that simple. Look in the telephone directories of two major cities, and you will find major discrepancies in the order of the listings. Another example is filing under the letters "Mc." *Mc* is not one of the 26 letters of the alphabet; however, it is included in some alphabetic filing systems and not in others.

ARMA Rules

The most important filing concept to remember is: **All filing is done to retrieve information**. To retrieve information efficiently, a set of rules must be followed. Different businesses have different needs for information retrieval. Not every business follows a universal set of rules for alphabetic filing because the goals and needs of each business vary. The Association of Records Managers and Administrators, Inc. (ARMA) has published *Alphabetic Filing Rules,* containing standard rules for storing records alphabetically. ARMA is an organization designed to help professionals in records management perform their jobs easier and better. By using ARMA's simplified rules, businesses have a place to start in setting up an efficient alphabetic storage system.

Why are written rules needed for filing?

ARMA's Simplified Filing Standard Rules are shown in Figure 2-1. The rules in this chapter and in Chapter 3 are written to agree with the ARMA Simplified Filing Standard Rules and Specific Filing Guidelines.

Procedures for storing records alphabetically vary among organizations and among departments within organizations. Therefore, the filing procedures to be used in any *one* office must be determined, recorded, approved, and followed with no deviation. Without written rules for storing records alphabetically, procedures will vary with time, changes in personnel, and oral explanations. Unless those who maintain the records are consistent in following storage procedures, locating records will not be possible. **The real test of an efficient records storage system is being able to find records quickly once they have been stored.**

If you thoroughly understand the indexing rules in this textbook, you will be able to adjust to any exceptions encountered in the specific office where you may work. Records managers who adopt these rules for their offices will find them understandable, logical, workable, and comprehensive enough to provide answers to the majority of storage questions that arise.

In this chapter, you will use three of the six steps for storing alphabetically: indexing, coding, and cross-referencing. Chapter 5 explains all six of the alphabetic storing procedures.

The Association of Records Managers and Administrators, Inc. (ARMA), the professional organization for the records management field, recommends the following Simplified Filing Standard Rules for consistency in filing.

1. Alphabetize by arranging files in unit-by-unit order and letter-by-letter within each unit.

2. Each filing unit in a filing segment is to be considered. This includes prepositions, conjunctions, and articles. The only exception is when the word *the* is the first filing unit in a filing segment. In this case, *the* is the last filing unit. Spell out all symbols—e.g., &, $, #—and file alphabetically.

3. File "nothing before something." File single unit filing segments before multiple unit filing segments.

4. Ignore all punctuation when alphabetizing. This includes periods, commas, dashes, hyphens, apostrophes, etc. Hyphenated words are considered one unit.

5. Arabic and Roman numbers are filed sequentially before alphabetic characters. All Arabic numerals precede all Roman numerals.

6. Acronyms, abbreviations, and radio and television station call letters are filed as one unit.

7. File under the most commonly used name or title. Cross-reference under other names or titles that might be used in an information request.

Figure 2-1   **ARMA Simplified Filing Standard Rules**

Indexing

What is indexing?

Indexing is the mental process of determining the filing segment (or name) by which a record is to be stored. The **filing segment** is the name by which a record is stored and requested. In alphabetic storage, indexing means determining the name that is to be used in filing.

The indexing step is more difficult when correspondence is being stored than when cards are being put in alphabetic order. On a card, the name to use for filing is easily recognized; on correspondence, the name may appear in various places on a record. Because accurate indexing is necessary for quick retrieval, the indexing step is extremely important. *Careful, accurate indexing is perhaps the most exacting step in the storage procedure.* In an alphabetic arrangement, the selection of the right name by which to store (the filing segment) means that the record will be found quickly when it is needed. If the wrong name is selected, much time will be wasted trying to locate the record when it is eventually requested.

To select the filing segment, keep the following in mind: The name most likely to be used in asking for the record, usually the most important one, is the one to use for storage.

Take a look at the examples in Figure 2-2. Several new terms are introduced in this figure: *Key Unit, Unit 2, Unit 3,* and *Unit 4.* These units are the **indexing units** of the filing segment; in other words, the indexing units are the various words that make up the filing segment. The **key unit** is the first unit of the filing segment. Units 2, 3, 4, and so on are the next units by which the placement of the record is further determined. The use of these terms is helpful when determining how an item is to be filed. By mentally identifying the key and succeeding units, you are making a complex process simpler and easier to handle.

What is a filing segment?

What are indexing units?

Coding

Coding is the physical marking of a record to indicate the name, number, or subject by which it is to be stored. Coding is a physical act, as contrasted

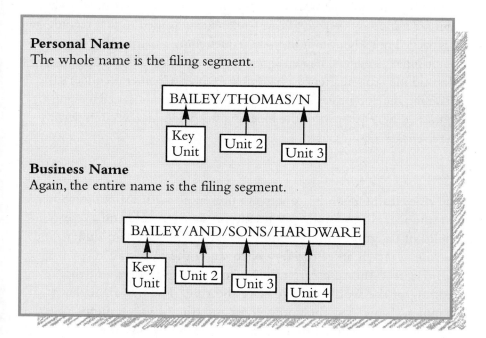

Personal Name
The whole name is the filing segment.

BAILEY/THOMAS/N

Key Unit | Unit 2 | Unit 3

Business Name
Again, the entire name is the filing segment.

BAILEY/AND/SONS/HARDWARE

Key Unit | Unit 2 | Unit 3 | Unit 4

Figure 2-2   **Coded Filing Segments, Key Unit, and Succeeding Units**

What is coding?

with indexing, which is a mental determination. Coding procedures for this textbook are to place a diagonal (/) between each word in the filing segment, underline the key unit, and then number each succeeding unit (i.e., 2, 3, 4), which you have mentally identified in the indexing process. When the records are coded, the indexing order of the filing segment is marked. The **indexing order** is the order in which units of the filing segment are considered when a record is stored.

To code properly, a set of rules for alphabetic storage must be faithfully followed. **Indexing rules** are the written procedures that describe how the filing segments are ordered. The indexing rules that follow give you a good start in following appropriate alphabetic storage procedures.

Cross-Referencing

While indexing a record, the filer may determine that the record could be requested by a name other than the one selected for coding. Because that record may be requested by the *other* name or names that were not coded, a cross-reference should be prepared. A **cross-reference** is an aid used in finding a record stored by a filing segment other than the one selected for storing. The record is stored under the name the filer determines to be the most important (*key unit*). Cross-referencing is used so that records can be retrieved quickly, even if they are requested by a name other than the one originally coded. Chapter 2 presents the first five alphabetic indexing rules and the cross-references that go with them. Chapter 3 contains the remaining indexing rules and their cross-references. Cross-referencing is mentioned here as a part of the indexing step and is discussed in detail after the rules are presented.

Indexing Rules

The rules for alphabetic storage are presented with examples to help you understand how to apply them. Study each rule and the examples of its application carefully; above all, be sure you understand the rule. Here is an effective way to study the indexing rules:

First, read the rule carefully. Make sure you understand the meaning of the words used to state the rule. Then, look at the examples. Note that the complete name (the filing segment) is given at the left. Then the name is separated into indexing units at the right according to the rule you are studying. Be sure you understand why the name has been separated into the indexing units shown.

In determining alphabetic order, compare the units in the filing segments for differences. If the key units are alike, move to the second units, the third units, and succeeding units until a difference occurs. The point of difference determines the correct alphabetic order. Marks that appear over or under some letters in foreign names are disregarded (such as Señora, Marçal, René, Valhallavägen). In this textbook, you will find an underscore in each example except the first one. This underscore indicates the letter of the unit that determines alphabetic order. Examples are numbered for ease in referring to them. Be sure you understand each rule before going to the next one.

What is an effective way to study alphabetic indexing rules?

Rule 1: Indexing Order of Units

A. Personal Names

A personal name is indexed in this manner: (1) the surname (last name) is the key unit, (2) the given name (first name) or initial is the second unit, and (3) the middle name or initial is the third unit. If determining the surname is difficult, consider the last name as the surname.

A unit consisting of just an initial precedes a unit that consists of a complete name beginning with the same letter—*nothing before something*. Punctuation is omitted. Remember: The underscored letter shows the correct order.

What does "nothing before something" mean?

Examples of Rule 1A:

Filing Segment	Index Order of Units		
Name	**Key Unit**	**Unit 2**	**Unit 3**
1. Barbara N. Shelley	SHELLEY	BARBARA	N
2. Stephen K. Shelly	SHEL<u>L</u>Y	STEPHEN	K
3. Sylvia N. Sibert	S<u>I</u>BERT	SYLVIA	N
4. Doug E. Siebert	SI<u>E</u>BERT	DOUG	E
5. Dreana Lee Siebert	SIEBERT	D<u>R</u>EANA	LEE
6. E. Matthew Siebert	SIEBERT	<u>E</u>	MATTHEW
7. Edith Ann Siebert	SIEBERT	E<u>D</u>ITH	ANN
8. Matt E. Siebert	SIEBERT	<u>M</u>ATT	E
9. Julia E. Siebly	SIE<u>B</u>LY	JULIA	E
10. Phyllis S. Siebly	SIEBLY	<u>P</u>HYLLIS	S

What does "as written" mean?

B. Business Names

Business names are indexed *as written* using letterheads or trademarks as guides. Each word in a business name is a separate unit. Business names containing personal names are indexed as written.

Examples of Rule 1B:

Filing Segment	Index Order of Units			
Name	Key Unit	Unit 2	Unit 3	Unit 4
1. Sam Shade Freight Company	SAM	SHADE	FREIGHT	COMPANY
2. Shade Machinery Company	SHADE	MACHINERY	COMPANY	
3. Shade Metal Working	SHADE	METAL	WORKING	
4. Shady Grove Disposal Company	SHADY	GROVE	DISPOSAL	COMPANY
5. Silly Salley Toy Shop	SILLY	SALLEY	TOY	SHOP
6. Smallen Bookstore	SMALLEN	BOOKSTORE		
7. Smallen Family Steakhouse	SMALLEN	FAMILY	STEAKHOUSE	
8. Smalley National Bank	SMALLEY	NATIONAL	BANK	
9. Smile Awhile Gift Shop	SMILE	AWHILE	GIFT	SHOP
10. Stacey Lynn Beauty Shop	STACEY	LYNN	BEAUTY	SHOP

Check Your Knowledge of Rule 1

1. On a separate sheet of paper, code items a–j by placing a diagonal (/) between each unit in the filing segment, underlining the key unit, and then numbering the second and succeeding units.

   Example: 0. Mark / <u>Kennedy</u>
   (with a 2 above Kennedy)

   a. Anna Wong
   b. Albert Brown Hosiery
   c. Elbert Albert
   d. Li Wu Wong
   e. Elspeth Gregory
   f. Bill Green Car Company
   g. T. F. Sommers
   h. E. William Smith
   i. Glen Scott Cleaners
   j. Randy Sheridan Aviation

2. Are the two names in each of the following pairs in correct alphabetic order? If not, explain.

   a. Ross Clothing Store
      Charlotte Ross
   b. Andrew Rose
      Rose Garden Nursery
   c. Rose Dale
      Rosedale Custom Printing
   d. Linda Lindsay Natural Foods
      Roy A. Lindsay

e. Gene David
    David Gene Furniture Company
f. Dorothy Johnson
    Dorothy Johnsen
g. Martin Ulbert
    Josephine Urroz

h. Red Robin Restaurant
    Red Robin Bait Shop
i. Pioneer Museum
    Pioneer Cemetery
j. L. G. Baker
    Lila G. Baker

Rule 2: Minor Words and Symbols in Business Names

Articles, prepositions, conjunctions, and symbols are considered separate indexing units. Symbols are considered as spelled in full. When the word "The" appears as the first word of a business name, it is considered the last indexing unit.

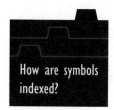

How are symbols indexed?

Articles: A, AN, THE

Prepositions: AT, IN, OUT, ON, OFF, BY, TO, WITH, FOR, OF, OVER

Conjunctions: AND, BUT, OR, NOR

Symbols: &, ¢, $, #, % (AND, CENT OR CENTS, DOLLAR OR DOLLARS, NUMBER OR POUND, PERCENT)

Examples of Rule 2:

Filing Segment	Index Order of Units			
Name	**Key Unit**	**Unit 2**	**Unit 3**	**Unit 4**
1. A Cutting Place	A	CUTTING	PLACE	
2. An Excellent Shop	AN	EXCELLENT	SHOP	
3. Bonzo the Clown	BONZO	THE	CLOWN	
4. Dollar Drug Store	DOLLAR	DRUG	STORE	
5. The $ Smart Shop	DOLLAR	SMART	SHOP	THE
6. Going My Way Motel	GOING	MY	WAY	MOTEL
7. Golf By The Shore	GOLF	BY	THE	SHORE
8. The Grand Hotel	GRAND	HOTEL	THE	
9. Hunt & Jones, Attorneys	HUNT	AND	JONES	ATTORNEYS
10. # One Drug Store	NUMBER	ONE	DRUG	STORE

Check Your Knowledge of Rule 2

1. On a separate sheet of paper, code items a–j by placing a diagonal (/) between each unit in the filing segment, underlining the key unit, and then numbering the second and succeeding units.

   a. The Chimney Sweeps
   b. The Crazy Chicken
   c. A Rainbow Shop
   d. An Unusual Mercantile
   e. C & R Office Supplies

   f. The Camp By The Sea
   g. Carson Hot Springs
   h. Clip & Curl Salon
   i. $ Saver Cleaners
   j. Cybersurf By The Hour

2. Write the letters beside the names to indicate the correct alphabetic order for items a–j on the same piece of paper.

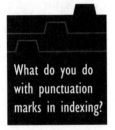

What do you do with punctuation marks in indexing?

Rule 3: Punctuation and Possessives

All punctuation is disregarded when indexing personal and business names. Commas, periods, hyphens, apostrophes, dashes, exclamation points, question marks, quotation marks, and diagonals (/) are disregarded, and names are indexed as written.

Examples of Rule 3:

| Filing Segment | Index Order of Units | | | |
Name	Key Unit	Unit 2	Unit 3	Unit 4
1. Alice's Custom Designs	ALICES	CUSTOM	DESIGNS	
2. Rosetta Allen-Carter	ALLENCARTER	ROSETTA		
3. Allen-Nelson Law Firm	ALLENNELSON	LAW	FIRM	
4. All-in-One Store	ALLINONE	STORE		
5. "A-OK" Pilot Shop	AOK	PILOT	SHOP	
6. The On/Off Freeway Hotel	ONOFF	FREEWAY	HOTEL	THE
7. Rob-Bob's Arcade Games	ROBBOBS	ARCADE	GAMES	
8. The Robin's Nest	ROBINS	NEST	THE	
9. Robin's Secret Hide-Away	ROBINS	SECRET	HIDEAWAY	
10. Whodonit? Mystery Tours	WHODONIT	MYSTERY	TOURS	

Check Your Knowledge of Rule 3

1. On a separate sheet of paper, code items a–j by placing a diagonal (/) between each unit of the filing segment, underlining the key unit, and then numbering the second and succeeding units.

a. Out-and-About Travel
b. Robin Poppino-Brown
c. The Spotted Cow Dairy
d. Inside/Outside Framers
e. Allison Beary-Caldwell

f. The Beary Good Store
g. $ Off Discount Store
h. All-Over-Town Delivery
i. #s Away Diet Center
j. Lambert & Wong Law Firm

2. Are the two names in each of the following pairs in correct alphabetic order? If not, explain.

a. Brenda's $ Saver
    Brenda Bertha
b. Rod-N-Reel Store
    Rodriguez & Gonzales Associates
c. Do-Rite General Contractors
    Do-Rite Builders
d. George & Son Electric
    George & Sons Alignment
e. Lamb-Western Company
    Lamb Industries
f. Temp-A-Cure Company
    Temp-Control Mechanics

g. Nor-West Growing Company
    Nor'Wester Novelties
h. Laura M. Swanson
    The Swan Shop
i. Heckman & Perez Law Firm
    David Heckman
j. Chi Kuo
    Ching-yu Kuo

Rule 4: Single Letters and Abbreviations

A. Personal Names

Initials in personal names are considered separate indexing units. Abbreviations of personal names (Wm., Jos., Thos.) and nicknames (Liz, Bill) are indexed as they are written.

B. Business Names

Single letters in business and organization names are indexed as written. If single letters are separated by spaces, index each letter as a separate unit. An acronym (a word formed from the first or first few letters of several words such as ARMA and ARCO) is indexed as one unit regardless of punctuation or spacing. Abbreviated words (Mfg., Corp., Inc.) and names (IBM, GE) are indexed as one unit regardless of punctuation or spacing. Radio and television station call letters (WBAP, KRDO) are indexed as one unit.

How do you index abbreviated personal names?

How do you index single letters in business names?

Examples of Rule 4:

Filing Segment	Index Order of Units			
Name	**Key Unit**	**Unit 2**	**Unit 3**	**Unit 4**
1. I C I Realty	I	C	I	REALTY
2. IBM	I<u>B</u>M			
3. K & O Security	<u>K</u>	AND	O	SECURITY
4. KKRS Radio Station	K<u>K</u>RS	RADIO	STATION	
5. K-Nine Klips	K<u>N</u>INE	KLIPS		
6. KOGO Television	K<u>O</u>GO	TELEVISION		
7. L A D Construction	<u>L</u>	A	D	CONSTRUCTION
8. LADD, Inc.	L<u>A</u>DD	INC		
9. U & I Nursery	<u>U</u>	AND	I	NURSERY
10. US Bancorp	U<u>S</u>	BANCORP		

Check Your Knowledge of Rule 4

1. On a separate sheet of paper, code items a–j by placing a diagonal (/) between each unit of the filing segment, underlining the key unit, and then numbering the second and succeeding units.

   a. IDEA Industries
   b. I & CM Auto Works
   c. I C A Corp.
   d. I Can Dig It Backhoe
   e. I Am Woman, Inc.

   f. I C Clear
   g. I Buy Antiques
   h. ICAP, Inc.
   i. ID Booth, Inc.
   j. I A B C Associates

2. Write the letters beside the names to indicate the correct alphabetic order for items a–j on the same piece of paper.

Rule 5: Titles and Suffixes

What are some suffixes for personal names?

A. Personal Names

A title before a name (Dr., Miss, Mr., Mrs., Ms., Prof.), a seniority suffix (II, III, Jr., Sr.), or a professional suffix (CRM, DDS, Mayor, M.D., Ph.D., Senator) after a name is the last indexing unit. Numeric suffixes (II, III) are filed before alphabetic suffixes (Jr., Mayor, Senator, Sr.). If a name contains both a title and a suffix, the title is the last unit.

Royal and religious titles followed by either a given name or a surname only (Father Leo, Princess Anne) are indexed and filed as written.

Note: *If a person's professional title appears after his or her name, it is referred to as a suffix—e.g., CPA, CRM, CMA, Senator.*

Examples of Rule 5A:

Filing Segment	Index Order of Units			
Name	**Key Unit**	**Unit 2**	**Unit 3**	**Unit 4**
1. Father John	FATHER	JOHN		
2. Ms. Ada Johnson, CPA	JOHNSON	ADA	CPA	MS
3. Dr. Ada Johnson	JOHNSON	ADA	DR	
4. Mr. Goro Nagai	NAGAI	GORO	MR	
5. Queen Anne	QUEEN	ANNE		
6. Sister Mary	SISTER	MARY		
7. Father John Smith	SMITH	JOHN	FATHER	
8. John Smith, Jr.	SMITH	JOHN	JR	
9. John P. Smith	SMITH	JOHN	P	
10. John P. Smith II	SMITH	JOHN	P	II
11. John P. Smith III	SMITH	JOHN	P	III
12. John Smith, Sr.	SMITH	JOHN	SR	
13. Sister Mary Nina Smith	SMITH	MARY	NINA	SISTER
14. Miss Suzi Yang	YANG	SUZI	MISS	
15. Mrs. Suzi Yang	YANG	SUZI	MRS	
16. Ms. Suzi Yang	YANG	SUZI	MS	

B. Business Names

Titles in business names are indexed as written.

Examples of Rule 5B:

Filing Segment	Index Order of Units			
Name	**Key Unit**	**Unit 2**	**Unit 3**	**Unit 4**
1. Aunt Sally's Cookie Shop	AUNT	SALLYS	COOKIE	SHOP
2. Captain Roy Bean's Coffee	CAPTAIN	ROY	BEANS	COFFEE
3. Dr. Carla's Chimney Works	DR	CARLAS	CHIMNEY	WORKS
4. Father Time's Antiques	FATHER	TIMES	ANTIQUES	
5. Mister Oscar's Gym	MISTER	OSCARS	GYM	
6. Mr. Video Connection	MR	VIDEO	CONNECTION	
7. Mrs. Mom's Day Care	MRS	MOMS	DAY	CARE
8. Ms. Salon of Beauty	MS	SALON	OF	BEAUTY
9. Professor Owl's Pre-School	PROFESSOR	OWLS	PRESCHOOL	
10. Sisters of Charity	SISTERS	OF	CHARITY	

Check Your Knowledge of Rule 5

1. On a separate sheet of paper, code items a–j by placing a diagonal (/) between each unit of the filing segment, underlining the key unit, and then numbering the second and succeeding units.

   a. Father George
   b. Ms. Paula Gonzales, CRM
   c. Mrs. Char. Campbell, DVM
   d. Call/Hold Company
   e. COR Construction, Inc.
   f. WKRA Radio Station
   g. A & N Drop Box Service
   h. Friends-of-the-Road Trucking
   i. The Colonial Arms Apts.
   j. SERA Architects PC

2. Are the two names in each of the following pairs arranged in correct alphabetic order? If not, explain.

   a. The Magic Coffee Shop
      Magic $ Saver
   b. John Phillips, Sr.
      John Phillips, Jr.
   c. Mrs. Carmen Zapata
      Z-Pro Company
   d. XYZ Rentals, Inc.
      X M Chemical Co.
   e. Mrs. C's Chocolates
      MVP Pizza Shop
   f. The Yarn Barn
      Ye Olde Print Shop
   g. L-M Equipment Co.
      L & M Appliance Repair
   h. Sharon's "Of Course"
      Miss Sharon Oest
   i. The Office King
      The Office Doctor
   j. FAX-R-Us, Inc.
      FAX to You Company

3. Are the following names in alphabetic order? If so, indicate by writing "Yes." If not, write "No." Then determine the correct alphabetic order and show it by rearranging the numbers beside the names on a separate sheet of paper.

   Example: 0. 1. A-Z Rentals
   　　　　　　　2. AAA Used Cars
   　　　　　　　3. A. Wilson Enterprises

   Answer: No, 3, 2, 1

   a. 1. In & Out Diner
      2. ITC Truck Company
      3. I Do I Do Catering
   b. 1. Alice Nelson
      2. The Nelson Company
      3. Donald Nelson
   c. 1. Brother Alfonso Blanco
      2. Cynthia Blanco-White
      3. Forentino Blanco
   d. 1. Brett Gibson III
      2. Brett Gibson
      3. Brett Gibson II

e. 1. AMP Factory
   2. AMPAK, Inc.
   3. AMPCO Parking, Inc.

f. 1. Dr. Joji Chiba
   2. Joji Chiba, M.D.
   3. Mr. Joji Chiba, CMA

g. 1. Queen Anne
   2. The Queen's Closet
   3. Margaret F. Queen

h. 1. Professor Rebecca Bartels
   2. The Professor Book Store
   3. Professor T's Academy

i. 1. The Captain's Surf & Turf
   2. Captain Cynthia S. Wilson
   3. Cap'n Hook's Sea Food

j. 1. Janice Cooper, CPA
   2. Ms. Janice Cooper
   3. Sister Janice Cooper

Alphabetic Card Filing

Many offices use an alphabetic card file or a computer file to store information that is frequently referenced. Recall your own experiences when calling for utility services such as an electrical hookup. What is the first piece of information the customer service representative asked of you? If you heard key clicks after providing the information, chances are the person was using a computer to find your record. Depending on the size and type of office, computers may not be available to everyone. As technology advances and the cost of hardware and software decreases, more and more offices will be using computers to reference customer records. You must be prepared to use both manual and computer files.

In the next section, card records are defined. The advantages and disadvantages of using card records, as well as the instructions for preparing card records, are discussed.

What Is a Card Record?

In many offices, card record files of the names and addresses of people and businesses are kept in alphabetic arrangement. A **card record** is a piece of card stock used for storing information that is referenced often. The card stock provides the durability to withstand large volume usage. These cards are prepared according to the style the records manager selects so that they can be handled with maximum efficiency and ease.

To understand the advantages and disadvantages of using card records, remember the basic difference between card records and records kept in other forms. One main item or unit of information such as a

What is a unit record?

Business Efficiency Aids, Inc.

Figure 2-3   Card Record Storage

telephone number or an address is stored on each card. For this reason, a card has often been called a **unit record**, which is a record that contains one main item or piece of information. Each card is handled as a single item or unit record. The card storage cabinet shown in Figure 2-3 provides work space and easy access to hundreds of card records.

Advantages of Card Records.   Cards as unit records offer many advantages to the records manager. These advantages include the saving of space because of the size and the easy visibility of a card record. One employee can work with a great deal of information without moving to different file drawers. Also, because of their uniform size and thickness, cards are handled more easily than papers.

Card records offer several other advantages over records maintained on sheets of paper as lists of information that are subject to frequent change. With only one key information item on each card such as a customer name or the name of a cataloged library book, information is easy to locate. If a change occurs in a customer's address or if a new book is added or an old book is removed from the library stacks, new information can be quickly inserted and the obsolete information easily deleted on a card. The card can also be physically removed from the file.

What are the advantages of using card records?

40

Because only one main item of information appears on each card, the information can be easily rearranged in any sequence desired. For example, a sales department may need customer name cards arranged alphabetically by customer name. At another time, the cards may need to be rearranged by customer name according to the numeric codes assigned to products each customer purchased. In a third instance, the cards may be rearranged geographically by the sales territories in which each customer is located. Cards can also be divided into groups or stacks, which will allow several people to use the entire file at once.

Disadvantages of Card Records. Card records systems also have disadvantages. For example, cards that are removed from a file can easily get out of sequence, especially when a records user drops a stack. Small-sized cards are easily lost, misfiled, or misplaced when removed from a file. Under certain conditions, adding, deleting, or changing information on a card may be difficult without removing the card from the file. Keying information on the top or bottom margins of a card also may be a problem. When information is recorded on cards from another document, errors can easily occur if the person posting the information is careless or inattentive to detail. Time is also required to transfer information from one record to another. Preparation and maintenance of card records systems is labor-intensive (time-consuming).

Preparation of Cards

Information on each card must be presented in the same format. A standard format helps to ensure consistency and ease in finding the information. Word processing software programs facilitate using prepared forms that are commercially available. See Figure 2-4, page 42, for an example of a Rolodex™ form prepared on a computer and printed on a laser printer.

As you read the following explanation, refer frequently to Figure 2-5, page 43, which shows one style that is commonly used in either manual or computer-based systems.

1. Key the name of the person or business in uppercase letters with no punctuation in indexing order beginning on the third space

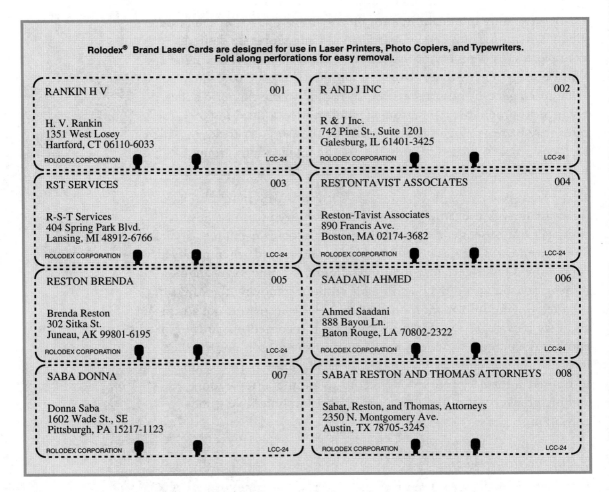

**Rolodex® Brand Laser Cards are designed for use in Laser Printers, Photo Copiers, and Typewriters.
Fold along perforations for easy removal.**

RANKIN H V	001	R AND J INC	002
H. V. Rankin 1351 West Losey Hartford, CT 06110-6033		R & J Inc. 742 Pine St., Suite 1201 Galesburg, IL 61401-3425	
ROLODEX CORPORATION	LCC-24	ROLODEX CORPORATION	LCC-24
RST SERVICES	003	RESTONTAVIST ASSOCIATES	004
R-S-T Services 404 Spring Park Blvd. Lansing, MI 48912-6766		Reston-Tavist Associates 890 Francis Ave. Boston, MA 02174-3682	
ROLODEX CORPORATION	LCC-24	ROLODEX CORPORATION	LCC-24
RESTON BRENDA	005	SAADANI AHMED	006
Brenda Reston 302 Sitka St. Juneau, AK 99801-6195		Ahmed Saadani 888 Bayou Ln. Baton Rouge, LA 70802-2322	
ROLODEX CORPORATION	LCC-24	ROLODEX CORPORATION	LCC-24
SABA DONNA	007	SABAT RESTON AND THOMAS ATTORNEYS	008
Donna Saba 1602 Wade St., SE Pittsburgh, PA 15217-1123		Sabat, Reston, and Thomas, Attorneys 2350 N. Montgomery Ave. Austin, TX 78705-3245	
ROLODEX CORPORATION	LCC-24	ROLODEX CORPORATION	LCC-24

Figure 2-4   Computer-Generated Name Cards

from the left edge of the card and on the third line from its top edge. The key unit is always the first word keyed (see A in Figure 2-5), followed by the second and succeeding units (see B in Figure 2-5). A person's title should be keyed if it is known (see C in Figure 2-5).

2. Key the name and address a triple space below the indexed name on Line 3 using upper- and lowercase letters and punctuation (see E in Figure 2-5).

3. Key the number code in the upper right corner of the card if the name on the card is to be used with a numeric system (see D in Figure 2-5).

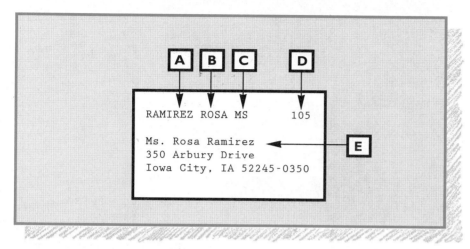

Figure 2-5   Name Card Preparation

Cross-Referencing

Some records of people and businesses may be requested by names that are different from those by which they were stored. This variation is particularly true if the key unit is difficult to determine. When a record is likely to be requested by any of several names, an aid called a *cross-reference* is prepared. A cross-reference shows the name in a form other than that used on the original record, and it indicates the storage location of the original record. The filer can then find requested records regardless of the name used in the request for those records. A cross-reference may be identical to all other records in size and color as shown in Figure 2-6, or it may be distinctively different in color to stand out clearly from the other records. Cross-reference cards are discussed in this chapter. Cross-reference sheets, used with correspondence records, are discussed in Chapter 5.

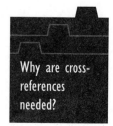

Why are cross-references needed?

Cross-referencing must be done with discretion. Too many cross-references crowd the files and may hinder rather than help retrieval. Each cross-reference requires valuable time to prepare, creates at least

Figure 2-6   **Locating Cross-References**

one additional card or computer entry that must be stored, and therefore requires additional space in a file.

Four types of personal names should be cross-referenced:

1. Unusual names
2. Hyphenated surnames
3. Alternate names
4. Similar names

Also, nine types of business names should be cross-referenced. Four will be presented in this chapter; the remainder, in Chapter 3.

1. Compound names
2. Abbreviations and acronyms
3. Popular and coined names
4. Hyphenated names

An explanation of the procedure to follow in cross-referencing each kind of name follows.

Personal Names

Cross-references should be prepared for the following types of personal names.

1. ***Unusual Names.*** When determining the surname is difficult, index
    the last name first on the original record. Prepare a cross-reference
    with the first name indexed first.

    On the original card for Gene David, David is the key unit, and
    Gene is the second unit. However, a request might come in for
    David Gene. The cross-reference would show Gene as the key unit
    and David as the second unit. Someone looking under Gene would
    find the cross-reference that shows the original record is filed under
    D for David. Study the examples in Figure 2-7.

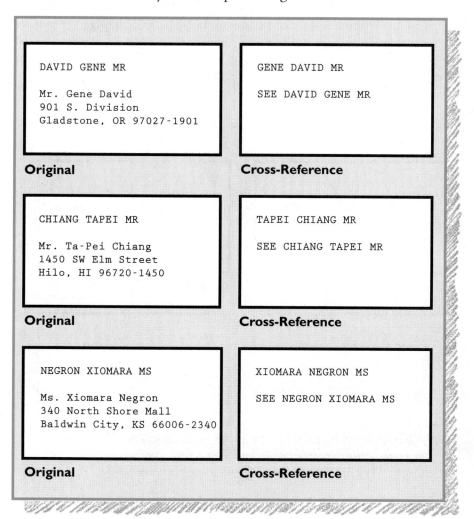

```
DAVID GENE MR

Mr. Gene David
901 S. Division
Gladstone, OR 97027-1901
```

Original

```
GENE DAVID MR

SEE DAVID GENE MR
```

Cross-Reference

```
CHIANG TAPEI MR

Mr. Ta-Pei Chiang
1450 SW Elm Street
Hilo, HI 96720-1450
```

Original

```
TAPEI CHIANG MR

SEE CHIANG TAPEI MR
```

Cross-Reference

```
NEGRON XIOMARA MS

Ms. Xiomara Negron
340 North Shore Mall
Baldwin City, KS 66006-2340
```

Original

```
XIOMARA NEGRON MS

SEE NEGRON XIOMARA MS
```

Cross-Reference

Figure 2-7 **Cross-Reference: Unusual Names**

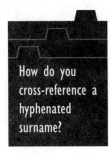

How do you cross-reference a hyphenated surname?

2. ***Hyphenated Surnames.*** Married women often use hyphenated surnames. For hyphenated surnames, a request for records could be in either of the two surnames. A cross-reference enables retrieval in either case. An example is Doreen Johnson-Hull shown in Figure 2-8. Remember that punctuation is ignored.

Many men use hyphenated surnames that are their family names. Because these men are known only by their hyphenated surnames, a cross-reference is not necessary. Some men adopt a hyphenated surname when they marry and may, in that case, be known by more than one name. A cross-reference is needed for accurate retrieval of records when a man changes his surname to a hyphenated surname. See Martin Stamp-Belke shown in Figure 2-8. You will be told when a cross-reference is needed for a man's name; otherwise, a cross-reference will not be required.

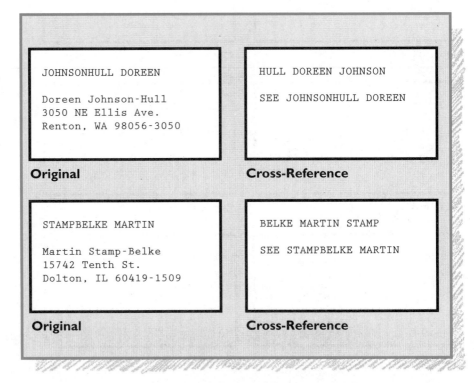

Figure 2-8   Cross-Reference: Hyphenated Surnames

3. *Alternate Names.* When a person is known by more than one name, you need to make cross-references. Examples are Peter Starkinsky doing business as Pete Star; and Mary Zavinella, DVM, who is also known as Mary Zavinella-Parks, Mrs. Arnold Parks, and Mrs. Mary Parks. (See Figure 2-9.)

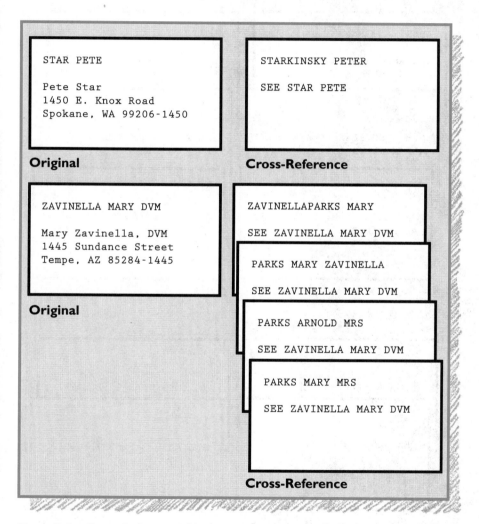

Figure 2-9   Cross-Reference: Alternate Names

4. *Similar Names.* A variety of spellings exist for some names like Alan and Bail. A SEE ALSO cross-reference is prepared for all possible spellings. If the card is not found under one spelling, the

filer checks the SEE ALSO card for other possible spellings. Figure 2-10 illustrates SEE ALSO cross-references for similar names.

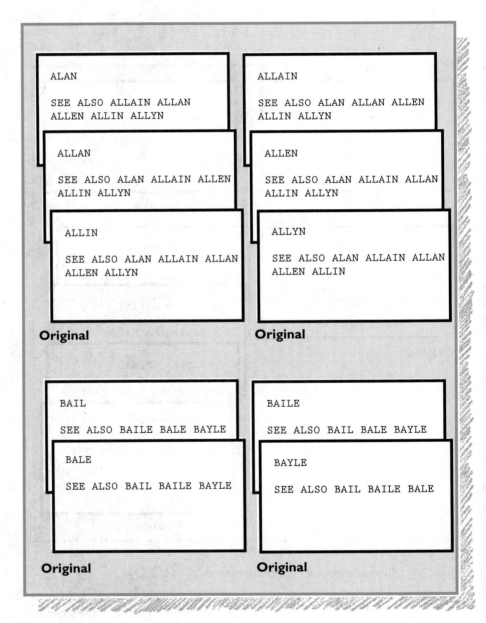

Figure 2-10   Cross-Reference: Similar Names

Business Names

Cross-references should be prepared for the following types of business names. The original name is the name appearing on the letterhead.

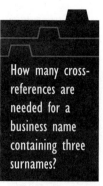

How many cross-references are needed for a business name containing three surnames?

1. ***Compound Names.*** When a business name includes two or more surnames, prepare a cross-reference for each surname other than the first. See Figure 2-11 for an example using McAllister, Craft, and Burns Attorneys.

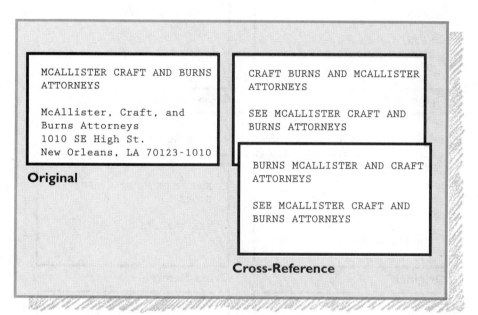

Figure 2-11   Cross-Reference: Compound Names

2. ***Abbreviations and Acronyms.*** When a business is commonly known by an abbreviation or an acronym, a cross-reference is prepared for the full name. Examples are IBM (International Business Machines Corporation) and MADD (Mothers Against Drunk Driving) shown in Figure 2-12.

3. ***Popular and Coined Names.*** A business is often known by its popular and/or coined name. A cross-reference will assist in retrieval. Figure 2-13 shows cross-references for Freddy's (Fred Meyer Department Store), Penney's (JCPenney Company, Inc.), and Smitty's (Smith's Home-Style Eatery).

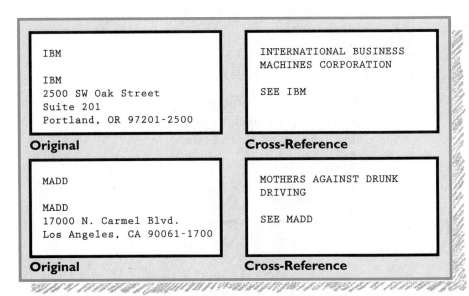

Figure 2-12   Cross-Reference: Abbreviations and Acronyms

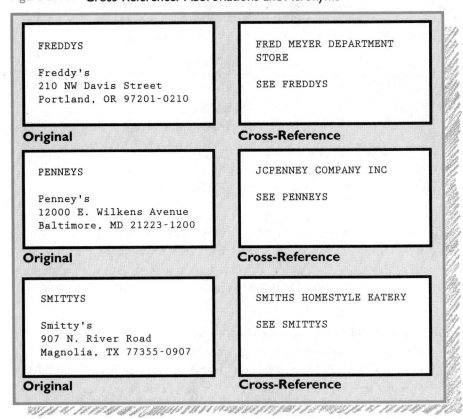

Figure 2-13   Cross-Reference: Popular and Coined Names

4. ***Hyphenated Names.*** Just as in personal names, business surnames with hyphens need to be cross-referenced for each surname combination. Examples are shown in Figure 2-14.

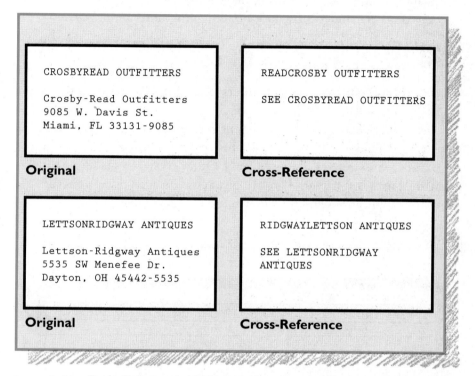

Figure 2-14 **Cross-Reference: Hyphenated Business Surnames**

Check Your Knowledge of Cross-Referencing

Which of the following names should have cross-references? Prepare cross-references as needed on a separate sheet of paper.

1. WKKP Radio Station
2. IBM (International Business Machines Corporation)
3. Bartel-Simmons Cattle Company
4. Nelson Allen
5. Mrs. Joanna Paulson-Childer
6. The Riverside Terrace
7. Akeo Saga, M.D.
8. Mom's (Mom's Cafe & Concert Hall)
9. Barnett, Wall & Wakui Brokerage
10. BBCC (Big Bend Community College)

Coding Cross-References

The name on the first line of a card is always used to determine placement in a file. This rule applies to original cards and to cross-reference cards. If the names on the cards are coded, diagonals are placed between the units, the key units are underlined, and the remaining units are numbered.

Current Trends in Records Management

As more offices add personal computers for support staff, more information will be stored in word processing, spreadsheet, or database files. The same principles of indexing and cross-referencing apply to computer software applications. Figure 2-15 shows a database program listing of similar name SEE ALSO cross-references for ALLEN. Other entries in the figure show individual names. Chapters 4 and 10 give more detailed discussions of computer applications and how they relate to records management.

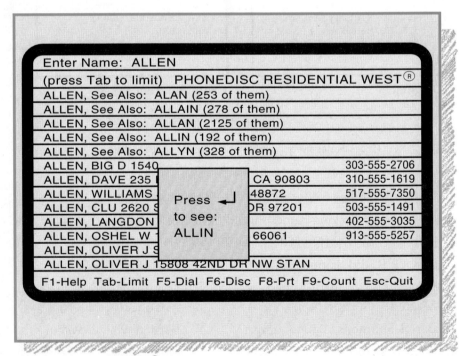

From PhoneDisc Residential® by Digital Directory Assistance, Inc., Bethesda, Maryland

Figure 2-15   **Cross-Reference: Computer Database**

Summary

A set of written indexing rules helps make filing consistent. If filing is consistent, retrieval is more likely. The ten indexing rules presented in this textbook are based on the ARMA Simplified Filing Standard Rules.

Indexing is the mental process of determining the filing segment or the name by which the record is to be stored. Coding is the physical process of marking the filing segment into indexing units. Insert diagonals between units, underline the key unit, and then number each succeeding unit when coding.

Personal names are indexed by the surname, the given name, and then the middle name or initial; business names are indexed as written on the letterhead. Minor words and symbols in business names are indexed as written and are considered separate indexing units. Spell out any symbols. If the word "The" is the first word in a business name, consider it the last indexing unit. All punctuation marks are ignored when indexing personal and business names.

Single letters and abbreviations are indexed as written for both personal and business names. If single letters in a business name are separated by spaces, each letter is considered a separate indexing unit. Personal titles and suffixes are indexed after the surname and given name. A suffix is indexed before a personal title when a person's name contains both. Titles in business names are indexed as written.

Card records can be prepared manually or by computer; in either case, consistency of format is important. Card records have advantages and disadvantages.

Cross-reference personal names that are unusual, hyphenated surnames, alternate names, and similarly spelled names. Cross-reference business names that contain more than one surname, abbreviations and acronyms, popular and coined names, and hyphenated surnames.

Current trends in records management indicate more offices using computers to store customer and other important business information. The same principles of indexing and coding apply to computer software applications.

Important Terms

alphabetic storage method
card record
coding
cross-reference
filing segment
indexing

indexing order
indexing rules
indexing units
key unit
storage (filing) method
unit record

Review and Discussion

1. Why is consistency in filing important? (Obj. 1)

2. Why are indexing rules important when filing names alphabetically? (Obj. 1)

3. In a personal name, what is the key unit? (Obj. 2)

4. How is the key unit of a business name determined? (Obj. 2)

5. Code and arrange the following names in alphabetic order. Justify your arrangement. (Obj. 2)
   a. Norman Andrews
   b. Norm's Painting Company
   c. Norma Anderson
   d. Norton Printing Company

6. Code and arrange the following names in alphabetic order. Justify your arrangement. (Obj. 3)
   a. Jordan & Pippin Produce
   b. The Jordan River Restaurant
   c. J/J Roller Express
   d. $ Off Store

7. Code and arrange the following names in alphabetic order. Justify your arrangement. (Obj. 4)
   a. Elizabeth Jones-Derwent
   b. Jones' Emporium
   c. "Jokes-R-Us"
   d. Johnson-Evans Hardware Store

8. Code and arrange the following names in alphabetic order. Justify your arrangement. (Obj. 5)
   a. UPS, Inc.
   b. U P S Associates
   c. Will Udey
   d. Wm. S. Udey

9. Code and arrange the following names in alphabetic order. Justify your arrangement. (Obj. 6)
   a. Mr. Ron Nelson, Jr.
   b. Ms. Rae Nielson
   c. Mrs. Rae Nielson, CPS
   d. Mr. Ron Nelson, Sr.

10. Give one advantage and one disadvantage for using a card record system. (Obj. 7)

11. Can you have too many cross-references? Explain. (Obj. 8)

12. Give two examples of types of personal names that should be cross-referenced. (Obj. 8)

13. Give two examples of types of business names that should be cross-referenced. (Obj. 8)

Applications (APP)

APP 2-1. Arranging Personal and Business Names in Alphabetic Indexing Order (Objs. 2-8)

A. Key or print in indexing order the following names on 5" by 3" cards or on slips of paper of that size. Key or print the number beside the name in the top right corner of the card. Key the name and address a double space below the indexed name.

B. Prepare cross-reference cards when necessary according to the guidelines provided in this chapter. On the cross-reference card, key or print the number beside the original name plus an "X."

C. Code each card for alphabetic filing.

D. Arrange all cards, including cross-references, in alphabetic order.

E. List the numbers keyed or printed on the cards that you have now arranged in alphabetic order in a vertical column on a separate sheet of paper.

F. Save the cards for use in Chapter 3.

Names:

1. H. V. Rankin, 1351 West Losey, Hartford, CT 06110-6033

2. R & J Inc., 742 Pine St., Suite 1201, Galesburg, IL 61401-3425

3. R-S-T Services, 404 Spring Park Blvd., Lansing, MI 48912-6766

4. Reston-Tavist Associates, 890 Francis Ave., Boston, MA 02174-3682

5. Brenda Reston, 302 Sitka St., Juneau, AK 99801-6195

6. Ahmed Saadani, 888 Bayou Lane, Baton Rouge, LA 70802-2322

7. Donna Saba, 1602 Wade St. SE, Pittsburgh, PA 15217-1123

8. Sabat, Reston, and Thomas, Attorneys, 2350 N. Montgomery Ave., Austin, TX 78705-3245

9. T/R Corporation, 455 SE Vineyard Lane, Lincoln, NE 68501-1273

10. Sylvia Resyowski Associates, Inc., 450 NW Lovejoy, San Francisco, CA 94102-6722

11. Sav-on Auto Repair, 4845 S. Bellevue Crescent, Chevy Chase, MD 20815-1101

12. Shear Impressions, 100 S. Potter Street, Jackson, MS 39202-1763

13. Satin-N-Lace Boutique, 414 W. Seventh Street, Andover, NH 03216-2233

14. Thomason Storage, Inc., 4700 E. Morningside Dr., Cincinnati, OH 45227-6511

15. Sav-On Oil Company, 44 Hillcrest, South Burlington, VT 05401-2217

16. TRI, Ltd., 1650 Northern Avenue, Bangor, ME 04401-1014

17. Sinoun Tha, 1750 S. Sunnyvale, Providence, RI 02909-1435

18. Linda A. Thatcher, 106 S. Elm St., Chicago, IL 60680-1876

19. "That's It!" Painting Co., 126 W. Grant Lane, Little Rock, AR 72211-5452

20. Sir Charles & Co., 217 S. Douglas Street, Dover, DE 19901-2235

APP 2-2. Using a Word Processing Software Program to Sort Records (Objs. 2-6, 8)

A. Open template file, CH2.AP2, into your favorite word processing software program.

B. The names used in App. 2-1 are listed in card number order. Each unit is separated from the next by a tab stop. The names will most likely *not* align. The Sort feature will still work, however. Use the

Sort feature of your word processing software to sort the key units in correct alphabetic order. ***Hint:*** *Remember to select or block the names only and not the heading line.*

C.   Did it work? In names having two identical key units, the second units may or may not be in correct alphabetic order. Sort again by *both* the Key Unit and Unit 2 columns. Print the list when the sort is correct.

Applying the Rules

Job 1, Card Filing, Rules 1-5. All supplies necessary for completing Job 1 and all other jobs in *Records Management Projects*, 6th ed., are contained in the practice set.

Chapter 3

Alphabetic Indexing Rules 6-10

Learning Objectives

1. Index, code, and arrange personal and business names with articles and particles.
2. Index, code, and arrange business names with numbers.
3. Index, code, and arrange the names of organizations and institutions.
4. Index, code, and arrange personal and business names that are identical.
5. Index, code, and arrange government names.
6. Prepare and arrange cross-references for business names.
7. Select appropriate subject categories to be used within an alphabetic arrangement.

Rule 6: Prefixes—Articles and Particles

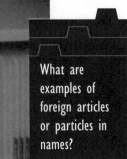

What are examples of foreign articles or particles in names?

A foreign article or particle in a personal or business name is combined with the part of the name following it to form a single indexing unit. The indexing order is not affected by a space between a prefix and the rest of the name, and the space is disregarded when indexing.

Examples of articles and particles are: a la, D', Da, De, Del, De la, Della, Den, Des, Di, Dos, Du, E', El, Fitz, Il, L', La, Las, Le, Les, Lo, Los, M', Mac, Mc, O', Per, Saint, San, Santa, Santo, St., Ste., Te, Ten, Ter, Van, Van de, Van der, Von, Von der.

Examples of Rule 6:

Filing Segment	Index Order of Units			
Name	Key Unit	Unit 2	Unit 3	Unit 4
1. Betty DuBarry's Pro Shop	BETTY	DUBARRYS	PRO	SHOP
2. Celeste D'Agostino	DAGOSTINO	CELESTE		
3. Gary Del Carrpio	DELCARRPIO	GARY		
4. E'Lan Suppliers, Inc.	ELAN	SUPPLIERS	INC	

58

Filing Segment	Index Order of Units			
Name	Key Unit	Unit 2	Unit 3	Unit 4
5. El Castor Industries, Ltd.	ELCASTOR	INDUSTRIES	LTD	
6. LaBar & McVey Brokers	LABAR	AND	MCVEY	BROKERS
7. LaPaloma Beauty Salon	LAPALOMA	BEAUTY	SALON	
8. Anne L'Auberge, CPA	LAUBERGE	ANNE	CPA	
9. Ms. Mayme LaVoy, CRM	LAVOY	MAYME	CRM	MS
10. McEwald Tax Service	MCEWALD	TAX	SERVICE	
11. Saint Claire's Arts & Crafts	SAINTCLAIRES	ARTS	AND	CRAFTS
12. Joseph Ste. Cyr	STECYR	JOSEPH		
13. Sylvia D'Bay's Studio	SYLVIA	DBAYS	STUDIO	
14. Susan TenClay, M.D.	TENCLAY	SUSAN	MD	
15. Van Der Hoff Seed Cleaning	VANDERHOFF	SEED	CLEANING	

Check Your Knowledge of Rule 6

1. On a separate sheet of paper, code items a–j by placing a diagonal (/) between each unit in the filing segment, underlining the key unit, and then numbering the second and succeeding units.

   a. Ms. Laura Von Lowe
   b. Van's Mobile Repair
   c. Ms. Wilma Ten Eck
   d. Van Dyke's Candy Shop
   e. Vanna's Dress Boutique

   f. Vanilla Fields, Inc.
   g. Miss Susan Van Meter
   h. Mr. Charles VanMeter, CMA
   i. VanNuys Service Center
   j. Vanessa's Sweet Shop

2. Write the letters beside the names to indicate the correct alphabetic order for items a–j on the same piece of paper.

Rule 7: Numbers in Business Names

Numbers spelled out (Seven Acres Inn) in business names are filed alphabetically. Numbers written in digits are filed before alphabetic letters or words (B4 Photographers comes before Beleau Building Co.). Names with numbers written in digits in the first units are filed in ascending order (lowest to highest number) before alphabetic names (229 Shop, 534 Club, Bank of Chicago). Arabic numerals are filed before Roman numerals (2, 3, II, III).

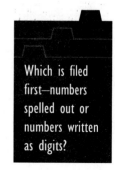

Which is filed first—numbers spelled out or numbers written as digits?

Names with inclusive numbers (33-37) are arranged by the first digit(s) only (33). Names with numbers appearing in other than the first position are filed alphabetically and immediately before a similar name without a number (Pier 36 Cafe, Pier and Port Cafe).

When indexing numbers written in digit form that contain *st*, *d*, and *th* (1st, 2d, 3d, 4th), ignore the letter endings and consider only the digits (1, 2, 3, 4).

Examples of Rule 7:

Filing Segment		Index Order of Units		
Name	**Key Unit**	**Unit 2**	**Unit 3**	**Unit 4**
1. 7 Day Food Mart	7	DAY	FOOD	MART
2. 21st Century Graphics, Inc.	21	CENTURY	GRAPHICS	INC
3. 24 Carrot Cake Bakery	24	CARROT	CAKE	BAKERY
4. 205 Auto Repairs	205	AUTO	REPAIRS	
5. 500-510 DeLaRose Court	500	DELAROSE	COURT	
6. The 500 DeLaRose Shop	500	DELAROSE	SHOP	THE
7. 1001 Book Store	1001	BOOK	STORE	
8. 12500 Windows, Inc.	12500	WINDOWS	INC	
9. XXI Club	XXI	CLUB		
10. Fifth Dimension, Inc.	FIFTH	DIMENSION	INC	
11. Highway 26 Cafe	HIGHWAY	26	CAFE	
12. I-5 Road Services	I5	ROAD	SERVICES	
13. I-80 Towing, Inc.	I80	TOWING	INC	
14. One Main Place	ONE	MAIN	PLACE	
15. Sixty-Six Grand Ave. Apts.	SIXTYSIX	GRAND	AVE	APTS

Check Your Knowledge of Rule 7

On a separate sheet of paper, code the following names by placing diagonals (/) between the units, underlining the key units, and then numbering the second and succeeding units. Write "Yes" if the names are in alphabetic order. Write "No" if the names are not in alphabetic order and show the correct order by rearranging the numbers. No. 1 has been coded and alphabetized for you.

a.
1. <u>EL-CO</u> / Enterprises (²)
2. Colleen / <u>Eller-McKinstry</u> (²)
3. <u>El Dorado</u> / Hotel (²)
  Ans: No, 1, 3, 2

b.
1. 50% Off Shop
2. V Roman Way
3. 21st Century Industries

c.
1. Labels 4 All, Inc.
2. LaBelle Styling Salon
3. Robert LaBelle

d.
1. Darrell J. McKenzie
2. McKenzie Construction Co.
3. McKenzie's Cafe

e. 1. Philip TenEyck, Jr.
   2. 10 Minute Delivery
   3. Philip TenEyck, Sr.

f. 1. Kelley de la Cross
   2. Kelly DeLacey
   3. Kelvin DelaCruz

g. 1. # 1 Deliveries
   2. A-1 Auto Sales
   3. 10 # Line Shop

h. 1. Frank Van Der Hout
   2. Walter Vander Hout
   3. Wm. Vanderhout

i. 1. Daniel LaDu
   2. Ladybug Day Care
   3. Joellen LaDuke

j. 1. The Elegant Gallery
   2. El Rancho Florists
   3. Ms. Anna Ellis

Rule 8: Organizations and Institutions

Banks and other financial institutions, clubs, colleges, hospitals, hotels, lodges, magazines, motels, museums, newspapers, religious institutions, schools, unions, universities, and other organizations and institutions are indexed and filed according to the names written on their letterheads.

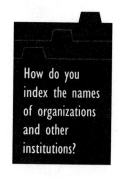

How do you index the names of organizations and other institutions?

Examples of Rule 8:

Filing Segment Name	Key Unit	Unit 2	Unit 3	Unit 4
1. 1st Christian Church	I	CHRISTIAN	CHURCH	
2. 1st National Bank	I	NATIONAL	BANK	
3. Assembly of God Church	ASSEMBLY	OF	GOD	CHURCH
4. Assn. of Iron Workers	ASSN	OF	IRON	WORKERS
5. Associated General Contractors	ASSOCIATED	GENERAL	CONTRACTORS	
6. The Bank of Idaho	BANK	OF	IDAHO	THE
7. Bank of Nova Scotia	BANK	OF	NOVA	SCOTIA
8. College of the Redwoods	COLLEGE	OF	THE	REDWOODS
9. Federated Farm Workers	FEDERATED	FARM	WORKERS	
10. Foundation for the Blind	FOUNDATION	FOR	THE	BLIND
11. The Homeless Institute	HOMELESS	INSTITUTE	THE	
12. Japanese Karate Association	JAPANESE	KARATE	ASSOCIATION	
13. Jewish Historical Society	JEWISH	HISTORICAL	SOCIETY	
14. JFK High School	JFK	HIGH	SCHOOL	
15. Journal of Photography	JOURNAL	OF	PHOTOGRAPHY	
16. Kiwanis Club	KIWANIS	CLUB		
17. New York Times	NEW	YORK	TIMES	
18. Pacific University	PACIFIC	UNIVERSITY		
19. Powers Modeling School	POWERS	MODELING	SCHOOL	
20. Public Employees Union	PUBLIC	EMPLOYEES	UNION	

Filing Segment	Index Order of Units			
Name	**Key Unit**	**Unit 2**	**Unit 3**	**Unit 4**
21. Rotary Club of Detroit	ROTARY	CLUB	OF	DETROIT
22. Rowe Jr. High School	ROWE	JR	HIGH	SCHOOL
23. The Sandman's Hotels	SANDMANS	HOTELS	THE	
24. School of the Arts	SCHOOL	OF	THE	ARTS
25. Spokane Community College	SPOKANE	COMMUNITY	COLLEGE	
26. St. Vincent's Medical Center	STVINCENTS	MEDICAL	CENTER	
27. University of Iowa	UNIVERSITY	OF	IOWA	
28. Western Society of Jesus	WESTERN	SOCIETY	OF	JESUS

Check Your Knowledge of Rule 8

1. On a separate sheet of paper, code the following names by placing diagonals (/) between the units, underlining the key units, and then numbering the second and succeeding units.

   a. Associated Psychotherapists of Northern California
   b. Association of Electricians
   c. Church of Religious Science
   d. Milwaukee First Church of Christ
   e. Berean Baptist Church
   f. Temple Beth Israel
   g. Woodlawn Medical Center
   h. Union Gospel Missionaries
   i. University Hospital
   j. Gonzaga University

2. Write the letters beside the names to indicate the correct alphabetic order for items a–j on the same piece of paper.

3. On the same sheet of paper, indicate whether the following pairs of names are in correct alphabetic order. If not, explain.

   a. International Organization of Masters, Mates & Pilots
      International Pentecostal Church
   b. International Brotherhood of Electrical Workers
      International Brotherhood of Carpenters
   c. American Cancer Society
      American Baptist Churches of Idaho
   d. American Legion Post 52
      American Red Cross, Southern Chapter
   e. American Association of Retired Persons, Chapter 78
      American Assn. of University Women

Rule 9: Identical Names

When personal names and names of businesses, institutions, and organizations are identical (including titles as explained in Rule 5), the filing order is determined by the addresses. Compare addresses in the following order:

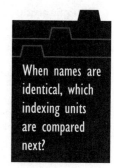

When names are identical, which indexing units are compared next?

1. City names

2. State or province names (if city names are identical)

3. Street names; include *Avenue, Boulevard, Drive, Street* (if city and state names are identical)

   a. When the first units of street names are written in digits (18th Street), the names are considered in ascending numeric order (1, 2, 3) and placed together before alphabetic street names (18th Street, 24th Avenue, 36 Grant Blvd., Academy Blvd.).

   b. Street names with compass directions (North, South, East, and West) are considered as written (SE Park Avenue, South Park Avenue). Street numbers written as digits after compass directions are considered before alphabetic street names (East 8th, East Main, Sandusky, SE Eighth, Southeast Eighth).

4. House or building numbers (if city, state, and street names are identical)

   a. House and building numbers written as digits are considered in ascending numeric order (8 Riverside Terrace, 912 Riverside Terrace) and placed together before spelled-out building names (The Riverside Terrace).

   b. If a street address and a building name are included in an address, disregard the building name.

   c. ZIP Codes are not considered in determining filing order.

Examples of Rule 9:
Names of Cities Used to Determine Filing Order

Filing Segment		Index Order of Units		
Name	Key Unit	Unit 2	Unit 3	Unit 4
1. First State Bank Elko, Nevada	FIRST	STATE	BANK	ELKO
2. First State Bank Reno, Nevada	FIRST	STATE	BANK	RENO

Names of States and Provinces Used to Determine Filing Order

Filing Segment	Index Order of Units				
Name	Key Unit	Unit 2	Unit 3	Unit 4	Unit 5
3. My-Own Beauty Shop Miami, FL	MYOWN	BEAUTY	SHOP	MIAMI	<u>F</u>L
4. My-Own Beauty Shop Miami, MB (Manitoba)	MYOWN	BEAUTY	SHOP	MIAMI	<u>M</u>B
5. Sandy's Motel Gladstone, MI	SANDYS	MOTEL	GLADSTONE	<u>M</u>I	
6. Sandy's Motel Gladstone, NJ	SANDYS	MOTEL	GLADSTONE	<u>N</u>J	

Names of Streets and Building Numbers Used to Determine Filing Order

Filing Segment	Index Order of Units						
Name	Key Unit	Unit 2	Unit 3	Unit 4	Unit 5	Unit 6	Unit 7
7. May's Cafe 4350 - 12 St. Tulsa, OK	MAYS	CAFE	TULSA	OK	<u>1</u>2	ST	
8. May's Cafe 350 - 36 St. Tulsa, OK	MAYS	CAFE	TULSA	OK	<u>3</u>6	ST	
9. May's Cafe 18650 Grant Ave. Tulsa, OK	MAYS	CAFE	TULSA	OK	<u>G</u>RANT	AVE	
10. May's Cafe 12500 Grant St. Tulsa, OK	MAYS	CAFE	TULSA	OK	GRANT	<u>S</u>T	12500
11. May's Cafe 17000 Grant St. Tulsa, OK	MAYS	CAFE	TULSA	OK	GRANT	ST	<u>17000</u>
12. May's Cafe 175 NE 13 St. Tulsa, OK	MAYS	CAFE	TULSA	OK	<u>N</u>E	13	ST
13. May's Cafe 405 NE Ninth St. Tulsa, OK	MAYS	CAFE	TULSA	OK	NE	<u>N</u>INTH	ST
14. May's Cafe 985 Silver Elm Dr. Tulsa, OK	MAYS	CAFE	TULSA	OK	<u>S</u>ILVER	ELM	DR

Check Your Knowledge of Rule 9

On a separate sheet of paper, code the following names by placing diagonals (/) between the units, underlining the key units, and then numbering the succeeding units. Next, determine whether the pairs are in correct alphabetic order. Write "Yes" or "No."

a. 1st Church of Christ
150 SE Concord
Dallas, OR

1st Church of Christ
725 N 48 Street
Dallas, TX

b. Diana Banks
4550 Elm Street
Dayton, OH

Diana Banks
975 Cedar Street
Dayton, OH

c. The Inquirer
870 N Main Street
Granite, OK

The Inquirer
370 Main Street
Granite, OR

d. The Corner Market
115 SE 8 Street
Pittsburgh, PA

The Corner Market
1150 SE 8 Street
Pittsburgh, PA

e. Bi-Rite $ Saver
8th and Grand Streets
Auburn, NH

Bi-Rite $ Saver
16875 Main Street
Auburn, WV

f. US National Bank
210 N Brentwood Blvd.
Los Angeles, CA

US National Bank
150 S Brentwood Avenue
Los Angeles, CA

Rule 10: Government Names

Government names are indexed first by the name of the governmental unit—country, state, county, or city. Next, index the distinctive name of the department, bureau, office, or board. The words "Office of," "Department of," "Bureau of," etc., are separate indexing units when they are part of the official name.

Note: *If "of" is not a part of the official name as written, it is not added.*

A. Federal

The first three indexing units of a United States (federal) government agency name are *United States Government*. Note that the examples start with Unit 4.

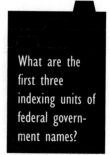

What are the first three indexing units of federal government names?

Examples of Rule 10A:

		Key Unit UNITED	Unit 2 STATES	Unit 3 GOVERNMENT		
Filing Segment		**Index Order of Units**				
Name	**Unit 4**	**Unit 5**	**Unit 6**	**Unit 7**	**Unit 8**
1. Portland Office General Accounting Office	GENERAL	ACCOUNTING	OFFICE	PORTLAND	OFFICE
2. Bureau of Prisons Justice Department	JUSTICE	DEPARTMENT	PRISONS	BUREAU	OF
3. Department of Labor Employment Standards	LABOR	DEPARTMENT	OF	EMPLOYMENT	STANDARDS

Check Your Knowledge of Rule 10A:

1. On a separate piece of paper, code items a-e by placing diagonals (/) between the indexing units, underlining the key units, and then numbering all succeeding units.

   a. National Park Service, Department of the Interior (federal government)

   b. Seattle Field Office, Food and Nutrition Service, Department of Agriculture (federal government)

   c. Water Quality Section, Environmental Protection Agency (federal government)

   d. Pacific NW Regional Center, National Archives and Records Administration (federal government)

   e. Suislaw National Forest, U.S. Forest Service, Department of Agriculture (federal government)

2. Write the letters beside the names to indicate the correct alphabetic order for items a-e on the same piece of paper.

B. State and Local

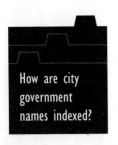

How are city government names indexed?

The first indexing units are the names of the state, province, county, parish, city, town, township, or village. Next, index the most distinctive name of the department, board, bureau, office, or government/political division. The words "State of," "County of," "City of," "Department of," etc., are added only *if needed* for clarity and if in the official name. Each word is considered a separate indexing unit.

Examples of Rule 10B

Filing Segment Name	Index Order of Units					
	Unit 1	Unit 2	Unit 3	Unit 4	Unit 5	Unit 6
1. Banking Office Dept. of Commerce (State Government) Juneau, AK	ALASKA	COMMERCE	DEPT	OF	BANKING	OFFICE
2. Dept. of Public Safety (State Government) Phoenix, AZ	ARIZONA	PUBLIC	SAFETY	DEPT	OF	
3. Highway Div. Benton County Corvallis, OR	BENTON	COUNTY	HIGHWAY	DIV		
4. Seattle Bridge Maint. Engineering Dept. Seattle, WA	SEATTLE	ENGINEERING	DEPT	BRIDGE	MAINT	
5. Planning Commission Starland Municipal Dist. Drumheller, AB (Alberta)	STARLAND	MUNICIPAL	DIST	PLANNING	COMMISSION	

Check Your Knowledge of Rule 10B

1. On a separate piece of paper, code items a-e by placing diagonals (/) between the units, underlining the key units, and then numbering all succeeding units.

   a. Beaverton Police Dept., Beaverton, Michigan
   b. Baker County Public Works, Baker City, Oregon
   c. Assessments and Taxation, Washington County, Hillsboro, Oregon
   d. Finance Division, Iowa Dept. of Revenue, Des Moines, Iowa
   e. Des Moines Fire Dept., Des Moines, Iowa

2. Write the letters beside the names to indicate the correct alphabetic order for items a-e on the same piece of paper.

C. Foreign

The distinctive English name is the first indexing unit for foreign government names. Then, index the remainder of the formal name of the government, *if needed* and if it is in the official name (CHINA REPUBLIC OF). Branches, departments, and divisions follow in order by their distinctive names. States, colonies, provinces, cities, and other divisions of foreign governments are filed by their distinctive or official names as spelled in English.

How are foreign government names indexed?

Examples of Rule 10C:

Foreign Government Name	English Translation in Indexed Order*
1. Jumhuriyah Misr al-Arabiya	EGYPT ARAB REPUBLIC OF
2. Republique Francaise	FRENCH REPUBLIC
3. Bundesrepublik Deutschland	GERMANY FEDERAL REPUBLIC OF
4. Bharat	INDIA REPUBLIC OF
5. Nippon	JAPAN

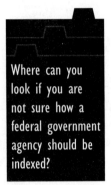

Where can you look if you are not sure how a federal government agency should be indexed?

Note: The *United States Government Manual* and the *Congressional Directory*, published annually, report a current list of United States government agencies and offices. *Countries, Dependencies, Areas of Special Sovereignty, and Their Principal Administrative Divisions*, published by the U.S. Department of Commerce, National Bureau of Standards, provides a list of geographic and political entities of the world and associated standard codes. The *State Information Book* by Susan Lukowski provides an up-to-date list of state departments and their addresses. The *World Almanac and Book of Facts*, updated annually, includes facts and statistics on many foreign nations and is a helpful source that gives the English spellings of many foreign names. Your local and/or college library should have these reference books.

Check Your Knowledge of Rule 10C

1. On a separate piece of paper, code items a-e by placing diagonals (/) between the units, underlining the key units, and then numbering all succeeding units.

Foreign Government	English Translation
a. Dawlet al-Qatar	State of Qatar
b. République Gabonaise	Republic of Gabon
c. Republika Hrvatska	Republic of Croatia
d. República del Ecuador	Republic of Ecuador
e. Kazak Respublikasy	Republic of Kazakhstan

2. Write the letters beside the names to indicate the correct alphabetic order for items a-e on the same piece of paper.

Check Your Knowledge of Rules 6–10

1. On a separate sheet of paper, code the following names. Place diagonals (/) between the units, underline the key units, and then number all succeeding units.

a. Nat'l. Assn. of Chiropractors
b. Independent Order of Fraternities
c. 1st Methodist Church
d. The Eugene Register Guard
e. International Dunes Hotel
f. American Confederation of Bakers
g. Building Dept., Athens, GA (City Government)
h. Bureau of Tourism, Lyoveldio Island (Iceland)
i. American Society of Engineers
j. International Association of Diabetics
k. Association of Handicapped Citizens
l. Sisters of Mercy Medical Center
m. Bureau of Land Management, Department of the Interior (federal government)
n. Brotherhood of Wood Workers
o. Neighbors of Meadowcraft

2. Write the letters beside the names to indicate the correct alphabetic order for items a–o on the same piece of paper.

3. On a separate sheet of paper, code the following names by placing diagonals (/) between the units, underlining the key units, and then numbering the succeeding units. Next, indicate whether the pairs are in correct alphabetic order by writing "Yes" or "No."

a. St. Mary's Academy
St. Mary's Church

b. 21 Skidoo Gallery
The 21 Club

c. Smith Elementary School
Smith Community College

d. Water Dept. Buxton, ND
Water Dept. Buxton, NC

e. Central State Bank
1430 Plymouth St.
Alamo, ND

Central State Bank
350 E First Avenue
Alamo, TN

f. Daily News, Combs, KY
Daily News, Combs, AK

g. Elliniki Dimokratia
(Greece Democracy)
Wanda Greco

h. School of Arts and Crafts
School of the Arts

i. San Carlos Apartments
Mr. Tatsumi Sanada

j. Freedom Museum
Historical Commission
Columbus, OH (State Govt.)

Archives & Records
Historical Commission
Columbus, OH (State Govt.)

Cross-References to Business Names

In Chapter 2, you learned that cross-references should be prepared for business names that are (1) compound names, (2) abbreviations and acronyms, (3) popular and coined names, and (4) hyphenated names. In this chapter, you will learn to prepare cross-references for the following types of business names:

5. Divisions and subsidiaries

6. Changed names

7. Similar names

8. Foreign business names

9. Foreign government names

An explanation of the procedure to follow in cross-referencing each kind of name follows.

The original record is stored in one place according to the alphabetic rules being used. A cross-reference is made, if necessary, for any of the reasons discussed here and in Chapter 2. The cross-reference will, in all probability, be on a label affixed to the tab of a guide or on a sheet of paper inserted into a folder. The cross-reference guide or the cross-reference sheet may be a distinctive color so that it is easy to find.

Divisions and Subsidiaries

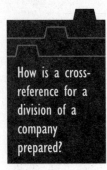

How is a cross-reference for a division of a company prepared?

When one company is a subsidiary or a division or branch of another company, the name appearing on the letterhead of the branch or subsidiary is the one indexed on the original record. A cross-reference is made under the name of the parent company. West One Bank is a division of US Bancorp; Key West Bank is a subsidiary of US Bancorp. (See Figure 3-1.)

Changed Names

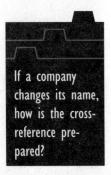

If a company changes its name, how is the cross-reference prepared?

A company may change its name. Consequently, its records must then be changed to indicate the name change and to ensure that the new name will be used for storage purposes. If only a few records are already in storage, they are usually refiled under the new name, and the former name is marked as a cross-reference. If many records are filed under the former name, a permanent cross-reference is placed at the beginning of the records for the former name. Any new records are placed under the new name. Examples are shown in Figure 3-2: Cellular One changed its name to AT&T Wireless, and The Carpet Barn changed its name to Floors to Go.

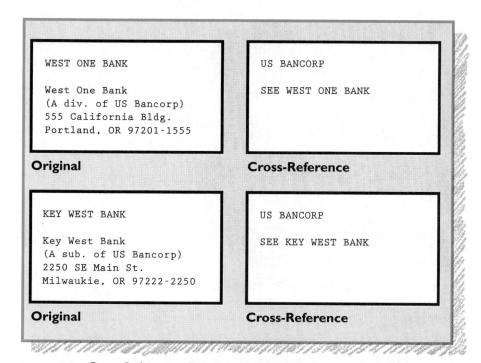

Figure 3-1 Cross-Reference: Divisions and Subsidiaries

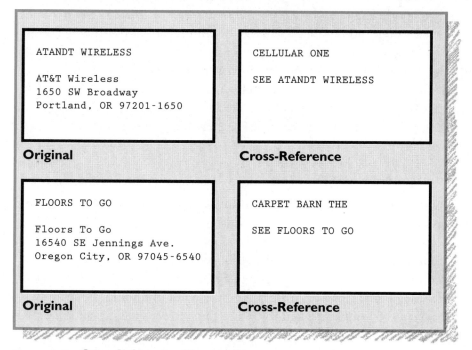

Figure 3-2 Cross-Reference: Changed Names

Figure 3-3   Cross-References in Vertical Files

Similar Names

What is an example of a similar business name?

Similar names for a business include examples like Northwest or North West, Southeast or South East, Goodwill or Good Will, and All State or Allstate. If a name could be considered either as one unit or as two units, it is a good candidate for a cross-reference. A SEE ALSO cross-reference is used to remind the filer to check the files for other possible spellings. The complete business name is not cross-referenced—only the similar name. For example, Allstate Properties, Inc., is the complete name of the business; a SEE ALSO cross-reference is prepared for All State, SEE ALSO Allstate. For the business name North West Lumber Supply, a cross-reference for Northwest, SEE ALSO North West, is prepared. (See Figure 3-4.)

Foreign Business Names

In what language is the original record of a foreign business name filed?

The original spelling of a foreign business name is often written in the foreign language, which is then translated into English for coding. The English translation is written on the document to be stored, and the document is stored under the English spelling. When a request for records is written in the native language, the filer will find that a cross-reference bearing the original spelling is an aid in finding the records. Special care should be taken to ensure the correct spellings and markings because these may differ greatly from the English form. Examples are shown in Figure 3-5.

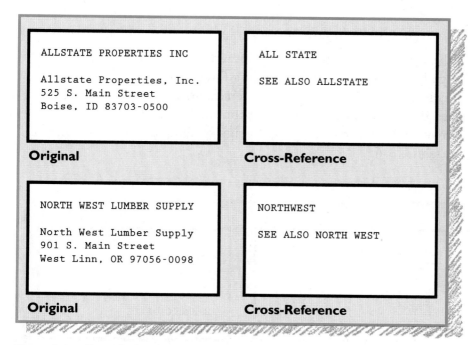

Figure 3-4   Cross-Reference: Similar Names

Figure 3-5   Cross-Reference: Foreign Business Names

In what language is a cross-reference prepared for a foreign government name?

Foreign Government Names

The name of a foreign government and its agencies, similar to foreign businesses, is often written in a foreign language. Write the English translation of the government name on each document to be stored. Store all documents under the English spelling. A cross-reference is prepared using the foreign spelling. Examples are shown in Figure 3-6.

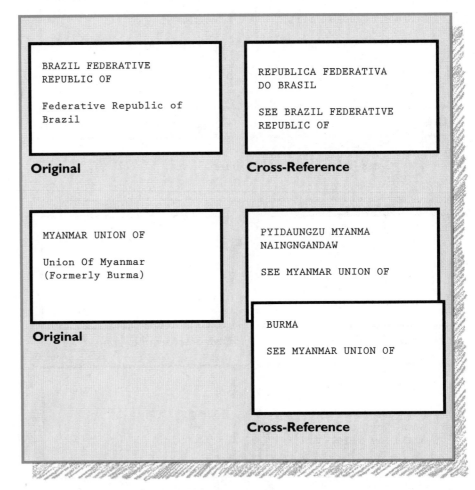

Figure 3-6   **Cross-Reference: Foreign Government Names**

Check Your Knowledge of Cross-References of Business Names

On a separate sheet of paper, prepare a cross-reference for each name that needs one.

1. Societe Europeene des Satellite Translated: European Society of Satellites

2. Dade County Public Works, Miami, Florida

3. St. Catherine Catholic Church

4. Los Angeles Police Department

5. All State Security Systems

6. Patent Scaffolding Co., A Div. of Hardco Corp.

7. Anchorage Daily News

8. Ministry of Defense, United Kingdom

9. Po Chien Distributing Company changed its name to Chien Distribution, Inc.

10. Southwest Mfg. Co.

Subjects Within Alphabetic Arrangement

Within an alphabetic arrangement, records may sometimes be stored and retrieved more conveniently by a subject title than by a specific name. Beware, however, of using so many subjects that the arrangement becomes primarily a subject arrangement with alphabetic names as subdivisions! A few typical examples of acceptable subjects to use within an otherwise alphabetic name arrangement are:

1. *Applications.* The job for which individuals are applying is more important than names of the applicants.

2. *Bids or projects.* All records pertaining to the same bid or the same project are kept together under the project or bid title.

3. *Special promotions or celebrations.* All records relating to a specific event are grouped together by subject.

Figure 3-7   Subject Titles Within Alphabetic Files

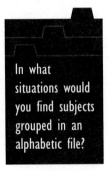

In what situations would you find subjects grouped in an alphabetic file?

4. ***Branch office memos and other information sent to many different offices.*** Material of this nature is grouped together to keep storage containers from becoming filled with duplicate records filed in many different places.

The filing procedure for the subject storage method is explained in detail in Chapter 7. Its application in this chapter consists of writing the subject title on the record if it does not already appear there.

When coding a record, the main subject is the key unit. Subdivisions of the main subject are considered as successive units. The name of the correspondent (individual or company name) is considered last.

For example, on all records pertaining to applications, the word APPLICATIONS is written as the key unit. The specific job applied for is a subdivision of that main subject and is the next unit (CASHIER in the first example). Further subdivisions may be necessary (see RECORDS CLERK in the fifth example and OFFICE CLERK in the third example). The applicant's name is coded last.

Index Order of Units

Key Unit	Unit 2	Unit 3	Unit 4	Unit 5
1. APPLICATIONS	CASHIER	ADAMS	HOLLY	
2. APPLICATIONS	CASHIER	FUNG	KAREN	
3. APPLICATIONS	OFFICE	CLERK	PACE	CHERYL
4. APPLICATIONS	OFFICE	CLERK	OWINGS	JERRY
5. APPLICATIONS	RECORDS	CLERK	CHARLES	SUE
6. APPLICATIONS	RECORDS	CLERK	JORDAN	VICKY
7. APPLICATIONS	SECRETARY	LASELLE	DIXIE	
8. APPLICATIONS	SECRETARY	MCCOLLUM	BILL	

Summary

The second half of the alphabetic filing rules addresses additional kinds of personal and business names as well as government names. A prefix (article or particle) is combined with the part of the name following it regardless of space.

Numbers spelled out in business names are alphabetized. Numbers written in digit form are filed numerically in ascending order before alphabetic names. Arabic numbers are filed before Roman numerals. Inclusive numbers are filed by the first digit(s) only.

Organizations and other institutions are indexed as written on letterheads. When names are identical, use the address to determine filing order. Start with the city, then state; use the street name last. If a difference still has not occurred in these units of the name, use the house or building number to determine the order.

Government names are indexed first by the name of the governmental unit (country, state, county, or city). The first three indexing units in federal government names are UNITED STATES GOVERNMENT. The next units are the distinctive name of the department, office, or bureau. The words "Office of," "Department of," etc., are separate indexing units only when those words are part of the official name.

Cross-references are prepared for businesses that are a division or subsidiary of another company, changed business names, similar names, foreign business names, and foreign governments.

Within an alphabetic file, subject files are appropriate for applications, bids or projects, special promotions or celebrations, or branch office memos.

Review and Discussion

1. Code and arrange the following names in alphabetic order and justify your arrangement. (Obj. 1)
   a. Dolores DeLa Torre
   b. D-E Tree Surgery
   c. Francis De La Torre
   d. Ardis Dela Torre
   e. Della's Music Studio

2. Code and arrange the following names in alphabetic order and justify your arrangement. (Obj. 2)
   a. 3 Rs Nursery School
   b. 100 Rays Tanning Salon
   c. 26 Freeway Hotel
   d. 7 Rs Landscaping, Inc.

3. Code and arrange the following names in alphabetic order and justify your arrangement. (Obj. 3)
   a. St. Peter's Orthodox Church
   b. St. Paul First National Bank
   c. The St. Paul Times
   d. St. Peter's Children's Home
   e. St. Paul's Chapter of the American Red Cross

4. What determines the alphabetic arrangement of common names that are identical such as John Smith or Washington High School? (Objs. 3 and 4)

5. Index, code, and arrange the following federal government names in alphabetic order. **Hint:** *The first three units in each name are the same.* (Obj. 5)
   a. Animal Damage Control, Animal and Plant Health Inspection, Department of Agriculture
   b. Air Quality Section, Nevada Operations Office, Environmental Protection Agency
   c. U.S. Customs Service, Department of the Treasury
   d. Bureau of Prisons, Department of Justice
   e. Federal Aviation Administration, Department of Transportation

    f. Federal Protective Service, General Services Administration

    g. Bureau of Engraving and Printing, Department of the Treasury

    h. Bureau of Public Affairs, Department of State

    i. Fish and Wildlife Service, Regional Office, Department of the Interior

    j. Antitrust Division, Department of Justice

6. When arranging city, county, province, or state government names alphabetically, what are the key units? (Obj. 5)

7. Which of the following items need cross-references? Explain why cross-references are needed and prepare the necessary cross-references. (Obj. 6)

    a. Transportacion Maritima Mexicana (Mexican Shipping Line)

    b. O'Connor Construction changed its name to Buildings by O'Connor

    c. Goodwill Computer Institute

    d. Pre-Fab Housing, a subsidiary of Wymax Construction Company, Inc.

    e. Koninkrijk Belgie (Kingdom of Belgium)

8. Why are subject categories sometimes used in an alphabetically arranged name file? Give at least two examples of subjects that might be found in an alphabetic file. (Obj. 7)

Applications (APP)

APP 3-1. *Arranging Cards in Alphabetic Order (Objs. 1-6)*

Critical Thinking

A. Key or print the following names (item H) in indexing order on 5" by 3" cards or on slips of paper that size. Also key or print the number of the name in the top right corner of the card. Key the name and address a double space below the indexed name.

B. Prepare cross-reference cards when necessary according to the guidelines given in this chapter. Key the original number and an "X" to indicate a cross-reference.

C. Code each card for alphabetic filing.

D. Arrange all cards, including cross-references, in alphabetic order.

E. List the numbers on the cards that you have now arranged in alphabetic order in a vertical column on a separate sheet of paper.

F. Check your work, correct any errors, and interfile these cards with those you prepared for App. 2-1 in Chapter 2.

G. List the numbers of all the cards from Chapters 2 and 3 that you have arranged in alphabetic order (cross-references included) in a vertical column on a separate sheet of paper.

H. Names:

21. Towanda Baptist Church, 330 Beech Ave., Towanda, PA 18848-0330

22. 9 to 5 Uniform Shop, 1250 S. Mill St., Dutton, VA 23050-5142

23. Dennis St. Amand, 2800 Bowman Rd., Baskett, KY 42402-3801

24. Transportation Dept., Turkiye Cumhuriyeti (Republic of Turkey)

25. St. Bernard's Pet Shop, 145 Ross St., Lebanon, MO 65536-1089

26. South West Investment Properties, 350 N. Silas St., Auburn, AL 36830-4521

27. The Republican, 3560 Main St., Republic, MI 49879-1243

28. TSR, a Div. of Republic Mfg., Inc., 6354 N. Vineyard, Marion, NY 14505-6543

29. Republic Fire Dept., 250 N. Main St., Republic, MO 65738-0250

30. The Republican, 9520 Ashton Way, Republic, WA 99166-5102

31. 57 Street Club, 19450 - 57 Street, Somerton, AZ 85350-5700

32. Shelby Public Works, 220 S. Main Street, Shelby, MT 59474-0220

33. Department of Tourism, Respubliki i Tojikiston (Republic of Tajikistan)

34. Shelby Police Dept., 35 Greenway Plaza, Shelby, AR 72662-3520

35. Ms. Margaret Ten Pass, CPS, 442 Lark Avenue, San Antonio, TX 78263-4400

36. St. Bernard's Pet Shop, 450 S. Harris Street, Lebanon, IL 62254-4700

37. Towanda Brotherhood of Iron Workers, 255 Exeter, Towanda, IL 61776-2550

38. State Savings Bank, 16750 S. McLoughlin Blvd., Marion, NC 28752-1675

39. Ryan's Barber Shop, 30250 N. Harris Street, Montgomery, IN 47558-4350

40. Reno Police Dept., 4350 Cedar Street, Reno, NV 89509-0032

APP 3-2. Using a Word Processing Software Program to Sort Records (Objs. 1-6)

A. Open template file CH3.AP2 into your favorite word processing software program.

B. The names used in App. 3-1 are listed in card number order. Indexing units are separated by tab stops. The names will most likely *not* align. The Sort feature will still work, however. Use the Sort feature of your word processing software to sort by Key Unit, then Unit 2, then Unit 3, and then Unit 4 (if your software allows this). Print a copy of the resulting list.

C. Use the Insert File or Open feature to combine the App. 2-2 and App. 3-2 files into one file. Sort the combined file to have a complete list of the 40 names. Print the resulting list.

Applying the Rules

Job 2, Card Filing, Rules 6-10
Job 3, Card Filing, Review Rules 1-10

Chapter 4

Alphabetic Indexing Rules for Computer Applications

Learning Objectives

1. Describe how ASCII values affect computer sorting.
2. Analyze and adjust filing segments for input into computer application software.
3. Identify computer application software that perform alphabetic sorting.
4. Identify current trends in records management.

How Computers Sort Data

Why use a computer for office operations?

Why use a computer for any office operation? The computer can classify, sort, and repeat processes tirelessly and accurately for long periods of time. The computer quickly performs sorting operations and can store more data in less space. It pays great attention to detail and can "remember" faster and better than humans **if** the input is accurate.

This chapter concludes the "rules" chapters about alphabetic storage procedures. In Chapters 2 and 3, you were introduced to standard alphabetic indexing rules for personal and business names. In this chapter, you will learn how to enter names into a computer to achieve correct alphabetic order when the names are sorted (alphabetized).

The Units As Written column in Example 1 shows a computer sort of example names from Rules 1-10 in Chapters 2 and 3. The names were keyed into the computer as they were written. Example 2 shows the same list of names (in all caps and no punctuation) keyed into the computer in indexing order. Notice the difference in the alphabetic order of the examples. What causes the difference? To understand the difference, you need some background on how the computer recognizes information.

Example 1	Example 2
Units As Written	**Indexing Order of Units**
"A-OK" Smart Shop	007 GNOMES MINING CO
# Off Diet Center	099 HIGHWAY SERVICE
$ Value Store	205 SHOPPING CENTER
205 Shopping Center	AOK SMART SHOP
7 Gnomes Mining Co.	DOLLAR VALUE STORE
99 Highway Service	ELAMIGO RESTAURANT
E'Lan Fashion Boutique	ELAN FASHION BOUTIQUE
El Amigo Restaurant	POUNDS OFF DIET CENTER

ASCII Values

The American Standard Code for Information Interchange (ASCII, pronounced "Ask E") was developed to give computers a logical way to recognize and analyze data. **ASCII** assigns specific numeric values to the first 128 characters of the 256 possible character combinations. Each symbol, space, number, uppercase letter, and lowercase letter has a unique numeric value. Notice the order of the decimal numbers and the ASCII characters in the ASCII Values Chart shown in Figure 4-1 on page 84. Computers of any size can be used to sort records. The notebook computer shown in Figure 4-2 easily sorts data according to ASCII values.

According to the ASCII values, which is arranged first—an uppercase *A* or a lowercase *a*?

Sort by ASCII Values

What do the ASCII values have to do with alphabetic indexing rules? For one thing, a computer only uses mathematical operations to process information. When you manually sort a list of names, you look at the letters to determine the order. A computer reads *each* character as an ASCII value. Because these values are numbers, the computer places the lowest value, or number, first. Then it sorts the numbers from lowest to highest. A computer sorts symbols such as $, %, and / before numbers written as digits because symbols have a lower numeric value. Since capital (uppercase) letters have a lower value than lowercase letters, a computer arranges uppercase letters first in an alphabetic sort.

If a filing segment began with a space, a computer would sort it before any filing segment that begins with a symbol, a number, an uppercase letter, or a lowercase letter. If two filing segments were the same, but one was in uppercase letters and the other was in lowercase

The first 31 decimal numbers are reserved for nonprinting characters, sometimes known as control characters.

Decimal Number	ASCII Character	Decimal Number	ASCII Character	Decimal Number	ASCII Character
32	Space	64	@	96	'
33	!	65	A	97	a
34	"	66	B	98	b
35	#	67	C	99	c
36	$	68	D	100	d
37	%	69	E	101	e
38	&	70	F	102	f
39	'	71	G	103	g
40	(	72	H	104	h
41	)	73	I	105	i
42	*	74	J	106	j
43	+	75	K	107	k
44	,	76	L	108	l
45	-	77	M	109	m
46	.	78	N	110	n
47	/	79	O	111	o
48	0	80	P	112	p
49	1	81	Q	113	q
50	2	82	R	114	r
51	3	83	S	115	s
52	4	84	T	116	t
53	5	85	U	117	u
54	6	86	V	118	v
55	7	87	W	119	w
56	8	88	X	120	x
57	9	89	Y	121	y
58	:	90	Z	122	z
59	;	91	[	123	{
60	<	92	\	124		
61	=	93	]	125	}
62	>	94	^	126	~
63	?	95	_	127	DEL

Figure 4-1   ASCII Values Chart

Photo by Alan Brown/Photonics Graphics

Figure 4-2   **Notebook Computer**

letters, a computer would sort and list the uppercase letters before the lowercase letters.

By understanding how a computer reads the ASCII values, you can make your computer input more accurate and the output more predictable.

Alphabetic Indexing Rules for Computer Applications

Whether you are indexing and coding filing segments for a manual storage system or for computerized storage, the choice of the filing segment is vitally important. Careful attention to detail, consistent application of the alphabetic indexing rules, and knowledge of how a computer processes words are important points to remember. This section deals with the considerations for computer input of filing segments.

Some overall assumptions about computer input are:

1. Key each indexing unit into a separate field.

2. Key indexing units in uppercase letters with no punctuation.

3. Spell out all symbols.

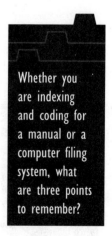

Whether you are indexing and coding for a manual or a computer filing system, what are three points to remember?

Rule 5: Titles and Suffixes

How do you key Roman numerals for computer application input?

Names with titles and suffixes are indexed according to Rule 5, Chapter 2; names with numeric titles are filed before names with alphabetic titles. The computer reads Roman numerals as uppercase letters and sorts them after numbers. Therefore, key Roman numerals as Arabic numbers (1, 2, 3, 4, 5, 6, etc.). The following table shows examples of titles and suffixes with Roman numerals keyed as Arabic numbers and as letters and how a computer sorted them. For example, CPA is filed before Roman numeral II. This list is **not** in correct order because some Roman numerals were keyed as letters.

No.	Key Unit	Unit 2	Unit 3	Unit 4
1	RODRIGUEZ	WILLIAM	F	1
2	RODRIGUEZ	WILLIAM	F	2
3	RODRIGUEZ	WILLIAM	F	CPA
4	RODRIGUEZ	WILLIAM	F	II
5	RODRIGUEZ	WILLIAM	F	III
6	RODRIGUEZ	WILLIAM	F	JR
7	RODRIGUEZ	WILLIAM	F	MAYOR
8	RODRIGUEZ	WILLIAM	F	MR
9	RODRIGUEZ	WILLIAM	F	SR

Rule 7: Numbers in Business Names

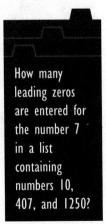

How many leading zeros are entered for the number 7 in a list containing numbers 10, 407, and 1250?

Numbers written as digits should be keyed so that all numbers have an equal number of digits and align on the right. A zero added to the front of a number to have it sort in numeric order is known as a **leading zero**. Most people know that 2 comes before 10. To the computer, which reads from left to right, 1 is first, then 10 through 19, then 2, followed by 20 through 29, continuing to 100. By adding a zero before a one-digit number, you are forcing the computer to read the number as a two-digit number. In Example 1 below, the numbers 14, 7, and 205 are out of order because the computer reads from the left. In Example 2, the numbers with leading zeros sort correctly.

Example 1			Example 2		
Key Unit	**Unit 2**	**Unit 3**	**Key Unit**	**Unit 2**	**Unit 3**
14	CARROT	BAKERY	007	SEAS	RESTAURANT
205	AUTO	SERVICE	014	CARROT	BAKERY
7	SEAS	RESTAURANT	200	AUTO	SERVICE

Rule 9: Identical Names

Identical names are indexed according to Rule 9, Chapter 3. Remember: The address determines alphabetic order—first by the city name, then the state, then the street name, and last the building number. The field structure to match Rule 9 includes separate City, State, and Street fields. If a building number will determine a filing order, a Building Number field is needed. Be sure to add leading zeros in a Building Number field. In Example 1 below, the Address field contained both the building numbers and the street names. The computer sorted by the numbers, which did not result in the correct order. In Example 2, a Building Number field was used to separate the street name from the building number, and leading zeros were added. The sort is now correct.

What fields are needed to sort identical names correctly?

Example 1				Example 2		
ADDRESS	**CITY**	**ST**	**BLDG NO**	**ADDRESS**	**CITY**	**ST**
145 CEDAR STREET	SELMA	AL	025	ASH STREET	SELMA	AL
201 ASH STREET	SELMA	AL	201	ASH STREET	SELMA	AL
25 ASH STREET	SELMA	AL	145	CEDAR STREET	SELMA	AL

Computer Application Software

When microcomputers were introduced to businesses in the mid-1980s, the application software were limited in what they could do. Now, the database, spreadsheet, and word processing application software for personal computers are almost unlimited in their pro-

Can you use a word processing program to create a database file?

cessing ability. Spreadsheet software can double as a database; word processing software can double as a spreadsheet and a database. Consequently, similarities are common among the spreadsheet, database, and word processing applications when sorting a list of names alphabetically. The next section describes the components that allow these computer application software to sort.

Setting Up the Sort

A computer **database** is a collection of facts or information organized especially for rapid search and retrieval of specific facts or information. Large mainframe computers have been using databases and database files for years. A variety of database programs are available for personal computers as well. With more powerful software, a table in a word processing program, as well as a spreadsheet in a spreadsheet program, functions as a database file.

When you have a list of names to sort alphabetically using a computer application, you need to separate the filing segments into indexing units. Each indexing unit becomes a field. A **field** is a combination of characters to form words, numbers, or a meaningful code. Your first name, middle name, and last name could each be a field. Your date of birth, social security number, telephone number, the day you started school, and the month and year you finished high school are all examples of facts about you, and each could be a field. Each indexing unit is a field in a list of names to be alphabetized.

What is a field?

Depending on the application software program you are using, fields usually have a name and a specified number of characters, and they contain a defined type of information. In a word processing table, the name of the field is usually at the top of the column. The first row in a spreadsheet usually contains the name of the field. A field is named when the database is defined in a database software program. The length of the field can be changed easily in both word processing and spreadsheet programs; a database program may not easily accommodate a field length change. The type of information that fields typically contain is either text or numbers. In a more sophisticated database program, the type of information can include dates or logical fields. A Date field usually is keyed in the mm/dd/yy (month/day/year) format. Software developers are changing the Date field to the mm/dd/yyyy format to accommodate the year 2000 (10/21/2000).

When the fields have been determined and filled with information, the finished product is called a *computer record*. A **computer record** is the total collection of fields or specific pieces of information about one person or one item within a file. When all facts about one person are put together in a computer application, a record has been created. For instance, all the specific facts about you listed in one place is a record in a database. In the examples that follow, each row is a record.

What is a computer record?

When all records of similar items, like the names of students in a class or the names of customers of a business, are joined together, a file is created. Because a **file** is a collection of related records, it can be called a *database*.

Sorting Alphabetically

Computer software programs often used in records management applications include word processing, database, and spreadsheet software. This section shows an example sort from each type of application software.

Figure 4-3, page 90 shows the result of an alphabetic name sort from a word processing program, Microsoft Word for Windows®. Notice that the names are in uppercase letters. Each indexing unit is in a separate column. Word processing programs differ in how their sort feature works. Usually, you choose the number of columns to be sorted. You must also choose the order, either ascending (1-10, A-Z) or descending (10-1, Z-A). Just as you look first to the key unit, then to unit 2, and so on to determine alphabetic order, the computer will compare the first column, then the second column, and then the third, and so on.

What is ascending order?

A spreadsheet example using Microsoft Excel® is shown in Figure 4-4, page 91. Similar to word processing programs, you must choose the number of columns to sort and whether the order will be ascending or

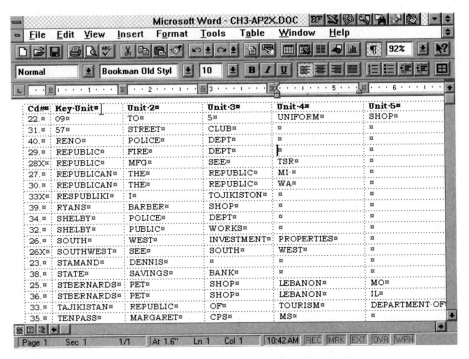

Figure 4-3   Result of a Word Processing Alphabetic Sort

descending. Any units containing numbers automatically align on the right in a spreadsheet application.

A database application sort result using Microsoft Access® is shown in Figure 4-5, page 92. When a field is chosen for sorting, ascending or descending order can also be chosen. All units are included in the sort. Also, more units could be added to the sort list if necessary. Depending on which sort operations are needed, one application software will most likely work better than another. For simple alphabetizing, any one of the three application software will work.

Working Within a Computer's Operating System

Whether an application program is run from a mainframe, minicomputer, or microcomputer, it performs according to the operating system of the computer. An **operating system** is the link

	A	B	C	D	E	F
1	Cd#	Key Unit	Unit 2	Unit 3	Unit 4	Unit 5
2	22		9 TO		5 UNIFORM	SHOP
3	31		57 STREET	CLUB		
4	40	RENO	POLICE	DEPT		
5	29	REPUBLIC	FIRE	DEPT		
6	28X	REPUBLIC	MFG	INC		
7	27	REPUBLICAN	THE	REPUBLIC	MI	
8	30	REPUBLICAN	THE	REPUBLIC	WA	
9	33X	RESPUBLIKI	I	TOJIKISTON		
10	39	RYANS	BARBER	SHOP		
11	34	SHELBY	POLICE	DEPT		
12	32	SHELBY	PUBLIC	WORKS		
13	26	SOUTH	WEST	INVESTMENT	PROPERTIES	
14	23	STAMAND	DENNIS			
15	38	STATE	SAVINGS	BANK		
16	36	STBERNARDS	PET	SHOP	LEBANON	IL
17	25	STBERNARDS	PET	SHOP	LEBANON	MO
18	33	TAJIKISTAN	REPUBLIC	OF	TOURISM	DEPARTMENT OF

Sheet1 / Sheet2 / Sheet3 / Sheet4 / Sheet5 / Sheet6

Figure 4-4   Result of a Spreadsheet Alphabetic Sort

between the computer hardware, the user, and the application software. The most common operating system for IBM and IBM-compatible microcomputers built from 1981 through 1995 is MS-DOS®, an acronym for **M**icro**s**oft **D**isk **O**perating **S**ystem. Windows™ 3.1 by Microsoft is an interface between the operating system and humans. Windows 95™ is an operating system and an interface for humans at the same time. The Windows program was designed to help humans interact more efficiently with the computer. Other operating systems specific to the type of computer and microprocessor are also available. For instance, the Apple Macintosh® operating system is called *The System.* The IBM PS/2™ operating system is called OS/2™.

When you actually begin working with any computer application software, each document you create must have a filename.

What is an operating system on a computer?

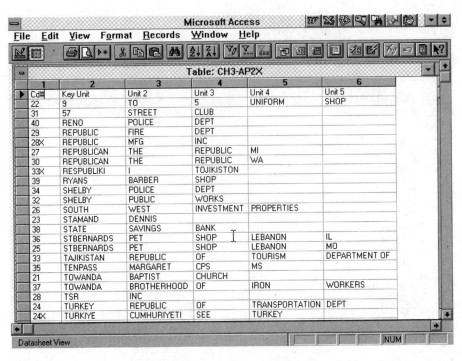

Figure 4-5 Result of a Database Alphabetic Sort

A **filename**, a unique name given to a file stored for computer use, must follow the computer's operating system rules. Current MS-DOS versions (6.X) limit the filename to eight characters. These characters can include all letters of the alphabet, A through Z; digits, 0 through 9; and these special characters: ! @ # $ % ^ & ( ) - _ { } ~ '. You may not use mathematic and common punctuation symbols such as * + = : ; " , . ? / and space or tab. Windows 95 allows longer filenames, as does the Macintosh.

In addition to the eight characters of the filename, a three-letter extension can be used. In some application programs, however, the extension is assigned by the software program and cannot be changed. For example, a file that contains database records will often have an extension of DBF or DTA; a report may have an extension of RPT or REP; and mailing labels might have an extension of LBL. Extensions can be helpful in identifying files stored on your disk.

Hard drives of 500 megabytes or larger are common in personal computers of today. By convention, floppy drives are identified as A or B, and hard drives are identified as C, D, or E. Most personal computers of today have one floppy drive and one hard drive. (See Figure 4-6.) The floppy drive is called Drive A, and the hard drive is called Drive C. Dividing disk space into directories is an important part of managing your computer's information. A **directory** is a subdivision of a disk that the computer's operating system creates. Each set or group of records created for a specific purpose should be in a separate directory. Each directory is then divided into files. For example, you could have a directory for this class called RM (for Records Management) on your computer's C Drive. You could create a file called CHAP4.DOC and save it to the RM directory. The

What is a directory on a computer?

Photo by Alan Brown/Photonics Graphics

Figure 4-6   **Disk being inserted into disk drive.**

full filename for this document would be C:\RM\CHAP4.DOC. Notice that a backwards diagonal (\) is used to separate the drive, the directory, and the filename. Chapter 10 discusses electronic file naming in detail.

Current Trends in Records Management

Many records departments use one of the three types of computer application software discussed earlier to create a database index of their paper and/or nonpaper records. For example, a database that contains the names, addresses, and telephone numbers of customers of a symphony could be created. The actual records would be sales records in paper form. A database would allow rapid creation of mailing labels to notify customers of special concerts or other events to help generate more sales.

Another example of using computer application software to assist in records management is creating an index in database form that lists the shared directories of the network server. Local Area Networks (LAN) are common in many businesses. The use of a LAN allows the sharing of correspondence, forms, and other computer records. Chapter 10 discusses LANs and automated records in detail. A database index listing the names of the common directories and the type of records stored in each directory is helpful in maintaining order in electronic files.

For example, a state government records employee created a word processing database to keep track of file lists/subject lists. In the following example, the first column lists the subject file. The second column contains a description of the directory's contents. The name of the directory where the electronic records are stored is shown in the last column. Extensive cross-references are made so that the information can be stored and retrieved correctly. Chapter 7 contains a thorough discussion of subject filing.

Subject File	Electronic Records Directory	Directory Name
Employment Agencies	Labor (Bureau of) Subject File	Labor
Employment of Handicapped	Compensation (Bureau of) File	Compstn
Disabled, See Also	Employment of Handicapped	Emp-hand
Handicapped, See Also	Employment of Handicapped	Emp-hand

Another use of computer application software to assist in records management is in an archive records center, which potentially stores many types of records from many types of businesses. Archival storage and retention is discussed in Chapter 6. The key to fast, accurate retrieval is being able to go directly to the correct storage shelf and box to locate the record. A database index of the company name, type and date of records, and the location of the storage box helps the records center employee quickly find the correct record. For example, a request arrives from the A–One Accounting Co. to find an invoice from February 1986. By using the database, you can quickly find A–One Accounting Co., and then find the location of the box that holds that record. A sample of such a database is listed below.

Company	Record Type	Record Dates	Row	Shelf	Box
A-One Accounting Co.	Invoices	1/1/86 to 12/31/86	14	3	14
Baker Hardware Store	Sales Receipts	1/1/87 to 6/30/87	80	4	81

Records managers continue to look to technology to make the management of records faster and more efficient. Using computer application software to create databases is one way to find information quickly.

Summary

A computer sorts words based on the numeric values of the letters as determined by the ASCII values. Symbols are sorted before numbers, and all capital (uppercase) letters are sorted before lowercase letters. Whether you are indexing and coding for a manual or a computer filing system, attention to detail, consistent application of the alphabetic indexing rules, and knowledge of how a computer processes words are important points to remember.

When keying records into computer application software, use all caps with no punctuation, key each indexing unit into a separate field, and spell out all symbols. In addition, key Roman numerals as Arabic numbers. Add leading zeros so that numbers align on the right in business names. If you have identical names, set up separate fields for the city, state, street name, and building number.

Word processing, spreadsheet, and database application software can each create a database file to sort alphabetically. To sort correctly, each indexing unit becomes a field. All fields about one person or one item are a record. When sorting, you must choose the field by which to sort and the order of the sort (ascending or descending).

When creating any document, you must save it by giving it a filename. The computer's operating system determines the specific rules for naming the file. Creating directories on the computer's hard drive helps you better manage the information contained on the hard drive. Current trends in records management show the use of computer application software to create databases to help locate paper or nonpaper records.

Important Terms

ASCII

computer record

database

directory

field

file

filename

leading zero

operating system

Review and Discussion

1. What does an ASCII value represent? (Obj. 1)

2. With your knowledge of ASCII values, what adjustments to your input into a computer are necessary? (Obj. 1)

3. Code the following names. Then, describe how you would key each name into a computer application software to achieve correct sorting of the list of names. (Obj. 2)

   a. #1 Rentals
   b. 21st and Main Cafe
   c. 110 Main Place Gallery
   d. $ Days Again!
   e. KOST Radio Station
   f. Dan's Diving Supplies

4. Code each of the following filing segments. Then, describe how you would adjust each for input into a computer application software for correct sorting of all the names. (Obj. 2)

   a. U & I Antiques, Inc.
   b. Henry Hastings, CRM
   c. St. Andrew's Elementary School
   d. 35 North Plains Mall
   e. $ and ¢ Store
   f. Henry Hastings III
   g. Mary Miller, 123 First Street, Gordon, Alaska
      Mary Miller, 123 Cedar Street, Gordon, Alaska

5. Which types of computer application software can perform alphabetic sorts? (Obj. 3)

6. Name at least one way that computer application software is used in records management. (Obj. 4)

Applications (APP)

APP 4-1. Adjust the Input in a Computer Application (Obj. 3)

A. Open the template file, CH4.AP1, into your favorite word processing software program. Correct the input. If you do not have access to a computer, code and then arrange the names in the correct alphabetic order. The file contains the following names:

No.	Key Unit	Unit 2	Unit 3	Unit 4
1	1	$	Store	
2	G	&	A	Apparel
3	10-4	Cafe		
4	Gabby's	Paging	Service	
5	50	%	Off	Stores
6	Mr.	Charles	Gable	
7	1	Hour	Cleaners	
8	Charles	Gable	II	
9	G	4	Associates	
10	2001	Caterers		
11	1040	Tax	Preparation	
12	Charles	Gable	Jr.	
13	20-20	Optometry		
14	Charles	Gable	Sr.	
15	1st	Federal	Credit	Union
16	Charles	Gable	III	
17	2	4	1	Pizza
18	Melanie	Gibson	Springfield	OR
19	2	Day	Video	
20	Melanie	Gibson	Springfield	IL

B. Sort the file. Is the file in correct alphabetic order? If not, check your input and sort again. Save the file as CH4B.AP1. When the file is correct, print a copy.

APP 4-2.   Import a Word Processing File into a Spreadsheet (Obj. 3)

A.   Open your favorite spreadsheet application software.
B.   Insert or copy and paste the template file CH4.AP1 into a blank spreadsheet.
C.   Correct the input, and then sort the spreadsheet.
D.   Print when the sort is in correct alphabetic order.

Applying the Rules

Job 3, Card Filing Review, Rules 1–10

Chapter 5

Alphabetic Records Storage

Learning Objectives

1. Explain the terms used in correspondence records storage systems.
2. Identify the basic types of equipment and supplies for correspondence records storage.
3. Describe the criteria for selecting storage equipment and supplies.
4. Discuss the advantages and disadvantages of the alphabetic method of records storage.
5. Explain the necessity for careful selection and design of an alphabetic records storage system.
6. Explain how color can be used in correspondence records storage.
7. Apply the six procedures for storing correspondence.
8. Explain how a tickler file is used.
9. Identify techniques to find lost or misfiled records.

Overview and Terminology of Correspondence Records Storage

So far in your study of *Records Management*, Sixth Edition, you have learned to index, code, and cross-reference card records. Beginning with this chapter, you will start to work with correspondence—the type of records found in all kinds of businesses. Business letters, forms, reports, and memorandums are all part of the daily correspondence that businesses transact. Even though the use of electronic records continues to grow in business offices, the use of paper is expected to double in the next ten years.[1] Paper as a popular records medium will continue to be used in many business offices. Thus, the discussion in this chapter focuses on the use of equipment and supplies for paper records. Chapter 10 discusses electronic systems used in records management; Appendix B discusses other types of records and their equipment and supplies.

---

[1]Nancy Dunn Cosgrove, "The Paperless Office: Still a Myth in the Nineties," *The Office*, April 1993, p. 25.

What is business correspondence?

You will continue to index, code, and cross-reference according to the ten alphabetic indexing rules presented in Chapters 2 and 3. In this chapter, you will learn three other steps in alphabetic storage procedures: inspecting, sorting, and storing.

In Chapter 1, you learned how the information explosion has increased the number of business records. The goal of records management is to get the right record to the right person at the right time at the lowest possible cost. You have discovered that a set of written rules for alphabetic indexing provides consistency for storing and retrieving records. Consistent application of the alphabetic indexing rules is only one part of an efficient records management program. Using effective, appropriate equipment and supplies is another. This chapter introduces various records storage equipment and supplies available and describes selection criteria.

You are familiar with some of the specific terms and meanings regarding storage procedures in records management. Part of your understanding of this chapter includes the following definitions:

1. **System. System,** as used in records storage, means any storage plan devised by a storage equipment manufacturer. However, the term *system* has a broader meaning when used in a management context. (See Figure 10-1, page 261).

2. **Storage. Storage** is the actual placement of records into a folder, on a section of a magnetic disk, or on a shelf according to a plan. The term *filing* may be used to mean storage, but filing is usually associated with paper records only.

3. **Storage (Filing) Method.** A **storage (filing) method** is a systematic way of storing records according to one of the following arrangements: alphabetic, subject, numeric, geographic, or chronologic. The focus in this chapter is the **alphabetic storage method**—a method of storing records arranged according to the letters of the alphabet.

4. **Storage Procedures. Storage procedures** are a series of steps for the orderly arrangement of records as required by a specific storage method.

The storage method discussed here and in previous chapters has been alphabetic. Records management professionals do not agree on the number of methods of records storage. Some say there are just two: alphabetic and numeric. These professionals do not consider subject and geographic methods as separate methods because subjects and geographic names are filed alphabetically. Other records professionals add a third method: alphanumeric. Still others add a fourth: chronologic. To make storage methods easy for you to understand, this textbook will consider four methods: alphabetic, subject, numeric, and geographic. With the exception of chronologic storage, each of these methods uses alphabetic concepts in its operation. The other storage methods are described in detail in Chapters 7, 8, and 9.

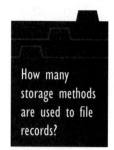

How many storage methods are used to file records?

ARMA (Association of Records Managers and Administrators, Inc.), the professional organization for records management, offers many helpful publications designed to simplify records management procedures. In this chapter, you will note reference to ARMA's *Filing Procedures Guideline*. ARMA committee members prepared this guideline, which addresses the best and most efficient storage procedures. As with the ARMA *Alphabetic Filing Rules*, the *Filing Procedures Guideline* describes procedures to help achieve the consistency so important to records storage and retrieval efficiency.

Paper Correspondence Records Storage Equipment and Supplies

You have heard the adage, "A place for everything, and everything in its place." The records manager or person in charge of purchasing the equipment and supplies for the records center must certainly heed this advice! The filing systems industry has wholesale sales in excess of $8 million annually. What types of equipment and supplies are used most often in the office? What is the specific vocabulary for records management equipment and supplies?

Storage Equipment

Types of storage equipment most commonly used for paper records are: (1) vertical file cabinets, (2) lateral file cabinets, (3) shelf files, and (4) mobile shelf files. Other types of storage equipment and their special uses are discussed in later chapters.

Vertical File Cabinets.   A **vertical file cabinet** is storage equipment that is deeper than it is wide. Files can be arranged front to back or side to side. Vertical file cabinets are the conventional storage cabinets in one- to five-drawer designs. The popular four-drawer vertical file cabinet is shown in Figure 5-1a. The type and volume of records to be stored will determine the width, depth, number, and size of drawers. The most common sizes of vertical file cabinet drawers are for cards, letters, and legal records.

Lateral File Cabinets.   A **lateral file cabinet** is storage equipment that is wider than it is deep. Files can be arranged front to back or side by side. A lateral file has drawers that open from the long side and looks like a chest of drawers or a bookshelf with doors. Figure 5-1b shows a five-drawer lateral file cabinet with roll-back drawer fronts.

Because the long (narrow) side opens, lateral file cabinets are particularly well suited to narrow aisle spaces. They are available in a variety of shapes and sizes, depending on the number and depth of the drawers.

Shelf Files.   A **shelf file** is side open-shelving equipment in which records are accessed horizontally. Shelf files may be the open style or have roll-back or roll-down fronts. Shelves may be arranged in rotary form (see Figure 5-1c) or as a stationary bookshelf (see Figure 5-1d). They may also be mobile with shelves that move as needed for storage and retrieval (see Figures 5-2a and 5-2b).

White Office Systems

Figure 5-1a   **Vertical File Cabinet**   Figure 5-1b   **Lateral File Cabinet**

Richards-Wilcox Office Systems Group

Figure 5-1c   **Rotary Shelf Files**

Acme Design Technology

Figure 5-1d   **Shelf Files**

Mobile Shelving.   With **mobile shelving**, records containers (folders and boxes, as a rule) are stored on shelves that move on tracks attached to the floor. In some cases, the shelving units are not motorized, and the operator must physically move them. More often, the units are electrically powered, which saves the operator both time and energy. One type of mobile shelving is the **mobile aisle system** (see Figures 5-2a and 5-2b), which is electrically powered so that shelves can be moved to create an aisle between any two shelving units.

In some movable shelving equipment, the shelves slide from side to side as shown in Figure 5-2b. The records on shelves behind the moved shelves are then exposed for use.

Courtesy of TAB Products Co.

Figure 5-2a   Mobile Aisle System

Courtesy of TAB Products Co.

Figure 5-2b   Side-to-Side Mobile Shelving

Motorized rotary storage rotates horizontally around a central hub similar to the movement of seats on a Ferris wheel. Shelves that house documents in folders, cards, or microforms are available in sideways positions similar to lateral files or in the regular forward position. (See Figure B-9 in Appendix B.)

Comparison of Space Used and File Capacity. When choosing storage containers, a comparison of floor space used and file capacity is useful for determining cost-effectiveness. Figure 5-3 uses the number of filing inches compared to the amount of floor space required in each of the storage containers shown. Notice the drawer-pull space needed for vertical and lateral file cabinets compared to no drawer-pull area needed for shelf files. If you had 10,000 records to store, 150 total square feet and 24 vertical file cabinets are required. For lateral four-drawer cabinets, 140 total square feet and 16 cabinets are used. For open-shelf cabinets, only 69 total square feet and 10 cabinets are needed. Open-shelf cabinets save space and are more accessible.

Which type of cabinet requires the least amount of aisle space?

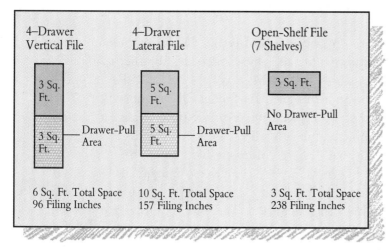

Figure 5-3   **Floor Space Consumption vs. Filing Capacity**

Storage Supplies

Efficient storage and retrieval requires the use of not only the right equipment, but also the right supplies. The principal supplies used in manual storage of paper records are discussed briefly in this section.

Guides. A **guide** is a rigid divider with a projecting tab that is used to identify a section of a file and to facilitate reference. Guides are made of heavy material such as pressboard, plastic, or lightweight metal. Some guides have reinforced tabs of metal or acetate to give added strength for longer wear. Tabs and tab cuts are discussed in detail on page 112.

What purpose do guides serve?

The proper placement of guides eliminates the need to spend time searching through similar names to find the part of the alphabet needed. The same set of guides may be used year after year with no change, or they may be added to or changed as the quantity of records expands. Because of their thickness and sturdy construction, guides serve also to keep the contents of a container (drawer or box) upright. When contents stand upright, neatness and efficiency of storage and retrieval result.

If too few guides are used, unnecessary time is spent looking for the correct place to store or to find a record. Using too many guides that are unevenly distributed throughout the files can also slow storage and retrieval because the eye must look at so many tabs to find the right storage section. Several filing authorities recommend using about 20 guides for each drawer in a file cabinet or for each 28 inches of stored records.

Primary Guides. A **primary guide** is a divider that identifies a main division or section of a file and always precedes all other materials in a section. In Figure 5-4, the NAMES WITH NUMBERS, A, and B guides, in first position, are primary guides. Remember Rule 7 about business names beginning with numbers? Numbers are filed before letters of the alphabet; the NAMES WITH NUMBERS guide and NAMES WITH NUMBERS folder are filed before the A guide. If the volume of stored correspondence with many individuals or firms is comparatively small, only primary guides need to be used to indicate the alphabetic sections. In systems that use color extensively, only primary guides with the letters of the alphabet may be used.

Guide sets that divide the alphabet into many different segments are available from manufacturers of filing supplies. The simplest set is a 23- or 25-division set, the latter having a tab for each letter from A to W, a tab labeled Mc, and a last tab with the combination XYZ. Figure 5-5 compares an 80-division and a 120-division breakdown of guides printed by manufacturers.

The number of alphabet guides furnished by different manufacturers may vary even though each plan may divide the alphabet into 40 subdivisions. Manufacturers may elect to omit Mc, subdivide letters differently, or combine different letters. Before purchasing a set of guides, the records manager needs to examine the manufacturer's alphabetic subdivisions to see if the subdivisions fit specific office requirements.

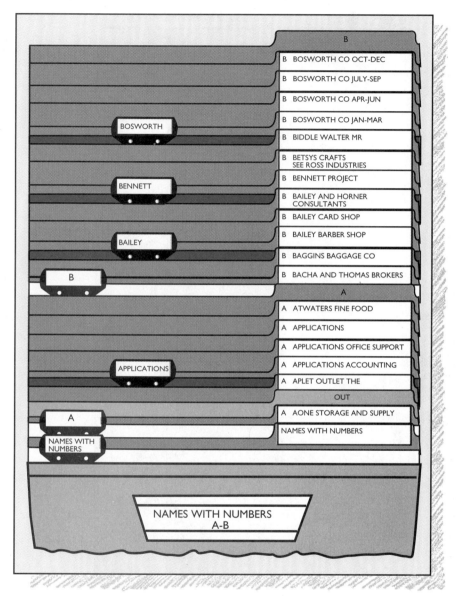

Figure 5-4   One Section of an Alphabetic Arrangement

Some alphabetic guides may be purchased with preprinted tabs. Others have tabs with slotted holders into which labels are inserted. (The guides in Figure 5-4 are slotted holders.)

80 Div. A to Z				120 Div. A to Z					
A	1	L	41	A	1	Gr	41	Pe	81
An	2	Le	42	Al	2	H	42	Pi	82
B	3	Li	43	An	3	Han	43	Pl	83
Be	4	Lo	44	As	4	Has	44	Pr	84
Bi	5	M	45	B	5	He	45	Pu	85
Bo	6	Map	46	Bar	6	Hen	46	Q	86
Br	7	McA	47	Bas	7	Hi	47	R	87
Bro	8	McH	48	Be	8	Ho	48	Re	88
Bu	9	McN	49	Ber	9	Hon	49	Ri	89
C	10	Me	50	Bl	10	Hu	50	Ro	90
Ce	11	Mi	51	Bo	11	I	51	Rog	91
Co	12	Mo	52	Br	12	J	52	Ru	92
Coo	13	N	53	Bre	13	Jo	53	S	93
Cr	14	O	54	Bro	14	K	54	Sch	94
D	15	P	55	Bu	15	Ke	55	Scho	95
De	16	Pl	56	C	16	Ki	56	Se	96
Do	17	Q	57	Car	17	Kl	57	Sh	97
Dr	18	R	58	Ce	18	Kr	58	Shi	98
E	19	Re	59	Ci	19	L	59	Si	99
En	20	Ro	60	Co	20	Lar	60	Sm	100
F	21	S	61	Com	21	Le	61	Sn	101
Fi	22	Sch	62	Cop	22	Len	62	Sp	102
Fo	23	Se	63	Cr	23	Li	63	St	103
G	24	Sh	64	Cu	24	Lo	64	Sti	104
Ge	25	Si	65	D	25	M	65	Su	105
Gi	26	Sm	66	De	26	Map	66	T	106
Gr	27	St	67	Di	27	McA	67	Th	107
H	28	Sti	68	Do	28	McD	68	Tr	108
Har	29	Su	69	Du	29	McH	69	U	109
Has	30	T	70	E	30	McN	70	V	110
He	31	To	71	El	31	Me	71	W	111
Her	32	U	72	Er	32	Mi	72	Wam	112
Hi	33	V	73	F	33	Mo	73	We	113
Ho	34	W	74	Fi	34	Mu	74	Wh	114
Hu	35	We	75	Fo	35	N	75	Wi	115
I	36	Wh	76	Fr	36	Ne	76	Wil	116
J	37	Wi	77	G	37	No	77	Wim	117
K	38	Wo	78	Ge	38	O	78	Wo	118
Ki	39	X-Y	79	Gi	39	On	79	X-Y	119
Kr	40	Z	80	Go	40	P	80	Z	120

Esselte Pendaflex Corporation

Figure 5-5 Comparison of Guide Sets for A to Z Indexes

Special Guides. To lead the eye more quickly to a specific place in a file, a **special** or **auxiliary guide** may be used. This guide may:

1. Indicate the location of the folder of an individual or a company containing a large amount of correspondence. In Figure 5-4, the

guides labeled BENNETT and BOSWORTH are special (auxiliary) name guides.

2. Introduce a special section of subjects such as one pertaining to Applications, Bids, Conferences, Exhibits, Projects, or Speeches that may be found in an alphabetic name arrangement. Figure 5-4 shows a special subject guide, APPLICATIONS, placed in alphabetic order in the A section. All correspondence concerning applications for positions in accounting and office support is stored behind APPLICA-TIONS in properly labeled folders.

3. Introduce a section reserved for names that have the same first index-ing unit. In Figure 5-4, the BAILEY special name guide leads the eye to the section with numerous folders labeled with BAILEY as the first indexing unit.

The tabs on guides for open-shelf equipment are at the side (see Figure 5-6). Because materials stored in open-shelf equipment are visible at one edge instead of across the top (as is true in drawer files), the alphabetic or other divi-sions must extend from the side of the guide so that they can be seen easily. The printing on these side-guide tabs may be read from either side.

Folders. A **folder** is a container used to hold and to protect stored re-cords in an orderly manner and is usually made of heavy material such as manila, Kraft, plastic, or pressboard. Folders are creased approximately in half; the back is higher than the front. A folder may be reinforced across the top of the back edge because a folder is usually grasped by that edge and that is the place receiving the greatest wear.

How are folders used in records storage?

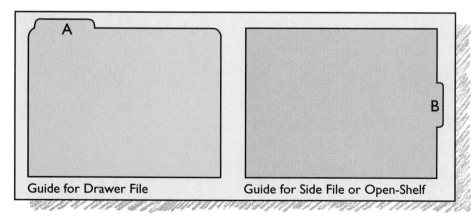

| Guide for Drawer File | Guide for Side File or Open-Shelf |

Figure 5-6   **Guides Used in Drawer Cabinets and Open-Shelf Files**

A **tab** is a portion of a folder or guide that extends above the regular height or beyond the regular width of the folder upon which the caption appears. (See "Labels," page 118.) Folder and guide tabs are available in different sizes or *cuts*. A **tab cut** is the length of the tab expressed as a proportion of the width or height of the folder or guide. A tab extending across the complete width of a folder is called *straight cut* (see Figure 5-7). *One-third cut* tabs extend only one-third the width of a folder and may be in any of three positions (see Figure 5-7).

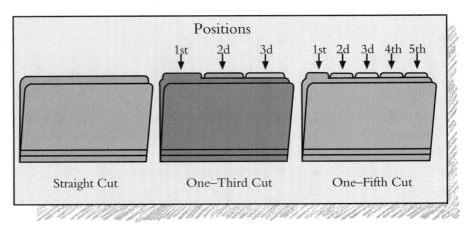

Figure 5-7   **Commonly Used Folder Cuts and Positions**

Position refers to the location of the tab on a guide or folder. First position means the tab is at the left; second position means the tab is second from the left; and so on. *Straight-line arrangement* aligns folder tabs in one position; for example, all tabs are third position (see Figure 5-4). *Staggered arrangement* follows a series of several different positions of folder tabs from left to right according to a set pattern (see Figure 5-7, above). Straight-line arrangement is preferred because of ease in reading label captions; the eye travels faster in a straight line than when it jumps back and forth from left to right. The most efficient position for folders is third with third-cut tabs, and the most efficient position for guides is either first or second with fifth-cut tabs as shown in Figure 5-4.

Tabs on folders for open-shelf equipment are on the side edge (see Figure 5-8) in various positions according to the manufacturer's system or the customer's preference.

Folders behind every guide are used to keep like records together. The three main types of folders used in alphabetic storage are general folders, individual folders, and special folders.

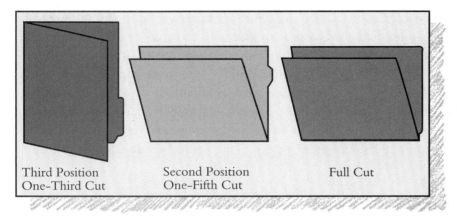

Third Position
One-Third Cut

Second Position
One-Fifth Cut

Full Cut

Figure 5-8   Open-Shelf File Folders

General Folders.   Every primary guide has a correspondingly labeled folder, called a *general folder,* bearing the same caption as that on the guide. A **general folder** contains records to and from correspondents with a small volume so that an individual folder or folders are not necessary. In Figure 5-4, the A folder is a general folder and is the last folder in that section. General folders often are color coded for greater visibility.

Records are arranged inside a general folder alphabetically by the correspondents' names. Then, the most recently dated record is placed on top within each correspondent's records (see Figure 5-9).

Figure 5-9   Arrangement of Records in a General Folder

Individual Folders.   An **individual folder** is used to store the records of an individual correspondent. Records are arranged chronologically within an individual folder with the most recently dated record on top. In Figure 5–4, all individual folders are third–cut, third position.

Records pertaining to one correspondent are removed from the general folder and placed in an individual folder when the number of records accumulates to a predetermined number. Individual folders are placed in alphabetic order between the primary guide and its general folder.

Special Folders.   A **special folder** follows an auxiliary or special guide in an alphabetic arrangement. In Figure 5–4, three special folders are shown: two behind APPLICATIONS and one behind BENNETT. Within the APPLICATIONS ACCOUNTING folder, all records pertaining to accounting positions are arranged first by the names of the applicants. If an applicant has more than one record in the folder, those records are arranged by date with the most recent date on top. Within the BENNETT PROJECT folder, records are arranged by date with the most recent one on top.

Care of Folders.   Proper care of folders will help make stored records readily accessible. When records start to "ride up" in any folder, too many papers are in the folder. The number of records that will fit into one folder obviously depends on the thickness of the papers. Records should never protrude from the folder edges and should always be inserted with their tops to the left. The most useful and most often recommended folders have *score marks* (indented or raised lines or series of marks) along the bottom edge to allow for expansion of the folder. As it becomes filled, the folder is refolded along a score mark and expanded to give it a flat base on which to rest. Most folders can be expanded from 3/4 to 1 inch. If folders are refolded at the score marks (see Figure 5–10), the danger of folders bending and sliding under others is reduced, papers do not curl readily, and a neater looking file results.

A folder lasts longer and is easier to use if it is not stuffed beyond its capacity. If too many papers are contained in an individual folder, a second folder is prepared for that correspondent. The folders are then labeled to show that the records are arranged chronologically in them (see the four BOSWORTH CO folders in Figure 5–4). Sometimes the

What is a general folder? an individual folder? a special folder?

Why are score marks on file folders?

114

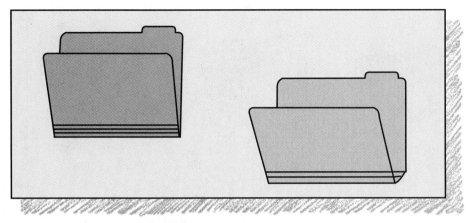

Figure 5-10   **Flat Folder and Expanded Folder**

papers are redistributed in folders by subjects instead of by dates, as is the case with APPLICATIONS in Figure 5-4.

New folders may be needed because:

1. A new group of names is to be added to a file.

2. Older folders have become full, and additional ones must be added to take care of the overload.

3. Enough records have accumulated for certain correspondents so that their records can be removed from the general folders and put into individual folders.

4. Folders have worn out from heavy use and must be replaced.

5. The regular time of the year has arrived for replacing folders and transferring infrequently used folders to inactive storage. Further explanation of records transfer is contained in Chapter 6.

Other types of folders often used in offices include:

1. The **suspension** or **hanging folder** has built-in hooks that hang from parallel bars on the sides of the storage equipment (see Figure 5-11, left).

2. The **bellows (expansion) folder** is made with creases along its bottom and sides so that it can expand like an accordion. These folders are used when the volume of stored records is small (see Figure 5-11, middle).

When are new folders needed?

115

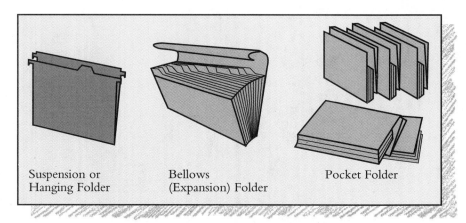

Figure 5-11   Special Folders Used to Store Paper Records

3. The **pocket folder** has a great deal more expansion at the bottom than that of the ordinary folder (see Figure 5–11, right). A pocket folder is useful for transporting as well as for storing records.

Follower Blocks or Compressors.   Failing to use proper means to hold drawer contents upright causes folders to bend and to slide under one another. Folders are kept upright by using the proper number of guides and by correctly using a follower block behind the guides and folders. A **follower block (compressor)** is a device at the back of a container that may be moved to allow for contraction or expansion of its contents (see Figure 5–12). A follower block that is too loose will allow the drawer contents to sag; one that is too tight will make filing and retrieving a folder difficult. In an overcompressed drawer, as in an overcrowded drawer, locating and removing a single sheet of paper is almost impossible. Instead of follower

What is the purpose of a follower block in a file drawer?

Figure 5-12   Follower Block (Compressor)

blocks, some file drawers have slim steel upright dividers placed permanently throughout the file drawer to keep the contents vertical.

OUT Indicators.　　OUT indicators are control devices that show the location of borrowed records at all times. They contain a form for writing the name of the person who borrowed the record, the date it was borrowed, a brief statement of its contents, and the date it should be returned to storage. When a borrowed record is returned to storage, the OUT indicator is removed to be reused, thrown away, or saved and later used to check the activity at the files or to determine which records are active or inactive. The more commonly used indicators are OUT guides, OUT folders, and OUT sheets; examples are shown in Figures 5-13a, 5-13b, and 5-13c.

What is an OUT guide? OUT folder? OUT sheet?

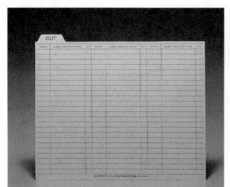

Courtesy of TAB Products Co.

Figure 5-13a **OUT Guide**

Courtesy of TAB Products Co.

Figure 5-13b **OUT Folder**

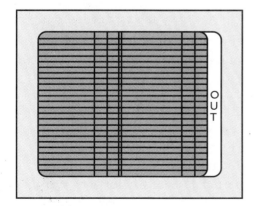

Figure 5-13c **OUT Sheet**

OUT Guide. An **OUT guide** is a special guide used to replace any record that has been removed from storage and to indicate what was taken and by whom. When the borrowed record is returned, the filer can quickly find the exact place from which the record was taken. An OUT guide is made of the same sturdy material as other guides with the word OUT printed on its tab in a large size and in a distinctive color. In Figure 5-4, an OUT guide is located between the AONE STORAGE AND SUPPLY and the APLET OUTLET THE individual folders.

OUT Folder. An **OUT folder** is a special folder used to replace a complete folder that has been removed from storage. This folder has a pocket or slot into which a small card is placed bearing the same information concerning who took the folder, the date it was taken, its contents, and the date it should be returned to storage. The OUT folder remains in the file as a temporary storage place for records that will be transferred to the permanent folder when it is returned to storage.

OUT Sheet. An **OUT sheet** is a form that is inserted in place of a record or records removed from a folder. An OUT sheet is often the same size and color as an OUT guide, but its thickness is that of a sheet of paper. An OUT sheet also remains in the file until the borrowed material is returned to storage.

Labels. Containers, guides, and folders that help you store records efficiently must be labeled to guide the eye to the appropriate storage location. A **label** is a device by which the contents of a drawer, shelf, folder, or a section of records is identified. A **caption** is the content identifying information on a label. Label captions may be typewritten or computer-printed with briefly worded, inclusive, and clear descriptions of the contents of the container, guide, or folder.

Container Labels. The labels on drawers, shelf files, or other storage containers should be as briefly worded, inclusive, and as clear as possible. The containers usually have holders on the outside where card stock labels can be inserted. Various colors are available on perforated card stock sheets. The ARMA *Filing Procedures Guide-*

line recommends centering the information for the container in uppercase letters with no punctuation. The caption on the drawer illustrated in Figure 5-4 reads NAMES WITH NUMBERS, A-B, indicating that records of correspondents whose names are within the A and B sections of the alphabet are stored in that drawer. Names in which the key units are numbers written as digits are filed before all alphabetic names.

Guide Labels. Labels on guides consist of words, letters, or numbers (or some combination of these items). In Figure 5-4, the guides shown have window tabs into which keyed information has been inserted (NAMES WITH NUMBERS, A, APPLICATIONS, B, BAILEY, BENNETT, BOSWORTH). Some guides come with preprinted information. The ARMA *Filing Procedures Guideline* recommends keying guide captions two spaces from the top edge and two spaces from the left edge in uppercase letters with no punctuation. Single letters of the alphabet may be centered on guide labels if preferred.

Folder Labels. Pressure-sensitive adhesive labels in continuous folded strips or in separate strips may be prepared and affixed to folders rapidly. A colored stripe across the top is often used on a white or buff-colored label. Many filing supply vendors have computer application software that generates labels. Sheets of labels for computer generation usually contain columns of labels across an 8 1/2" by 11" sheet. Names are entered into the computer application software, label sheets are loaded into the printer, and printed labels are produced. Some vendors have thermal or laser printers that will print durable laminated labels. Figures 5-14a, 5-14b, and 5-14c illustrate a computer-generated labeling system.

A bar code is often generated along with a name on a label. When a bar code is used, a tracking system is implemented that keeps "track" of a file at all times. When a file is checked out, some type of scanner reads the bar code. Bar code technology is discussed in detail in Chapter 10. Information about the file and who checked it out is then updated and recorded in a computer program. Sometimes another label strip is generated for OUT indicators. A large law firm in the Midwest uses a system of this

Courtesy of EDP/Colorflex

Figure 5-14a **Colorflex Computer-Generated Labeling System**

Courtesy of EDP/Colorflex

Figure 5-14b **Colorflex Labels**

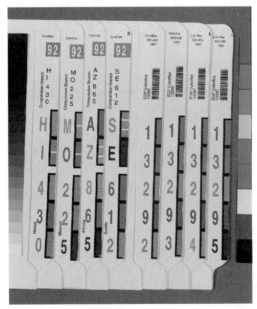

Courtesy of EDP/Colorflex

Figure 5-14c **Detail of Colorflex Labels**

What format does ARMA recommend for folder labels?

type, and its retrieval rates are 99 percent. Refer to Chapter 6 for more on bar code tracking.

The ARMA *Filing Procedures Guideline* recommends keying folder labels two spaces from the left edge and as near the top of the label or the bottom of the color bar as possible. Wraparound side-tab labels for lateral file cabinets are keyed both above and below the color bar separator so that the information is readable from both sides. The letter of the alphabet is keyed first, followed by five spaces, then the actual filing segment is keyed. In all cases, the label is keyed in uppercase letters with no punctuation as shown in Figure 5-15a.

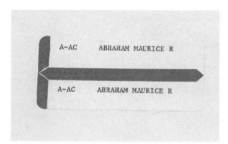

Photo by Erik Von Fischer/Photonics Graphics

Figure 5-15a   **Keyed Folder Label**

Labels supplied by Engineered Data Products, Inc.

Figure 5-15b   **Preprinted Folder Labels**

When new folders are prepared, placement of the labels and the format should be the same as those on other folders (see Figure 5-15b). Consistency in the placement and format of labels helps achieve faster retrieval of a required folder. One way to achieve uniform placement of labels is as follows: When a new box of folders is opened, remove all the folders, keep them tightly together, and stand them upright on a flat surface. Place a ruler or stiff card over the tab edges at the spot where all the labels are to be affixed. Make a pencil mark across the top edge of all the tabs. A very small pencil mark will show on each of the tabs at the same place and will serve as a guide for attaching all the labels.

Sorters.   A **sorter** is a device used to hold records temporarily and to separate them into alphabetic or numeric categories to be stored later. The records are organized in a roughly alphabetic order so that they may be stored quickly when time is available for the storage function. The type of sorter used in any office depends on the volume of records to be stored.

One sorter that will accommodate records with one dimension as large as ten inches such as checks, sales slips, time cards, correspondence, and ledger sheets is shown in Figure 5-16.

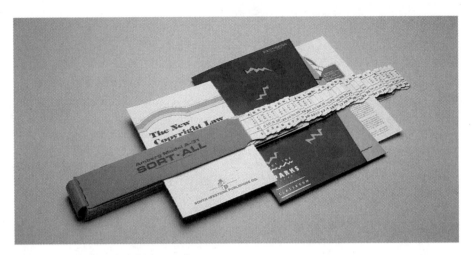

Figure 5-16   **General Purpose Sorter**

Other specialized supplies are discussed in later chapters of the textbook as their use becomes necessary. The supplies just explained and illustrated are basic ones and applicable to all storage methods.

Selection of Storage Equipment and Supplies

What are the benefits of using the right type and quality of storage equipment and supplies?

Efficiency, increased productivity, and overall savings result when the right type, size, number, and quality of storage equipment and supplies are used. Records managers should keep themselves up to date on new and improved products by reading business periodicals, trade magazines, and manufacturer's catalogs and brochures; by attending business shows; and by participating in professional records management association meetings.

The selection of storage equipment and supplies requires that each of the following interrelated factors be considered:

1. *Type and volume of records to be stored and retrieved.* An inventory of what is to be stored may reveal papers, cards, books, disks, microrecords, architectural drawings, computer printouts, etc. Such an inventory will also show the current volume of records already stored. Future volume must be forecast as well as any anticipated changes in method of storage such as the possibility of microfilming or imaging records. Records inventory is presented in more detail in Chapter 6.

2. *Degree of required protection of records.* Confidential or classified records may require equipment with locks; irreplaceable records will need fireproof or fire-resistant storage equipment.

3. *Efficiency and ease of use of equipment and systems.* The ease with which records can be found is another consideration. The simpler the system is to understand, the easier it is to use. Also, less training of new employees is needed when the system is a simple one. Time saved by personnel who store and retrieve records means dollars saved. The ease of expansion or modification of a system or the addition of compatible equipment will be important in meeting the changing needs of an organization.

4. *Space considerations.* Floor-weight restrictions, usage of space to the ceiling (air space), or the advisability of counter-type equipment or something in between, and the possibility of transferring part of the records to offsite storage facilities affect space that, in an office, is costly. The effect of new equipment on present layout and workflow should also be considered.

5. *Cost.* After all other criteria have been examined, cost and the company budget may be the final determinants as to which equipment and supplies may be acquired. The astute records manager realizes that the least expensive equipment and supplies may not provide the most economical records storage. Quality in construction and in materials is important; inferior materials or lightweight stock may need frequent and costly replacement. In determining costs, keep in mind the following points:
   a. Cost of the personnel needed to work with the records.
   b. Compatibility of supplies and equipment.
   c. Advisability of using local vendors rather than purchasing from out-of-town vendors.
   d. Possibility of discounts for quantity purchases.
   e. Feasibility of choosing used, rather than new, equipment.
   f. Volume of records that can be stored within the equipment. Lateral, shelf, or rotary equipment can house more square feet of records than can conventional drawer file cabinets in the same square footage of floor space.

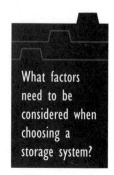

What factors need to be considered when choosing a storage system?

You may need to add other factors to your list of considerations because of the special needs of your organization. Also, consult with users of the same equipment that you are considering acquiring. They can describe some of the benefits or problems associated with the equipment.

Correspondence Storage Procedures

This last section of the chapter reviews the advantages and disadvantages of alphabetic records storage; some criteria for selecting an alphabetic storage system; and, finally, procedures for storing correspondence alphabetically.

Advantages and Disadvantages of Alphabetic Records Storage

The advantages of alphabetic records storage are as follows:

1. Alphabetic filing does not require an index and is, therefore, a direct access filing method. **Direct access** is a method of accessing records without prior use of an index or a list of names in the files. In other words, you look directly for a specific name in a file without referring to an index.

2. All records for correspondent names that begin with numbers written as digits are filed before all alphabetic names according to alphabetic indexing Rule 7, which facilitates storage and re-trieval.

3. The dictionary (A to Z) order of arrangement is simple to understand.

4. Storage is easy if standard procedures are followed.

5. Misfiles are easily checked by examining alphabetic sequence.

6. Costs of operation may be lower than for other methods because of the direct access feature.

The disadvantages of alphabetic records storage are as follows:

1. Misfiling is prevalent when rules for alphabetic storage have not been established and when filers follow their own preferences.

2. Similar names may cause confusion, especially when spellings are not precise.

3. Transposition of some letters of the alphabet is easy, causing filing sequence to be out of order.

4. Selecting the wrong name for storage can result in lost records.

5. Names on folders are instantly seen by anyone who happens to glance at an open storage container. Consequently, confidential or classified records are not secure.

Selection and Design of Alphabetic Records Storage Systems

At the time a new office is opened, the records manager must make a decision on the kind of storage system to be selected or designed. For established offices, the system in use may prove to be ineffective because it no longer serves the needs of those who request records. If records are requested by names of individuals, businesses, and organizations with few subjects, then an alphabetic system is best for that office.

When selecting the alphabetic storage method, the records manager should exercise utmost care in the selection or design because, once installed, the method is likely to be used for a long time. To select an alphabetic storage system, or to redesign one, the records manager should know:

1. The total volume of records to be stored.

2. The number of records in each alphabetic section and which letters of the alphabet contain a large number of records.

3. The expected activity in the files—an estimate of how many times records may be requested.

4. The length of time records are to be kept.

5. The efficiency of the filing personnel.

6. The training time available for personnel.

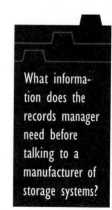

What information does the records manager need before talking to a manufacturer of storage systems?

In some cases, the person in charge of the records may seek the help of a records management consultant or a representative of a filing system manufacturer. These people study the information needs of the office, consult with the person in charge of the records, and make recommendations.

The person in charge of the records must keep the needs of the office in mind and not be swayed by the beauty of a system, the expert sales techniques of a representative, or the apparent low cost of a system. The ultimate test of any successful storage system (alphabetic or any other) is whether records that have been stored within the system can be found quickly when needed.

Examples of Alphabetic Records Storage Systems

Many different manufacturers create storage supplies and systems. The use of color enhances the effectiveness of a records storage system. For instance, all key units that begin with A are stored in blue folders with red labels. If you see a yellow folder among the blue folders, you know that something is misfiled, and you can immediately place the yellow folder with other yellow folders.

How is color used in storage systems?

The use of color has two meanings: (1) **color coding**, where different colors are used to divide the alphabetic sections in the system; and (2) **color accenting**, where different colors are used for the different supplies in the system—one color for guides, various colors for folders, one color for OUT indicators, and specific colors of labels or stripes on labels. Both color coding and color accenting are found in the systems illustrated here.

Many manufacturers have produced trade-name alphabetic systems with special characteristics intended to speed records storage and retrieval and to provide a double-check against misfiling. These systems use color extensively, as you will see in the following illustrations. Other trade-name alphabetic systems are available; the ones shown here are representative of the systems available.

To gain a maximum understanding of each system, study the text material carefully and refer to the illustrations frequently.

TAB Products Co. TAB Products Co., 1400 Page Mill Road, Palo Alto, CA 94303, uses color in simple to complex filing systems. TAB's AlphaCode is shown in Figures 5-17a and 5-17b. The color bars correspond to the first letters of the correspondent's name. TAB claims 40 percent faster retrieval because the use of color eliminates the need to stop and read letters. Notice the blocks of color. For instance, the C guide shows the same first color; the CO guide shows a different second color on the label. Misfiles would stand out because the color pattern would be broken.

TAB's AlphaCode assigns a letter and color for the key unit of the filing segment and then a second color for the second letter of the key unit. Supplies for the AlphaCode come in handy rolls of adhesive labels. The folders are ordinary manila color. However, the records manager can choose to have TAB generate computer AlphaCode folders from the company's list, tape, or disk. Or, TAB now offers computer application software that generates a company's information on labels. The generated label contains all the letters and colors and is applied in one motion.

Other TAB systems assign a letter and color for the key unit of the filing segment, a second color for the second letter of the key unit, and a third color for the first letter of the second unit.

Courtesy of TAB Products Co.

Figure 5-17a   **TAB's AlphaCode System**

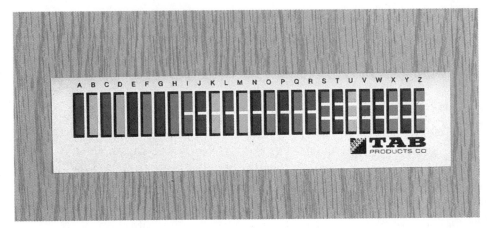

Courtesy of TAB Products Co.

Figure 5-17b   **TAB's Color Coding System**

Smead Manufacturing Company.   Smead Manufacturing Company, Hastings, Minnesota, uses color in its Alpha–Z indexing system shown in Figures 5-18a, 5-18b, and 5-18c. Smead claims that Alpha–Z is the most widely used alphabetic color coding system. Colors are assigned to each letter of the alphabet as a colored bar on white labels. File titles are keyed on the labels, which wrap around the tab of the file folder. The colored bars form a band of color for all folders beginning with that letter, which makes misfiles easy to locate quickly.

For alphabetic filing of 1,000 records or fewer, a color band, plus the alphabetic letter in the same color, is enough for effective color coding as shown in Figures 5-18a and 5-18b. Larger systems use additional colored labels for the third character of the folder title to break the color line for the different letters as shown in Figure 5-18c. Computer-generated labels may also be used to create the colored labels.

Procedures for Storing Correspondence Records

The actual storing operation is an exacting responsibility that must be done with concentration and the knowledge that a mistake may be costly. No matter whether records storage is centralized, decentralized, or centrally controlled, the filing procedures remain the same: Records

128

Courtesy of Smead Manufacturing Co.

Figure 5-18a **Smead's Alpha-Z System
on Open Shelf**

Courtesy of Smead Manufacturing Co.

Figure 5-18b **Smead's Alpha-Z
System in a
Lateral File**

Courtesy of Smead Manufacturing Co.

Figure 5-18c **Smead's Alpha-Z System**

must be (1) inspected, (2) indexed, (3) coded, (4) cross-referenced if necessary, (5) sorted, and (6) stored (see Figure 5-19). Therefore, the filer must enjoy detailed work, be dexterous, have a good memory, be willing to follow set procedures, be interested in developing new and better procedures, and realize the importance of correctly storing all records so that they may be found immediately when needed. Each procedure is discussed in the following section.

Inspecting. Checking a record for its "readiness to be filed" is known as **inspecting**. A business record must not be stored until its contents have been noted by someone with authority. Storing must not take place before whatever needs to be done with the record has been done. Anyone who stores records should be absolutely certain that the actions required by the contents of the records have been taken or noted in a reminder system such as a tickler file. This way, the records will be brought to the attention of the proper person at a future date. (See page

	Inspecting	Look for release mark!
	Indexing	Most important step!
	Coding	Mark the filing segment.
	Cross-Referencing	Think! Use the rules.
	Sorting	Rough sort. Then, fine sort. Coordinate these steps to handle the record just once.
	Storing	Prepare record for storage. Check again to match filing segments. Most recent date on top.

Figure 5-19 **Storage Procedures for Correspondence Records**

139.) Storing records before their contents have been noted and before appropriate action has been taken can sometimes cause embarrassment to a business and might even result in financial loss or loss of goodwill.

The copy of an outgoing letter or other communication would appear ready to be stored when the filer receives it for storage. But in most offices every original (or incoming) record to be stored must bear a **release mark** showing that the record is ready for storage (see JJ on Figure 5-20). The person who has prepared the reply or otherwise handled the matter usually puts on the record this release mark, which may be initials, a code or check mark, a punched symbol, a stamped notation, a lightly drawn pencil line through the contents, or some other agreed-upon mark. A missing mark is a signal to the filer to inquire why the release mark is missing. A date/time stamp (see OCT 23, 19-- 10:30 AM in Figure 5-20) is not a release mark. The person who opens mail often stamps the correspondence with a date/time stamp showing the date and time received for reference purposes only.

A cardinal rule that all filers must observe, therefore, is:

Be sure that the record to be stored has been released for storage.

How do you know when a record is ready to be stored?

Indexing. Because you have indexed filing segments on cards, you know that indexing is a mental process. On correspondence, the name (filing segment) may appear in various places. As you know, the selection of the right name by which to store the record means that the record will be found quickly when it is needed. If the wrong name is selected, much time will be wasted trying to locate the record when it is eventually requested. Here are some rules to keep in mind when indexing correspondence—incoming and outgoing:

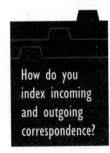

How do you index incoming and outgoing correspondence?

Incoming Correspondence

1. On incoming correspondence, the name for storage purposes is usually in the letterhead.

2. If a letterhead has no relationship with the contents of the letter, the writer's location or the writer's business connection is used. The letterhead name is disregarded for filing purposes. An example is a letter written on hotel stationery by a person who is out of town on a business trip.

3. Incoming correspondence on plain paper (paper without a letterhead—usually personal) is most likely to be called for by the name in the signature line, which will then be the one used for storage.

4. When both the company name and the writer's name seem to be of equal importance, the company name is used.

Outgoing Correspondence

1. On the file copy of an outgoing letter, the most important name is usually the one contained in the inside address.

2. When both the company name and an individual's name are contained in the inside address of the file copy of an outgoing letter, the company name is used for filing unless the letter is personal or unless a name in the body is the correct name to index.

3. On the copy of a personal letter, the writer's name may be the most important and should be used for storage.

If a special subject is used in an alphabetic arrangement (such as Applications), the subject is given precedence over both company and individual names appearing in the correspondence. Often, the subject name is written on the correspondence at the top right.

Sometimes two names seem equally important. One name is selected as the name by which the record is to be stored, and the other name is cross-referenced according to the rules learned in Chapters 2 and 3. In case of real doubt as to the most important name, clarification should be requested from the records supervisor or the department from which the record came. If a records manual is in use in the office, it should be consulted.

Coding. The filer is often responsible for coding the record. The filing segment may be coded in any one of several ways. Figure 5–20 shows diagonals placed between the units, the key unit underlined, and the remaining units numbered. In some offices, a colored pencil is used for coding to make the code stand out; in other offices, coding is done with a pencil to keep distracting marks at a minimum.

Coding saves time when refiling is necessary. If an uncoded record is removed from storage and returned at a later date to be refiled, it must be reindexed and recoded.

What are the advantages to coding records?

Cross-Referencing. The same cross-reference rules learned in Chapters 2 and 3 apply for storing correspondence. Here's an example:

Assume that the letter shown in Figure 5-20 comes to the filer for storage. The record is indexed and coded for Investment Strategies, Inc., by placing diagonals between the units, underlining the key unit, and numbering the other units. The letter is then coded for cross-referencing because it may be called for by Trotter Poll Company. A wavy line is drawn under Trotter Poll Company; diagonals are placed between the units; all units are numbered; and an X is written in the margin. The cross-reference coding marks are slightly different from those used for the regular coding of a record. Figure 5-21 shows the cross-reference sheet prepared for the letter shown in Figure 5-20.

A separate cross-reference sheet, as shown in Figure 5-21, may be prepared for the alternative name, or an extra copy of the original record may be coded for cross-reference purposes. The cross-reference sheet shown in Figure 5-21 is a type that may be printed in quantity and used as needed. Note that the name at the top of the cross-reference sheet is coded for storage in exactly the same way as is any record—diagonals are placed between the units, the key unit is underlined with a straight line, and the succeeding units are numbered.

At times a permanent cross-reference replaces an individual folder to direct the filer to the correct storage place. A **permanent cross-reference** is a guide with a tab in the same position as the tabs on the individual folders. The caption on the tab of the permanent cross-reference consists of the name by which the cross-reference is filed, the word SEE, and the name by which the correspondence may be found. In Figure 5-4, a permanent cross-reference guide for BETSYS CRAFTS SEE ROSS INDUSTRIES appears in proper alphabetic sequence in the file drawer.

A permanent cross-reference may be used, for instance, when a company changes its name. The company's folder is removed from the file, the name is changed on the folder, and the folder is refiled under the new name. A permanent cross-reference guide is prepared under the original name and is placed in the position of the original folder in the file. For example, assume that EMORY AND PHILLIPS changes its name to RIVERSIDE DISTRIBUTION CO. The EMORY AND PHILLIPS folder is removed from the file, the name on the folder is changed to RIVERSIDE DISTRIBUTION CO, and the folder is filed under the new name. A permanent cross-reference guide is made and filed in the E section of the file:

CROSS-REFERENCE SHEET

Name or Subject 3
Trotter Poll Company

Date of Record
October 21, 19--

Regarding
Survey of customers regarding investment objectives

SEE

Name or Subject
Investment Strategies, Inc.

Date Filed *10/23/19--*   By *J. Phelps*

Figure 5-21   Cross-Reference Sheet for Letter Shown in Figure 5-20

Investment Strategies, Inc.

150 SW Salmon Ave., Suite 200
Portland, OR 97202-0015
(503) 555-0992
(503) 555-0991 FAX

OCT 23, 19-- 10:30 AM

October 21, 19--

Ms. Joan Jensen, Manager
1040 Tax Express
1500 SW Cedar Ave.
Portland, OR 97204-1500

Dear Ms. Jensen:

We are very interested in forming a type of partnership for your customers. We would like to help your customers by offering advice on investments for both short-term and long-term goals.

To help us get an idea of what your customers need, we have hired the Trotter Poll Company to conduct a survey of the investment objectives of your customers.

In the near future Trotter Poll Company will send to each of your customers a questionnaire that will provide spaces for the listing of annual income, approximate annual expenses, amount available for savings and investment, investment objectives, and other pertinent information. Trotter Poll Company will analyze the data received from all those who return the questionnaire and will then make recommendations for types of investments your customers should make.

We shall greatly appreciate your cooperation in this matter.

Sincerely yours,

James Washington

James Washington
Investment Counselor

pas

Figure 5-20   Letter Properly Released and Coded

135

EMORY AND PHILLIPS

SEE RIVERSIDE DISTRIBUTION CO

Sorting.   **Sorting** is the act of arranging records in the sequence in which they are to be filed or stored. In most instances, a sorting step precedes the actual storing. Sorting should be done as soon as possible after coding and cross–referencing, especially if storage must be delayed. Sometimes coding and rough sorting are done in sequence. When **rough sorting**, records are arranged according to sections but in random order within the sections. After each record has been coded, it is rough sorted into a pile of like pieces—all A, B, Cs are together; all D, E, Fs are together; and so on. Records having filing segments that are numbers written as digits are rough sorted into 100s, 200s, and so on. Coordination of inspection, indexing, coding, and sorting means handling each record only once. If a record is needed before it has been filed, it can be found with less delay if records have been rough sorted instead of being put in a stack on a desk or in a "to-be-filed" basket.

A delay in sorting until all records have been coded means handling each record twice, consumes more time and energy, and results in greater record-handling costs. If sorting is delayed until all coding is finished, the records may then be grouped into another rough-sort arrangement: all the As together in no special order; all the Bs together at random; all the Cs together in mixed order; all 100s in random order; all 200s in random order; and so forth. This sorting may be done on top of a desk or table with the records placed in separate piles. The sorting will be easier if a desktop sorter that has holders or pockets for various sections of the alphabet is used.

After the records have been rough sorted according to the alphabetic sections, they are removed section by section, alphabetized properly within each section, and replaced in order in the sorter for temporary storage. This step is often called **fine sorting,** or arranging records in exact sequence prior to storing. The records in all sections have thus been alphabetized and are now ready to be stored. Records with numeric key units are arranged in numeric order prior to storing. The records are removed in sequence from all divisions of the sorter and taken to the storage containers.

What is the difference between rough sorting and fine sorting?

Using these rough and fine sorting procedures saves time. By handling each paper once when inspecting, indexing, coding, cross-referencing, and rough sorting, wasted motion will be minimized because all records are in strict alphabetic or numeric order. The greater the number of records to be stored, the more precise or fine the sorting should be to make the work easier, quicker, and less tiring.

Storing. **Storing** is the actual placement of records into containers, a physical task of great importance in an office. A misfiled record is often a lost record; and a lost record means loss of time, money, and peace of mind while searching for the record.

The time at which records are actually put into the storage containers depends on the work load during the day. In some offices, storing is the job performed first in the morning; in others, all storing is done in the early afternoon; in others, storing is the last task performed each day. In still other offices, storing is done when records are ready and when a lull in other work occurs. In a centralized filing department, storage takes place all day every day—storing, retrieving, and restoring without any lulls.

Prior to the actual storage of records, the filer must remember to:

1. Remove paper clips from records to be stored.

2. Staple records together (if they belong together) in the upper right corner so that other records kept in the folder will not be inserted between them by mistake.

3. Mend torn records.

4. Unfold folded records to conserve storage space unless the folded records fit the container better than when unfolded.

What preparation is needed before storing a record?

Then, when at the storage equipment, the filer should:

1. Glance quickly at the container label to locate the place to begin storage.

2. After locating the place, scan the guides until the proper alphabetic section is reached. All records having numeric key units will be stored at the front of the alphabetic file.

3. Pull the guides forward with one hand, while the other hand searches quickly for the correct folder.

4. Check for an individual or a special folder for the filing segment. If none of these folders are in the file, locate the general folder.

5. Slightly raise the folder into which the record is to be placed. Avoid pulling the folder up by its tab, however, as continual pulling will separate the tab from its folder. If the folder is raised, the record will be inserted into the folder and not in front of or behind it.

6. Glance quickly at the label and the top record in the folder to verify further that the piece to be stored is placed correctly because all records in the folder will bear the same coded name.

7. Place each record in the folder with its top to the left (see Figure 5-22). When the folder is removed from storage and placed on a desk to be used, the folder is opened like a book with the tab edge to the right; all the records in it are then in proper reading position.

8. Jog the folder to straighten the records if they are uneven.

Figure 5-22   **Proper Insertion of Papers into a File Folder**

9. Never open more than one drawer in a cabinet at the same time. A cabinet can fall forward when it becomes overbalanced because two or three loaded drawers are open.

Special points to remember include:

1. The most recently dated record in an individual folder is always placed at the front and, therefore, is on top when the folder is opened. The record bearing the oldest date is the one at the back of the folder.

2. Records that are removed from a folder and later refiled must be placed in their correct chronologic sequence, not on top of the contents of the folder.

3. Records within a general folder are arranged first alphabetically by correspondents' names and then by date within each correspondent's records. The most recently dated record is, therefore, on top of each group (see Figure 5-9).

Use of a Tickler File

A **tickler file** is a chronologic arrangement of information that "tickles" the memory and serves as a reminder that specific action must be taken on a specific date. Other names sometimes used to describe such a file are *bring-up file*, *suspense file*, and *pending file*. The basic arrangement of a tickler file is always the same: chronologic. A manual arrangement usually takes the form of a series of 12 guides with the names of the months of the year printed on their tabs. One set of guides or folders with tabs printed with 1 through 31 for the days of the month is also used. A computer tickler file is usually in the form of a calendar or schedule program. Card and folder tickler files are shown in Figure 5-23.

Many office workers use a tickler system to remind them of yearly events such as birthdays and anniversaries; membership expiration dates and dues payments; insurance premium payments; weekly, monthly, or annual meetings; subscription expiration dates; and the dates on which certificates of deposit or bonds are due. In records management, tickler files can be used to keep track of records that are borrowed or that do not have release marks.

What is the purpose of a tickler file?

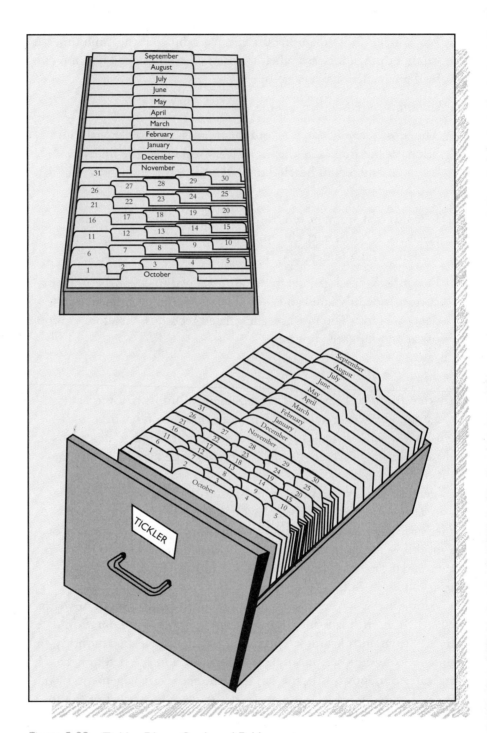

Figure 5-23   Tickler Files—Cards and Folders

On the last day of each month, the person in charge of the tickler file checks through the date cards/folders to be certain that nothing has been inadvertently overlooked during the month. Then, all the papers from behind the next month's guide are removed and redistributed behind the daily guides (numbered 1 through 31). At the end of October, for instance, the spaces behind all the daily guides would be checked, the October guide would be moved to the back of the file, and the November guide would be put in the front. All reminders that were filed behind November would then be redistributed behind the daily guides according to the dates on the reminders.

The tickler file must be the first item checked each day by the person in charge of it. Information on the notes found in the tickler file serves as a reminder to act or follow through on specific instructions.

Misfiled and Lost Records

Even with care, some records are misfiled and become lost. Over 7 percent of all paper documents in any office are lost. Companies spend about $120 to track down a misfiled document.[2] Electronic files are also misplaced; the cost estimate per knowledge worker is $4,500 per year.[3] Paying attention to detail and following established, written rules for filing help eliminate lost and misfiled documents.

If storage is done haphazardly or with no concern for the importance of following consistent procedures, lost records are even more numerous. Lack of attention to spelling, careless insertion of records into the storage equipment, and distractions often cause records to be misfiled and, therefore, "lost."

Experienced filers use the following techniques in trying to find missing records:

1. Look in the folders immediately in front of and behind the correct folder.

2. Look between the folders.

3. Look under all the folders, where the record may have slipped to the bottom of the drawer or shelf.

---

[2]_____, *The Office Professional*, Vol. 14, No. 9, September 15, 1994.
[3]Larry Bates, "Records Managers Need a Game Plan for the PC Era," *Managing Office Technology*, November 1994, pp. 51-52.

4. Look completely through the correct folder because alphabetic or other order of sequence may have been neglected due to carelessness or haste.

5. Look in the general folder, in addition to searching in the individual folder.

6. Check the transposition of names (DAVID MILLER instead of MILLER DAVID).

7. Look for the second, third, or succeeding units of a filing segment rather than for the key unit.

8. Check for misfiling because of misreading of letters—e for i, n for m, t for l, k for h, C for G, etc.

9. Check for alternate spellings (JON, JAHN).

10. Look under other vowels (for a name beginning with Ha, look also under He, Hi, Ho, and Hu).

11. Look for a double letter instead of a single one (or the reverse).

12. Look for Anglicized forms of a name (Miller, Moller, or Muller for Mueller).

13. Check for transposition of numbers (35 instead of 53).

14. Look in the year preceding or following the one in question.

15. Look in a related subject if the subject method is used.

16. Be aware that the records may be en route to storage.

17. Look in the sorter.

18. Ask the person in whose desk or briefcase the record may be to search for it!

What techniques are used to locate lost or misfiled records?

If every search fails to produce the missing record, some records managers try to reconstruct the record from memory, rekeying as much as is known. This information is placed in a folder labeled LOST along with the name on the original folder. This new folder is stored in its correct place as a constant reminder to the filer to be on the alert for the missing record.

Efficient correspondence records storage is the result of:

1. Good planning to choose the right equipment, supplies, and system.

2. Proper training of personnel who recognize the value of the release mark, know and consistently apply the rules for alphabetic indexing, code papers carefully, prepare cross-references skillfully, invariably sort papers before storing, and carefully store records in their proper containers.

3. Constant, concerned supervision by records managers or others responsible for the storage and retrieval functions.

Summary

Chapter 5 discusses the differences among a filing system, storage, storage method, and storage procedures. The four most common types of filing equipment are vertical files, lateral files, shelf files, and mobile shelf files. The most common supplies needed for correspondence storage are guides, folders, labels, and OUT indicators.

The criteria for selecting equipment and supplies include these interrelated factors: type and volume of records to be stored and retrieved; degree of protection required; efficiency and ease of use of equipment and systems; space considerations; and cost.

The alphabetic storage method is a direct access method; attention to detail and consistent application of written rules make this method easy to use. Many manufacturers of storage supplies use color as a means to increase efficiency in storing and retrieving. The six procedures for storing correspondence records are inspecting, indexing, coding, cross-referencing, sorting, and storing. A tickler file is used as a reminder for tasks to be done daily. Tips for finding lost or misfiled records included looking around, under, between, and in other folders; checking for alternate spellings, other vowel combinations, and double letters; and being aware that the record may be temporarily in the sorter or in transit to storage.

Important Terms

bellows (expansion) folder
caption
color accenting
color coding
direct access
fine sorting
folder
follower block (compressor)
general folder
guide
individual folder
inspecting
label
lateral file cabinet
mobile aisle system
mobile shelving
motorized rotary storage
OUT folder
OUT guide
OUT sheet
permanent cross-reference

pocket folder
position
primary guide
release mark
rough sorting
shelf file
sorter
sorting
special folder
special (auxiliary) guide
storage
storage (filing) method
storage procedures
storing
suspension (hanging) folder
system
tab
tab cut
tickler file
vertical file cabinet

Review and Discussion

1. Compare and contrast the terms *storage system* and *storage method*. (Obj. 1)

2. List and briefly describe four types of commonly used storage equipment for correspondence records. (Obj. 2)

3. List and briefly describe five important supplies used in records storage. (Obj. 2)

4. Why is the straight-line arrangement of tabs on folders and guides easier to use than the staggered arrangement? (Obj. 2)

5. What five criteria should be considered when choosing storage equipment and supplies? (Obj. 3)

6. Discuss the advantages and disadvantages of the alphabetic storage method. (Obj. 4)

7. Why should users carefully inspect and study an alphabetic records storage system before purchasing it? (Obj. 5)

8. Explain how color can be used in correspondence records storage. (Obj. 6)

9. List and briefly describe (in order) the six steps to store a record properly. (Obj. 7)

10. What kinds of release marks might you find on records that are ready to be stored? (Obj. 7)

11. What is a tickler file and how is one arranged? (Obj. 8)

12. List at least five procedures to try to locate a "lost" or "misfiled" record. (Obj. 9)

Applications (APP)

APP 5-1. Coding Correspondence (Obj. 7)

On the copy of an outgoing letter, both the company name and the individual's name appear in the following inside address. Which name is coded for storage? Why?

Dr. Joyce Phosgene, President
Callous Records Equipment, Inc.
Coney Towers #47
Dallas, TX 75202-1847

APP 5-2. Changing Storage Equipment (Objs. 2, 3, and 5)

You and one or two of your classmates have formed a records management consulting company. The Fly-By-Night Charter Co. has asked your company for a consultation about its storage equipment. You and your team visited the Fly-By-Night office and noted the following:

1. Correspondence is stored alphabetically in traditional four-drawer vertical file cabinets.

2. Everyone in the office has access to the file cabinets.

3. Ten to 20 stored records are retrieved daily, one paper at a time.

   You and your team need to analyze the Fly-By-Night Charter Co.'s current equipment and determine whether anything should be changed. Would open-shelf files work better? Why do you think so? What factors would contribute to your decision? What other resources are available to help your team assemble the facts needed to propose a solution for Fly-By-Night Charter Co.? Create a proposal for Fly-By-Night Charter Co. to change their filing equipment.

APP 5-3. Observe Records Storage Equipment and Supplies in Use (Objs. 2, 3, 5, and 6)

Arrange for you and one or two of your classmates to visit a local office to observe the records storage equipment and supplies. Make a list of the equipment and supplies that the office is using to store paper records. If office workers are available, ask them the following questions.

1. What type of supplies are used? Are the current supplies adequate for their usage?

2. What type of equipment is being used? Is the current equipment adequate for their usage?

3. What changes would you make in terms of equipment or supplies?

4. Do you have input when equipment or supplies are purchased? If so, what types of choices did you make and how did you make your choices?

Be prepared to give an oral summary of your visit to the class.

Applying the Rules

Job 4, Correspondence Filing, Rules 1–5
Job 5, Correspondence Filing, Rules 6–10
Job 6, Correspondence Filing, Rules 1–10, and Tickler File Usage

Chapter 6

Records Retention, Retrieval, and Transfer

Learning Objectives

1. Explain the use of a retention schedule.
2. Explain requisition, retrieval, charge-out, and follow-up procedures.
3. Explain the classifications of records, two transfer methods, and transfer procedures.
4. Describe records center control procedures.
5. Describe how bar codes can be used when retrieving records.

Records Retention

As you will recall from Chapter 1, *maintenance* and *disposition* of records are two phases in the record life cycle (see Figure 6-1). Maintenance includes storing, retrieving, and protecting records; and disposition includes transferring, retaining, or destroying records. These two phases, as they relate to the retention, retrieval, and transfer of records, are discussed in this chapter.

Records retention refers to established policies and procedures relating to *what* documents to keep, *where* the documents are kept, and *how long* these documents are to be kept. Ideally, the retention of a record is known when the record is created. Retention is part of the *disposition phase* in the record life cycle. However, another facet of retention is determining where and in what condition and environment documents are stored, which is part of the *maintenance stage* of the record life cycle. The next section describes how records are inventoried to determine how long to keep them.

What is records retention?

Records Inventory

A **records inventory** is a detailed listing of the volume of an organization's records. It includes quantity, type, function, location, and frequency of use of the records obtained from a records survey. Knowing what records and nonrecords a company has in storage helps to prepare an accurate retention and destruction schedule.

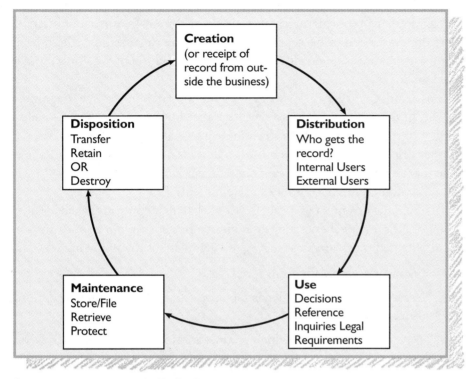

Figure 6-1   **The Record Life Cycle**

An **official record** is one that is legally recognized as establishing some fact. Another name for an official record is **record copy,** or the official (usually the original) copy of a record that is retained for legal, operational, or historical purposes.   Convenience files, day files, and reference material are not considered official records and are referred to as *nonrecords*. Typically, nonrecords are created, modified, and destroyed without formal records management procedures and are not included in a records retention program. Nonrecords should not be retained past their usefulness.

What is the difference between official records and nonrecords?

For example, a document *printed* from an electronic file is often considered the "official record," rather than the file stored on electronic media, because of its readability, durability, and ease of use. The electronic file must still be retained for a week or two, and the printed document may be saved for two or three years, depending on its content.

Electronic mail (E-mail) is another example of nonrecords in many companies. Most electronic mail is sent between workers within one company and is often a means of transmitting other information, rather than being a record in and of itself. For example, an E-mail message advising the recipient that a report is attached to the E-mail message is not important and does not need to be kept. However, in some organizations, the transmittal information is significant when determining who sent what to whom and when.

Records managers must work with the information services departments in their organizations to develop official policies regarding E-mail retention. Some organizations routinely purge all E-mail after 30 days. Other organizations allow each user to determine what to retain as long as the user follows the organization's policy regarding retention. E-mail users must be trained to purge unneeded documents.

A records inventory is a valuable tool to help a company decide which filing method (alphabetic, subject, numeric, or geographic) to use. Information obtained from a records survey usually includes the following:

- Name and dates of records series.

- Location of records by department or office, then building, floor, and room, if necessary.

- Type of equipment in which records are stored—cabinets, shelves, or vaults.

- Number of cabinets, shelves, or other storage containers.

- How often records are referenced—daily, weekly, monthly, or annually—and why.

- Type of media on which the record is stored—paper, microfilm, electronic, or optical.

- Size of the records—letter, legal, tab/checks, other.

- Housing for the records—folders, binders, cassettes, etc.

- Value of the records—vital, important, useful, nonessential.

- Retention requirements.

Figure 6-2 shows a sample records inventory worksheet on which records are identified by series. A **records series** is a group of related records that are normally used and filed as a unit and can be evaluated as a unit to determine the records retention period. For example, invoices for the month of December illustrate a records series, as do bank statements retained for a year.

Once the records inventory is completed, the records manager determines the value of each record and then determines how long records are to be kept (retained). A **records retention schedule** is created from the

Records Inventory Worksheet													
Department: *Contracts*		**Division:** *Sales*			**Date:** *January 1, 19--*								
Records Series/Description	**Record Date**	**Location**	**Qty.**	**Usage***					**Value****				**Current Retention**
				D	**W**	**M**	**S**	**A**	**1**	**2**	**3**	**4**	
CONTRACTS ABBOTT AND MASSEY	1/93-12/93	104	2 fldrs			M				2			3 years
CONTRACTS ACORN HILL, INC.	1/93-12/93	104	1 fldr			M				2			3 years
CONTRACTS ADORABLE PRINTS	1/93-12/93	104	2 fldrs			M				2			3 years
CONTRACTS AFFORDABLE STYLE CO.	1/93-12/93	104	3 fldrs			M				2			3 years
CONTRACTS ANDERSON, RALPH H.	1/93-12/93	104	2 fldrs			M				2			3 years
CONTRACTS A (GENERAL FOLDER)	1/93-12/93	104	1 fldr			M				2			3 years

*D - Daily; W - Weekly; M - Monthly; S - Semiannually; A - Annually
** 1 - Vital; 2 - Important; 3 - Useful; 4 - Nonessential

Figure 6-2   **Records Inventory Worksheet**

records inventory and lists an organization's records along with the stated length of time the records must be kept.

Figure 6-3 shows a portion of a retention schedule. Many factors contribute to the creation of a retention schedule. Creating the records retention schedule is a cooperative effort among several departments in an organization: legal, tax, information management, and records management. Each department has unique needs that the retention schedule must meet. Without cooperative input from all departments in an organization, the retention schedule will not serve its purpose. In addition, the records manager must consider each of the following interrelated aspects when developing a retention schedule.

How is a records retention schedule used?

1. How long will the records be used?

2. In what form should the records be kept? How accessible should the records be?

3. When should the records be determined inactive? Which records should be transferred offsite and when? How will such records be accessed? Will transferred records maintain their integrity and security?

4. What are the applicable federal, state, and local laws?

5. What are the comparative costs for keeping the records or for not keeping the records?

Record	Years to Retain	Legal	
		Claims and Litigation of Torts and Breach of Contract	P
Accounting and Fiscal		Copyrights	P
Accounts Payable Invoices	3	Patents and Related Data	P
Accounts Payable Ledger	P	Trademarks	P
Accounts Receivable Ledger	3	**Office Supplies and Services**	
Balance Sheets	P	Inventories	I
Bank Deposit Books and Slips	3	Office Equipment Records	6
Bank Statements and Reconciliations	3	Requests for Services	I
Bonds and Records	P	Requisitions—Supplies	I
Cash Receipt Journals	7	**Personnel**	
Check Register	P	Applications, Changes, Terminations	5
Checks—Canceled, Payroll	2	Attendance Records	7
Checks—Canceled, Voucher	3	Health and Safety Bulletins	P
Cost Accounting Records	5	Injury Frequency Charts	P
Expense Reports—Employee	3	Time Cards	3
Financial Statements—Periodic	2	Training Manuals	P
Financial Statements—Certified	P	**Public Relations & Advertising**	
General Ledger	P	Advertising Activity Reports	5
Payroll Register	3	Community Affairs Records	P
Petty Cash Records	3	Employee Activities and Presentations	P
Profit and Loss Statements	P	Exhibits, Releases, Handouts	3
Administrative		Internal Publications (Record Copy)	P
Audit Reports—Public & Government	10	Layouts	I
		Manuscripts	I
Audit Reports—Internal	3	Public Information Activity	7
Audit Work Paper—Internal	3	Research Publications	P
Correspondence—Executive	P	**Traffic and Transportation**	
Correspondence—General Office	5	Aircraft Operating & Maintenance	P
Communications		Bills of Lading, Waybills	3
Bulletins—Communications	P	Delivery Reports	3
Messenger Records	I	Freight Bills	6
Postage Reports, Stamp Requisitions	I	Freight Claims	6
Postal Records—Registered & Insured Mail Logs, Meter Records	I	Receiving Documents	5
		Shipping and Related Documents	6
Telephone Records—Installation, Location, Rental Charges, Moves	P	Vehicle Operating and Maintenance	2

P = Permanent
Source: *Adapted from Olsten Temporary Services Pocket Retention Guide, 1993.*

Figure 6-3   Retention Schedule

6. When and how will the records be disposed of?

Once a record is stored, it does not stay in storage forever. Just think of the thousands of storage containers, shelves, and so forth that would be required in offices if that were the case! One critical part of creating the retention schedule is estimating the value of a record to a company and determining how long the record is useful. The next section discusses the value of records.

The Value of Records

Remember the four uses of records first discussed in Chapter 1? Records serve as the memory of a company and their purpose is either administrative, fiscal, legal, or historical. Another classification of records discussed in Chapter 1 was by value of the record to the firm. This classification is useful for making retention decisions. The four categories of records values are listed below with an extended definition for each.

1. *Nonessential.* Records that are not worth keeping such as bulk mail announcements, simple acknowledgments, routine telephone message forms, and bulletin board announcements.

2. *Useful.* Records for short-term storage of up to three years, used mainly for active files of business letters and interoffice memorandums, business reports, and bank statements.

3. *Important.* Records for long-term storage of, say, seven to ten years for retaining more important financial and sales data, credit histories, and statistical records.

4. *Vital.* Records for permanent storage such as student transcripts, customer profile records, and business ownership records, which have lasting value.

What is a vital record?

Information needed to create and keep a records retention schedule up to date can be obtained at little or no cost from various sources. The U.S. Government annually publishes the *Guide to Records Retention Requirements*, which is available from the Superintendent of Documents, U.S. Government Printing Office. Each of the 50 states has developed statutes of limitations that specify the time after which legal rights cannot be enforced by civil action in the courts. Once a record reaches an age beyond which the statute of limitations applies, the record has no value as evidence in a court of law.

Do nonpaper records need to follow a records retention schedule?

Records retention and destruction schedules are based on the value of the *information* contained in the records, not on the storage media. All records media—paper, magnetic, and image—need retention schedules. Storage conditions and environment, however, are important considerations for each type of records media.

Records users need to comply with the records retention schedule. Increased storage efficiency and lower storage costs are two benefits of following a records retention policy. Following transfer and destruction timetables reduces clutter and shortens retrieval time because fewer records will be contained in storage. Additional space will be available for current records needed for day-to-day decision making. The next part of the chapter discusses the records retrieval process.

Records Retrieval

Retrieval is the process of searching for and finding records and/or information. For example, a common storage and retrieval activity is that of finding a name and telephone number in a telephone directory or database. The storage method is an alphabetic listing of names on the pages of a book; the system is a table search (scanning of tabulated telephone lists) according to name. Similarly, nonfiction library books are stored on shelves in numbered sequence, and the shelves are searched by reference number to retrieve a desired book.

What is retrieval?

Retrieval of a record or of information from it can be done in three ways:

1. *Manually.* A person goes to a storage container and removes by hand a record wanted or makes a note of the information requested from it.

2. *Mechanically.* A person uses some mechanical means such as pressing the correct buttons to rotate movable shelves to the correct location of a record, manually removing the record, or recording information requested from it.

3. *Electronically.* A person uses some means such as a computer to locate a record. The physical record may not need to be removed from storage; but the requester is informed as to where it can be found, or the information requested is shown to the requester in some way, perhaps on a screen, or sent via electronic mail.

Requests for stored records may be made orally (from the next desk, over the telephone or intercom, or by messenger) or in writing (by fax, by E-mail, by memo, by letter, or on a special form). The request may be delivered in person, sent by some mechanical means such as a conveyor system, or sent electronically by fax or E-mail. A typical request, for example, might be, "Please get me the most recent letter from Nature's Foods that forecasts the amount of bird food that will be produced next quarter." Or, "Let me have the videotape of the president's annual report to the stockholders." Or, perhaps, "Get me the microfilm of the current price list for patio enclosures." All these records have previously been stored manually according to an established storage method. The letter, videotape, or microfilm must be retrieved from storage and given to the requester quickly. Every minute of delay in finding a record is costly—in user or requester waiting time and in filer searching time—to say nothing of possible loss of business as an ultimate result.

How are records requested?

If filer and requester use the same filing segment for storing and for requesting a record, the system works well. If, for instance, records relating to a company named Huffman Refrigerator were stored under Huffman but requested under Refrigeration Company, retrieval would be extremely difficult because the searcher would look in the R section of the storage instead of the H section. Consequently, good cross-referencing is necessary.

Retrieval and Restorage Cycle

The same basic steps for retrieving are used for handling manual records. Only the specific operating procedures differ. The crucial step, the point at which a problem is most likely to arise, is in Step 1 with the words used to request a record. Ideally, the person who stores the record should be the one who searches for and removes it from storage when it is requested. Realistically, however, one person may store the record and someone else may retrieve it when that record or information is requested.

Steps in the retrieval process:

1. Request a stored record or records series—requester or records center personnel prepares requisition form.

2. Check index for location of stored record(s).

3. Search for the record or records series.

4. Retrieve (locate) the record or records series.

5. Remove the record(s) from storage.

6. Charge out the record(s) to the requester. Insert OUT indicator in place of record(s) removed from storage. Complete charge-out log.

7. Send the record(s) to the requester.

8. Follow up the borrowed record(s).

9. Receive the record(s) for restorage.

10. Store the record(s) again. Remove OUT indicator. Update charge-out log.

Effective records control enables the records manager or searcher to retrieve requested records on the first try and to answer correctly these questions:

1. *Who* took the records?

2. *What* records are out of storage?

3. *When* were the records taken?

4. *Where* will the records be refiled when they are returned to storage?

5. *How long* will the records be out of storage?

Requisition, Charge-Out, and Follow-Up Procedures

Effective records control includes following standard procedures for requesting records, charging them out, and seeing that they are returned, referred to as *requisition, charge-out,* and *follow-up.*

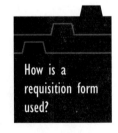

How is a requisition form used?

Requisition Procedures. Requesting a record by preparing a requisition is the first step in the retrieval sequence. A **requisition** is a written request for a record or for information from a record. Even if the borrower orally requests the information or record, that request is put into writing and referred to as a *requisition.* The form may be (1) prepared by the requester or (2) completed by the filer from information given orally or in writing by the requester. Two of these forms are described next.

Requisition Form. One of the most frequently used requisition forms is a 5" by 3" or 6" by 4" card or slip of paper printed with blanks to be filled in. Figure 6-4 shows an example of such a requisition.

By studying Figure 6-4, you see that this form answers the five records retention questions (Who? What? When? Where? How long?) discussed previously. This form may be prepared in duplicate: The original stays in the folder from which the document was retrieved to serve as an OUT indicator;

Records Request	
Name on Record	Date of Record
Date Taken	Date to Be Returned
Requester	Extension
Department	
White copy in folder; blue is reminder copy.	

Usually prepared as a duplicate—original stays in folder; copy serves as a reminder.

Figure 6-4   Requisition Form

the copy (usually placed in a tickler file as discussed in Chapter 5) serves as a reminder to be sure that the record is returned on time.

On-Call (Wanted) Form.   Occasionally, another user will request a record that has already been borrowed. A requisition form replaces the record in the file and identifies who has the record and when it will be returned. The filer should notify the second requester that the record is on loan and when it is scheduled to be returned. If the request is urgent, the filer will notify the original borrower that someone else wants the record and ask that it be returned to storage. The notification may be made orally and/or in writing on an on-call form or a wanted form. An **on-call form** (or **wanted form**) is a written request for a record that is *out* of the file. (See Figure 6-5.) This form is similar to an OUT form.

	ON CALL			
WANTED BY		**PAPERS WANTED**		**DELIVERED**
DATE	NAME	DATE	DESCRIPTION	DATE
9-9	*Wm. Nixon*	8-15	*Acctg. Dept. Budget Figures*	

Prepared as a duplicate—one copy to borrower; one copy is attached to the original OUT indicator in storage.

Figure 6-5   On-Call (or Wanted) Form

Two copies of an on-call form are made—one copy goes to the borrower; the other is attached to the original OUT indicator in storage. As soon as the borrowed record is returned to storage, it is charged out to the second borrower by the standard method of charge-out or by noting on the on-call form the date on which the record was delivered to the second borrower. (Note the Delivered column at the right of the card in Figure 6-5.)

In some technologies such as optical disk storage systems, requested information is retrieved and sent to the requester electronically. If the records center is some distance from the requester, the record is faxed to the user. In both cases, the official record is not removed from its file. No follow-up procedures are needed at that point because the official record is still in storage.

Confidential Records Requests. All stored records are considered valuable, or they would not be stored. Some are so valuable that they are marked *Confidential, Classified, Secret, Vital,* or *Personal.* Do *not* release these types of records from storage without proper authorization—follow the standard office procedure. In some offices, a written request bearing the signature of a designated company officer is required for the release of such records. In an electronic system, access to confidential records is limited to those users who know the password. If a copy of a confidential record is sent electronically, it might be encrypted (the words are scrambled by code) to prevent unauthorized access. When the requester receives the encrypted file, he or she must know the code to unscramble the file before reading it.

Some records may be so valuable or confidential that they are not to be removed from storage under any circumstances. Requesters must inspect these records at the storage container. This inspection is not accompanied by any requisition form other than the required signature of someone in authority before the inspection is allowed.

What procedures are followed for confidential records?

Charge-Out Procedures. **Charge-out** is a control procedure to establish the current location of a record when it is not in the records center, by manual or automated system. A record is charged-out to the borrower who is held responsible for returning it to storage by an agreed-upon date. A standard procedure for charging out and following up records should be observed in every instance, regardless of who removes material from storage. Less than one minute is needed to note the name of a person who borrows a record, while hours can be spent searching for a lost or misplaced record. Borrowers seem to be more conscientious about returning records to storage when they know that records have been charged out

Why use a charge-out procedure?

in their name. Typically, the supplies needed to charge out records consist of the following:

1. OUT indicators to show that records have been removed from storage.

2. Carrier folders to transport borrowed records while the original folder remains in the file.

3. Charge-out log.

   In automated systems, records are indexed and bar coded to identify their place in the file and other information. When the requester has presented his or her bar code identifier and the file is located, the bar code on the record is scanned. An electronic form is created that indicates which record is checked out to whom and for how long. Copies of the form may be printed or kept electronically. A bar code of the form may be printed to be affixed to an OUT indicator and placed in the requested record's "spot." When the record is returned, the bar code is scanned again, the OUT indicator located, the record returned to the file, and the requester "cleared" of any borrowed records.

OUT Indicators.   When a requested record is found, it is removed from storage and an OUT form is inserted in place of the record. An OUT form shows where to refile the record when it is returned. OUT indicators are explained in Chapter 5.

Disposing of OUT Indicators.   When a borrowed record is returned to storage, the OUT form inserted while the record was gone must be re-moved immediately. If the charge-out information was written on the OUT form itself, this information is crossed out, and the form is stored for reuse. In some offices, OUT forms are kept for tallying purposes to see how many records are being requested, to determine the work load of employees, and to see which records are being used frequently and which are not. Totals may be kept daily, weekly, monthly, or yearly as determined by the standard office procedure in effect. Requisition forms that are removed from files may be destroyed. Any duplicate copies of OUT forms should be located and immediately destroyed.

Follow-Up Procedures.   Whoever is responsible for retrieving records from storage and charging them out is also responsible for checking on their return. **Follow-up** is checking on the return of borrowed records within a reasonable (or specified) time. The length of time records may be borrowed from storage depends on (1) the type of business, (2) the number of requests received for the records, (3) the use of a copying machine, and (4) the value of the records.

Experience shows that the longer records remain out of the files, the more difficult their return becomes. Many businesses stipulate a week to ten days, with two weeks being the absolute maximum amount of time records may be borrowed. Other businesses allow less time because records can be copied easily and quickly, and the original may be returned to storage within a few hours. Extra copies should be destroyed when they are no longer needed. Following-up on a borrowed record may mean calling a borrower as a reminder that records must be returned to storage or sending a written request that the borrowed records be returned. If no other requests for the same records have been received, the date the records are to be returned may be extended.

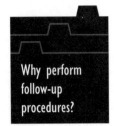

Why perform follow-up procedures?

Following Up Confidential Records. The rule concerning confidential records is generally that the records (if they may be borrowed at all) must be returned to storage each night. A special memory device is often used as a reminder to see that these records are returned. The same charge-out procedures used for other records are also used for confidential records. However, an *additional* reminder to obtain the record before the end of the day is also used. Because the memory jogger must remind the filer that confidential records are out of storage and must be returned, it needs to be something unusual. This reminder may be a note prominently displayed, a special flag, or a signal on the filer's desk.

Charge-Out Log. Usually, a company will have a charge-out log on which information for all records leaving storage is recorded. A **charge-out log** is a written or electronic form used for recording the following information:

1. *What* record was taken (correspondent name on the record and date of the record).

2. *When* the record was taken (date borrowed).

3. *Who* took the record (name of person, extension number).

4. *Date due.*

5. *Date returned.*

6. *Date overdue notice was sent.*

7. *Extended* date due.

CHARGE-OUT LOG									
Name on Record	**Date of Record**	**Name of Person Borrowing Record**	**Ext. No.**	**Date Borrowed**	**Date Due**	**Date Returned**	**Date Overdue Notice Sent**	**Extended Date Due**
Connors Sports Equipment	1/15	L. Burns	5501	2/1	2/8	2/4		
Cyber Quest, Inc.	12/28	V. Ginn	5695	2/2	2/9	2/9		
Olson's Restaurant	1/30	J. Daniels	5235	2/3	2/10		2/10	2/17
Mayme's Hair Design	1/27	M. Tran	5260	2/4	2/11	2/5		

Figure 6-6   Charge-Out Log

Keep the log current and use it in the follow-up procedure. Refer to Figure 6-6 above for an example of a charge-out log.

Records Transfer

Records transfer refers to the physical movement of active records from the office to inactive or archive storage areas. The basis for making the decision to transfer records is the frequency of use of the records.

Records analysts define three degrees of records activity:

1. **Active record**.   A record needed to carry out an organization's day-to-day business; used three or more times a month. Such records are stored in very accessible equipment in the active storage area.

2. **Inactive record**.   A record that does not have to be readily available but must be kept for legal, fiscal, or historical purposes; referred to fewer than 15 times a year. Inactive records are stored in a less expensive storage area.

3. **Archive record**.   A record that has continuing or historical value to an organization and is preserved permanently. Archives can have many uses: maintain public relations; prepare commemorative histories; preserve corporate history; provide financial, legal, personnel, product, or research information; provide policy direction. Archive records are stored in less expensive storage areas, often at an offsite location.

Careful management of stored records requires that established procedures be followed. Procedures to handle all situations should be described

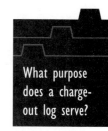

What purpose does a charge-out log serve?

What is the difference between inactive and archive records?

in the policies and procedures manual developed for the organization. In most cases, only the current year's records plus those of the past year are needed in the active files. However, several other factors must be considered when making transfer decisions.

First of all, transfer helps reduce equipment costs because inactive records may be stored in cardboard containers that are less expensive than the steel cabinets used for storage of active materials. Second, the cabinets or shelves formerly used by the transferred files provide additional space for the active files. Finally, efficiency of storage and retrieval of active files is improved because crowded files have been eliminated; and, as a result, the work space in drawers, cabinets, or shelves has been increased.

In the disposition phase of the record life cycle, decisions are made to (1) destroy the record, (2) retain the record permanently, or (3) transfer the record to inactive storage. Records transfer is made according to a retention schedule that was described earlier. If records are transferred, the main basis for making that decision is often the active or inactive use of the record. The following reasons also greatly influence when and why transfer takes place:

1. No more active records storage space is available.

2. Costs of more storage equipment and extra office space are rising and less costly areas of nearby storage or offsite storage become attractive alternatives.

3. Stored records are no longer being requested and, therefore, are ready for transfer.

4. Work loads have lightened, and time is available for records transfer activity.

5. Case or project records have reached a closing or ending time (the contract has expired, the legal case is settled or closed).

6. Established company policy requires every department to transfer records at a stated time.

Once transfer is decided upon, the records manager must find answers to four important questions:

1. *What* records are to be moved?

2. *How* are the records to be prepared for transfer?

When should a records transfer take place?

3. *When* are the records to be transferred?

4. *Where* are the transferred records to be stored?

The answers to the first three questions will depend on the transfer method selected and the company's records retention schedule. The answer to *where* will depend on the method selected *and* on the availability of in-house or offsite records storage areas. After answering these questions, the records manager then follows perpetual or periodic transfer procedures to move the selected records.

Transfer Methods

Two of the most common methods of transferring records are the perpetual transfer method and the periodic transfer method. Each is discussed along with the procedures required to ensure efficient transfer.

Perpetual Transfer Method. Under the **perpetual transfer method**, records are continuously transferred from active storage to inactive storage areas whenever the records are no longer needed for reference. Examples of records that can be transferred by the perpetual method include student records after graduation; legal cases that are settled; research projects when results are finalized; medical records of cases no longer needing attention; prison and law-enforcement case records; and construction or architectural jobs that are finished.

Electronic records and nonrecords should be perpetually transferred from storage on a hard drive to storage on cassette tape or floppy disks. E-mail messages should be routinely deleted if they are not official records.

The perpetual transfer method is not recommended for business correspondence or records that are often referred to and that must be quickly available.

Periodic Transfer Method. The **periodic transfer method** is a method of transferring active records at the end of a stated time period, usually one year, to inactive storage. Guides remain in the active storage containers. However, new folders are made for records that are then allowed to accumulate in active storage until the next transfer period. A commonly used periodic method of transferring records at the end of one time period, usually once or twice a year, is called the **one-period transfer method**. At the end of *one period of time* (six months or a year),

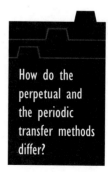

How do the perpetual and the periodic transfer methods differ?

records are transferred. The main advantage of this method is the ease of operation. The main disadvantage is that some frequently requested records will be in inactive storage, and time will be lost in making frequent trips to the inactive storage area. At times, records of some correspondents will need to be retrieved from both active and inactive storage if the requested records cover several time periods.

Transfer Procedures

Once the transfer method has been determined, transfer procedures are communicated to every department. The records manager must see that adequate storage equipment is available and at the correct place to receive transferred records before the actual transfer begins.

Records are either transferred to inactive or archive (permanent) storage. Inactive storage indicates that the record may be infrequently referenced; at the end of the retention period, inactive records are destroyed. The **retention period** is the length of time, usually based on an estimate of the frequency of use for current and anticipated business, that records should be retained in offices or records centers before they are transferred to an archives or otherwise disposed of.

Archive storage indicates that the record must be kept permanently; however, the records may still be referenced. Because some of the records may have historical value, a special display area may be created for those records. Often records are transferred to a **records center**, which is a centralized area usually in a lower cost facility for housing and servicing inactive records whose reference rate does not warrant their retention in the prime office area. Whether the records are classified as inactive or archive, the transfer procedures are the same.

Preparing records for transfer involves completing the necessary forms (see Figure 6-7) and boxing the records for inactive or archive storage. The forms used will vary; Figure 6-7 shows a records transmittal form. Note that the form should be keyed or clearly handwritten because it will be attached to the outside of the storage box and used to locate inactive records that may be requested at a later date. Also note that on the form is information about the storage box's contents such as a description, the time span the records cover, the department name, and the retention data.

At the time records are transferred, the transferring department completes a multicopy set of the records transfer form. The transferring department retains one copy when the box is in transit to storage. The original and

1		**Transmittal of Records to Records Center**								

1	2	**Department** *Administration*
3	4	**Office** *Purchasing*
5	6	**Address** *LeGinn Bldg.* *Rm. 201*

Shaded Areas for Records Mgmt. Use Only

2		3	4	5	6		7	8	9	10
Box Number		**Description of Records** (exact description of contents of each box)	**Rec Disp Auth No**	**Dept Sched Item No**	**Year of Record**		**Location in Records Ctr.**	**Ret Per**	**Disp Year**	**Disp**
Current Year	**Sequential Number**				**Beg**	**End**				
19--	*2140*	*Purchase Requisitions*	*98*	*PUR110*	*92*	*93*				
19--	*2141*	*Purchase Orders*	*98*	*PUR120*	*92*	*93*				

11. Date Transferred *1/10/--*	**Signature of Person Releasing Records** *M. L. Hornsby*	**Telephone:** *X5696*	**Received in Records Center By:** *Bob Burns*	**Date:** *1/10/--*

Form 97-240 (Rev. 96)   Distribution: White & Yellow - Records Center: Pink - File Copy

Figure 6-7   Records Transmittal Form

two copies accompany the box to inactive storage where the box is logged in and its location on the storage shelves is noted on all copies. One copy of the form is returned to the transferring department for reference when a record from that box is required. The copy that was first retained in the transferring department is now destroyed.

Information from the records transfer form is either keyed into or read into automated equipment such as bar codes (discussed further in Chapter 10). When records are borrowed from inactive or archival storage, the same controls are needed as used in active storage—requisition, charge-out, and follow-up.

If the records center does not provide boxes of uniform size in which to store records to be transferred, the records manager must see that all departments use the same size box to facilitate stacking and to use space most economically. Transfer cases are made of heavy fiberboard with sliding drawers. Transfer boxes, also of heavy fiberboard, have lift-up or lift-off tops or lift-out sides and are more difficult to retrieve records from than are transfer cases. Refer to Figures 6-8a and 6-8b for illustrations of boxes stored in inactive records centers.

Courtesy of Iron Mountain

Figure 6-8a　Inactive Storage Center

Courtesy of Penco Products, Inc.

Figure 6-8b　Inactive Storage Center

Records Center Control Procedures

Whether inactive or archival records are stored offsite or within the same building as active records, several control procedures need to be in place to ensure the appropriate security and retrieval of the records.

Inactive Records Index

First and most important, the records must be located. A records center may house several different organizations' records; an in-house records center houses records for all departments. In either case, many different records series are stored on a space available basis. Therefore, like records series with different dates probably will not be stored near each other. If a request is made for an inactive record, the filer must locate the box of records quickly to find the requested record.

What is the purpose of an inactive records index?

To aid in locating inactive records, an inactive records index is maintained. The **inactive records index,** an index of all records in the inactive records storage center, lists details about the records: dates the records were created, description of the records series, department, authorization for transfer to inactive storage, location in the records storage center, retention period, and disposition date.

This information can be manually or electronically maintained and is often a continuation of the records transmittal form (see Figure 6-7), which contains all the information needed for an inactive records index. The records center employee completes the location part of the form by checking the available space in the center and assigning space for the box(es). A copy of the records transmittal form is affixed to the box containing the records; and another copy of the transmittal form is filed in the destruction date file (discussed later).

Charge-Out and Follow-Up File

As with active records, charge-out and follow-up procedures must be followed for inactive and archive records. When the Human Resources Department requests the payroll records for July 1, 1997, through December 31, 1997, a requisition form is completed. The filer scans the inactive records index. After noting the location of the box of records, the filer physically goes to that location in the center, finds the correct box, and then removes the correct record. One copy of the requisition form is used as an OUT indicator and is placed in the box. Last, the charge-out and follow-up file is completed.

The **charge-out and follow-up file** is a tickler file that contains the requisition forms filed by dates that records are due back in the inactive records center. If a record is not returned by the date due, written reminders, telephone calls, or E-mail messages are used to remind the borrower to return the record(s) to the center.

Destruction Date File

The **destruction date file** is a tickler file containing copies of forms completed when records are received in the records center. When a records retention schedule is created, destruction dates are determined. The destruction date is recorded on the records transmittal form (see column 10 in Figure 6-7). Another copy of the transmittal form can be used in the destruction date file.

How is a destruction date file used?

When the destruction date arrives, an authorization to destroy the records is completed. The manager of the department who owns the records signs an authorization form that is kept on file in the records center. Notice the fourth column on the records transmittal form in Figure 6-7 identifies a records disposal authorization number. This number is assigned when the records are transferred. If a written authorization is on file, the number in that column is all that is needed.

Records can be destroyed by shredding, pulping (shredded and mixed with water, then bailed), recycling, or other legally approved methods. Many organizations are contracting service providers to destroy their records because of cost-effectiveness.

Destruction File

Whether a service or company employees destroy the records, the actual destruction must be witnessed or proof must be provided by a certificate of destruction. A **destruction file** contains information on the actual destruction of inactive records. After the records are destroyed, forms in the destruction date file are moved to the destruction file and are filed by department names and dates.

Records managers maintain and dispose of records as part of the record life cycle. Proper control procedures ensure that the right record is available to the right person at the right time.

Current Trends in Records Management

The need to retrieve a record as quickly as possible has led to the development of tracking software. Tracking systems often use bar codes to help in retrieval and to eliminate the need for keying input each time a record is requested. Because pertinent information is not keyed each time, input errors are virtually eliminated when bar codes are used. Whether the record is classified as active, inactive, or archive, a tracking system allows instant recall of facts, location, and in some cases, the record itself. Most tracking systems use a database setup where management at the document, folder, or box level is possible.

Why have tracking systems been developed?

Figure 6-9 illustrates Triadd Software Corporation's (Bothell, Washington) tracking software. Notice the fields used for each of the three levels of tracking. The software automatically applies retention dates from previously entered retention schedule data. Notice the various codes and descriptions. The descriptions and other fields allow powerful searching and finding capabilities. The information required for charge-out and follow-up procedures is included on the screens. Because the records tracking systems offer complete records management control, more organizations are turning to tracking technology to help ensure faster, more accurate retrieval of stored information. See Chapter 12 for more detailed information about tracking software as a means of controlling records.

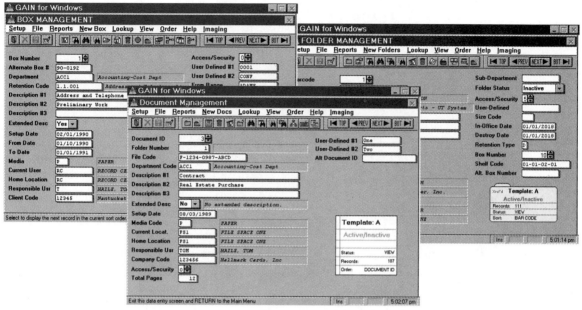

Triadd Software Corporation

Figure 6-9 Records Tracking Software

Summary

The first step in developing a records retention policy is to conduct a records inventory to determine the frequency of use, location, size, and other facts about official records. From the completed inventory, create a records retention schedule showing how long a records series needs to be retained. Create a retention schedule for all official records regardless of the media on which they are stored.

Records retrieval in its simplest form is retrieving information from a record or file. Standard retrieval procedures should be in place to ensure protection of the records. When a request for a record is made, complete a requisition form. Find the record and send it to the requester. If a record is removed from the storage container, the filer prepares a charge-out form. After a specified length of time, perform follow-up procedures to ensure the proper return of the record to its storage container.

By following the retention schedule, records that are no longer active are transferred to inactive storage by perpetual transfer or periodic transfer methods. Again, follow procedures to ensure proper tracking of the records. Final transfer of records is either to archival storage or destruction.

Records centers use an inactive records index to keep track of the location of the records and destruction dates. Similar charge-out and follow-up procedures are needed in records centers. In addition, records centers have destruction date files so that records are destroyed according to the retention schedule. A destruction file is maintained to provide proof of records destruction.

Computer application software is available to keep track of records at the document, folder, or box level. Records management programs that combine document tracking software and bar coding are being used more often in today's businesses for faster, more accurate retrieval.

Important Terms

active record

archive record

charge-out

charge-out and follow-up file

charge-out log

destruction date file

destruction file

follow-up

inactive record

inactive records index

official record

on-call (wanted) form

one-period transfer method

periodic transfer method

perpetual transfer method

record copy

records center

records inventory

records retention

records retention schedule

records series

records transfer

requisition

retention period

retrieval

Review and Discussion

1. What is the purpose of a records retention schedule? How is it created? (Obj. 1)

2. How is a records retention schedule used? How can using a retention schedule contribute to cost savings? (Obj. 1)

3. Name at least three ways that requests for stored records are made. (Obj. 2)

4. Explain the steps in a manual charge-out procedure. (Obj. 2)

5. What is the purpose of using follow-up procedures? (Obj. 2)

6. Describe the three classifications of records based on the degree of file activity. (Obj. 3)

7. Why is transferring records necessary? (Obj. 3)

8. What are four important questions to be answered before records transfer takes place? (Obj. 3)

9. Describe the two most common methods of records transfer. (Obj. 3)

10. Explain the steps for a records transfer. (Obj. 3)

11. Describe records center control procedures. (Obj. 4)

12. Describe how bar codes can be used in records retrieval. (Obj. 5)

Applications (APP)

APP 6-1. *Solving Retrieval Problems (Objs. 1-3)*

You and at least two other students are consulting with Arnold and Burns, a small certified public accounting firm, where two CPAs, one junior accountant, and two administrative assistants work. The two administrative assistants are responsible for keeping the records stored so that they can be found quickly. All five people in the office have access to the files—removing and refiling records as needed. The two administrative assistants do the refiling about 50 percent of the time.

Because the office is small, no controls are presently being used; no one knows who has a client's records except to ask. Misfiling occurs frequently because someone is in a hurry when records are refiled, and the administrative assistants spend unproductive time searching for records that should be in storage but are not.

What kind of records procedures would you recommend? Would additional supplies or equipment provide adequate control of records? What does your group recommend to help Arnold and Burns become more productive? Be prepared to give an oral presentation of your recommendations.

APP 6-2. Recommending Records Transfer Methods (Obj. 3)

What method of records transfer would you recommend for each of the following records situations? Explain your decision.

1. Medical clinic office: Medical case files of deceased patients.

2. Law office: Client folders with ten years' accumulation of records.

3. Department store: Correspondence and billing records of customers, kept for five years in active storage.

4. Shopping center developer: All folders related to a shopping center that has just been completed, all space rented, and the Grand Opening held last Saturday. Folders are those of contractors, lessees, insurance carriers, and governmental agencies that contain permits.

APP 6-3. Setting Up a Computer Application for Archive Storage (Objs. 1, 3, 4)

You and at least two of your classmates have decided to open a records storage center for archive records for various businesses. Prepare a computer form for records center personnel to use when storing and receiving records. Use your favorite software application to set up columns for information about the records that will help you locate the actual records in your center. Consider identifying the company that owns the records, the area of the warehouse, the row, the shelf, box, records series, dates of the records, and the destruction date as part of the information in your document. Name the file CH6.AP3 and save the file on your template disk. Print a copy of the form.

Applying the Rules

Job 7, Requisition and Charge-Out Procedures
Job 8, Transfer Procedures

Part 3

Subject, Numeric, and Geographic Storage and Retrieval

Part 3 focuses on subject, numeric, and geographic records storage and retrieval. The subject and geographic records storage methods are extensions of the alphabetic records storage method. Numeric records storage is truly indirect access filing and is portrayed as a method especially adaptable to electronic records media storage. All three filing methods represent essential skills for organizing records and information in a records management program.

Chapter 7

Subject Records Storage

Learning Objectives

1. Define the subject records storage method.
2. Explain when the subject records storage method is needed.
3. List advantages and disadvantages of filing by subject.
4. Describe the dictionary and encyclopedic subject file arrangements.
5. List the supplies needed for subject records storage.
6. Describe four indexes used in the subject filing method.
7. Prepare a relative index.
8. Store and retrieve records by the subject method.
9. Describe a procedure for preparing a computer index.

Need for a Subject Records Storage Method

In Part 2 of this textbook, you studied the alphabetic method of storing records by name—names of individuals, businesses, and organizations. Two other alphabetic filing methods are also possible; namely, the subject and geographic methods. You will study geographic records storage in Chapter 9. The focus of Chapter 7 is subject records storage: its basic nature, when to use it, who uses it, and how to use it.

The Subject Records Storage Method

Storing and retrieving records by subject matter or topic is known as the **subject records storage method**. File users expect related records to be stored together. Therefore, categories of records are often established by subject, topic, department, services, products, or projects. When you file records alphabetically by name, some records are best kept together by subjects such as APPLICATIONS, PROJECTS, and BRANCH OFFICE MEMOS. As you study more filing methods, you will learn how filing methods are combined to provide efficient records storage and retrieval systems.

When Subject Records Storage Is Used

The ARMA International guideline *Subject Filing* contains an in-depth discussion of subject records storage. This document recommends using subject filing when other systems will not be effective or when documents cannot be filed by any other single filing characteristic. For example, you may reasonably expect all information related to filing equipment to be in one file location. If you file letters, memos, brochures, flyers, and other material related to office equipment by personal or business names that may appear on those documents, you spread the information throughout the filing system. Such a method is not effective. Instead, file all information related to office equipment under the subject OFFICE EQUIPMENT.

Some records simply do not contain personal or business names, which makes filing such records by name impossible. Such records, however, may refer to a topic, project, or subject and should be filed accordingly.

When file users request records by subject, the records should be filed by subject. Subjects are easy to recall, and subject records storage is the only logical, efficient method of storing and retrieving some records. Your telephone directory Yellow Pages is a good example of what a remarkable memory aid subjects can be.

Why store records by subject?

Imagine each of the following situations: (1) You go to your basement, find a broken water pipe, and are knee-deep in water. (2) You cannot complete your federal income tax return. (3) You need to buy a new car. (4) You need to talk to a lawyer. (5) Your washing machine just stopped working. (6) Now you need a nearby bank or a doctor. Individuals and businesses that could help you are listed alphabetically in the white pages of your telephone directory. However, were you thinking of names in those situations? More likely, you were thinking PLUMBER! ACCOUNTANT or INCOME TAX! CAR or AUTOMOBILE! LAWYER! WASHING MACHINE! BANK or DOCTOR!

In the Yellow Pages of metropolitan telephone directories, you can locate a nearby bank by looking up the subject BANKS. Banks are listed alphabetically. Suburban banks are often listed first by their locations (geographic filing) and finally alphabetically by bank name. Subject, geographic, and alphabetic name filing methods are combined in the classified index of your telephone directory; you can locate a local bank quickly. By the way, when you are looking for a particular subject, do not be surprised if you are directed to search elsewhere for it. For example, when you look up LAWYERS, you are directed to see ATTORNEYS. Office workers sometimes use alternate, synonymous terms for a single topic when filing by subject. Therefore, cross-references and useful indexes are necessary with subject filing, as is explained later. For now, remember these important subject filing guidelines:

1. Select subject titles that best reflect stored records and that are easy to remember.

2. Provide for the occasional use of alternate, synonymous, or related subject titles.

3. Consider combining filing methods when subdividing and subsorting records in large subject filing systems. For example, subdivide records first by subject and then alphabetically by location or name, numerically by record or document number, or chronologically by date.

Why combine filing methods?

Where Subject Records Storage Is Used

Whether you are in the kitchen using a cookbook or in the office at your computer, you are likely using some kind of subject record file. The subject records storage method is used somewhere in almost every office. Subject filing is suitable for filing correspondence, reports, catalogs, clippings, research data, excessively long inventory lists, or product development plans, just to name a few examples. Here are some of the types of organizations and their uses of the subject records storage method:

1. Department stores that keep all records together relating to such subjects as advertising, appliances, clothing, customers, home furnishings, housewares, special promotions, store maintenance, and window displays.

2. School offices where records are stored according to such subjects as accidents, accreditation, athletics, budget, cafeteria, curriculum, graduation, library, personnel certification, and student records.

3. Airplane manufacturers where records may be stored according to the types of planes being manufactured.

4. Construction companies whose records are stored by such types of construction as apartment houses, bridges, condominiums, individual homes, multifamily homes, office buildings, and roads.

5. Organizations in which purchasing agents keep records according to the names of products being bought or being considered for purchase: dryers, freezers, microwave ovens, refrigerators, and washers.

Who stores records by subject?

Information stored on other media such as computer disks, microforms, optical disks, and audio and visual cassettes is often categorized appropriately by subject, topic, product, or particular business function. A manual file folder with the subject title STUDENT RECORDS may be converted to a computer file named STDNTRCD. Computer disks, microforms, compact disks, and other electronic records require the same considerations as paper records when selecting a filing method. Subject records storage is the easiest and simplest method to implement with such records. Workstation computer disks commonly are labeled and filed alphabetically by such subject titles as INVENTORY, LETTERS AND MEMOS, MAILING LISTS, REPORTS, SALES FORECASTING, etc. Because information stored on electronic media is not readable without special equipment, the subject titles must describe the media contents in a way that not only reflects the information stored, but also is easy to remember.

Advantages and Disadvantages of Subject Records Storage

The greatest advantage of subject records storage is also its greatest disadvantage. A proponent of subject records storage claims that records are best remembered and retrieved by subject. This statement is true; however, not everyone remembers the exact subject title, or heading, selected to file the records every time. That is why in practice, subject files can become the most *individualized* filing systems in an office, making their use difficult for all file users. Following are some advantages and disadvantages of the method.

Advantages

Storing records by subjects saves time when records related to a specific topic, product, or project that requires managerial decisions are grouped, rather than separated in folders and filed alphabetically by correspondents' names.

Subject files are expanded easily by adding subdivisions to main subjects. For example, if OFFICE EQUIPMENT were a main subject and COPIERS, CHAIRS, DESKS, and FILES were subdivisions, new subdivisions for COMPUTERS, LASER PRINTERS, and SCANNERS could be added easily.

Disadvantages

Main subject titles and subdivisions in subject files have a tendency to grow until subjects begin to overlap. Selecting subject titles that are concise, clearly defined, and uniformly stated is sometimes difficult. Unless selected subject titles are used consistently to code records, filers will find storage and retrieval difficult. The development and installation of a subject records storage system may require the assistance of an experienced records analyst to examine stored records and to create well-defined subject titles for them.

Why is subject records storage expensive?

The subject records storage method is the most expensive method to maintain because it requires experienced filers. Preparation of materials for subject storage always takes longer than for any other storage method because the content of every record must be read thoroughly and carefully.

The disadvantages of the subject method can be many if the file is poorly planned and maintained. However, the disadvantages are minimized when you select an appropriate arrangement of guides and folders, prepare the necessary indexes, and apply proper procedures to store and to retrieve records. Suggestions for the arrangement of records stored by subject follow.

Arrangements of Records Stored by Subject

The standard arrangements for subject records storage are (1) the dictionary arrangement and (2) the encyclopedic arrangement. Both arrangements are explained and illustrated in the following pages.

Dictionary Arrangement

What is a dictionary arrangement?

In the **dictionary arrangement**, subject folders are arranged behind A-to-Z primary guides in correct alphabetic order by subject title. The dictionary subject arrangement is generally recommended when the volume of records is no greater than two file drawers. The nature of the records stored is a more important determinant of arrangement, however. When subjects do not require subdivisions, the dictionary arrangement is used, regardless of the number of records. Figure 7-1 shows a small office file arranged in dictionary order. A-to-Z guides are one-fifth cut and occupy first position in the file. Special guides are one-fifth cut and are in second position. Two special guides in Figure 7-1 are CREDIT CARDS and TAXES. These special subject guides mark exceptionally active subjects, making them conspicuous and, therefore, easier to find. OUT guides and all general folders are one-third cut and occupy the

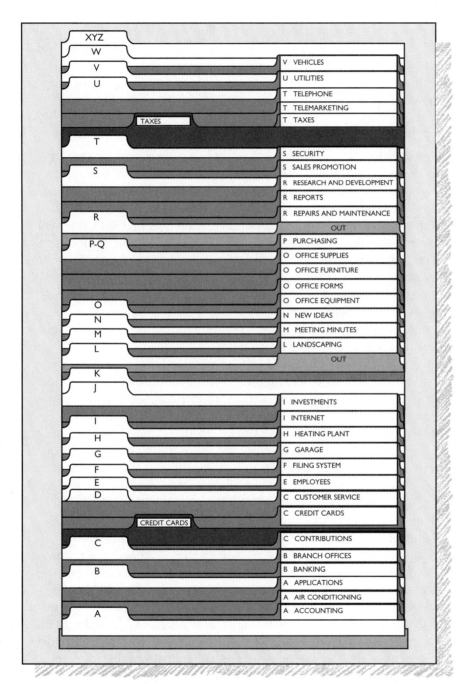

Figure 7-1   Dictionary Arrangement of Subjects

third position in the file. So far, subdividing general subjects into more specific subdivisions has not been necessary. If records accumulate and make dividing the general subjects into more specific subdivisions necessary, the arrangement would no longer be considered a dictionary arrangement.

Encyclopedic Arrangement

The **encyclopedic arrangement** is a subject filing arrangement in which broad main subject titles are arranged in alphabetic order with subdivisions arranged alphabetically under the title to which they relate. Figures 7-2a and 7-2b show an encyclopedic arrangement of the subject file shown in Figure 7-1. As the number of records increases, the file arrangement requires specific subject subdivisions for quicker access to filed records. Study the guide and folder captions in the four-drawer file in Figures 7-2a and 7-2b. Main subject labels have been prepared and inserted into the metal holders of the one-fifth cut, first-position, primary guide tabs. Secondary guides are in second position. The secondary guides are also one-fifth cut tab guides with labels bearing the main subject *subdivisions*. The secondary guides may include the primary guide captions such as those illustrated in Figure 7-3. Because guides are not removed from the file, repeating the main subject title on the secondary guide is not necessary. Sometimes in subject filing, less is better; reading lengthy and unnecessary labeling is time-consuming.

· What is an encyclopedic arrangement?

On the other hand, the *folder* label captions include complete subject titles: main, secondary, and, if necessary, specific subject titles. A comprehensive folder label assures that a borrowed folder will be returned to its correct file location. The tab cut of the folders depends on the length of the subject titles. One-third cut folders are recommended, but unusually long subject titles may require half-cut folders.

Most of the general subject folders have been maintained in the encyclopedic file arrangement shown in Figures 7-2a and 7-2b. Specific subject folders have been added, however, where subjects have been subdivided. Note the general subject folder for TAXES. Although subdivision folders for FEDERAL, SALES, and STATE taxes have been added, the general TAX folder remains. The general TAX folder holds records pertaining to any other tax information— i.e., city tax, import and export tax, etc. Apparently, the predetermined number of records has not accumulated to warrant a specific tax folder for those records.

The secondary subject guides have accompanying specific subject folders. See OFFICE SUPPLIES in Figure 7-2b. The general subject

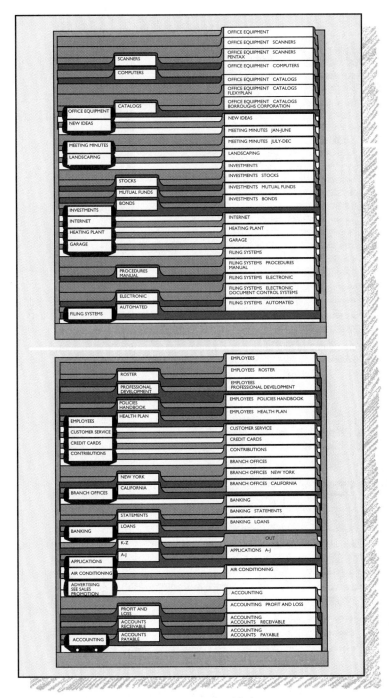

Figure 7-2a   Encyclopedic Arrangement of Subjects

181

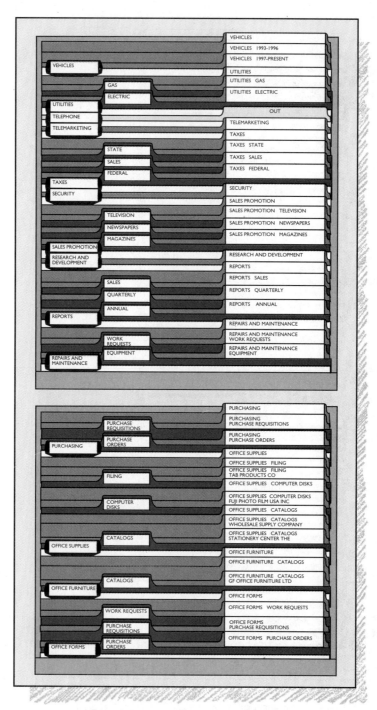

Figure 7-2b   Encyclopedic Arrangement of Subjects

folder for OFFICE SUPPLIES appears at the end of the OFFICE SUPPLIES section and is used for storing information that does not fit into any of the established subdivisions. Subdivisions have been added for CATALOGS, COMPUTER DISKS, and FILING. Each subdivision has a specific subject folder. In addition, two individual folders have been added for individual vendor catalogs: one for The Stationery Center and one for Wholesale Supply Company. Can you spot other individual folders added to the system? Store any information other than that related to the specific subject folders in the OFFICE SUPPLIES general folder placed at the end of the section. Checking general folders from time to time to see if any records can be transferred to more specific subject folders or even individual folders, especially for frequently requested records, is recommended.

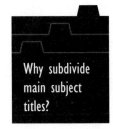

Why subdivide main subject titles?

When general folders become crowded and no specific subject subdivisions are possible, other means of subdividing records may be used. Notice that the APPLICATIONS general folders are subdivided alphabetically A–J and K–Z in Figure 7-2a. The VEHICLES general subject is subdivided by the model years of the vehicles. Although a specific folder for each vehicle could have been prepared, infrequent retrieval of such records apparently does not warrant specific folders.

As you can see from studying the file illustrations, predicting the subjects and subject subdivisions that will be needed in an office file is unlikely. The nature of the organization, the kinds of records stored, and how the office staff uses and requests stored information determine the subject titles and subdivisions of stored records.

OUT indicators are in third position with all folders. These third-cut OUT guides are usually of some distinctive color and stand out to show the location of a removed folder. Color can be used effectively with subject filing. Each subject will often have a color band that is repeated on all guides and folders of that subject. Sometimes, all captions of one subject will be one color, the color changing when the subject title changes. A third possibility is that each subject will have guides and folders of one color only; another color will be used for guides and folders of the next subject. Another effective use of color is to use color folders for all general subject folders.

Why use color in a subject file?

Although the use of color can speed the filing process and reduce misfiles in any filing system, color does not take the place of careful selection of meaningful subject titles in a subject records storage system.

Supplies for Subject Records Storage

Supplies used for the subject arrangement include guides, folders, labels, and OUT indicators, which were explained in Chapter 5. Preparing guide and folder label captions is slightly more challenging in subject records storage. A closer look at guide and folder label captions follows.

Guides and Labels

The subject titles used determine the guides used in subject records storage. If subject titles are long, subject codes or abbreviations can be used. Subject coding is explained in more detail on page 190. Figure 7-3 shows an example of primary and secondary guides. The primary guide caption contains the main subject title; the secondary guide contains the main subject and its subdivision. Because guides are not removed from a storage container, a primary guide caption may be omitted on a secondary guide, as shown in the file sample in Figures 7-2a and 7-2b. Prepare guide labels on a typewriter or a computer. Key primary guide label captions two spaces from the left edge and two spaces from the top of the label. Key the information in uppercase letters with no punctuation. Key secondary guide *subdivisions* five spaces to the right of the main subject title *or* under the first letter of the first line. Once you have decided whether to use complete subject titles, abbreviated titles, or subject codes, be consistent when preparing guide labels. If you mix the styles of the captions, you will complicate an already time-intensive filing method.

Figure 7-3   **Primary and Secondary Guide Labels**

Folders and Labels

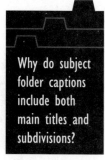

Why do subject folder captions include both main titles and subdivisions?

Folder label captions include the main subject title and all necessary subdivisions. As discussed previously, comprehensive label captions assure that borrowed folders are returned to their correct file locations. One-third cut folders are preferred. However, lengthy titles may require longer folder tabs. Key the folder label caption on a typewriter or a computer. Key the main subject title two spaces from the left edge and as near the top of the label or the bottom of a color bar as possible. Key the subdivision five spaces to the right of the main subject title *or* under the first letter of the first line. Key in uppercase letters with no punctuation as shown in Figure 7-4. The size of the label, of course, should match the width of the folder tab. Be precise and consistent with folder label preparation. Attention to this detail creates a neat, readable, straight-line filing system.

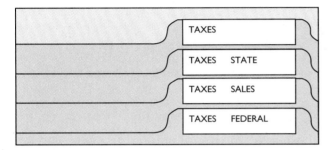

Figure 7-4 **Subject Folder Labels**

OUT Indicators

An OUT guide appears in the file sample in Figure 7-1. You may want to review briefly OUT indicators and the charge-out and follow-up procedures discussed in Chapters 5 and 6. Follow the same procedures for subject filing that you applied in alphabetic name filing. The only difference is that you will use subject titles, rather than individual or organization names, to identify records.

Indexes for the Subject Records Storage Method

The selection of a word or phrase to use as a subject title (the filing segment) is of prime importance when using the subject records storage method. One person should be responsible for selecting subject titles. That person must be thoroughly familiar with the material to be stored and must have considerable knowledge of every phase of the operations and activities of the business. If all file users have authority to add subject titles to a subject filing system, soon the same type of material becomes

185

stored under two or more synonymous terms. Such storage of related records in two or more places not only separates records that should be stored together, but also makes retrieval of all related records difficult.

The subject title must be short and clearly descriptive of the material it represents. Once a subject title has been chosen, it must be used by everyone in the organization. Additional subject titles must be chosen so that they do not duplicate or overlap any subject previously used.

Need for Indexes

Good subject selection requires:

1. *Agreement* by file users on the subjects to be used.

2. *Flexibility* to allow for growth within the subjects chosen and for expansion to include new material.

3. *Simplicity* so that records users can understand the system.

Why are indexes necessary?

Once subject titles have been selected, they must be consistently used by all file users. Ensure consistent use of selected subject titles by preparing necessary indexes.

You learned in Chapter 5 that a direct access filing system is one in which you look directly for a specific name in a file without having to refer to an index. An **index** is a systematic guide that allows access to specific items contained within a larger body of information. Because you may not know all subjects used in a subject file, you cannot go directly to a file to locate a record. A subject file requires an index and is, therefore, considered an indirect access filing method. **Indirect access** is a method of locating records requiring prior use of an index. Users must refer to an index to determine the subject and the location of a record before they can store or retrieve the record from the main file.

Preparation of Indexes

Indexes are printed lists keyed on sheets of paper, cards, or some kind of visible file (described in Appendix B). An index prepared on sheets of paper or on visible strips is easier to see at a glance than are indexes keyed on individual cards. However, adding and deleting subjects on visible strips or cards are easier than adding and deleting from printed sheets. If you prepare the index in a word processing or other computer application software, you can make additions, deletions, and corrections quickly and easily. The computer also sorts for you and makes maintaining an up-to-date index easy. The Search feature of your computer application software allows you to search and find a specific subject with a single keystroke.

Four types of indexes are valuable, and often necessary, when using the subject records storage method. They are the master index, also referred to as the *master list*, *subject index*, or *subject list*; the relative index; the numeric index; and the name index.

Master Index.   A **master index** is a printed alphabetic listing in file order of all subjects (filing segments) used as subject titles in the filing system. Update the index as new subjects are added and old ones are eliminated or modified. When new subjects are added, refer to the index to avoid any subject title duplications. Figure 7-5 is a master index of the portion of file illustrated in Figure 7-2. Store the index at the beginning

What is a master index?

Accounting	Heating Plant	Repairs and Maintenance
Accounts Payable	Internet	Equipment
Accounts Receivable	Investments	Work Requests
Profit and Loss	Bonds	Reports
Air Conditioning	Mutual Funds	Annual
Applications*	Stocks	Quarterly
Banking	Landscaping	Sales
Loans	Meeting Minutes*	Research and Development
Statements	New Ideas	Sales Promotion
Branch Offices	Office Equipment	Magazines
California	Catalogs	Newspapers
New York	Computers	Television
Contributions	Scanners	Security
Credit Cards	Office Forms	Taxes
Customer Service	Purchase Orders	Federal
Employees	Purchase Requisitions	Sales
Health Plan	Work Requests	State
Policies Handbook	Office Furniture	Telemarketing
Professional Development	Catalogs	Telephone
Roster	Office Supplies	Utilities
Filing Systems	Catalogs	Electric
Automated	Computer Disks	Gas
Electronic	Filing	Vehicles*
Procedures Manual	Purchasing	
Garage	Purchase Orders	
	Purchase Requisitions	

*Not necessary to show divided folders in the master index.

Figure 7-5   Subject File Master Index

of the file for ready access to all users. It is an outline of the file contents. Without a master index, file users would have to scan drawers of records to locate subject titles. New file users can familiarize themselves with the subject storage system quickly by referring to a master index. In addition, reference to the master index assures users that only preselected subject titles are used for filing and retrieving records.

Relative Index. A more complex subject file may require a relative index. A **relative index** is a dictionary-type listing of *all* possible words and combinations of words by which records may be requested. The word *relative* is used because the index includes not only the actual subject titles used in the system, but also any *related* subject titles that some filers may use to store and retrieve records. Study the relative index in Figure 7-6. Notice the entry for Advertising. (Advertising is not used as a subject title in the system.) The relative index refers the filer to Sales Promotion—the subject title selected for storing and retrieving advertising materials. This type of index is a vast cross-reference device because it contains all the subjects by which a record might be requested. When someone requests a record by a subject that is not the one selected for use in the system, check the relative index to see if that requested subject has been included. If not, add the requested subject to the index listing with the correct subject title beside it. The relative index may contain SEE and SEE ALSO cross-references as well. These notations help in suggesting related materials and alternate file locations.

What is a relative index?

Numeric Index. The numeric index will become more meaningful to you after Chapter 8, where you will learn to assign numbers to subject file headings. Numbers are faster to file and retrieve because you can read numbers more quickly than words and letters. When numbers are used to identify specific subjects, a numeric index is needed. A **numeric index** is a current list of all files by the file numbers. Such an index shows the numbers assigned to subject titles and avoids duplication of numbers when new subjects are added to the storage system.

Name Index. Subject records storage does not customarily require an alphabetic index of names of individuals or companies. However, correspondence filed in a subject arrangement *does* require a name index. A **name index** is a listing of correspondents' names stored in a subject file. The name and address of each correspondent are included in the index, as well as the subject under which each name is stored. The names are arranged alphabetically on printed sheets or cards. Because records are sometimes requested by an individual or a company name, a

Is a name index really necessary?

Subject Title	Filed Under	Subject Title	Filed Under
Accounting	Accounting	Meeting Minutes	Meeting Minutes
Accounts Payable	Accounting		
Accounts Receivable	Accounting	Mutual Funds	Investments
Advertising	Sales Promotion	New Ideas	New Ideas
Air Conditioning	Air Conditioning	New York Branch	Branch Offices
Annual Reports	Reports	Newspaper Advertising	Sales Promotion
Applications	Applications	Office Equipment	Office Equipment
Automated Filing Systems	Filing Systems		
Banking	Banking	Office Forms	Office Forms
Bonds	Investments	Office Furniture	Office Furniture
Branch Offices	Branch Offices	Office Supplies	Office Supplies
Building Maintenance	Repairs and Maintenance	Policies Handbook	Filing Systems
		Professional Development	Employees
California Branch	Branch Offices	Profit and Loss	Accounting
Cars	Vehicles	Purchase Orders	SEE Office Forms Purchasing
Catalogs	SEE Office Equipment Office Furniture Office Supplies	Purchase Requisitions	SEE Office Forms Purchasing
Computer Disks	Office Supplies	Purchasing	Purchasing
Computers	Office Equipment		
Contributions	Contributions	Quarterly Reports	Reports
Credit Cards	Credit Cards	Repairs and Maintenance	Repairs and Maintenance
Customer Service	Customer Service		
		Reports	Reports
Electric	Utilities	Research and Development	Research and Development
Electronic Filing Systems	Filing Systems		
Employee Roster	Employees	Roster	Employees
Employees	Employees	Sales Promotion	Sales Promotion
Equipment	Office Equipment	Sales Reports	Reports
Equipment Repair	Repairs and Maintenance	Sales Taxes	Taxes
		Scanners	Office Equipment
Federal Taxes	Taxes		
Filing Equipment	Office Equipment	Security	Security
Filing Procedures Manual	Filing Systems	State Taxes	Taxes
Filing Supplies	Office Supplies	Statements	Banking
Filing Systems	Filing Systems	Stocks	Investments
Forms	Office Forms	Taxes	Taxes
Garage	Garage	Telemarketing	Telemarketing
Gas	Utilities	Telephone	Telephone
Health Plan	Employees	Television Advertising	Sales Promotion
Heating Plant	Heating Plant	Utilities	Utilities
Internet	Internet	Vans	Vehicles
Investments	Investments	Vehicles	Vehicles
Landscaping	Landscaping	Work Requests	SEE Office Forms Repairs and Maintenance
Loans	Banking		
Magazine Advertising	Sales Promotion		

Figure 7-6   Subject File Relative Index

name index containing this information can save time that would otherwise be spent searching for a record by subject.

Storage and Retrieval Procedures for the Subject Records Storage Method

All the steps studied in Chapter 5 for storing and retrieving correspondence records are as important in the subject records storage method as they are in any other storage method. A brief description of each step, together with an explanation of its importance to the subject method, follows.

Inspecting

In any storage system, inspect every record to see that it has been released for storage. Do not store a record until someone with authority has indicated that it is ready for storage. In Figure 7-7, JJ is the release mark used to indicate that the letter is ready for storage.

Indexing

Indexing, or classifying, records consumes more time with the subject records storage method than with any other storage method. Examine the contents of each record carefully to determine the filing segment under which it is to be stored. If a record relates to only one subject, indexing is comparatively simple. Just select the correct subject from the index. If someone else has previously indicated the subject under which a record is to be stored, recheck the accuracy of the subject selection.

If a record contains information about more than one subject, you must determine the most important subject by which to store the record. Then cross-reference the other subject(s).

Coding

Code the main subject title and any subdivisions by placing diagonals between the units, underlining the key unit, and numbering the succeeding units in the selected words (filing segment) where they appear on the record. Code the correspondent's name by placing diagonals between the units and continuing the numbering of the units. If the subject is not mentioned, write it legibly at the top of the record. Some filers prefer simply to write the filing segment in color in the upper right of the record. The subject title is, therefore, more visible in the file. When more than one subject is indicated, code only the most important one; cross-reference all other subjects in some distinctive manner. For

How do you code a record for subject filing?

example, the subject to cross-reference in Figure 7-7 is underscored with a wavy line, and an X is placed in the margin opposite the subject. The correct cross-reference subject title and subtitle SALES PROMOTION TELEVISION are written and coded in the margin; diagonals are placed between the units, and all filing units are numbered.

Do not rely on memory to determine the subject under which a record should be stored. Consult the master or relative index to be sure that you have selected and coded the filing segment correctly. Coding in an alphabetic subject filing system may include an entire subject title such as PERSONNEL. Abbreviations can simplify coding in a complex subject filing system. Create an abbreviation with the first alphabetic character of the subject title followed by the next one or two consonants such as PRS for PERSONNEL. Or use the first character of each word in a multiple-word subject heading such as RRS for RECORDS RETENTION SCHEDULE. Consistency is essential when developing a subject code system in which two- to six-character abbreviations are used. Everyone using the system must understand the codes and how to develop new ones when necessary. Be sure to write subject letter codes on each record and include them on individual folder label captions.

Cross-Referencing

A cross-reference may be needed for a stored record. After coding the document for the cross-reference, as suggested previously, prepare a cross-reference sheet such as the one shown in Figure 7-8. Those looking for the document under its alternate subject title SALES PRO-MOTION TELEVISION are referred to the original record file location SALES PROMOTION MAGAZINE. If a record refers to several important subjects, consider filing photocopies of the record under the different subject titles involved. This procedure eliminates the need for preparing cross-reference sheets for that record. Sometimes a permanent cross-reference guide is placed in the storage container. In Figure 7-2a, for example, a permanent guide labeled ADVERTISING SEE SALES PROMOTION has been placed in the file after ACCOUNTING. Do not file records behind the permanent SEE guide, however. The SEE guide is there only to direct you to the correct storage location.

Sorting

Use some kind of A-to-Z sorter to sort records to be stored alphabetically by subject. Sort records by main subject titles; subsort records by subdivisions as well. Sorting records before filing saves a lot of time. You

Why sort records before storing?

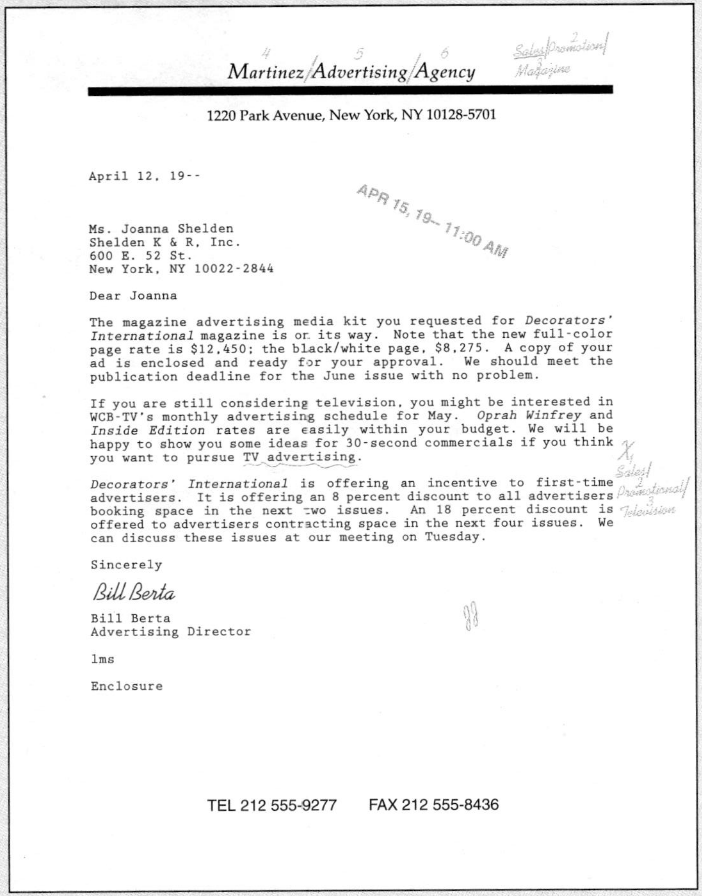

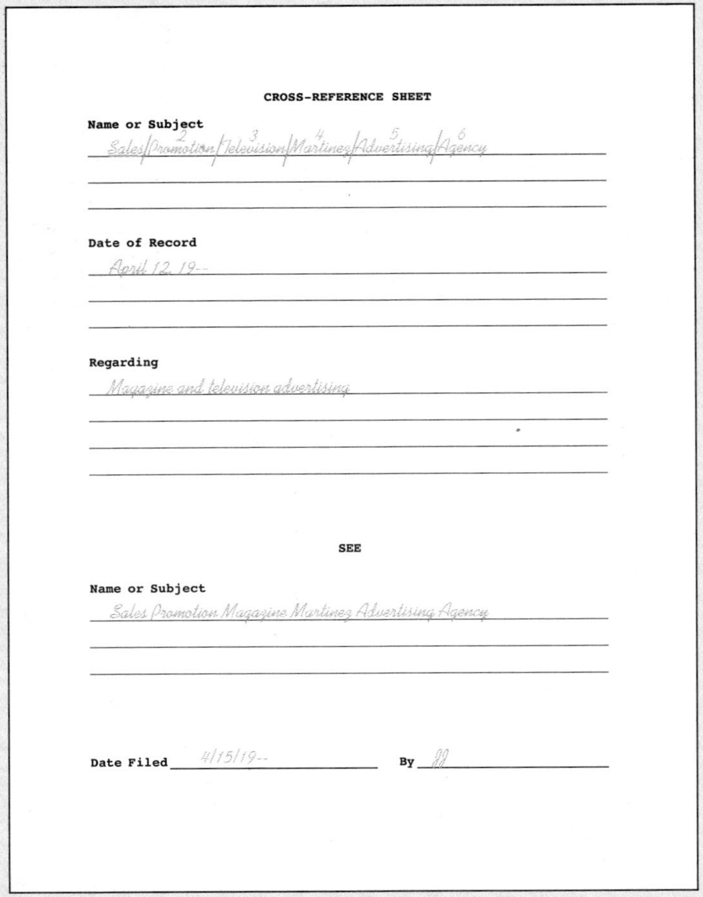

CROSS-REFERENCE SHEET

Name or Subject

Sales/Promotion/Television/Martinez/Advertising/Agency

Date of Record

April 12, 19--

Regarding

Magazine and television advertising

SEE

Name or Subject

Sales Promotion Magazine Martinez Advertising Agency

Date Filed ___4/15/19--___ By _JB_

Figure 7-8   Cross-Reference Sheet for Subject Records Storage

Martinez/Advertising/Agency

1220 Park Avenue, New York, NY 10128-5701

APR 15, 19-- 11:00 AM

April 12, 19--

Ms. Joanna Shelden
Shelden K & R, Inc.
600 E. 52 St.
New York, NY 10022-2844

Dear Joanna

The magazine advertising media kit you requested for *Decorators' International* magazine is on its way. Note that the new full-color page rate is $12,450; the black/white page, $8,275. A copy of your ad is enclosed and ready for your approval. We should meet the publication deadline for the June issue with no problem.

If you are still considering television, you might be interested in WCB-TV's monthly advertising schedule for May. *Oprah Winfrey* and *Inside Edition* rates are easily within your budget. We will be happy to show you some ideas for 30-second commercials if you think you want to pursue TV advertising.

Decorators' International is offering an incentive to first-time advertisers. It is offering an 8 percent discount to all advertisers booking space in the next two issues. An 18 percent discount is offered to advertisers contracting space in the next four issues. We can discuss these issues at our meeting on Tuesday.

Sincerely

Bill Berta

Bill Berta
Advertising Director

lms

Enclosure

TEL 212 555-9277   FAX 212 555-8436

Figure 7-7   Record Coded for Subject Records Storage

will be able to file straight through a filing system rather than bouncing backward and forward through stored records.

Storing

Careful placement of records into folders is always important. Be sure that the folder label subject caption agrees with the filing segment coded on the record. Raise the folder slightly before inserting the record to be sure the record enters the folder completely. Remove papers that are in disarray, jog them, and return them neatly into the folder. Records in shelf-stored folders need constant straightening. Papers sticking out of folders can obscure guide and folder label captions.

When filing correspondence in subject folders, file records in alphabetic order according to the names of the correspondents. Then for each correspondent, arrange the records by the date keyed on the document with the *most recent date in front.*

Retrieving

Retrieval procedures for the subject records storage method are the same as those used in any other storage method. Knowing who has taken the records, the contents of those records, when the records were borrowed, and when the records will be returned is the only way to maintain control over a retrieval system. Follow-up also is necessary to assure that records are returned, to extend the charge-out time, or to call someone's attention to matters needing consideration in the future.

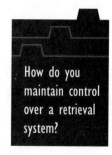

How do you maintain control over a retrieval system?

Current Trends in Records Management

Indexes are used in a variety of ways in filing methods. The master index and the relative index are illustrated in this chapter. In Chapters 8 and 9, you will learn about other indexes used to store and retrieve records.

You have already learned that an index is a systematic guide that allows access to specific items contained within a larger body of information. Common to all indexes is (1) a specific list of items and (2) a second body of information that shows location. Therefore, the index requires at least two columns of information. Indexes may be prepared on index cards; however, card indexes are rarely seen today. Because computers are so prevalent, the trend is to prepare indexes on the computer. Any computer application software capable of sorting tabular columns is adequate for preparing indexes.

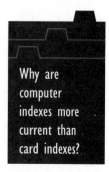

Why are computer indexes more current than card indexes?

Computer indexes are always current because additions, deletions, and changes are made easily. The preparation of a computer index requires four simple steps. (1) Key the information in two tabular columns, (2) sort the columns, (3) refine the layout, and (4) print the index.

After it has been sorted, the index is simply two columns of data and not very attractive. Some computer application software will allow more refinement of the index layout than others. Figure 7-9 shows the computer screen of the relative index with some minor cosmetic changes. The changes improve the appearance of the index and make it easier to use. A main heading and column headings were added. The tab set was changed to a dot leader tab that automatically inserted leaders between the columns to guide your eye to the second column. Repetitive subject titles were deleted, dot leaders turned off, and SEE references added instead.

The index can be printed in a two-column format to look like Figure 7-6 on page 189. Copies of the index should be available to file users and at the storage area as well. Computer-generated indexes are just one more way the computer can assist in the manual storage and retrieval of subject records.

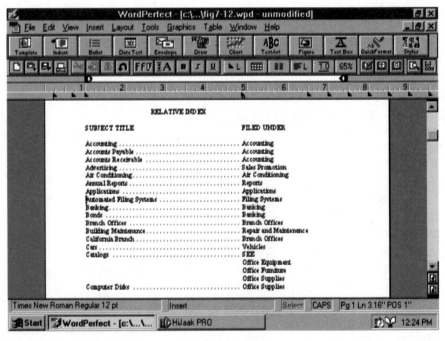

Figure 7-9   Computer Screen of Relative Index

Summary

Storing records by subject is sometimes the only filing method possible with some records. Either records are needed and requested by a particular subject, topic, or project; or they do not have any other identifying characteristics by which to file them. Benefits of storing like records in one location are numerous. However, subject records storage systems become highly individualized if they are not carefully controlled and monitored by an individual who is most familiar with the office records and the information needs of the office staff.

The dictionary and encyclopedic arrangements are used in subject records storage systems. Deciding which arrangement to use depends on (1) the nature of the records and (2) the volume of records. Use the dictionary arrangement when main subject titles do not require subdivisions. The encyclopedic arrangement is usually the choice for large subject records storage systems. Faster information retrieval is possible when primary subject titles are subdivided into more specific subject categories.

The subject records storage method requires the use of indexes and is, therefore, considered an indirect access filing method. The master index is an outline of the file and lists all subject titles and subdivisions in alphabetic order as they appear in the file. The relative index lists <u>all</u> subject titles and subdivisions in an alphabetic, dictionary order. Alternate, synonymous titles by which some filers may request subjects are listed as well. The relative index shows the correct subject file location of all listed subject titles. A numeric index is needed when numbers are assigned to subject titles; a name index for correspondents' names is needed when correspondence is filed by subject.

Maintain control over the subject records storage system by carefully inspecting, indexing, coding, preparing necessary cross-references, sorting, and storing records. Maintain a charge-out record of all borrowed records and a follow-up system that ensures their safe return to storage.

Card indexes readily convert to computer indexes. Prepare indexes on the computer if possible. The use of any computer application software capable of sorting tabular columns simplifies the preparation and maintenance of updated file indexes.

Important Terms

dictionary arrangement
encyclopedic arrangement
index
indirect access
master index

name index
numeric index
relative index
subject records storage method

Review and Discussion

1. Describe the subject records storage method and explain why the method is more expensive than other storage methods. (Obj. 1)

2. Describe two records storage situations or environments where records stored by subject would be a preferred storage method. (Obj. 2)

3. List three advantages and three disadvantages of the subject records storage method. (Obj. 3)

4. Name two possible arrangements of subject records storage and explain how the two arrangements differ. (Obj. 4)

5. What supplies are needed when using the subject records storage method? Describe how guide and folder label captions are keyed. (Obj. 5)

6. Name and describe four possible indexes used with subject records storage. (Obj. 6)

7. Compare the master index and the relative index. Explain what modifications are required to convert a master index to a relative index. Unless otherwise instructed, describe the steps using either a word processor or a computer to make the conversion. (Obj. 7)

8. Explain how correspondence (letters, memos) are stored in a subject records storage system. (Obj. 8.)

9. Describe a procedure for preparing a computer-generated index. (Obj. 9)

Applications (APP)

APP 7-1. *Filing and Retrieving Records by the Subject Method (Obj. 8)*

Refer to Figure 7-2, Encyclopedic Arrangement of Subjects, to file/retrieve the records described below. Indicate the possible file locations by giving the complete folder label captions for each. If more than one location is possible, list all possible folders.

1. A record of a recent repair made to an office window and the cost of the repair.

2. Information on office shredders; a possible purchase is pending.

3. This month's meeting minutes.

4. The employee roster. You need to add a name to it.

5. Information on a new secretarial chair you want to purchase.

6. A blank purchase requisition to request the purchase of a secretarial chair you found in No. 5.

7. File a paid electric bill.

8. Check on current radio advertising rates.

9. File a quarterly *sales* report.

10. Find a copy of a purchase order you submitted for computer disks.

APP 7-2. Create a Relative Index (Obj. 7)

1. Open the template file CH7.AP2 into your favorite word processing software program. The document is a subject file master index.

2. Convert the master index to a relative index for the subject records storage system. Do not re-enter any data.

3. If your equipment allows, reduce the font size and change to a two-column (newspaper) format for the relative index. You may need to adjust the tab set to achieve a layout similar to Figure 7-6 Try it! Print a copy.

Applying the Rules

Job 9, Subject Correspondence Filing

Chapter 8

Numeric Records Storage

Learning Objectives

1. List reasons for storing records by a numeric method.
2. List and describe the basic components of the consecutive numeric storage method.
3. Describe the procedures for storing records by the consecutive numbering method.
4. Describe the conversion process from alphabetic storage arrangement to consecutive numeric storage arrangement.
5. State the advantages and disadvantages of consecutive numeric records storage.
6. Explain the difference between consecutive and nonconsecutive numbering storage methods.
7. Explain how to sort numeric records for consecutive, terminal-digit, and middle-digit numeric storage.
8. Describe how records are stored chronologically.
9. Describe block numeric coding.
10. Explain duplex-numeric, decimal-numeric, and alphanumeric coding.
11. Describe trends in computer numeric data storage and manipulation.

Overview of Numeric Records Storage

The alphabetic and subject methods of records storage were discussed in previous chapters. This chapter explains a third method by which to store records—numeric storage method. As its name suggests, the **numeric records storage method** is a storage method in which records are assigned numbers and then arranged in one of various numeric sequences. Reasons for using a numeric storage method will become evident as you study this chapter. Two major reasons are: (1) the unlimited set of numbers available (compared with the limitation of 26 *alphabetic* characters), and (2) the ease with which people recognize and use numbers. Computers manage numbers with greater speed than humans. Therefore, you will be reminded frequently of the computer's amazing ability to search, sort, manipulate, and retrieve numeric data.

Numbers are commonly used for identification and for classifying data in everyday work routines. However, not too long ago, many people believed that using numbers to identify individuals was dehumanizing. Today, most people appreciate the speed and accuracy that computers and numbers bring to routine business transactions. Entering numbers into a computer is faster than pronouncing and spelling names for identification purposes. If you are already listed in a company's database, your computer record is located by a search of one or more data fields in the record. ZIP Codes are often used to locate an individual's computer record. A ZIP Code search calls up everyone with that ZIP Code; therefore, a second field search may be needed to locate a record. Because they are more specific than ZIP Codes and easier to remember than account numbers, telephone numbers are sometimes used to search and locate individual computer records.

Order clerks at your local pizza shop know your name, address, and the kind of pizza you last ordered after they enter your telephone number into the shop's computer. The video store clerk enters your telephone number into the store's computer, scans a movie jacket with a hand-held scanner, and sends you to the cash register. That series of tasks tells the clerk who you are, where you live, what movie you rented, when you rented it, and when it is due back. Numbers are commonly used to identify the following:

Why use so many numbers?

- Bank checks and accounts
- Charge accounts
- Drivers' licenses
- Hospitalization/health plans
- Insurance policies
- Legal cases
- Permits of many kinds (boating hunting, fishing)

- Post office boxes
- Products and product parts
- Residential addresses
- Safe-deposit boxes
- School courses
- Social security records
- Student records

By now, are you convinced that numbers play an important part in everyday lives? The last time you passed through a checkout of a supermarket or large department store, a clerk may have electronically scanned your merchandise. Scanners read products marked with Universal

Who uses numeric records storage?

Product Codes, and computers interpret and manipulate the codes to produce a variety of meaningful data. You have an instant product description and total cost of your purchases; and the store has instant, meaningful merchandise sales and inventory information. Other organizations that use the numeric storage method include the following:

1. Insurance companies store records by policy and claim numbers.

2. Social welfare agencies maintain records by case numbers.

3. Firms in the building trades use contract or job numbers and stock or parts numbers.

4. Architects assign numbers to their clients' projects to ensure clear-cut identification of all pieces of correspondence and other records about contracts and projects.

5. State automobile license departments and social security offices arrange records by number because of their large-scale operations.

6. Physicians, dentists, and veterinarians assign numbers to patient history records and to X-ray records.

7. Companies sometimes store personnel records by either employee numbers or social security numbers.

8. Savings and loan associations and banks store records by numbers assigned to mortgages and loans.

This chapter contains a detailed description of the basic features of numeric arrangements and the procedures for storing records numerically.

Consecutive Numbering Method

What is consecutive numbering?

Numbers arranged in sequence is the easiest and most widely used numeric storage method. Also called *serial* or *sequential numbering*, the **consecutive numbering method** is a storage method in which consecutively numbered records are arranged in ascending number order—from lowest to highest numbers. Numbers begin with 1, 100, 1000 or any other number and progress upward. For example, office forms, such as invoices, sales tickets, and purchase orders, frequently are numbered in consecutive order. Although these forms may be completed at various locations within a business, the forms ultimately are stored together in consecutive numeric sequence.

Customer and client records—including correspondence—are sometimes stored by consecutive numbers. Because an index must be referenced first to locate a numbered record in the numbered file, the numeric records storage method is considered an indirect access method. Because of this indirect access, numeric filing is ideal for storing disks, tapes, cassettes, and other electronic records where label space for record identification is often limited.

Look at Dataware's® numeric label designs for the optical disk and magnetic tape cartridges in Figure 8-1. The records are usually stored in consecutive numeric order. An index is prepared to show the contents of the records and their assigned file code numbers. The index will list records by name, subject, creator, date, department, location, function, or possibly by some combination of these. Indexes are necessary to locate the records, just as indexes are needed to find books in your library. The books are labeled with an alphanumeric code and stored in sequential order. The books are then located by referencing an index—i.e., title index, author index, or subject index. Indexes required for numeric records storage are discussed in detail later.

Why are indexes necessary?

The need for efficient electronic records storage has brought about a keen and renewed interest in this powerful, useful filing method. Although the focus of the consecutive numbering method described next is for paper records, you can easily adapt many of the storage concepts to electronic records storage.

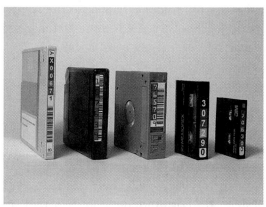

Courtesy of Dataware® Corporation

Figure 8-1 **Dataware® Magnetic and Optical Records Media Labels**

Basic Components of Consecutive Numbering

The components of the consecutive numbering method consist of (1) a numbered file, (2) an alphabetic file, (3) an accession log, and (4) an alphabetic index. The following supplies are needed:

1. Numbered guides and folders for the numbered file.

2. Alphabetic guides and folders for the general alphabetic file.

3. Index cards (or computer) for an accession log.

4. Index cards (or computer) for an alphabetic index.

Numbered Guides and Folders. Figure 8-2 (back) shows a file drawer of consecutively numbered individual correspondent file folders in a straight-line arrangement. Primary guides, numbered 100 and 110, divide the drawer into easy-to-find numeric segments. Guide captions are available in a variety of formats. Guides may have numbers already printed on their tabs; numbered labels may be inserted into blank slots on the tabs; self-adhesive numbers may be attached to blank tabs; or numbers may be keyed on guide labels or stamped on with a numbering machine. Avoid handwriting or hand printing on guide labels. Handwriting on labels lacks uniformity of placement and style, making the captions unattractive and difficult to read.

In Figure 8-2, consecutively numbered individual folders 100 through 109 are placed behind corresponding guide number section 100. Usually one guide is provided for every ten folders. Folders at the right also show the correspondents' names because secrecy is not a factor in this file. Although office policy may require names, in addition to assigned file code numbers, the names are not in alphabetic order. Names are assigned file code numbers, and the numbers are arranged in consecutive order.

Alphabetic Guides and Folders. You might wonder what a general alphabetic file is doing in numeric records storage. A general alphabetic file, found in many numeric arrangements, holds records of correspondents whose volume of correspondence is very small. Some offices prepare individually numbered folders for correspondents as their files are entered. Then, a general alphabetic file is not needed. However, in most offices, individually numbered folders are not prepared until a predetermined number of pieces of correspondence (usually five or

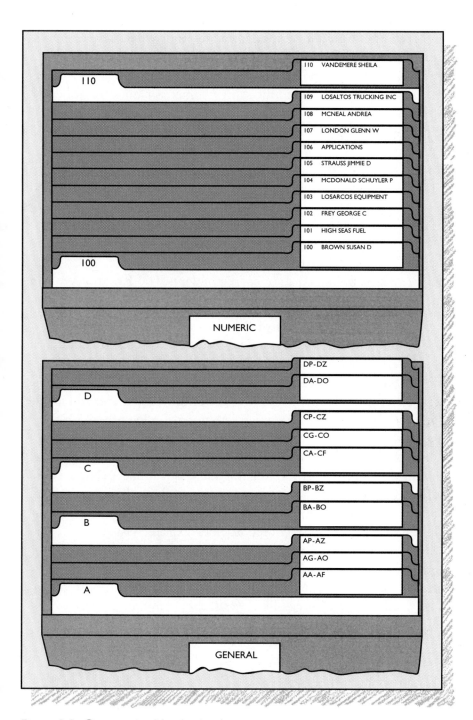

Figure 8-2 **Consecutive Numbering Arrangement**

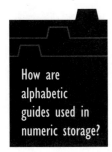

How are alphabetic guides used in numeric storage?

more) have accumulated for one correspondent or when a correspondent's file is *expected* to be very active. Until an individual numbered folder is prepared, correspondence is stored in general alphabetic folders in the general alphabetic file in the same manner as names are stored by the alphabetic method.

Because expansion occurs at the end of a consecutively numbered arrangement, placement of the general alphabetic file section at the beginning of the file is recommended. In Figure 8-2 (front), the general alphabetic file contains a centered primary guide labeled GENERAL. In large systems, this primary guide is followed by alphabetic lettered guides to show the alphabetic divisions. In small systems, alphabetic lettered guides may not be needed; instead, folders with alphabetic captions are arranged in alphabetic order behind the GENERAL guide. The general alphabetic folders hold records of correspondents who have not yet been assigned numbers.

Accession Log. The **accession log**, also called an *accession book* or *numeric file list*, is a serial list of numbers assigned to records in a numeric storage system. Figure 8-3 shows an accession log. In paper storage systems, the log provides (1) the number codes assigned to correspondents, subjects, or documents; (2) the date of the assignment; and (3) the next number available for assignment. An accession log prevents a filer from assigning the same number twice.

What is an accession log?

Only complete names, not addresses, are needed in the accession log because the log is used only for assigning file code numbers. The accession log is not used to locate correspondent names or to locate code numbers *previously* assigned to correspondents. That information is instantly available in the alphabetic card or computer index explained later.

Filers can use index cards or a book for the accession log, but a computer-generated accession log is simpler to prepare and easier to keep updated. Any computer application software—spreadsheet, database, or word processing—can be used. If the computer program sorts and moves tabular columns, the accession log and the alphabetic computer index can be created from the same data input. Some software programs have a line numbering feature that will assign the next available number automatically.

Alphabetic Index. Numeric records storage cannot function without an **alphabetic index**, which contains the names of and cross-references

```
                        ACCESSION LOG


  File No.   Name of Correspondent or Subject        Date


   100       BROWN SUSAN D                           9/03/--
   101       HIGH SEAS FUEL                          9/03/--
   102       FREY GEORGE C                           9/04/--
   103       LOSARCOS EQUIPMENT                      9/04/--
   104       MCDONALD SCHUYLER P                     9/04/--
   105       STRAUSS JIMMIE D                        9/11/--
   106       APPLICATIONS                            9/12/--
   107       LONDON GLENN W                          9/12/--
   108       MCNEAL ANDREA                           9/13/--
   109       LOSALTOS TRUCKING INC                   9/17/--
   110       VANDEMERE SHEILA                        9/17/--
   111       MCNEAL JOYCE                            9/18/--
   112       LARUSSA COMPUTER CENTER                 9/18/--
   113       MAYER ALICE H                           9/18/--
   114       MITCHELL LESA G                         9/19/--
   115       LASATER SHEILA M                        9/24/--
   116       MIAMOTO ERIA A                          9/24/--
   117       LASBRISAS FABRICS INC                   9/25/--
   118       HIGH TECH SOLUTIONS                     9/25/--
   119       VANDEWATER HAROLD P                     9/25/--
   120       LOSADA ANDREW                           9/26/--
   121       MCANDREWS MARK                          9/27/--
   122       APACHE ADVERTISING AGENCY               9/27/--
```

Figure 8-3 **Computer Accession Log**

for correspondents or any subjects used in a numeric file. The index shows the correspondents' assigned file codes if their records are stored in the numbered file or a G file folder designation if the correspondents' records are stored in the general alphabetic file. Filers reference the alphabetic index to determine whether correspondents are actually in the system and the location of their records. The index may be kept on cards (see Figure 8-6, page 210), but a computer list is easier to maintain. Figure 8-4 is a printout of an alphabetic index prepared from the accession log in Figure 8-3. Simply by alphabetizing the *name* column and arranging it as the first column or field, the accession log becomes an alphabetic index.

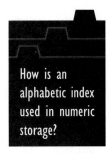

How is an alphabetic index used in numeric storage?

```
                    ALPHABETIC INDEX

APACHE ADVERTISING AGENCY        122
APPLICATIONS                     106
BROWN SUSAN D                    100
COOK MARIETTA                    G
FREY GEORGE C                    102
HIGH SEAS FUEL                   101
HIGH TECH SOLUTIONS             118
LARUSSA COMPUTER CENTER         112
LASATER SHEILA M                115
LASBRISAS FABRICS INC           117
LASTRADA PRODUCTS INC           122X   SEE APACHE
                                       ADVERTISING AGENCY

LATIMER MICHAEL J               G
LONDON GLENN W                  107
LOSADA ANDREW                   120
LOSALTOS TRUCKING INC           109
LOSARCOS EQUIPMENT              103
MAYER ALICE H                   113
MCANDREWS MARK                  121
MCDONALD SCHUYLER P             104
MCNEAL ANDREA                   108
MCNEAL JOYCE                    111
MCNEAL JOYCE MS                 G
MIAMOTO ERIA A                  116
MITCHELL LESA G                 114
STRAUSS JIMMIE D                105
VANDEMERE SHEILA                110
VANDEWATER HAROLD P             119
```

Figure 8-4 **Computer Alphabetic Index**

In some offices, correspondents whose records are stored in the general alphabetic file may not be included in the alphabetic index. However, because the index is the first reference a filer uses to learn the location of a requested name or subject in the numbered file, including all names in the index is a good practice. A record filed in the general alphabetic file is shown in the index with a G (GENERAL) instead of a file code number. Because each correspondent is assigned either a different file code number or a G, the alphabetic index is the important file location "memory" for all file users; take care to keep the index accurate and up to date.

Storage and Retrieval Procedures for Consecutive Numbering

The steps for storage (inspecting, indexing, coding, cross-referencing, sorting, and storing) and retrieval (requisitioning, charging out, and following up) are as important in the numeric method as they are in all other storage methods. The procedures to follow in storing and retrieving records in numeric systems are discussed next.

Inspecting and Indexing.   Inspect records for release marks. Then index to determine the name or subject by which to store each record.

Coding.   Code for numeric storage in two steps: (1) code the filing segment and (2) assign a file code number or the letter G (GENERAL) to the record.

Why is coding a two-step process?

If the alphabetic coding of the name or subject has been done previously, check the coding for accuracy. If the coding has not been done, mark the record to fit the practice of the office. If cross-references are needed, code the cross-reference name or subject and include a notation to that effect (usually an X written on the record).

A rough preliminary alphabetic sort at this time will speed the storing process because reference to the alphabetic index is the next step. Consult the alphabetic index to see whether a card or a computer entry has already been prepared for that correspondent or subject. If so, either a file code number or the letter G (GENERAL) will have been assigned.

Correspondents or Subjects with Numbers Already Assigned.   Code the record with the file code number found in the alphabetic index. Write the number at the top right on the record and place the coded record in a numeric sorter for storage later. The letter in Figure 8-5a shows the name coded and the number already assigned to the name of that organization. The number 122 is written in the upper right corner of the letter.

Correspondents or Subjects with the Letter G Already Assigned.   If the alphabetic index shows a G for the name or subject, the record has been stored in the general alphabetic file. Code the record with a G in the upper right corner. Then place the record in an alphabetic sorter for later storage in the general alphabetic file. The letter in Figure 8-5b shows the G coding.

New Correspondents or Subjects with No Assigned File Code.   If a correspondent or subject is not listed in the alphabetic index, write the letter G in the upper right corner of the document. The letter in Figure 8–5b shows a document coded for the general alphabetic file. Make a card or computer entry for the new correspondent or subject and indicate the file location to be G. File the card in its correct alphabetic sequence in the alphabetic card index. Key computer entries in correct alphabetic sequence.

To assign file code numbers to a correspondent or subject, follow these steps:

1. Consult the accession log and write or key the correspondent's name or the subject on the first unused numbered line. Record the current date.

2. Write the assigned code number on the record in the upper right corner.

3. Make an alphabetic index entry for the correspondent or subject. Include all required information for the correspondent and the file code number assigned. For subjects, key the subject and the assigned number.

4. If any cross-references are needed, prepare a cross-reference entry in the alphabetic index.

5. Prepare a new folder with the file code number on its tab, as well as the correspondent's name or the subject if office policy requires.

6. Place the record in the folder with the top to the left.

7. Place the folder in the sorter for storage in the numbered file later.

Cross-Referencing.   Follow the same rules and procedures explained in Chapters 2 and 3 to cross-reference names and subjects. Do not store cross-references in numbered file folders. Instead, enter all necessary cross-references in the alphabetic index where the filer looks first. Figure 8-6 shows an original card entry and a cross-reference made for a card index. The letter in Figure 8-5a shows a cross-reference notation made on a document. Consider using a card of distinctive color to emphasize a cross-reference in a card index; consider bold print or underlining to show cross-references in a computer index, as shown in Figure 8-4. The cross-reference shows the number assigned to the original file entry, followed by an X to indicate clearly that it is a cross-reference entry.

Where are cross-references filed?

Michael /D. / Larson /Group

3909 21 St., New York, NY 10022-1445 (212)555-9497

DEC 21, 19 – 3:15 PM

December 18, 19–

Ms. Joanna Shelden
Shelden K & R. Inc.
600 E. 52 St.
New York, NY 10022-2844

Dear Ms. Shelden

Last week I met with your friend Joel Duffy regarding the renova-
tion of our office complex at 3909 21 St., here in the city. He
suggested that I look at your work on the Theater Arts Building
because he thought it was close to the kind of makeover we are
thinking about doing here.

Well, several of us toured the building last week and agreed it
is an impressive piece of work. We would like to know what you
and your staff would propose for us. We have very specific needs
in mind and some creative projects that we would like to leave to
you.

Let me know how you would like to proceed. We would prefer a
meeting at our location, where we can show you the kinds of
changes in layout, in communication services, and office equipment we have in mind. We are also eager to hear your suggestions
and hope that you can prepare a proposal by the end of January.

Now that we have agreed to renovate, we are eager to get started.
We are looking forward to an early meeting time that will be
convenient for your people and our staff.

Sincerely

Michael D. Larson

Michael D. Larson

jmo

Figure 8-5b Coded Correspondence for Numeric
Method, Alphabetic File

Apache Advertising Agency
80 Second Avenue
New York, NY 10022-1421
TEL: (212) 555-0346   FAX: (212) 555-0687

NOV 21, 19 – 11:03 AM

November 19. 19–

Ms. Joanna Shelden
Shelden K & R. Inc.
600 E. 52 Street
New York, NY 10022-2844

Dear Ms. Shelden

Your co-op ad with La Strada/Products/Inc. is well under way.
La Strada is more than a little excited about the advertising
tie-in with you as well. We have a two-page ad for spring
distribution we would like to share with you and John Ashley,
Advertising Director at La Strada.

John is really eager to complete the work on this campaign. By
the way, La Strada is also willing to supply a personal appearance of one of its product designers for your spring exhibition.
La Strada has agreed to pay $37,000 for the first spring ad if
you will handle all production costs. We can work out these
arrangements in more detail at our joint meeting.

Shelden K & R. Inc.. and La Strada Products, Inc.. are uniquely
compatible, Joanna. This cooperative effort creates a far more
dynamic campaign for today's market than what we could have
developed from an independent effort. We are eager to show you
what we have done.

I will call you in a few days to arrange a convenient time for a
joint ad and presentation.

Sincerely

APACHE ADVERTISING AGENCY

Mia Black

Mia Black. Advertising Coordinator

jsf

Figure 8-5a Coded Correspondence for Numeric
Method, Numbered File

209

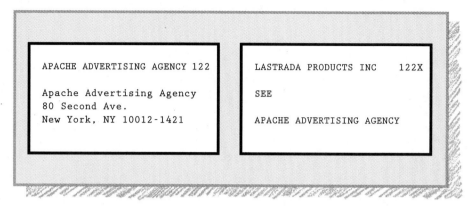

```
APACHE ADVERTISING AGENCY 122          LASTRADA PRODUCTS INC    122X

Apache Advertising Agency              SEE
80 Second Ave.
New York, NY 10012-1421                APACHE ADVERTISING AGENCY
```

Figure 8-6 **Original and Cross-Reference Cards for Alphabetic Index**

Why sort
records before
storing?

Sorting. If you rough sorted as you prepared the records, move the sorter and its contents to the storage area. However, if you prefer to perform like tasks together, *sort all records after* you have indexed, coded, and prepared necessary cross-references. A quick sorting before storage saves time. Stacking the records randomly in groups by hundreds, for example, eliminates moving back and forth from drawer to drawer or shelf to shelf while storing records.

Storing. Store all records coded with numbers in correspondingly numbered folders with the most recent date on top. Store records coded G in the general alphabetic folders. Store them first alphabetically according to the units in the filing segments and then by dates within each name group with the most recent date on top.

Office policy determines the point at which accumulated records in the general alphabetic file require the assignment of a permanent code number. When that accumulation point has occurred, remove the records from the general alphabetic file and take the following steps:

1. Consult the accession log to determine the next available number and enter the name of the correspondent or the subject in the accession log beside that number. Record the current date.

2. Locate the alphabetic index entry already prepared with the subject or the correspondent's name, showing the code letter G.

3. Change the G to the assigned number by crossing out the G and writing the assigned number above it or beside it on the card; on the computer, simply delete the G and insert the code number.

4. Locate all cross-references for the subject or correspondent's name. Change the G to the assigned number followed by an X on the cross-reference entries in either the card or computer alphabetic index.

5. Recode all records with the newly assigned number, crossing out the G and writing the number beside it.

6. Prepare a new folder with the assigned number on its tab (and, possibly, the correspondent's name or the subject).

7. Place all records in the new folder with the most recently dated record on top.

8. Place the numbered folder in its correct numeric sequence in storage.

Retrieving. Whenever you remove records from numeric storage, use requisitions, charge-out cards or slips, and OUT indicators in the same way you used them for alphabetic and subject records storage. Follow-up procedures to locate borrowed records include the use of a tickler file or another reminder system. To ensure the safe return of borrowed records, follow the same procedures described in Chapter 6.

Conversion from Alphabetic Storage to Consecutive Numeric Storage

An organization may decide that a numeric arrangement would provide quicker records storage and retrieval than would an existing alphabetic arrangement. An organization may decide to change from alphabetic storage to consecutively numbered storage for security reasons. A number on a storage container or file folder does not convey information to inquisitive people, but a name on a folder is instantly recognizable to anyone who sees it. Or, an office may prefer an indirect access storage method that allows for a variety of useful indexes to locate stored records such as the storage method your school library uses. Whatever the reason for a conversion, the procedure is not difficult; it is only time-consuming.

Steps to follow in converting from an alphabetic arrangement to a consecutively numbered arrangement are as follows:

1. Prepare numbered guides for every 10 folders in storage according to the sequence of numbers decided upon such as 1–10–20; 100–110–120; 1000–1010–1020; etc.

2. Remove each individual folder from storage and assign a code number from the accession log. Make the filing segment notation (the name of each correspondent or of any subject) in the accession log beside the assigned number. Record the current date.

3. Prepare a numbered label and affix it to the folder or add the newly assigned number to the older label. (*Caution:* Do not remove general folders from alphabetic storage as explained later.)

4. Key each filing segment and all necessary cross-references either on index cards for the alphabetic card index or in the computer alphabetic index. Key the assigned file code number on each card or in each computer entry for reference purposes. Key the file code number and an X on cross-reference cards or in computer entries; use bold or underlining for computer cross-reference entries as well.

5. Remove cross-reference sheets and SEE ALSO references from the individual folders because the cross-reference cards or computer entries in the indexes now take the place of those sheets.

6. Remove any permanent cross-reference guides within the group of folders being converted to the numeric method and make cross-reference cards or computer entries bearing the same information as on the guides.

7. Place all cards, including cross-reference cards, in the card index alphabetically by name or subject. Sort all computer entries in the computer index in ascending alphabetic order.

8. Code each record in every folder with its newly assigned file code number in the upper right corner of the record.

9. Return the numbered folders to storage in correct numeric sequence.

10. Create the general alphabetic file by coding all remaining records with the letter G. (All individual folders have been removed from alphabetic storage, converted to numbered folders, and refiled numerically.)

11. Key an index card or a computer entry for the name of each correspondent or for the subject in every general folder. Place the card in the index file in alphabetic order. If you are using a computer alphabetic index, sort the index again after making the last entry.

Advantages and Disadvantages of Consecutive Numbering

Every storage method has advantages and disadvantages. Consecutive numbering is no exception.

Advantages.   This indirect access method has earned greater respect than some other filing methods for storing electronic records where labeling space is often limited. A simple numeric code identifies tapes, cassettes, disks, and the like. Then the records can be indexed by originator's name, department, subject, special project, or any other meaningful category. The alphabetic index can be as comprehensive as necessary to identify and locate records. Even when disks and tapes are reused, the file code number remains the same; only the index is updated.

Why are electronic records stored by number?

The consecutive numeric method offers many advantages to paper records storage. Some of the advantages apply to electronic records media as well. Advantages include the following:

1. Refiling of numerically coded records is rapid because the majority of people know the sequence of numbers better and faster than they know the sequence of alphabet letters.

2. Expansion is easy and unlimited. New numbers are assigned without disturbing the arrangement of existing folders or other stored records media.

3. Transfer of inactive records is easy, especially in offices where case numbers or contract numbers are used. The oldest cases or contracts or the oldest cassettes or disks have the lowest numbers and are stored together.

4. All cross-references are in the alphabetic index and do not congest the main numbered records in drawers or on shelves.

5. Numeric captions on guides, folders, electronic records, and other records storage media are secure from curious eyes or intentional information seekers. When storage security is needed for medical patients, research projects, formulas, or clients' names, such information can be excluded from label captions.

6. Orders, invoices, ledger accounts, and correspondence for one customer all bear the same numeric code, keeping related records together. Fewer errors may occur when matching invoice and payment, for example.

7. A complete list of correspondents' names, addresses, and other information is instantly available from the alphabetic index.

8. Time and effort in labeling are minimized because numbers can be affixed more quickly than can names, subjects, or project titles. Available folders and electronic records media may be numbered in advance of their use.

9. Misfiled records are easily detected because numbers out of sequence are usually easier to detect than are misfiled records arranged alphabetically.

Disadvantages. Disadvantages of the consecutive numbering method include the following:

1. Numeric storage access is indirect because reference to an alphabetic index is necessary. Whenever more steps are required to store records, more mistakes can occur.

2. More guides are necessary for the numeric method than for other storage methods; therefore, the cost of supplies for numeric storage may be somewhat higher.

3. Congestion around an alphabetic card index may occur when more than one person makes frequent reference to its contents. This problem may or may not occur with a computer alphabetic index, depending on how many computers and/or updated printed copies of the index are available.

4. Because each record must be checked against an alphabetic index, alphabetic sorting must be done first. Then resorting numerically is done prior to storage. This double sorting requires extra time.

5. Because new records are added in consecutive order, records with the highest numbers are typically the most current and most active records. Several people simultaneously referencing the more current records can, therefore, cause congestion at the end of the storage area.

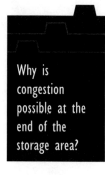

Why is congestion possible at the end of the storage area?

Nonconsecutive Numbering Methods

Nonconsecutive numbering is a system of numbers that either has no logical sequence or has a logical sequence from which blocks of numbers have been omitted. These methods include terminal-digit, middle-digit, and chronologic storage.

Terminal-Digit Storage

Developed to avoid the disadvantage of working with large numbers manually, the terminal-digit storage method also overcame the disadvantage of congestion that can occur at the end of a consecutive numeric storage area. The terminal-digit storage method is used most effectively with thousands of folders whose numbers have reached at least five digits (10,000 or more). The words *terminal digit* refer to the end digits of a number (091 38 <u>0297</u>). Numbers may be assigned sequentially, or the digit groups may mean something specific. The first group of numbers may be a customer identification number; the second group may indicate a sales district, salesperson, or department; the third group may indicate a date, branch office, or department. The number may be a product number in which various groups of numbers refer to a sales department and/or a particular manufacturer or wholesaler. The numbers can mean a great deal, or they can be simply a sequentially assigned file code number.

Terminal-digit storage is a numeric storage method in which the last two or three digits of each number are used as the primary division under which a record is filed. Groups of numbers are read from right to left. The digits in the number are usually separated into groups by a space or hyphen. If separated by spaces, computer sorting is possible with some software. Each part of the number becomes a separate "word" sort in the numeric data field.

What is terminal-digit storage?

The groups of numbers are identified as primary, secondary, and tertiary numbers reading from right to left.

02	24	51
(tertiary)	(secondary)	(primary)

An arrangement of numbers in terminal-digit sequence would look like the following; the numbers in bold determine the correct numeric order:

786 67 **1258** (file front)	303 **99** 2891	502 64 **9284**
331 55 **2187**	947 28 **6314**	498 64 **9485**
189 40 **2891**	287 **29** 6314	**502** 64 9485 (file end)

215

The primary numbers usually indicate a drawer or shelf number. If the volume of records stored is great, more than one drawer or shelf may be needed to hold all records with numbers ending in the same terminal digits. Figure 8-7 shows the arrangement of folders or numbered cards in a portion of Drawer 51. All records within that drawer have numbers ending in 51. The numbers of the secondary digits determine the primary guide captions. The section of the drawer shown begins with guide 24-51; actually if space had permitted, the entire 51 section would show guide 00-51 at the beginning of the drawer. The records are arranged behind each guide by the tertiary numbers, or the digits at the extreme LEFT of the number.

As new folders are stored, new guides are added to separate each group of 10 folders. In Figure 8-8, the first section of the file shown in Figure 8-7 (the 24-51 section) has expanded by the addition of folders numbered <u>10</u>-24-51 through <u>19</u>-24-51. The tertiary numbers now have increased from 00 through 07 to 00 through 22. Therefore, secondary guides 00, 10, and 20 were added in first position, and the primary guides moved to the prominent center position of the file drawer.

When sequentially numbered records such as 02 25 51 and 02 25 52 are added to terminal-digit storage, these new, typically more active records are filed in *different* file locations. Distributing current records throughout a storage area avoids congestion in one particular storage area. Remember: In consecutive numeric storage, these records would be stored next to each another at the end of the storage area.

Do not confuse terminal-digit storage with the consecutive numeric storage of large, six-digit numbers often used in electronic records media storage. When six-digit numbers are stored *consecutively*, the last two digits in the number become rack numbers—the number placed on the rack just below a stored cartridge, cassette, or tape. The last two digits 01 in the number 789<u>201</u> do not occur again until 789<u>301</u>—100 records away. Therefore, once you have arrived in the file section of 7893, the last two digits fixed to the storage rack become the important numbers for record identification.

Middle-Digit Storage

Middle-digit storage is another method of nonconsecutive numbering. Similar to terminal-digit storage, this method also avoids working with large numbers and overcomes the disadvantage of congestion at the end

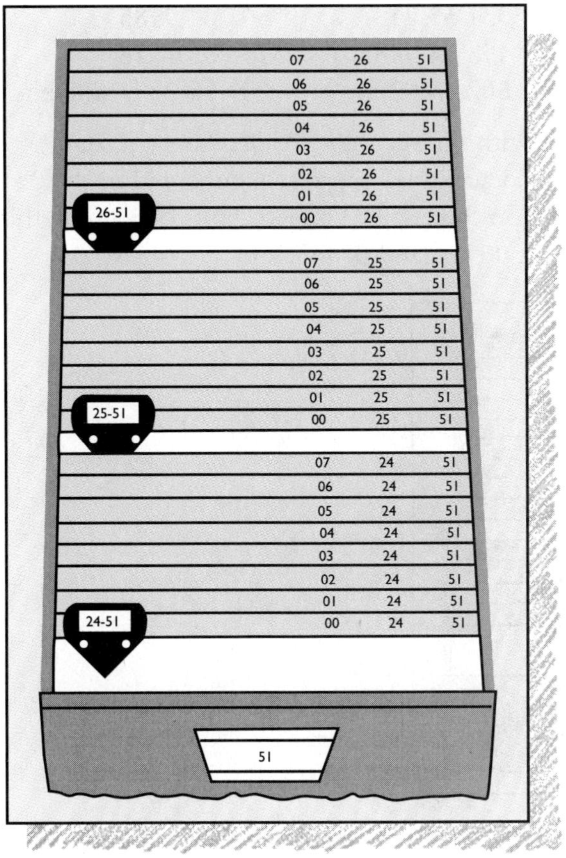

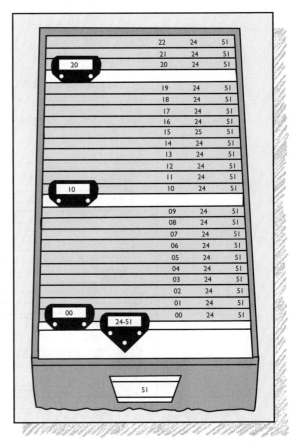

Figure 8-7 **Terminal-Digit Arrangement**

Figure 8-8 **Expansion of Terminal-Digit Arrangement**

of the storage area. The words *middle-digit* refer to the middle group of digits in a large number.

Middle-digit storage is a numeric storage method in which the middle two or three digits of each number are used as the primary division under which a record is filed. Groups of numbers are read from the middle to left to right. Numbers to the left are secondary; numbers to the right are tertiary, or last.

02   24   51

(secondary)   (primary)   (tertiary)

An arrangement of numbers in middle-digit sequence would look like the following; the numbers in bold determine the correct numeric order:

947 **28** 6314 (file front)   331 **55** 2187   502 64 **9485**

287 **29** 6314   498 **64** 9485   786 **67** 1258

189 **40** 2891   **502** 64 9284   303 **99** 2891 (file end)

In Figure 8-9, all records with middle digits 33 are stored in one section. The digits on the left determine record sequence within the 33 drawer, followed by the digits on the right. The left digits determine the primary guide captions **05**-33, **06**-33, and **07**-33.

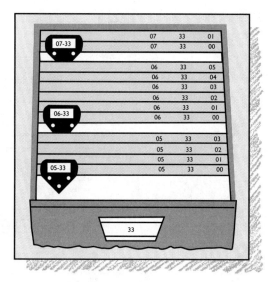

Figure 8-9 **Middle-Digit Arrangement**

In the middle-digit method, blocks of sequentially numbered records are kept together. However, records are distributed through the files in blocks of 100. Records numbered 10<u>34</u>00 to 10<u>34</u>99 are filed together in one section; 10<u>35</u>00 to 10<u>35</u>99, in the next file section. The middle-digit method has additional value when the middle digits identify someone or something specific and when related records need to be kept together. If the middle digits represent a sales representative or a sales district, for example, all records for that individual or location are kept together in one block.

Why use middle-digit storage?

Chronologic Storage

Chronologic storage is filing records by calendar date with the most recent date always on top. Exact chronologic storage is not well suited to correspondence because of the need for keeping together all records from, to, and about one individual or organization. Chronologic storage is often used for daily reports, deposit tickets, freight bills, statements, and order sheets, which may be best stored by date.

The chronologic principle is followed in all methods of storage as records are placed in their folders. The most current records are at the front of the folder, thereby keeping the most recent records in the most accessible place. Tickler files are another form of chronologic storage. You may want to refer to the discussion of tickler files in Chapter 5.

Numeric Coding Systems

Numbers are sometimes added to encyclopedic arrangements of subject and geographic filing methods. Numbers help eliminate misfiles in subject and geographic files containing main subject divisions and many subdivisions. The numeric coding systems described in the following sections allow for coding the necessary subdivisions.

Block Numeric Coding

Block numeric coding is a coding system based on the assignment of groups of numbers to represent primary and secondary subjects such as the encyclopedic arrangement of the subject file in Chapter 7. The major subject divisions are assigned a block of round numbers such as 100, 200, 300. Then each subdivision is assigned a block of numbers within the major block of round numbers such as 110, 120, 130. The more file expansion expected, the larger the blocks of numbers will be. The subdivision 110, for example, allows for additional subject subdivisions of subjects (111 to 119). If blocks of numbers were assigned to the subject file illustrated in Figure 7-2, pages 181–182, the block number allotments might look like this:

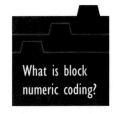

What is block numeric coding?

```
100  ACCOUNTING
       110  ACCOUNTS PAYABLE
       120  ACCOUNTS RECEIVABLE
       130  PROFIT AND LOSS
150  AIR CONDITIONING
200  APPLICATIONS
250  BANKING
       260  LOANS
       270  STATEMENTS
300  BRANCH OFFICES
       . . .
```

Duplex-Numeric Coding

Is duplex-numeric coding numeric or alphabetic?

Like block numeric coding, duplex-numeric coding is also used in subject or geographic filing systems that contain major categories and subdivisions. **Duplex-numeric coding** is a coding system using numbers (or sometimes letters) with two or more parts separated by a dash, space, or comma. An unlimited number of subdivisions is possible with this coding system. Subject subdivisions are added *sequentially*, however, and may not follow a strict alphabetic order. Notice that PAST BUDGETS comes before FUTURE NEEDS in the following example because FUTURE NEEDS was added to the file *after* PAST BUDGETS:

    10 BUDGETS
        10-1   ACCOUNTING DEPARTMENT
            10-1-1   PAST BUDGETS
            10-1-2   FUTURE NEEDS
            10-1-3   RECEIPTS
        10-2   DATA PROCESSING DEPARTMENT
            10-2-1   PAST BUDGETS
            10-2-2   FUTURE NEEDS
        10-3   ENGINEERING DEPARTMENT
            10-3-1   PAST BUDGETS

        . . .

Decimal-Numeric Coding

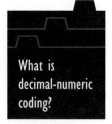

What is decimal-numeric coding?

Decimal-numeric coding is a system for coding records numerically in units of 10. An unlimited number of subdivisions is permitted through the use of digits to the right of the decimal point. This method was first used in 1873 by Dr. Melvil Dewey for classifying library materials. The system has nine general classes or main divisions (100-900). A tenth division (000) is used for records too general to be placed in any of the nine main divisions. Each main division may be divided into nine or fewer parts (110, 120, to 190). These nine parts can be divided further into nine additional groups (111, 112, to 119). Decimals are added for further divisions (111.1, 111.1.1). The Dewey decimal classification is not commonly used in the office. However, the use of decimals to subdivide records is a practical alternative to the dashes, spaces, and commas used in duplex-numeric coding to subdivide records.

Alphanumeric Coding

Alphanumeric coding is a coding system that combines alphabetic and numeric characters. Main subjects are arranged alphabetically, and their subdivisions are assigned a number. After all main subjects are determined, they are given a number (usually in groups of 10 or 100 to provide for expansion). More elaborate variations of this system may use both letters and numbers and have numerous subdivisions.

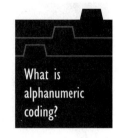

What is alphanumeric coding?

```
MGT -   MANAGEMENT
    MGT-01   RECORDS MANAGEMENT
        MGT-01-01   FILING EQUIPMENT
        MGT-01-02   FILING SYSTEMS
            MGT-01-02-01   AUTOMATED
            MGT-01-02-02   ELECTRONIC
            MGT-01-02-03   PROCEDURES MANUAL
        MGT-01-03   RETENTION SCHEDULE
    MGT-02   SALES MANAGEMENT
        MGT-02-01   ADVERTISING
        . . .
```

Current Trends in Records Management

The computer has changed forever the way in which offices control records storage and retrieval systems and perform routine tasks. Many current trends in records management are the result of some new technology or computer application software. The computer's power to store information is well known. However, its power to manipulate (sort and rearrange) and present numeric data in useful patterns is still being discovered. Two software features to look for in this regard are (1) the hard space and (2) the individual word sort within a data field. Both of these features are explained next.

You have learned that indexing order is not affected by spacing between a prefix and the rest of the name (LaSalle and La Salle). Although both names are indexed as one unit, it is sometimes important to know how such names are normally written. In the accession log in Figure 8-10, compound names like Los Altos and Mc Neal are keyed with spaces and not closed up in the usual manner for correct sorting (LOSALTOS and MCNEAL). Actually, hard spaces were used in these names. A **hard space** is a computer character code used to keep two or more parts of a name, phrase, date, or number together. Therefore, names entered with hard spaces look like compound names. However, the names are viewed by the computer as ONE word—a single filing unit—important for computer sorting of names with prefixes. A hard space assures a correct alphabetic name sort and maintains the correct spelling of such names. Check your computer application software manual for this feature and for instructions on how to create it.

Some computer application software will sort individual "words" keyed into a single data field left-to-right order, right-to-left order, or

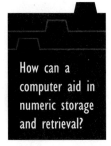

How can a computer aid in numeric storage and retrieval?

```
                            ACCESSION LOG


    File No.    Name of Correspondent or Subject        Date


      100       BROWN  SUSAN  D                         9/03/--
      101       HIGH  SEAS  FUEL                        9/03/--
      102       FREY  GEORGE  C                         9/04/--
      103       LOS  ARCOS  EQUIPMENT                   9/04/--
      104       MC  DONALD  SCHUYLER  P                 9/04/--
      105       STRAUSS  JIMMIE  D                      9/11/--
      106       APPLICATIONS                            9/12/--
      107       LONDON  GLENN  W                        9/12/--
      108       MCNEAL  ANDREA                          9/13/--
      109       LOS  ALTOS  TRUCKING  INC               9/17/--
      110       VANDEMERE  SHEILA                       9/17/--
      111       MC  NEAL  JOYCE                         9/18/--
      112       LARUSSA  COMPUTER  CENTER               9/18/--
      113       MAYER  ALICE  H                         9/18/--
      114       MITCHELL  LESA  G                       9/19/--
      115       LASATER  SHEILA  M                      9/24/--
      116       MIAMOTO  ERIA  A                        9/24/--
      117       LAS  BRISAS  FABRICS  INC               9/25/--
      118       HIGH  TECH  SOLUTIONS                   9/25/--
      119       VAN  DE  WATER  HAROLD  P               9/25/--
      120       LOSADA  ANDREW                          9/26/--
      121       MCANDREWS  MARK                         9/27/--
      122       APACHE  ADVERTISING  AGENCY             9/27/--
```

Figure 8-10 Computer Accession Log Using Hard Spaces

any other order. For example, the computer reads a numeric data field 991 53 8748 as three "words." The numbers can be sorted left to right (Word 1, Word 2, Word 3) for consecutive numeric order; right to left (Word 3, Word 2, Word 1) for terminal digit order; or Word 2, Word 1, Word 3 for middle-digit order. Large numbers can be sorted in any order without having to key parts of the number in separate data fields as is often necessary.

Have you checked your mailbox lately? All mail you receive with PAID Bulk Rate in the stamp location was presorted by ZIP Code. Sorting mailing addresses by ZIP Code is necessary to take advantage of low-rate, bulk mailing services. The mail can be manually hand sorted, of course. However, computer-generated mailing labels can be sorted by ZIP Code without the need to key the ZIP Code in a separate data field. Figure 8-11 shows mailing labels sorted by ZIP Codes. Some software will sort *the last "word" in a CITY/STATE/ZIP data field*. For example, city, state, and ZIP Code data fields such as Norwalk, CT 06850-3932

MAILING LABELS SORTED BY ZIP CODES	
Los Altos Trucking, Inc. 466 Houston Rd. Boston, MA 02172-3772	Mr. George C. Frey 41 Broad St. New York, NY 10004-3672
High Seas Fuel 522 Oakwood Terrace Norwalk, CT 06850-3932	Ms. Joyce Mc Neal 824 Arlington Blvd. Philadelphia, PA 19121-3428
Mr. Jimmie D. Strauss 3841 East Crescent Avenue Upper Saddle River, NJ 07458-3864	Mr. Mark McAndrews 241 Seneca St. Charleston, WV 25304-3820
Ms. Joyce Mc Neal 881 Jamaica Ave. Trenton, NJ 08601-3993	Mr. Michael J. Latimer 1062 Wells St. Sumter, SC 29150-3819

Figure 8-11 Mailing Labels Sorted by ZIP Codes

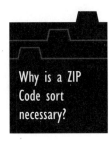

(three words); New York, NY 10004-3672 (four words); and Upper Saddle River, NJ 07458-3864 (five words) sort by ZIP Codes—regardless of the number of words preceding the ZIP Code.

The computer has eliminated the need to key the same data into the computer more than one time. For example, the accession log and alphabetic index shown earlier in this chapter are good examples of producing two documents from one input of data. Continue to explore computer application software and how it can help with future routine records management tasks.

Summary

Although some individuals still may resent a society that identifies people, products, and everything in between by some kind of numbering system, most appreciate the speed by which accurate transactions are possible by using numbers. The consecutive numeric storage is an indirect access method that allows records to be stored by a simple numeric file code and provides the flexibility of creating one or more indexes to locate them.

The increasing demand for electronic records storage has resulted in a keen and renewed interest in this powerful numeric storage method. Color-coded numeric labels are available for all kinds of electronic records, as well as for file folders.

Nonconsecutive numeric storage is rarely seen in offices today. However, in large manual numeric systems, terminal-digit storage creates a more even distribution of consecutively numbered records throughout a numeric system, and middle-digit storage allows blocks of related records to be stored together sequentially. Computers have simplified the control of large numbers in numeric storage systems.

The chronologic storage method is used in just about every filing method. Because dates, like numbers and letters, are sequential, they continue to be an important factor in developing efficient retrieval systems. Block numeric, duplex-numeric, decimal-numeric, and alphanumeric coding provide a means to code numerically encyclopedic arrangements of subject and geographic files, creating faster and more accurate records storage and retrieval systems.

The computer has simplified numeric records storage control. The computer must be appreciated not only for its ability to store numeric data, but also for its ability to sort and manipulate data in a variety of useful formats. Computers have simplified the preparation of accession logs and alphabetic indexes that control numeric storage systems.

Important Terms

accession log

alphabetic index

alphanumeric coding

block numeric coding

chronologic storage

consecutive numbering method

decimal-numeric coding

duplex-numeric coding

hard space

middle-digit storage

nonconsecutive numbering

numeric storage method

terminal-digit storage

Review and Discussion

1. List three reasons for storing records by the numeric method. (Obj. 1)

2. What does a school library storage method have in common with consecutive numeric records storage? (Obj. 2)

3. List the four basic components of consecutive numeric storage. Explain the primary function of each. (Obj. 2)

4. Is the numeric method a direct or an indirect access filing method? What is the difference between the two? (Obj. 2)

5. Why is it recommended that a general alphabetic file be placed at the beginning, rather than at the end, of a consecutively numbered storage arrangement? (Obj. 2)

6. What are the procedures for storing records by the consecutive numbering method? (Obj. 3)

7. What functions do an alphabetic index and an accession log serve in the numeric storage method? (Obj. 3)

8. Explain why records in numeric records storage are coded with the letter G, a crossed-out G with a number (G̸125), or just a number (122). (Obj. 3)

9. How are cross-references prepared in the consecutive numbering method? How are they numbered? (Obj. 3)

10. In converting from an alphabetic arrangement to a consecutively numbered arrangement, you will not assign numbers to the general folders in alphabetic storage. Where will these folders be located in

the numeric storage arrangement? Will records in these folders be coded with a number? Why or why not? (Obj. 4).

11. List at least three advantages and three disadvantages of consecutive numeric records storage. (Obj. 5)

12. What is the difference between the consecutive numbering method and a nonconsecutive numbering method of storing records? (Obj. 6)

13. Explain how numbers are sorted in consecutive numbering and terminal-digit and middle-digit nonconsecutive numbering methods. (Obj. 7)

14. Explain chronologic storage and how it is used. (Obj. 8)

15. What is block numeric coding? (Obj. 9)

16. Explain the similarities of the duplex-numeric, decimal-numeric, and alphanumeric coding systems. (Obj. 10)

17. Describe two features of computer application software that can benefit numeric data storage and manipulation. (Obj. 11)

Applications (APP)

Collaborative   Template

APP 8-1. *Computer Disks and Files Out of Control (Obj. 11)*

Your friend, Mary Carpenter, walks into your office carrying computer disks numbered 1 to 5. She is distraught because finding the data files she has recorded on five disks is time-consuming. Mary had no difficulty finding files when she had just one disk, two, or even three. Now that the disks are accumulating, she can't find anything anymore. Mary asks for your help in creating a system that allows her to find her files *without* moving any files. Her explanations of file contents are in parentheses after the filenames.

You find the following data files on each of the five disks:

DISK 1
    SALSFRCST.RPT (Sales Forecast Report)
    SALSANNL.RPT (Annual Sales Report)
    WRKORD.FRM (In-house Work Order 8/12)
    WRKORD1.FRM (In-house Work Order 8/12)

MCKAY.CRS (Mr. McKay's Dictation 8/15)
JANSEN.CRS (Mr. Jansen's Dictation 8/24)
ADMINIS.BDG (Administrative Budget)
EMPDRTRY.LST (Employee Telephone Directory)

DISK 2

WARMEMRL.CNT (War Memorial Contract)
MDARTBLD.CNT (Medical Arts Bldg. Contract)
THETRART.PRO (Theatre Arts Bldg. Proposal)
POYOUNG.FRM (Young & Lewis Purchase Order)
POSTCNTR.FRM (Stationery Center Purchase Order)
EMPLOYEE.LST (List of Employees)
PRSPCUST.LBL (Prospective Customer Mailing Labels)
ADMINIS.RPT (Administration Report)
PRICE.LST (Price List)

DISK 3

EMPLOYEE.LBL (Employee Mailing Labels)
PRSPCUS.DTA (Prospective Customer Data File)
EMPLOYEE.DTA (Employee Data File)
CLIENT.DTA (Client Data File)
MCKAY.CRS (Mr. McKay's Dictation 8/22)
ABBRAHM.CRS (Mr. Abbrahms' Dictation 8/24)
SLSQRTL.RPT (Quarterly Sales Report 8/24)
KAUFMAN.PRO (Kaufman, Inc., Proposal)

DISK 4

WILLIS.CRS (Mr. Willis' Dictation 9/5)
COMPCNTR.BDG (Computer Center Budget)
SLSMRKTG.BDG (Sales & Marketing Budget)
SLSQRTL.RPT (Quarterly Sales Report 11/24)
THETRART.BDS (Theatre Arts Bldg. Bid)
WRKORD.FRM (In-house Work Order 11/27)
POSMEAD.FRM (Smead Purchase Order)
WALMART.PRO (Wal-Mart Proposal)
THETRART.CNT (Theatre Arts Bldg. Contract)

DISK 5

COANNUAL.RPT (Company Annual Report)
KAUFMAN.CNT (Kaufman, Inc., Contract)

MCKAY.CRS (Mr. McKay's Dictation 12/4)
ABBRAHM.CRS (Mr. Abbrahms' Dictation 12/8)
PRCORP.BDS (P & R Corporation Bid)
DELANEY.BDS (Delaney Chemical, Inc., Bid)
POIBM.FRM (IBM Purchase Order)
INVKAUFM.FRM (Kaufman, Inc., Invoice)
INVTHART.FRM (Theatre Arts Bldg. Invoice)
SLSPROM.BDG (Sales Promotion Budget)

Mary tells you that she tried to be consistent in naming the files. For example, she has used meaningful codes for filename extensions. She explains her coding system as follows:

BDG = Budgets	FRM = Forms
BDS = Bids	LBL = Labels
CNT = Contracts	LST = Lists
CRS = Correspondence	PRO = Proposals
DTA = Data	RPT = Reports

Based on what you know about subject filing and have learned about useful indexes, prepare an index for Mary that will help her find files quickly. Prepare a 5" by 3" card index or key a computer index. Name the file CH8.AP1. Print a copy of the computer index. What suggestions can you make to simplify Mary's data disk storage in the future?

Collaborative

Template

APP 8-2. Analyzing a Numeric Method of Storage (Obj. 5)

Request a copy of your school's class schedule. In a short report, analyze what system (or systems) is used to identify the different departments, courses within that department, and the various sections of a single course. Include in your report at least one positive statement about the system used and at least one improvement you would recommend. Key your report in file CH8.AP2, check the spelling, and print a copy.

Practice Set

Applying the Rules

Job 10, Consecutive Numeric Correspondence Filing
Job 11, Terminal-Digit Numeric Correspondence Filing

Chapter 9
Geographic Records Storage

Learning Objectives

1. Explain the need for geographic records storage.
2. Name the kinds of businesses that might use the geographic records storage method.
3. List advantages and disadvantages of the geographic records storage method.
4. Compare the difference between the dictionary and encyclopedic arrangements of geographic records.
5. Explain the differences between the lettered guide plan and the location name guide plan.
6. Describe an arrangement of guides and folders in the geographic records storage method.
7. Explain the use of an alphabetic index in the geographic records storage method.
8. Describe how indexing and coding for the geographic records storage method differ from indexing and coding for the alphabetic records storage method.
9. List the types of cross-references used in the geographic records storage method and how they are stored.
10. Describe what effect the Internet is likely to have on geographic records storage.

Need for Geographic Records Storage

Local neighborhoods were once served primarily by small businesses that had little need or concern to expand activities beyond their local communities. Businesses prospered or failed based on whether sales were good or not so good in the neighborhood. Today, the United States is a lean, "mean," high-tech production machine with a highly ranked competitive economy in which large corporations operate worldwide. Such global marketing has emerged for several reasons:

1. Emphasis on efficiency and high production that has resulted in more goods and services than can be consumed locally or domesti-

cally. Organizations now explore market possibilities beyond their immediate locations.

2. Improvements in transportation and shipping that have made the movement of goods easier throughout the world.

3. New trade agreements that have opened new world markets.

What has promoted global marketing?

4. High-tech communications and satellite networks that have brought the people of the world closer together. A New York organization conducts business activities as easily in Mexico, Japan, or Germany as it does in Ohio, California, or Idaho.

The importance of location in the day-to-day decisions of big business is clearly evident in a global economy. However, a domestic, local perspective of business reveals the same critical role that location plays in the success or failure of small, local enterprises. Look at the changes taking place in your own community. Why does a large super-market close in your neighborhood? Why does a large discount chain (box store) open in town? Why does a manufacturer move its operations from New York to Mexico? from California to Utah? or from Alabama to Taiwan? Why did your favorite pizza shop move from the north side of town to the south side? One principal part of the answer is *location*!

As you would expect, location plays an important role in organizational decision making. As business activities span wider geographic areas, decisions regarding those locations need to be made; and intelligent business decisions based on location are made by maintaining records by those locations. You do not have to be a marketing research analyst to figure out why skis sell better in Colorado or New York than they do in Florida or Arizona or why in-line skates sell better in urban locations than in rural locations. However, not all needed information regarding location is so obvious when organizations are considering expanding their market potential. For example: Why are production costs higher in one location than another? Is the climate of a location important to sales? What about the average age of the populations or their literacy and income levels? Good management decisions are based on reliable information; and when such information is needed, the records collected and stored by location provide it.

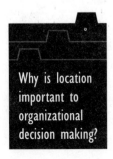

Why is location important to organizational decision making?

Now let us explore how geography (location) relates to your study of geographic records storage. You have already studied alphabetic storage by name and by subject. In this chapter, you will learn a third alphabetic storage method: by location. **Geographic records storage method** is a method of storing and retrieving records in alphabetic order by location of an individual, an organization, or a project.

Businesses that may store records by the geographic method include the following:

1. Multinational companies, or those businesses with plants, divisions, and customers outside the U.S. boundaries, whose records are arranged by region and then by country within a region.

2. The petroleum industry, mining companies, government offices, and other organizations that store maps and other related location- and land-oriented records.

3. Businesses that have many branches (possibly sales offices) at different geographic locations within the United States and often have a great deal of intracompany correspondence.

4. Businesses such as insurance companies, franchised operations, banks, and investment firms that are licensed to operate in specific states and whose records are kept according to those states.

5. Mail-order houses and publishers whose business is conducted through the U.S. mail and who refer to their customers' records first by geographic location or by a number (ZIP Code or Account No.) representing a specific location or region.

6. Companies that direct their advertising promotions to specific geographic areas such as the West Coast, East Coast, South, or North.

7. Utility companies (electricity, gas, telephone, water) whose customers are listed by street name and address first.

8. Real estate agencies that list their properties by areas. Sometimes the areas may be quite unusual such as islands, castles, and estates in foreign countries; sometimes the areas are divisions of countries or cities; and sometimes in a metropolitan area, the listings may be grouped by subdivision names or by street boundaries within the city itself.

9. Government agencies whose records might be stored according to geographic areas such as state, county, township, etc., depending on the scope of the governmental function.

Who uses geographic records storage?

Advantages and Disadvantages of the Geographic Records Storage Method

Similar to any storage method, the geographic records storage method has advantages and disadvantages. However, when records need to be stored by location, the advantages are highly evident, and the disadvantages are calmly tolerated.

Advantages of Geographic Records Storage

Why use geographic records storage?

Geographic records storage provides speedy reference to information specific to certain geographic areas needed for making sound decisions regarding those locations. For example, the number of stored records created in various geographic areas can be compared by examining the space required to store those records. An analysis of those records can be used constructively to note (1) areas with the most complaints; (2) aggressive selling effort or the lack of selling effort; (3) areas that need special attention to personnel, production, shipping costs, and the like; or (4) where territories need to be combined, separated, or subdivided. If territories need adjustments, geographic file guides and folders are easily rearranged. Each geographic area in storage is a unit or a group, and the shift of groups of records is easily accomplished by moving an entire group from one file location to another.

Disadvantages of Geographic Records Storage

One disadvantage of the geographic storage method is the complexity of the guide and folder arrangements that some large systems may require. Because the method may call for many subdivisions, a geographic arrangement requires more time to establish than an alphabetic arrangement. Storing and retrieving records can also be more time-consuming because reference must be made first to an area (such as a state), then to a location within that area (such as a city), and finally to a correspondent's address and name.

Another disadvantage is the need for an alphabetic index of all correspondents' names and addresses. If the location of a correspondent is not known, an alphabetic index must be referenced to learn the location before a record can be filed or retrieved from the geographic file. Similar to the subject storage method, the geographic storage method may require two operations to store and retrieve a record—a check of the index for the correct file location and then the actual search of the file. These disadvantages are insignificant, however, when compared to the important data geographic storage provides.

Geographic Records Storage Arrangements

The geographic arrangement that an office uses will depend on the following:

1. The type of business being operated.

2. The way by which records are referred (by state, by geographic region, by country, and so forth).

3. The geographic areas to which the records are related.

The geographic arrangement can be as simple as a file of city streets or countries of the world. More complex systems include subdivisions and are arranged in order from *major* to *minor* geographic units; for example, (1) country name, (2) state name or state equivalent (provinces, for example), (3) city name, and (4) correspondent's name. In general, the filing segment in geographic records storage includes geographic indexing units first, followed by the correspondent's name.

Two basic arrangements are commonly used in geographic storage: (1) the dictionary arrangement and (2) the encyclopedic arrangement. You have already studied the dictionary and encyclopedic arrangements in Chapter 7, Subject Records Storage. Your familiarity with these two arrangements will further your understanding of the discussion and illustrations that follow.

What are the two basic storage arrangements?

Dictionary Geographic Records Storage Arrangement

The **dictionary arrangement** is the arrangement of records in alphabetic order (A-Z). Use the dictionary arrangement when filing *single* geographic units such as all streets, all cities, all states, or all countries. Two guide plans are possible: the lettered guide plan or the location name guide plan.

Lettered Guide Plan. The **lettered guide plan** is an arrangement of geographic records in which primary guides are labeled with alphabetic

What are two commonly used guide plans?

letters. The lettered guide plan can be used in any geographic arrangement. If the volume of records stored geographically is very large, alphabetic guides will cut storage and retrieval time by guiding the eye quickly to the correct alphabetic section of storage.

Figure 9-1 shows a dictionary arrangement of records by country in a lettered guide plan. The primary guides are one–fifth cut lettered guides arranged in a straight line in the file drawer first position (from left to right). The general country folders are third-cut folders arranged in a straight line in the file drawer second position. As you can see, a lettered guide plan may be excessive in a file consisting of only a few but diverse names.

Location Name Guide Plan. The **location name guide plan** is an arrangement of geographic records in which primary guides are labeled with location names. When location names are few but diverse, use the location name guide plan.

Figure 9-2 shows a location name guide plan in a dictionary arrangement of foreign country names. The primary guides are one-fifth cut country name guides arranged in a straight line in the file drawer first position. The general country folders are one-third cut folders arranged in a straight line in second position down the right side of the file drawer. Figures 9-1 and 9-2 show the different guide plans in a dictionary arrangement of identical records.

Encyclopedic Geographic Records Storage Arrangement

The **encyclopedic arrangement** is the alphabetic arrangement of major geographic divisions *plus* one or more geographic *subdivisions* also arranged in alphabetic order. Similar to the dictionary storage arrangement, the encyclopedic arrangement makes use of either a lettered guide plan or a location name guide plan. Guides in a storage system provide sufficient guidance to speed the storage and retrieval of records. Guides should not dominate a storage area or become an efficiency barrier. Although lettered guides with closed captions require more thought when filing (A–D, E–H, I–P, etc.), they provide a means of using fewer lettered guides.

Figures 9-3 and 9-4 illustrate geographic records storage in an encyclopedic arrangement. Compare the guide plans used for these identical records: Figure 9-3 uses a lettered guide plan, and Figure 9-4 uses a location name guide plan. The major geographic units in the

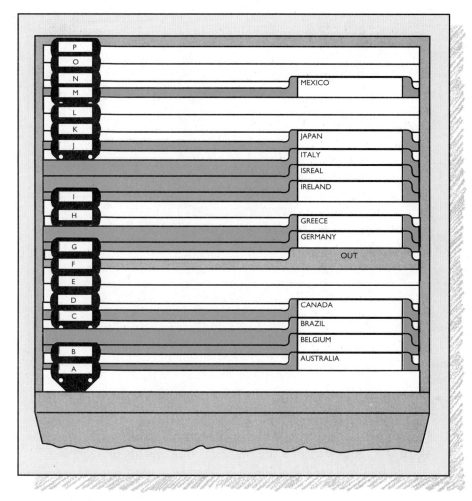

Figure 9-1 **Dictionary Arrangement of Records, Lettered Guide Plan**

illustrations are state names; the subdivisions are city names. Refer to the illustrations as you study the following detailed explanations of the file arrangements, the guide plans, and the folder contents.

Lettered Guide Plan. Figure 9-3 shows part of a drawer of New York and North Carolina records stored by the lettered guide plan. Refer to Figure 9-3 as you study the following arrangement description:

1. In first position in the drawer are one-fifth cut primary guides for the state names NEW YORK and NORTH CAROLINA, the largest geographic divisions in this storage plan.

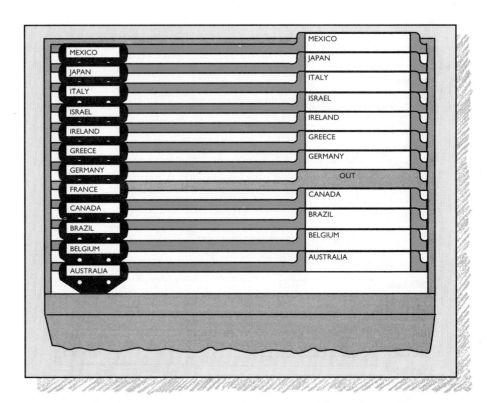

Figure 9-2   Dictionary Arrangement of Records, Location Name Guide Plan

2. In second position are the secondary guides, the one-fifth cut alphabetic guides that divide the states into alphabetic sections. Each guide indicates the alphabetic section within which records with city names beginning with that letter are stored. The guide tabs are numbered consecutively to keep them in correct order.

3. In third position are special guides. Special city guides indicate cities for which there is a considerable volume of records (ALBANY); A-M and N-Z provide a separation of correspondents' *names* in the ALBANY city section. These guides are one-fifth cut.

What kinds of folders are needed?

4. In fourth position as your eye moves left to right *in the drawer* are all the folders. Folders are one-third cut, third-position tab folders arranged in a straight line at the right of the file drawer. Notice the three kinds of folders used in this file arrangement: general alphabetic state folders, special city folders, and individual folders.

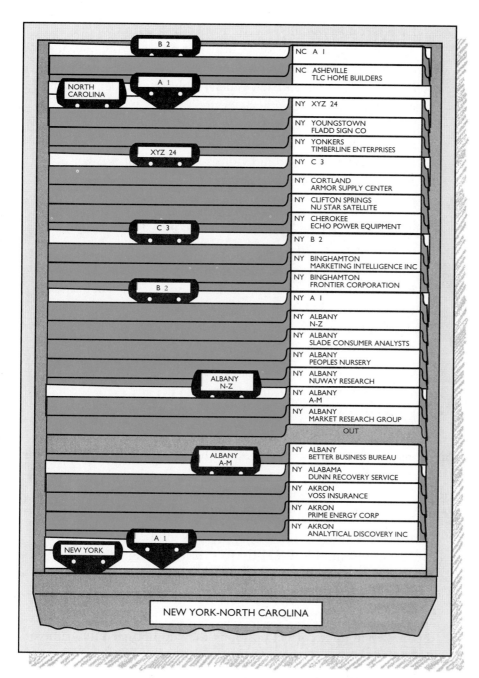

Figure 9-3   Encyclopedic Arrangement of Records, Lettered Guide Plan

a. Each secondary guide is accompanied by a corresponding general alphabetic city folder, which is placed at the end of that alphabetic section. The folder has the same caption as that of the secondary guide. Each general alphabetic folder contains records from correspondents located in cities with names beginning with the letter of the alphabet on the folder. For instance, the general A 1 folder might contain correspondence from organizations and individuals in cities such as Adams, Akron, Alabama, and Amsterdam but not from Albany because that city has its own special city folders.

b. The special city folders accompany the special city guides (NY ALBANY A-M and NY ALBANY N-Z).

c. Individual folders for correspondents are arranged alphabetically by city and then by correspondents' names. The label caption for individual folders includes the name of the correspondent's state and city on the first line. The correspondent's name is on the second line.

5. Also in fourth position in the drawer are OUT guides. The OUT guides are one-third cut, third-position guides and mark the location of a borrowed folder.

Location Name Guide Plan. Probably the most frequently found location name guide plan arrangement is that based on state names as the first filing segment. Figure 9-4 shows part of a drawer of New York and North Carolina records stored by the location name guide plan. Refer to Figure 9-4 as you study the following arrangement description:

1. In first position in the drawer are primary guides for state names NEW YORK and NORTH CAROLINA. The guides are one-fifth cut, first-position guides.

2. In second position are city guides. AKRON is the first city guide after the NEW YORK state guide. Because the city guides stay in the drawer in their correct positions, they do not need the name of the state on them. The guides are one-fifth cut, second-position guides.

3. In third position are special lettered guides A-M and N-Z. These special guides show an alphabetic division of correspondents' names

in the city of ALBANY section. Special guides help locate more quickly the very active or high-volume records. The guides are one-fifth cut, third-position guides.

4. In fourth position in the drawer are all folders. *General* folders are shaded in the illustration to distinguish them from *individual* folders. The folders are one-third cut, third-position folders. Notice that every city guide in the arrangement is accompanied by a corresponding general city folder bearing the same caption as the guide.

How are special guides used?

a. The general state folder for NEW YORK is at the end of the NEW YORK section. File correspondence from New York in this general state folder when no general folder for that city is in the file. Arrange the records alphabetically in the general state folder by city name first, followed by the correspondent's name. If correspondents' names are identical, use the street name and house number to determine correct order. Store all records from the same correspondent in chronologic order with the most recent record in front.

b. A general city folder is used for every city guide in the file drawer. Place the general city folder at the end of the city subdivision. ALBANY has two general city folders, one for correspondents' names beginning with A–M and a second general city folder for correspondents' names beginning with N–Z. Store all records in general city folders alphabetically by correspondent's name. Arrange records from the same correspondent with the most recent record in front. When records begin to accumulate for one correspondent, say five or more, consider opening an individual folder for that correspondent.

c. Individual folders for correspondents are arranged alphabetically by name within their state and city sections. The folder label captions include the state and city locations as well as the correspondents' names. Because folders will be removed from the file, the comprehensive caption helps prevent misfiles when borrowed records are returned to storage. Arrange records in individual folders with the most recent record in front. Be sure to store all records in folders with the top of the document at the left of the folder.

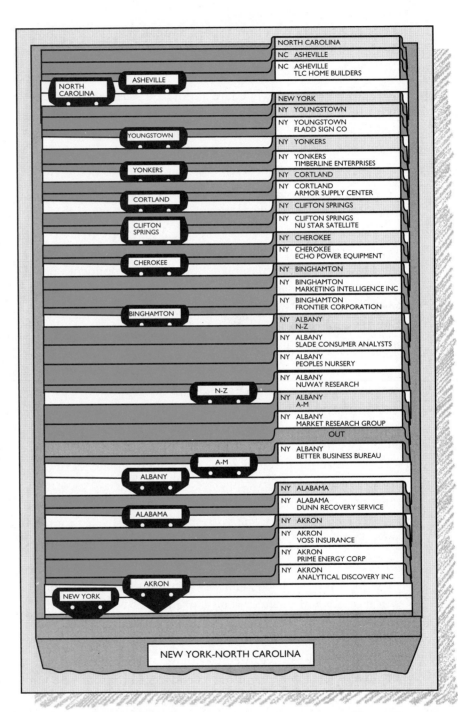

Figure 9-4   Encyclopedic Arrangement of Records, Location Name Guide Plan

5. Also in fourth position in the file drawer are one-third cut OUT guides, which show the location of borrowed records.

Geographic Records Storage Indexes

You are already familiar with indexes because you studied alphabetic and master indexes in Chapter 7, Subject Records Storage. Because geographic records are arranged first by location and then by company or individual names, the correspondent's location must be known before a record can be located. If the location of a correspondent is not known, then an alphabetic index is needed.

Alphabetic Index

The alphabetic index lists all correspondents in geographic storage and may be a printed list, a card file, or a computer list. However the index is maintained, the index must be easily updated and kept current. Names will be added and deleted, and names and addresses will change. Information in the index should include the correspondent's name and full address. Figure 9-5 is a sample of a computer alphabetic index for geographic records storage. The correspondents' names are in alphabetic order in the first column. The state, city, and street locations are shown in the remaining columns. All correspondents are listed in the index, including those whose records are stored in general city and state folders.

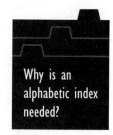

Why is an alphabetic index needed?

Master Index

If the alphabetic index is prepared on a computer, re-sorting and moving the columns produce a master index. A master index is a complete listing of all filing segments in the filing system. Figure 9-6 is a sample of a computer master index. The states were sorted first, then the city names, and finally the correspondents' names. The correspondents' names column was moved from the first column to the fourth column. The master index shows at a glance the geographic units covered in the filing system and is especially useful to new users of the file.

Geographic Records Storage and Retrieval Procedures

The supplies used in the geographic storage method are similar to those used in other storage methods. The supplies consist of guides, folders,

ALPHABETIC INDEX FOR GEOGRAPHIC RECORDS STORAGE			
CORRESPONDENT	STATE	CITY	STREET
ANALYTICAL DISCOVERY INC	NY	AKRON	4873 CENTER ST
ARMOR SUPPLY CENTER	NY	CORTLAND	1601 FOURTH ST
BETTER BUSINESS BUREAU	NY	ALBANY	150 ROWAN ST
COMPUTER MAGIC	NY	GENESEO	38 MAIN ST
DUNN RECOVERY SERVICE	NY	ALABAMA	60 JACKSON RD
ECHO POWER EQUIPMENT	NY	CHEROKEE	174 MILITARY RD
FLADD SIGN CO	NY	YOUNGSTOWN	30 CUMMINGS ST
FRONTIER CORPORATION	NY	BINGHAMTON	20 SHUMAN BLVD
KERRY COMPANY THE	NY	ALBANY	204 DELAWARE AVE
LUCKY STORES INC	NY	BINGHAMTON	145 ROSEMARY ST
MARKET RESEARCH GROUP	NY	ALBANY	4055 MOTOR AVE
MARKETING INTELLIGENCE INC	NY	BATH	451 DUNBAR RD
NU STAR SATELLITE	NY	CLIFTON SPRINGS	11 MAIN ST
NUWAY RESEARCH	NY	ALBANY	44 BROADWAY
PEOPLES NURSERY	NY	ALBANY	727 SECOND ST
PRIME ENERGY CORP	NY	AKRON	2470 MILES RD
SLADE CONSUMER ANALYSTS	NY	ALBANY	58 SYLVAN AVE
TIMBERLINE ENTERPRISES	NY	YONKERS	3034 WALL ST
TLC HOME BUILDERS	NC	ASHEVILLE	20 RIVER DR
VOSS INSURANCE	NY	AKRON	1422 EUCLID AVE

Figure 9-5   Alphabetic Index for Geographic Records Storage

OUT indicators, and an alphabetic index. You may want to review these filing supplies covered in Chapter 5 before continuing with the discussion of storage and retrieval procedures.

The same basic steps to store records in alphabetic, subject, and numeric methods (inspecting, indexing, coding, cross-referencing, sorting, and storing) are also followed in the geographic method. Small differences will be explained in the following paragraphs. Retrieval procedures (requisitioning, charging out, and following up) are also basically the same.

Inspecting and Indexing

Check to see that the record has been released for storage (inspect) and scan the letter for content to determine its proper place in storage

MASTER INDEX FOR GEOGRAPHIC RECORDS STORAGE

ST	CITY	STREET	CORRESPONDENT
NC	ASHEVILLE	20 RIVER DR	TLC HOME BUILDERS
NY	AKRON	4873 CENTER ST	ANALYTICAL DISCOVERY INC
NY	AKRON	2470 MILES RD	PRIME ENERGY CORP
NY	AKRON	1422 EUCLID AVE	VOSS INSURANCE
NY	ALABAMA	60 JACKSON RD	DUNN RECOVERY SERVICE
NY	ALBANY	150 ROWAN ST	BETTER BUSINESS BUREAU
NY	ALBANY	204 DELAWARE AVE	KERRY COMPANY THE
NY	ALBANY	4055 MOTOR AVE	MARKET RESEARCH GROUP
NY	ALBANY	44 BROADWAY	NUWAY RESEARCH
NY	ALBANY	727 SECOND ST	PEOPLES NURSERY
NY	ALBANY	58 SYLVAN AVE	SLADE CONSUMER ANALYSTS
NY	BATH	451 DUNBAR RD	MARKETING INTELLIGENCE INC
NY	BINGHAMTON	20 SHUMAN BLVD	FRONTIER CORPORATION
NY	BINGHAMTON	145 ROSEMARY ST	LUCKY STORES INC
NY	CHEROKEE	174 MILITARY RD	ECHO POWER EQUIPMENT
NY	CLIFTON SPRINGS	11 MAIN ST	NU STAR SATELLITE
NY	CORTLAND	1601 FOURTH ST	ARMOR SUPPLY CENTER
NY	GENESEO	38 MAIN ST	COMPUTER MAGIC
NY	YONKERS	3034 WALL ST	TIMBERLINE ENTERPRISES
NY	YOUNGSTOWN	30 CUMMINGS ST	FLADD SIGN CO

Figure 9-6   Master Index for Geographic Records Storage

(index). In Figure 9-7, the handwritten letters JK indicate that the letter is released for storage.

Coding

Code the document for geographic storage by marking the correspondent's *location* (address) first. Code by circling the filing segment (see Figure 9-7 Raleigh, NC). Write numbers above or below the filing segment to show the order for alphabetizing the indexing units. Then code the name of the correspondent by underlining the name, placing diagonals between the units, and numbering the succeeding units. Figure 9-7 shows a letter coded for the geographic storage method.

What is the first indexing unit?

Consult the alphabetic index after the coding is done to see whether the correspondent is currently in the system. If not, add the new correspondent's name and address to the index.

Cross-Referencing

What names require cross-references?

Cross-referencing is as necessary in the geographic storage method as it is in the alphabetic storage method. In Chapters 2 and 3, personal and business names that may require cross-references are listed. In this chapter, additional cross-references may be needed for (1) names of organizations having more than one address and (2) organizations located at one address and doing business under other names at other locations.

In the geographic storage method, insert cross-references into both the alphabetic index and the storage containers. In the alphabetic index, prepare an entry for every name by which a correspondent may be known or by which records may be requested. For the letter shown in Figure 9-7, a cross-reference shows a branch office located in another city—two locations where a filer might look for the Stratford Group, Inc., record.

In the storage containers, three types of cross-references may be used: (1) cross-reference sheets that are stored in folders to refer the filer to specific records, (2) cross-reference guides that are placed in storage as permanent cross-references, and (3) SEE ALSO cross-references on sheets or on folder tabs. Each of these cross-references is explained next.

A *cross-reference sheet* directs the filer to a specific record stored in a different location other than where the filer is searching. The cross-reference sheet in Figure 9-8 is made for the branch office indicated on the letter shown in Figure 9-7. The original letter is stored in the N section of geographic storage (NORTH CAROLINA), but the cross-reference sheet is stored in the C section (CALIFORNIA).

A *cross-reference guide* is a permanent marker in storage indicating that all records pertaining to that company name are stored elsewhere. For example, the cross-reference guide in Figure 9-9 shows that all records for Lockwood, Inc., are stored under the home office location Ann Arbor, MI, not the branch office location St. Clair Shores, MI. The words *Ann Arbor* must be written on each record when it is coded. The cross-reference guide is stored according to the location on the top line of its caption in alphabetic order with other geographically labeled guides and folders.

SEE ALSO cross-references are used to direct the filer to sources of related information. If a company has two addresses and records are stored under both addresses, two SEE ALSO cross-references would be used. For example, if Windsor Publishing Co., Inc., conducts business in Houston, TX, and also in Wichita Falls, TX, the references would indicate that information for this company can be found in two storage locations. If these SEE ALSO cross-references are sheets of paper, they are always kept as the first items in their respective folders so that they will not be overlooked (see Figure 9-10). Instead of being written on separate cross-reference sheets, this SEE ALSO information may be keyed on the tabs of the two folders for the Windsor Publishing Co., Inc. (see Figure 9-11).

How are SEE ALSO references prepared?

Sorting

Sort records alphabetically by location. Sort first by the largest geographic unit such as state name; then sort by the first subdivision such as city; finally, sort by the names of the correspondents, in alphabetic order.

Storing

Individual correspondents' folders, special city folders, alphabetic subdivisions of cities with their corresponding general folders, general folders for alphabetic grouping of cities, and general state or regional folders may be part of a geographic records storage arrangement. Therefore, placing a record in the wrong folder is easy to do. Because of the complexity of a geographic arrangement, be extremely careful when storing.

Lettered Guide Plan. Assuming that the arrangement is by state and city, look for the primary state guide. Then use the lettered guides to locate the alphabetic state section within which the city name falls. After finding that section, look for an individual correspondent's folder. If you find one, store the record in that folder in chronologic order with the most recent record on top.

If an individual folder for the correspondent is *not* in the file, look for a general city folder. If a general city folder is in the file, store the record according to the correspondent's name in the same manner as in an alphabetic arrangement. If a general city folder is *not* in the file, store the record in the general alphabetic folder within which the city name falls. Again, arrange the city names according to the rules for alphabetic indexing.

Within a city, arrange the names of correspondents alphabetically; group the records of one correspondent with the most recent date on top. If identically named correspondents reside in one city, follow the rules for filing identical names (see Chapters 2 and 3 for review).

Stratford/Group,/Inc.
Educational Consultants

49 Kimberly Lane, Raleigh, NC 76000-4127
PHONE (919) 555-2843 FAX (919) 555-3123

May 4, 19--

MAY 07, 19-- 9:05 AM

Dr. Michael L. Kelley
Alfred State College
Alfred, NY 14802-3643

Dear Dr. Kelley

Your request for 50 brochures explaining in detail the programmed learning materials we have available for use in summer workshop programs has been referred to our Burbank, California, Office.

Interest in this exciting and novel material has been extremely high, and we are pleased that professors are finding it so worthwhile. Because of the extraordinary number of requests for this brochure, it is temporarily out of stock. We expect a new supply within the next two weeks, however, and will send you 50 copies as soon as we receive them.

Thanks for letting us provide you with helpful materials for your workshop.

Sincerely

Johandra Linfoot

Johandra Linfoot
Educational Consultant

JK

dw

Branch Office: 2964 Broadway, Burbank,/CA 91500-1217 X

Figure 9-7 Letter Coded for Geographic Storage Method

CROSS-REFERENCE SHEET

Name or Subject
CA/Burbank
Stratford/Group,/Inc
2964 Broadway

Date of Record
May 4, 19--

Regarding
Programmed learning materials for summer workshop

SEE

Name or Subject
NC Raleigh
Stratford Group, Inc
49 Kimberly Lane

Date Filed *5/7/19--* **By** *JK*

Figure 9-8 Cross-Reference Sheet for Geographic Storage Method

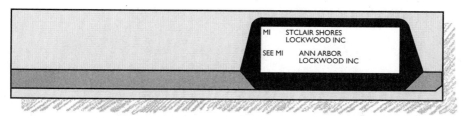

Figure 9-9   **Cross-Reference Guide for Geographic Storage Method**

When enough correspondence has accumulated to warrant making a separate folder for a specific city, a specific geographic section, or an individual correspondent, remove the records from the general folder and prepare a new folder with the geographic location on its tab as the first item of information. Then prepare a similarly labeled guide, if one is needed, for the folder. Finally, place the folder and guide in their alphabetic positions in storage.

Although requirements for preparing a separate folder for a specific geographic location vary, a good rule of thumb is this: When five or more records that pertain to one specific geographic location (such as a state, city, or a region) accumulate, prepare a separate folder for that location.

Location Name Guide Plan.   Again, assuming that the arrangement is by state and city, find the primary state guide and look for the correct city name on a secondary guide. If a city guide is present, search for an individual correspondent's folder. If one exists, store the record in the folder according to date.

If an individual folder is *not* in the file, store the record in the correct general city folder according to the geographic location of the correspondent and then by name in alphabetic order with the other records within the folder. If more than one record is stored for a correspondent, arrange the records chronologically with the most recent date on top.

If a general city folder is *not* in the file, place the record in the general state folder, first according to the alphabetic order of the city name and then by correspondent's name and street address (if necessary), according to the rules for alphabetic indexing.

Retrieving

Retrieving a record from the geographic arrangement involves these five steps:

CROSS-REFERENCE SHEET

Name or Subject
TX Houston
Windsor Publishing Co., Inc.
1313 North Sixth Street

Date of Record

SEE ALSO

Regarding

Name or Subject
TX Wichita Falls
Windsor Publishing Co., Inc.
2264 Evanston Avenue

Date Filed   11/4/19—   By   JK

CROSS-REFERENCE SHEET

Name or Subject
TX Wichita Falls
Windsor Publishing Co., Inc.
2264 Evanston Avenue

Date of Record

Regarding

SEE ALSO

Name or Subject
TX Houston
Windsor Publishing Co., Inc.
1313 North Sixth Street

Date Filed   11/4/19—   By   JK

Figure 9-10   Cross-Reference Sheets for SEE ALSO References

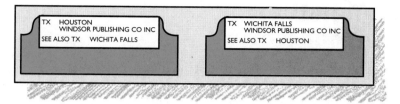

Figure 9-11   **SEE ALSO References on Folder Tabs**

1. Asking for the record (requisition).

2. Checking the alphabetic index to determine the location of the record.

3. Removing the record from the storage container.

4. Charging out the record by some means.

5. Following up to see that the record is returned to storage within a specified time.

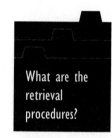

What are the retrieval procedures?

Requisition.   A requester may ask for a record from a geographic arrangement by location or by correspondent's name. If the request is made by location, finding the record should be simple. If the request is made by name, however, refer to the alphabetic index to locate the address by which the record was originally stored (unless your memory is supercharged and can supply this information without reference to the index!).

Charge-Out.   After you have located and retrieved the record, charge it out in the same manner that you charge out records from any other storage method. Be sure to insert an OUT indicator where you remove the record.

Follow-Up.   The follow-up procedures used to secure the return of borrowed records are the same for the geographic storage method as those used with any other storage method. Use a tickler file or another reminder system to be sure that records are returned to storage at designated times and to remind yourself of records that need to be brought to someone's attention in the future.

Current Trends in Records Management

A dynamic communications wonder to watch closely in the years ahead is the realization of a true international *information superhighway*—all computers interconnected globally. Paving the way for this phenomenon is the *Internet*—a computerized communications medium that has made a great impact on the transmittal of information *geographically*.

The Internet, also known as the *Net*, is the most open computer network in the world and is available to anyone who has Net access. Students use the Internet to pursue studies, to meet new friends, and to exchange letters and stories with students around the United States and in foreign countries. Anticipate a growth in records and information storage and retrieval responsibilities as education, government, business, and individuals with home PCs use the Internet as a fast and reliable means of moving information. Currently, an estimated 20 million users are on the Internet, with a monthly increase of 130,000 new users. Each month over 2,000 companies expand their operations on the Internet.[1]

With an estimated 100 million people connected to the Internet by 1998, businesses are taking very seriously a vehicle capable of reaching millions of people and transforming the world—or parts of it anyhow—into one large "shopping mall." The World Wide Web (WWW, or WEB) multimedia environment is capable of projecting text, color photos, interactive fill-in forms, and audio and video clips and, therefore, serves well as an advertising and marketing medium.

Companies are just learning how to take advantage of the evolving Internet opportunities to advertise and market their products and services and to reach potential customers around the world. Some businesses have already opened WEB "storefronts" or WEB sites. These commercial sites are set up as advertising places where companies provide information about their products. Figure 9-12 represents a site that ARMA International created to identify the organization and its mission.

The most important factor in sales is location. Therefore, businesses at the least will have to establish a positive, online presence to be competitive. They cannot ignore Internet advertising and marketing poten-

How will the Internet affect records management?

---

[1]Michael Dieckmann, "Doing Business on the World-Wide Web," *Managing Office Technology*, June 1995, pp. 41-44.

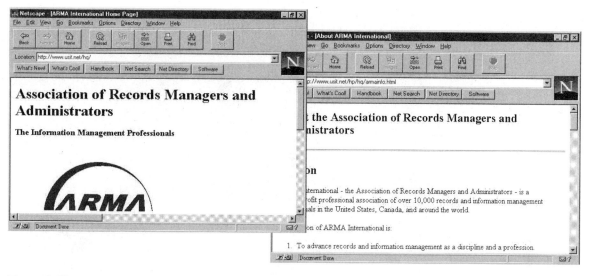

Figure 9-12   ARMA International World Wide Web Site

tial as millions more become Internet users over the next few years. Especially to small businesses, the Internet offers a more equal opportunity to compete with large businesses for new customers. As businesses learn to use the Internet effectively to reach new locations to market their goods and services worldwide, they will likely store and evaluate records by these new locations as well.

How will the Internet affect geographic records storage?

Summary

This chapter began with the reason businesses store records by location; namely, a geographic expansion of their marketable goods and services. This geographic dispersion of business activities resulted from increased production, better transportation, new trade agreements, and improved communications.

The advantages of examining records by various locations when necessary outweigh the disadvantages of extra supplies and procedures required for the geographic records storage method.

Two arrangements of records stored by geographic location are the dictionary and the encyclopedic arrangements. The arrangement used depends on whether subdivisions of the geographic units are necessary. Two guide plans include the lettered guide plan and the location name guide plan. Either method can be used in geographic file arrangements, but the storage of a small number of diverse names or the storage of a large number of similar names will likely determine the guide plan.

Indexes are prepared as needed. When correspondence is stored by the geographic method, an alphabetic index is needed. Except for indexing and coding, the storage and retrieval procedures are similar to those used for other storage methods. Indexing and coding require looking first at the location of the document and then the name, the document subject, or project title being stored.

The Internet, as a worldwide network of computer networks, is gaining global recognition for its domestic and global transmission of information. A greater need for geographic records storage will result as more organizations explore the Internet's potential for expanding their domestic and global markets and succeed in a wider distribution of their products and services.

Important Terms

dictionary arrangement
encyclopedic arrangement
geographic records storage method

lettered guide plan
location name guide plan

Review and Discussion

1. How has the developing global economy created a greater need for geographic records storage? (Obj. 1)

2. Name three kinds of businesses that are likely to use the geographic records storage method. (Obj. 2)

3. What are the advantages and disadvantages of the geographic records storage method? (Obj. 3)

4. Explain how the dictionary and encyclopedic arrangements of geographic records differ. (Obj. 4)

5. Explain the difference between the lettered guide plan and the location name guide plan. (Obj. 5)

6. Describe the arrangement of guides and folders in an encyclopedic arrangement of a geographic file using the lettered guide plan. The geographic units covered in the arrangement are state names and city names. (Obj. 6)

7. In your description of guides and folders in Question 6, did you include general STATE folders? Explain why you did or did not include them. (Obj. 6)

8. Explain how an alphabetic index is used in geographic records storage. (Obj. 7)

9. Explain how indexing and coding for the geographic records storage method are different from indexing and coding for the alphabetic records storage method. (Obj. 8)

10. List three types of cross-references used in the geographic records storage method and include where they are placed or stored in the filing system. (Obj. 9)

11. Explain what possible effect the Internet is likely to have on geographic records storage in the future. (Obj. 10)

Applications (APP)

APP 9-1. Selecting the Most Efficient Geographic Arrangement (Objs. 4–6)

Critical Thinking

Refer to the guide plans and file arrangements in Figures 9-1 through 9-4 as you complete this application. Recommend a geographic arrangement (dictionary or encyclopedic) and a guide plan (lettered or name) for each of the following situations. Explain the reason for your choice. Prepare a sketch of your recommended arrangement; remember that geographic files are arranged from the largest geographic units to the smallest. Show the placement of guides and folders used in the arrangement.

1. The home office of a large food processing/packing plant is located in Iowa. However, the company stores correspondence and records to and from suppliers, refineries, wholesalers, and branch offices in most cities in all 50 states.

2. A newspaper publisher in a large city maintains a file of *all* city streets. The street name file identifies paper carriers who distribute to those locations.

3. A garment manufacturer maintains records by its operations in ten cities. City locations include the following:

United States	Canada
Los Angeles, CA	Montreal, Quebec
Philadelphia, PA	Calgary, Alberta
Detroit, MI	London, Ontario

Mexico	Central America
Cuernavaca, Morelos	Managua, Nicaragua
Zamora, Michoacan	León, Nicaragua

APP 9-2. *Geographic Filing Procedures (Objs. 8–9)*

Key the names of the following correspondents in indexing order on your template disk. Save the list to filename CH9.AP2. Key any necessary cross-references. Indicate any cross-references or SEE ALSO references by keying an X beside the record number. Sort the names for geographic records storage. Assume the main filing segments are state, city, and correspondent's name or organization, in that order. If a computer is not available, prepare 5" by 3" cards for each correspondent; then index, code, and sort the cards for geographic records storage.

1. Indian River Community College
   3209 Virginia Ave.
   Fort Pierce, FL 33482-3209

2. Computer Land, Inc.
   Shepherd Rd.
   Springfield, IL 62708-0101

3. John Powers Electronics
   24 Delaware Ave.
   Rochester, NY 14623-2944

4. Portland Cement Co.
   12000 Lakeville Rd.
   Portland, OR 97219-4233

5. Wilkes Tree Farm
   400 Stanton Christiana Rd.
   Newark, DE 19713-0401

6. Ms. Beverly C. Monroe
   1000 Gordon Rd.
   Rochester, NY 14623-1089

7. Electric City, Inc.
   3201 Southwest Traffic Way
   Kansas City, MO 64111-3201

8. Abba D Plumbing
   901 S. National Ave.
   Springfield, MO 65804-0910

9. Penn Valley Community College
   3201 Southwest Traffic Way
   Kansas City, MO 64111-3201

10. Cerre Ceramic Studios
    7250 State Ave.
    Kansas City, KS 66112-7255

11. Toby Leese Tack Shop
    175 University Ave.
    Newark, NJ 07102-1175

12. John Powers Electronics
    10 State St.
    Rochester, NY 14623-2944

13. City Office Supplies
    4281 Drake St.
    Rochester, MI 66112-0698

14. Armstrong State College
    11935 Abercorn St.
    Savannah, GA 31419-1092

15. Pioneer Center Furniture
    560 Westport Rd.
    Kansas City, MO 64111-0568

16. Amy's Sports Center
    874 Dillingham Blvd.
    Honolulu, HI 96817-8743

17. Genesis Cinema
    1325 Lynch St.
    Jackson, MS 39203-1325

18. Computer Magic
    84 Center St.
    Springfield, MA 01100-2028

19. Computer Magic
    24 Fourth Ave.
    New York, NY 10018-4826

20. The Computer Store
    2847 14th St.
    New York, NY 10018-2032

Note: *Records for Nos. 3 and 12 and 18 and 19 are in separate file locations. A SEE ALSO reference is the only entry required because the records for these two businesses are in two file locations.*

Applying the Rules

Job 12, Geographic Filing

Part 4

Records Management Technology

10 *Automated Records Systems*
11 *Image Records*

Part 4 provides comprehensive coverage of current computer technology as applied in records management and image records systems. Computer hardware and software are presented from a systems approach. Current technology is described in areas such as networks, optical disk storage, computer output to laser disk (COLD), and scanners. Image systems discussions include both microforms and electronic records, as well as hybrid imaging systems integrating microfilm-based images with electronic image processing technologies.

Chapter 10
Automated Records Systems

Learning Objectives

1. Explain how computer technology promotes a systems approach to records management.
2. Describe the components of the five phases of a computer system: input, processing, output, control, and feedback.
3. Compare a stand-alone automated records system with a local area network and a wide area network.
4. Explain why standard records procedures are essential to the management and protection of electronic records.

Technology and Records Systems

Records technology refers to three elements essential to the operation of records systems: (1) machines (hardware), (2) procedures (people and processes), and (3) programs (software). Advances in computer hardware and software technologies are transforming the way organizations receive and process information. In Chapter 1, a *records system* is defined as a group of interrelated resources acting together according to a plan to accomplish the goals of the records management program. Computer hardware and software are resources that enable rapid data input, processing, information output, records storage, and information retrieval. Thus, technological advances in computers promote effective and efficient functioning of records systems. In spite of the improvements technology brings to records systems, however, the importance of people and processes cannot be overlooked. The best available technology can only operate effectively if trained personnel operate the system and if they follow appropriate policies and procedures.

Why is the use of computers increasing?

Systems Concept

How often the word *system* is used in our ordinary conversations! People frequently talk about educational systems, political systems, environmental systems, road systems, and other systems that relate to their lives. In records management, the primary concerns are *records*

258

systems that are a component of *information systems*. To understand records systems and the role that computer technology plays, you must first understand the systems concept and how subsystems, or parts of systems, work together to accomplish a task.

Systems and Subsystems.   Computers have given records managers and other information specialists a broader—and clearer—view of organizations and how their parts work together. The ability of computer technology to create, process, store, retrieve, and distribute information to all divisions or departments in a firm helps managers and workers in all departments to relate to the total organization and to see the relationships among departments. The phrase "seeing the whole picture" stems from the broad, company-wide view of a firm's operations made possible by use of the computer. Using a company-wide perspective to look at the interrelated parts when solving organizational problems is called a **systems approach**. A broad view of a *system* and of the relationships of its parts or *subsystems* provides a useful tool for the problem solver and, in particular, for the records manager.

What is meant by the term *systems approach?*

A **system** is made up of related components that interact to accomplish a task. Within a system, various groupings of interrelated components that accomplish one phase of a task are referred to as a **subsystem**. Related elements or **system components** are the resources necessary to accomplish the system task and include people, space, equipment, forms, related records, work procedures, and data. For example, *records storage* is a *subsystem* of a *records management system*, as described in Chapter 1. Each lower level of a system is called a *subsystem*. Other records management subsystems include records creation, distribution, usage, and disposition. You will recognize these subsystems as the phases of a record life cycle. However, regardless of their nature, *all systems have phases or subsystems necessary to complete the system task.*

Systems Environment.   A system and its subsystems operate within a certain setting or environment. A **systems environment** consists of circumstances, objects, or conditions surrounding a system. The *environment* has many interrelated subsystems that influence the system either directly or indirectly—i.e., economic, political, legal, or educational subsystems. These influences also affect records systems. For example, legal requirements affect the records retention schedule, and economic conditions permit or restrict the purchase of new technology. Each

What is a systems environment?

influence may also be considered a system with related components to accomplish a task.

Systems achieve tasks through a set of sequential or simultaneous phases that include *input*, *process*, *output*, *control*, and *feedback*. Operation begins with resources entered into a system (**input**). The operation of a system to change its input is the **process**, which produces the desired product or service (**output**). The standards for processing that a system uses to improve output is system **control**. Communication based on evaluation of output against quality and quantity standards is **feedback**. Figure 10-1 displays a system and its related components operating within a systems environment.

Let's see how these phases of a system work with a simple example— using a computer to create a new record, an annual budget.

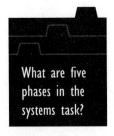

What are five phases in the systems task?

1. The *output* or task is a document that accurately reflects projected income and expenses and that can be used to monitor expenditures throughout the year. The document may be printed and become a hardcopy in the files, or it may be electronically stored to a data disk for computer retrieval as needed. (This phase is listed first, although it represents the final product. Understanding the task before beginning improves the likelihood that it will be accomplished and will meet expected standards.)

2. The *input* necessary to produce the output requires:

   a. A computer with word processing, spreadsheet, or database software and a printer.

   b. Data entered in the computer for income sources with estimated amounts and expense categories with estimated expenditures.

   c. The human knowledge, skill, time, and labor required to gather the data, to enter it into the computer, and to use software functions for totaling income items and projected expenses.

3. The *process(es)* to produce the desired output using the input resources listed in Step 2 above include:

   a. Selecting the necessary data from previous years' records and projecting income and expenses for next year's activities.

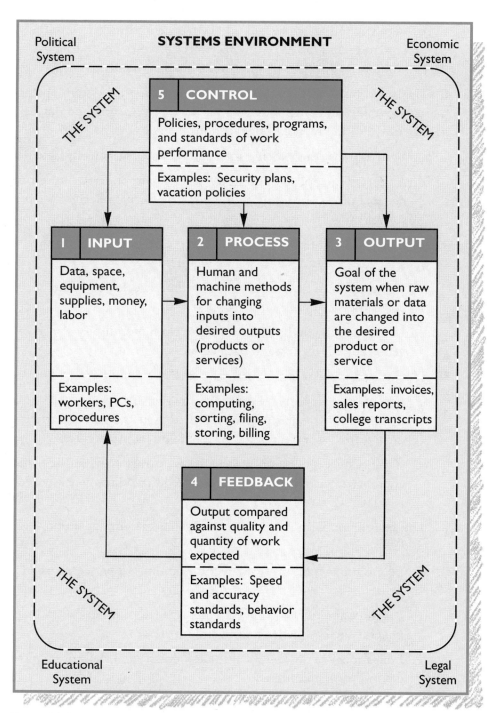

Figure 10-1   A Systems Environment and Operational Phases of a System

b. Performing the actual steps of keying the information into the computer and manipulating the software functions to total columns and to produce the annual budget report.

4. The *control* phase refers to actions needed to keep the system operating accurately and efficiently and may take place before and during processing of the record. These actions include:

a. Verifying that the expense total and income total are equal.

b. Adjusting the dollar amounts to either round or carry out to two decimal places according to the numeric format selected in the software.

c. Checking that text and data are entered according to software selection of settings and format requirements.

d. Using software features such as a spelling checker to verify correctness of information.

e. Looking at the budget report on the computer display screen to verify correct format and balance of income and expenses.

5. The *feedback* phase results in activities such as the following:

a. If the budget report is accepted as a reasonable estimate of income and expenditures, the report is used as a guide for the next year's expenditures and is stored with active records.

b. If the budget report is not accepted as correct or reasonable, the appropriate person(s) would be notified that adjustments should be made.

6. The *environment* within which the budgeting system operates includes:

a. Economic conditions that affect the amount of projected expenses.

b. Legal requirements that affect employer rates for personnel benefits such as social security and medicare.

c. Educational backgrounds, attitudes, morale, and skills of employees in the organization.

Remember that all phases of a system are interdependent—they must work together; the work of each one affects the work of others. Also, keep in mind that each phase in a system (input, process, output, control, and feedback) uses all the resources at hand to achieve a system task. Consequently, solving problems that arise in records management requires consideration of all these phases and how well they work together to achieve the final result.

The entire records management program may be considered a *records management system*. Records managers make repeated use of systems concepts when dealing with storage and retrieval or with any of the subsystems in the records management system. An understanding of systems concepts can help identify and solve records management system problems.

What is meant by *interdependence?*

Automated Records Systems

The word *automated* comes from **automation**, which means the self-operation, regulation, or control of a process, machine, equipment, or system. A records system in which the computer or computer-related equipment controls all or most of the records functions is an **automated records system.**

What is an automated records system?

Computer Systems

A computer receives, stores, and processes data. After they are processed into meaningful form, these data become information. Although a computer rapidly performs complex functions on data input, the basis of operation is a digital system involving only two states for electrical charges: on or off. Communication signals such as telephone messages or video pictures must be represented in this digital on-off manner before the computer can process them. Translating communication signals into a two-state form for computer input is referred to as **digitizing**.

The storage capacity and sophistication of processing varies somewhat among three major types of computers: mainframe, minicomputer, and microcomputer. A **mainframe computer** is a fast, large-capacity machine that organizations use to handle millions of transactions and data items. A **minicomputer** is a scaled-down version of the mainframe, has less data storage capacity, and operates at a slower speed. A **microcomputer** is a desktop or notebook (portable) computer that is widely used in offices, schools, and homes. The current capacity and speed of microcomputers competes successfully with minicomputers for most business functions.

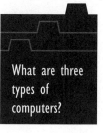

What are three types of computers?

What is digitizing?

What is hardware and software?

A computer and other equipment used with it are referred to as **hardware**. Hardware connected to a computer processing unit is referred to as a **peripheral device,** which commonly includes a keyboard, mouse, monitor, printer, and external modem. **Software** is a package of programmed instructions that direct a computer in machine language to perform specific tasks or procedures in an exact sequence. A computer system contains the required hardware and software to perform a task.

Similar to all systems, a computer system uses inputs, processes, outputs, controls, and feedback to perform a task. The next section describes computer technology that assists with creation, storage, and retrieval of records.

Data Input

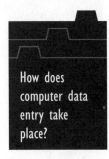

How does computer data entry take place?

Data may be defined as factual or statistical items. The computer has the capacity to sort, compute, and categorize data. Data that have been processed to communicate knowledge in meaningful ways for decision making are referred to as **information**. A software program determines the processing steps that a computer completes.

Computer data entry takes place through a variety of methods and devices. Entering data into a computer is input. Most data entry takes place through a computer keyboard; however, other input devices such as scanners, light pens, and modems are also used.

A **scanner** is a device that converts an image (text, graphic, or photograph) to electronic form for processing and storage. A scanner passes light over a document or object and converts it to dark and light dots that become digital code. Scanners may be hand–held devices that are passed over the item to be entered or a table model similar to a copying machine that scans the page from a flat surface. Figures 10–2a and 10–2b show these two types of scanners.

Another type of scanned input uses bar codes for computer data entry. A **bar code** is a coding system consisting of vertical lines or bars that, when read by an optical scanner, can be converted to machine-readable language. In records management, bar codes are used for record identification to track and maintain inventory control of records. An example of bar code usage is for prices or inventory numbers on products such as those in a supermarket. The Universal Product Code (UPC) used for bar coding has from 13 to 21 bars. Each bar can be *on* (present)

Typist Plus Graphics, Caere Corporation

Figure 10-2a   **Hand-Held Scanner**

Marstek, Inc.

Figure 10-2b   **Tabletop Scanner**

What is a bar code?

or *off* (absent). A **bar code reader** is a photoelectric scanner that translates bar code symbols into digital forms so that a computer can read them.

In records systems, scanning devices that translate characters into digital form for computer input include the following:

1. Magnetic-ink character recognition (MICR) uses magnetized ink to print characters on records such as the preprinted account numbers on checks. When MICR equipment such as a bank's check reader/sorter machine passes over the MICR characters, it produces a digitized signal that can be used as computer input.

2. Optical character recognition (OCR) uses a device such as a wand to read special preprinted characters and to convert them to digital form for computer data entry. A department store clerk uses OCR scanning to enter prices from products.

3. Intelligent character recognition (ICR) software converts handprinted characters to digitized data. The use of a scanner with ICR software enters handprinted records such as order forms or timesheets into computer storage for rapid retrieval.

Software packages now on the market not only can scan bar codes, magnetic-ink characters, pencil marks, preprinted characters, or handprinted characters, but they also can extract the data from the text and place it into a database. An example of current records software that uses scanners or fax machines to enter data directly from forms into a database or spreadsheet is Tele*form*® for Windows. Tele*form* software interprets handprinted upper- and lowercase characters, preprinted or keyed machine print, and checked or shaded bubbles or squares. The information that the scanner and software capture is stored in a data format as a database requires.

Two other images that can be scanned and saved to a database are signatures and SecureRead® fields. A **SecureRead field** is a shaded box that holds confidential information on a form. An example of data that might be placed in a SecureRead field could be a patient diagnosis on a medical record. The business form from which data are derived is also sorted and indexed or automatically deleted. Figure 10-3 illustrates coding system formats for handprinted data for ICR, bar code, and SecureRead.

Modems and fax machines provide other means of computer data input. A **modem** is an electronic device that transfers data from one

Figure 10-3   Coded Data that Can Be Read and Stored in a Database by a Scanner and Forms Processing Software

computer to another computer using telephone lines. The modem can be an electronic board placed inside the microprocessor (internal modem) as shown in Figure 10-4a or an external modem placed on the desk and connected to the microprocessor or central processing unit (see Figure 10-4b). Communication software used with modems translates the digital computer code from the sending computer into electronic signals used for telephone line transmission and then back to digital code for the receiving computer. Wireless cellular modems such as the one shown in Figure 10-4c give a traveling executive two-way access to a home-based computer. Wherever a person conducts business, a cellular modem handles business transactions such as entering purchase orders, reviewing customer records, or reading electronic mail.

Which type of modem can be used anywhere?

Another means of sending and receiving written messages over telephone lines and satellite relays is the facsimile machine, more commonly referred to as "fax." The **facsimile (fax) machine** is a device that transmits an exact reproduction of an image to another location electronically. A table-model fax machine scans an image and converts it to digital code, enabling transmission to another fax machine or to a computer with a fax modem and fax software. A fax modem and fax software installed as part of the computer system simulate a fax machine's input and output.

Courtesy of IBM Corporation

Figure 10-4a   Internal Modem

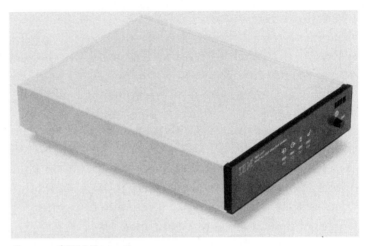

Courtesy of IBM Corporation

Figure 10-4b   **External Modem**

Courtesy of IBM Corporation

Figure 10-4c   **Cellular Wireless Modem**

Other computer input devices include the mouse or trackball, the light pen, touch screen, and pen–controlled, hand-held computers. A **mouse** or a **trackball** is a device used to move the cursor around on a display screen or to point and select specific operations that a computer is to perform. A mouse or trackball can also be used to create or edit graphic records. The **light pen**, another input device, is used for writing or sketching on a display screen. As the pen reacts to the light from the screen, the computer digitizes (converts to a numeric code) the image written or sketched for processing, storing, and printing. A **touch screen**, a sensitized computer display screen that receives input from the touch of a finger, is typically menu-driven and easy to use. A common example is an automatic teller machine that makes cash deposit or withdrawal records. A **personal digital assistant (PDA)**, a hand-held computer controlled by a pen similar to a stylus, processes handwritten commands and messages. Figure 10-5 shows a portable computer designed so the display screen folds down to convert to a pen computer. You can write or draw on the screen and store the pen input "as is" for signatures or convert the handwriting to digitized data.

What is a PDA?

Processing of Data

Following data input, the computer microprocessor processes the data or stores it for later retrieval and processing. Computer processing takes many forms. The processing phase performs numeric calculations, locates specific data items, and displays data in meaningful reports and formats. The microprocessor is sometimes called the **central processing unit (CPU)**. The processing of data requires a computer software program and memory or storage space.

Software Programs. Software programs determine the process performed on data input. Database software is designed to enable input of data into separate fields that allow data reorganization, summarization, and manipulation into various formats and reports. Database records management software may be off-the-shelf commercial software such as Access, dBase®, Paradox®, or Rbase®, or customized software developed by a programmer for a specific business. Word processing and desktop publishing software are used to create many types of records. Examples of word processing packages include WordPerfect, Microsoft Word, Ami Pro®, and MacWrite®. Numeric displays and calculations can be performed efficiently with spreadsheet software. Spreadsheet software, functioning similarly to a columnar worksheet, can be used to produce financial reports, sales projections, budgets, and accounting-related functions. Examples of spreadsheet software useful for records creation are Excel, Lotus 1-2-3®, and Quattro Pro®. Database, spreadsheet, and word processing software may be used for records creation and processing of records.

What are three major types of application software?

Courtesy of Momenta Computers

Figure 10-5   A Notebook Computer that Converts to a Pen
Computer for Writing or Drawing

Primary Computer Memory.   Processing data requires computer memory to hold the data during processing. The CPU can hold only a small amount of data at one time. Temporary internal computer storage that holds data being processed by a computer is called **primary memory** or **working memory**. Computers have two types of primary memory: read only memory and random access memory.

Read only memory (ROM) is a permanent storage location for instructions a computer needs each time it is turned on. These instructions remain intact when a computer is turned off. When a computer is turned on, the ROM instructions control initial display screen messages and a computer's interaction with the keyboard and other peripherals.

Random access memory (RAM) is a computer's working memory that serves as a temporary storage location for the software and data used at any one time during processing. A computer must have enough RAM to hold the software program and all data entered for one file. Increasingly complex software programs capable of more and more special functions have increased drastically the amount of RAM required for processing records. Because RAM is temporary storage, all data in RAM are eliminated when the power to a computer is interrupted. Primary memory is short-term storage. The amount of primary memory determines the total size of a program and data file that can be worked on at any given time.

What are two kinds of primary memory?

The temporary storage nature of RAM requires additional storage in a more permanent form to maintain information and data. Permanent storage of data takes place by transferring or moving (saving) the data or records from the processing units to disks or tape. The form of data storage must allow retrieval upon demand. A computer's disk drives perform this storage and retrieval function. The next section describes types of secondary computer storage systems.

Secondary Data Storage. **Secondary data storage** is an electronic medium (such as a floppy disk or hard disk) that a computer uses as a more permanent storage location for records transferred (saved) from its temporary working memory. A computer can locate and read information recorded on secondary storage media for further processing, or it can output this information as a printed copy. Other types of secondary storage media include optical disks, flash-memory cards, and magnetic tape. Secondary data storage serves as a computer input and output device. A computer reads information or documents from secondary storage devices (input) or stores information on disks, tapes, or memory cards (output). Computer storage devices are to electronic records as file cabinets are to paper records. Records managers must be knowledgeable of computer secondary storage devices to determine ways to extend electronic records storage and to select the most appropriate and efficient type of records storage.

Floppy Disks. A **floppy disk** is a piece of round plastic that stores data and records by electromagnetic charges. Most microcomputer users store some data on floppy disks in 3.5-inch or 5.25-inch sizes. Storage capacity of floppy disks ranges from 360 kilobytes (KB) (360,000 characters) to 2 megabytes (MB) (2,000,000 characters). The 5.25-inch floppy disk is rapidly fading from office use because the 3.5-inch disk has a greater storage capacity and is more durable. A disk drive on a computer reads the data from a floppy disk and temporarily brings it into the primary memory where data can be used or changed. Therefore, a floppy disk can be an input device as well as a storage device. When a computer disk drive saves data onto a disk, the data are stored in permanent form. Data read into the computer are not removed from the disk; the disk drive simply copies the data into the working memory. Data stays on a floppy disk until execution of a specific computer command deletes or replaces the file.

Which disk holds the most data—5.25- or 3.5-inch?

Hard Disks.   Manufacturers install at least one floppy disk drive and one hard disk drive on microcomputers. A **hard disk** consists of a thin, rigid metal platter covered with a substance that holds data in the form of magnetized spots. Internal hard disks are sealed within an enclosed unit inside the computer case that holds the microprocessor. An **external hard drive** sits on the desk beside the microprocessor and connects to it. Hard disk capacities for microcomputers generally range from 500MB (500 million characters) to 1 or 2 gigabytes (GB) (2 billion characters).

What is a hard disk?

Hard-Disk Cartridges.   An external hard drive or hard-disk cartridge drive may be added to a computer to increase the hard disk storage capacity. A **hard-disk cartridge** is a hard plastic case enclosing one or two storage platters that have read/write heads. The cartridge is inserted into an external cartridge disk drive connected to the microprocessor. The cartridge can be removed and carried in a briefcase. Hard-disk cartridges hold up to 1.2 gigabytes and may be used for backing up records to protect against data loss.

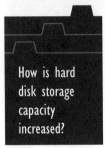

How is hard disk storage capacity increased?

Fixed-Disk Drives.   A **fixed-disk drive** is a high-speed, high-capacity disk drive housed in a cabinet and used with a mainframe or a minicomputer. As many as 20 to 100 fixed-disk drives may be connected to a mainframe computer. Secondary storage for large computer systems consists of a removable-pack hard-disk system containing from 6 to 20 hard disks in a sealed unit as shown in Figure 10-6.

Another type of mainframe storage is a RAID storage system. A **redundant array of inexpensive disks (RAID)** is a computer storage system that consists of over 100 disk drives in a single cabinet and that

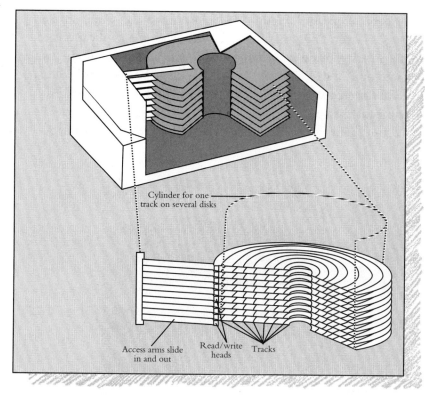

Figure 10-6   Sealed Storage Hard Disk Packs for Large Computer Systems

sends data simultaneously to a computer over parallel paths. The RAID system is reliable because if one disk drive fails, other drives take over.

Flash-Memory Cards.   A **flash-memory card** is a credit-card size variation of memory chips that can be placed inside a computer case in slots connecting to the system board. The card differs from the primary internal memory chips in the computer, however, in that it does not lose data when the electrical power is turned off. The circuitry on flash-memory cards can wear out; therefore, backup of the information to another storage device is important.

Optical Disks.   A high-capacity storage medium for microcomputers or large computers is the optical disk. An **optical disk** is a storage medium for digitally encoded information that is written and read by means of a laser. A **compact disk read only memory (CD-ROM)** is an optical disk that can be read only; it cannot be written on. CD-ROMs store databases, documents, directories, publications, and archival records

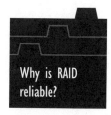

Why is RAID reliable?

What are flash-memory cards?

273

that do not need alteration. Figure 10-7 illustrates a CD-ROM drive, that holds up to seven CDs at a time, allowing multiple applications to be opened. A **write once read many (WORM) disk** is a nonerasable, nonrewritable optical disk. WORM disks hold 122 to 6,400MB of data and are useful for archival records because they cannot be altered. An **erasable optical disk** allows data to be erased and, therefore, provides for repeated use. This type of disk can store 281 to 3,200MB of data.

Courtesy of John Greenleigh/Apple Computer, Inc.

Figure 10-7 **A CD-ROM Drive**

A **magneto–optical disk** is a rewritable optical disk. By using magneto-optical disks, successive versions of large databases or documents and multimedia work can be stored on the same disk. The term **multimedia** means information that includes two or more data types: text, graphics, animation, video, or sound. Interaction of the user with the software is a computer multimedia characteristic. By clicking a button, touching a screen, or selecting a key on a keyboard, the computer user determines what part of the software program is activated. Because full-motion video requires huge amounts of storage, variations of disk storage are used for this purpose. One answer to high storage capacity requirements for multimedia is the laser videodisk. A **laser videodisk** is a device that stores sound and visual images by using a laser to burn small holes into a disk to expose a reflective surface. A laser disk player uses a light beam to pass over the disk as it spins. The holes are small; therefore, laser disks can store billions of characters. A laser disk the size of a 33 1/3 rpm record can store about 30 minutes of video on one side. Extended-play videodisks double this storage capacity. The smaller laser disk is a CD-ROM. Because laser disks cannot be changed after recording, they are not frequently used to store computer data.

What is meant by *multimedia?*

Because they are similar in shape, both magnetic and optical disks can be stored in a similar manner. Large-scale optical disk storage may be arranged in the form of a "jukebox" similar to the disk-pack arrangement of magnetic disks for large computers. Optical disk storage, because of its capacity for storage of large volumes of data, is likely to be used extensively as a storage medium in the future.

Digital Storage Technology. The search for more capacity in less space brings new forms of storage. Three advances currently under development that have implications for records storage are digital VCRs, bubble memory, and multiple-layer storage on compact disks. A **digital video cassette recorder (VCR)** is a device that stores video pictures, television pictures, and vast amounts of computer data; therefore, this medium promises to be an improvement for backup copies of hard disk data. **Bubble memory** is a type of computer memory consisting of small electromagnetic bubbles. Although currently expensive, this technology can handle extreme environmental conditions thus safeguarding data on a device only one or two square inches in size. Another computer storage advancement under development stores data in multiple layers on a single optical disk.

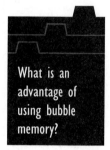

What is an advantage of using bubble memory?

The increasing use of multimedia records that require high-volume storage will result in further advances in storage technologies. Scanning technologies will also increase the demand for high-volume storage as more and more paper records are scanned into electronic format.

Backup Data Storage. A second copy, or backup copy, should be made of computer records for safekeeping. Magnetic tape is a common medium used to backup records. Magnetic-tape reels for large computers can hold up to 250MB of data. Essential records for large companies may be stored on reels of magnetic tape, placed in round metal boxes, and kept in special rooms such as tape libraries. Tape reel containers are usually assigned numbers and filed in numeric sequence. Color coding may be used to speed manual storage and retrieval of the containers.

What is a commonly used medium for backup records?

Cartridge tape units are used to back up data from a microcomputer hard disk. A **cartridge tape unit** may be an external magnetic tape unit connected to a computer or a quarter-inch cassette that fits into a standard hard-disk drive bay of a microcomputer. An external cartridge tape unit is shown in Figure 10-8a and cartridge tape storage in 10-8b. A quarter-inch minicartridge can store up to 250MB (250 million characters) of data. Digital audio tape can hold 2GB or more of data (two billion or more characters). Therefore, the digital audio-tape cassette can back up data from larger hard disk drives.

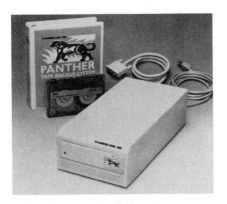

Courtesy of Extabyte Corporation

Figure 10-8a **External Tape Cartridge Equipment**

Courtesy of Tandberg Data, Inc.

Figure 10-8b **Cartridge Tape Storage**

What is sequential records storage?

Because of the volume of records held in a small amount of space, magnetic tape provides low-cost records storage. However, records in a tape file cannot be accessed directly. Magnetic tape records use sequential storage with an identifying code number such as employee number, customer number, or stock number that accompanies each record on a tape; such records can be updated on tape. **Sequential storage** is a method of organizing and accessing stored records in alphabetic or numeric order. The sequential nature of tape storage requires the read head to move through all preceding records to locate a specific record. For example, locating Janice Smith's record in an alphabetic grouping of records would require the tape read/write drive head to cycle through records from A to S before locating the record for Janice Smith.

Compression of computer files is a process that removes blank spaces between words, in margins, in boxed material, and in graphical material to conserve disk space. This technique helps manage the high-volume storage problem. Compression repackages data for storage or transmission. Compression of pictures or video requires removing parts of the repeated images or shades of color but retaining enough so that the absence of these details is not noticed. **Decompression** is the process of restoring compressed data in usable form for viewing or processing.

How are data compressed for electronic storage?

Computer Output

After a computer processes data, it can present the information in printed form, display it on a video monitor, or save it to a storage device. Visual or stored representations of processed information is referred to as *output*. Output devices include computer secondary storage devices, paper copies produced with printers, visual displays on a video screen or monitor, or digital voice recordings. Although paper copies remain a popular output of computers, more use is being made of electronic storage and display for frequently used information. Also, electronic communication from computer to computer, as well as high-volume records such as customer files, are likely to be printed in paper form only when required for a specific purpose. A paper copy of an electronic record is referred to as a **hardcopy**.

How can electronic mail reduce paper copies?

Modems and fax machines are output as well as input devices. These machines illustrate an emerging trend toward multifunctional peripheral equipment. For example, most modems now also have fax capabilities, and some stand-alone fax machines may serve as a modem, fax, printer, copier, and scanner. Refer to Chapter 12 for more on multifunctional equipment.

Processing Control

Controls must be present for a system to function efficiently and effectively. Computer systems require both human controls and technological controls; therefore, even a computer is not completely self-controlled. Human controls are most important because computers are tools that help people accomplish tasks. People must control the preparation and input of data into a computer so that errors and inaccurate input and output do not occur. Also, people must maintain reasonable turnaround time schedules by working efficiently. Finally, people must protect the information stored in the files, both for record safety and security.

Technological controls are maintained over a computer's operation by well-written and properly tested programs or computer instructions. A computer performs its processes in specific logical sequences and will not accept data input that does not conform to its programmed logic. In addition, internal controls are built into a computer's circuitry to improve the performance and to reduce problems.

How do controls affect computer operation?

Feedback

Feedback is information that helps evaluate the effectiveness of a process or of any step in a process. Computer systems software, as well as other software programs, displays feedback messages on the computer screen when errors occur. Computers can also be programmed to exchange messages with other devices connected to them—i.e., the computer screen displays a message that the printer is not ready when a file is sent to print if the printer has not been turned on or if it is out of paper. Feedback also comes from the human element with the computer user's evaluation of the completed process.

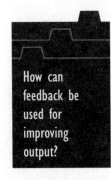

How can feedback be used for improving output?

Office Automation and Records Systems

In addition to creating, storing, and retrieving records in automated systems, the computer also plays a leading role in performing other information systems activities. With each new development in information technology, the office becomes more automated. Also, in each case, records are involved. Thus, each new application of automation to the field of records management expands the responsibilities of the records management staff. Keeping up with new technology and office automation methods as they affect records systems will continue to be a responsibility for records managers.

Stand-Alone Automated Records Systems

When automated systems first emerged, each piece of equipment operated as a separate, stand-alone system. Thus, a computer and its related equipment operated on an individual basis. If a firm had two computers, neither was connected to the other. Most microcomputers used in homes and in small offices are stand-alone systems. Today's managerial emphasis on work teams and on continuous improvement creates a demand for workers to share data. The increasing speed and memory capacity of microcomputers, along with software capable of producing varied reports from large databases, address this teamwork emphasis in the workplace. The next section discusses means of networking computers; that is, connecting them so they can share data and information, hardware, and software.

Office Automation Networks

Because the computer can be connected to the telephone system and to other communication systems (wired and wireless), communication takes place with other computers not only within a business but also worldwide. A **network** is a linkage of computers that allows computer users to share peripheral devices, programs, and data. A **local area network (LAN)** is a group of microcomputers or workstations within the same building or within one mile of each other that are connected to enable transmission of information to one another and to share hardware and software. LANs require a communications link and network operating system. A **file server** is a high-speed computer in a LAN that stores the programs and files that users share. Within a company, a LAN transmits computerized records of business operations to one or all network-linked computers. A **wide area network (WAN)**, on the other hand, is a communication link with computers scattered in a wide geographic region—a state, a country, or the world. The following paragraphs describe different types of local area and wide area networks.

Local Area Networks (LANs). The most commonly used type of LAN is the **client-server LAN** that links microcomputers, referred to as *clients*, to supplying devices called *servers*. A **server** is a computer that manages shared devices in a network. Examples of servers include: (1) a printer server that manages printers, (2) a microcomputer server that runs software, and (3) a file server that stores programs and data files that LAN users or clients share. Figure 10-9 illustrates a client-server LAN with two kinds of servers: a printer server and a file server.

For 25 or fewer computers, a peer-to-peer LAN may be used. A **peer-to-peer LAN** connects microcomputers in a network to enable

Why is sharing data among workers important?

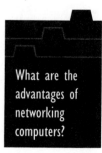

What are the advantages of networking computers?

direct communication with one another without using a server. This type of network is less expensive than the client–server network; however, it is slower when several people are using it at the same time.

Instead of telephone lines, LANs use cable or a connection system, either wired or wireless, to enable network computer users to have instant access to data from several different computers. Electronic mail or E-mail can be sent through LANs to selected network users or to everyone on the network. Through electronic mail, messages can be entered on a computer and read on other computers without requiring a paper copy. Electronic mail is one means of creating, distributing, and receiving records. A modem and a fax use telephone lines and can communicate with only one location at a time. Because they can make one electronic mail file available to many different users at the same time, LANs extend the ability for rapid communication to multiple receivers.

Wide Area Networks (WANs).   Wide area networks enable computers to send and to receive messages worldwide. Microwaves and satellites,

What is an advantage of a peer-to-peer LAN?

How is electronic mail used to create records?

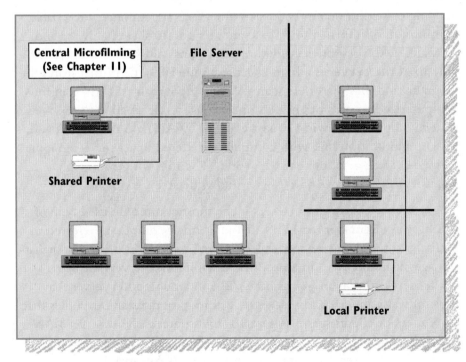

Figure 10-9   Local Area Networks (LANs) Enable Sharing of Software, Hardware, and Data

as well as wire and cable, are used to transmit wide area network messages. The ability to connect devices by telecommunications has opened a whole new world of communication. Computers use modems, software, and telephone lines to access commercial information services such as CompuServe®, Prodigy®, or America Online® for a small monthly fee. These services provide a means to send E-mail to other members of the same service regardless of their location. Most information services also provide gateways to electronic mail networks outside of their membership through access to the Internet. E-mail and special-interest discussion groups through the Internet allow international communication. In addition, the Internet offers extensive worldwide information research capabilities and access to an array of databases all over the world.

Records Management and Automation

Electronic communication and computer technology are changing the way business is done. How often do you place a telephone call and leave a message on voice mail? **Voice mail** is a computer-based message system (CBMS) that sends and receives voice messages electronically. Voice mail eliminates the need for written records because one-way voice messages are stored in a computer mailbox, and the receiver accesses the caller's voice message by entering a sequence of code numbers.

Electronic Records Procedures

The high volume of electronic records multiplies problems for records management unless records system procedures are adapted and consistently applied to electronic records, as well as to paper records. Electronic records must be indexed, coded, stored and retrieved. Cross-references may be necessary as well. Consistently followed procedures will ensure accurate, efficient storage and retrieval of records in any medium.

Why are records system procedures important for electronic records?

Indexing a computer record is the mental process of deciding the name or code by which it will be stored and retrieved. Coding the record is entering the record identifier code or filename for storage. Electronic files, particularly those files on floppy disks, are often carelessly identified with abbreviations as filenames that only the record creator could interpret. MINADVCO illustrates a filename that means nothing to anyone other than the person creating the name. Storing a description of the record with the filename aids retrieval.

Chapter 4 describes methods of organizing computer records into directories and subdirectories in a manner similar to arranging paper documents in file folders and storing them in separate file cabinet drawers. Consistency in naming files, subdirectories, and directories is important in locating computer records. An index or log of directories, subdirectories, and filename categories should be kept up to date and accessible to the people creating and storing electronic records. Assume that the filename illustrated in the paragraph above stands for minutes of advisory council. This file could be in a directory called ADVISORY with a subdirectory called MINUTES. The filename could be the month of the meeting or month and day (AUGUST18). The index or log would show all subdirectory names under the main directory, ADVI-SORY, and would give the uniform file extensions for files in that directory. The file manager in Windows automatically maintains a directory and filename index of files.

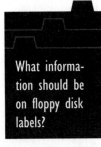

What information should be on floppy disk labels?

Floppy disks, cartridge tape units, optical disk cartridges, or other removable secondary storage devices must be clearly labeled. Labels should show the following information: (1) department or organization where the records were created; (2) name of the records series; (3) inclusive dates, numeric series, or other identifying information; (4) type of computer on which the records were created; and (5) name and version of the software used to create the records.

The work area or department of origination keeps active electronic files on hard disk drives or on removable storage devices. When these files are transferred to inactive storage, standard filing procedures should be followed.

For long-term archival storage, transfer from magnetic media to microfilm or optical disk may be desirable. The long-term permanent nature of magnetic storage media has not been determined. Because extreme temperature or proximity to magnetic charges can damage magnetic records, archival storage of vital records should be on a more permanent medium. Although optical disks have a predicted life of approximately 100 years, retrieval of records from optical disk storage requires computer equipment and software. Computer equipment and software can become obsolete, which affects retrieval of records created on that hardware and software. Newer versions of some software and hardware accept earlier versions and save the records in the new version. However, media format may change, which will make locating the specific type of disk drive difficult. Examples of this change are the tape disk drives and the 5.25-inch disk drives that no longer are included as standard features on new computers. For these reasons, microfilm storage remains a popular medium for long-term storage of vital records. Microfilm and other archival storage media and equipment are described in Chapter 11.

Why are archival records transferred from magnetic storage?

Records Protection

Safeguarding records against intentional or unintentional destruction or damage and protecting record confidentiality are known as **records protection**. Protection of records and their proper use and control must be maintained, regardless of the records media. Providing safety and security of electronic records differs somewhat from paper records. Both safety and security of electronic records are discussed in this section.

Records Safety. Records safety refers to protecting records from physical hazards existing in an office environment. The following procedures apply to controlling and protecting records from physical hazards:

1. *Adopt protective measures for the hardware and software.* These measures include protecting magnetic records from changes (surges) in electrical voltage and physically locking areas containing computer files and equipment to protect against misuse or theft. Care should be taken in handling floppy disks to protect against damage. High humidity or extreme heat or cold can result in damage to electronic records; therefore, control of extreme temperature, humidity, and air circulation helps protect these records. Adequate protection should also be in place for natural disasters such as floods, fires, and earth-quakes. Protection from natural disasters involves advance planning to select a second equipment site for emergency operation and duplicate copies of vital records for these alternate locations.

2. *Convert records stored on magnetic media to hardcopy, optical disks, or microforms if the records are to be retained for long time periods.* As discussed in the previous section, the shelf life of automated magnetic records may be limited, depending on storage conditions. Therefore, magnetic media should not be used for long-term storage of vital records.

Where should backup files be stored?

What measures can prevent computer viruses?

3. *Protect against loss of files.* Establish a policy of backing up computer files and storing the copies in fireproof cabinets or in an offsite location. Duplicating automated records with backup copies can be done quickly and inexpensively. Backing up records is good insurance that the records will be available when needed.

4. *Take special measures to prevent computer "viruses."* A **computer virus** is a special computer program created for illicit reasons and used to distort or to erase electronic records. Safety measures involve:

   a. Using virus detectors regularly.

   b. Making backup copies of each software package as soon as it is opened.

   c. Making copies daily of data entered.

   Always checking for viruses on data disks from outside sources helps eliminate data damage from viruses.

Records Security. Records security is protection from unauthorized access to the information stored on records. Generally accepted safety measures include the following practices:

1. *Developing a security policy to ensure the safe, reliable operation of the records system.* Such a policy is based on a detailed study of equipment used, records functions performed, information contained in the principal records, employees' access to the records, and current security devices.

2. *Conducting security checks and, when necessary, bonding personnel who use the system hardware and software.* The automated records security policy should include close supervision of the work plus holding employees personally accountable for the proper maintenance of company equipment and information.

3. *Providing deterrents to crime.* Some firms have a security warning programmed into their computers for display on terminal screens. An effective method of controlling access to a computer room is a card reader/combination lock system into which employees must insert their cards and key in their personal codes before the door will open.

4. *Protecting data stored on disks or tapes.* To protect company data against unauthorized use, safeguards such as passwords, digital signatures, encryption systems, or call-back may be used.

    a. A **password** is a special word, code, or symbol that is required to access a computer system. Passwords are not sufficient protection because they can be stolen or guessed. You should not use a real word or a variation of your name, your date of birth, or a word that might logically be guessed. The best password is a mix of letters, numbers, and punctuation marks in a random sequence of at least eight characters.

Why is your name not a good computer password?

    b. A **digital signature** consists of a string of characters and numbers added as a code on electronic documents being transmitted by computer. The receiving computer performs a mathematical operation on the character string to verify its validity.

    c. An **encryption system** scrambles data in a predetermined manner at the sending point to protect confidential records. The destination computer decodes the data. SecureRead, a specialized type of encryption system, hides data in a shaded block on the record. Special software on the receiving computer will decode the data.

    d. A **call-back system** is a records protection procedure requiring the individual requesting data from a computer system to hang up after a telephone request and to wait for the computer to call back. In call-back systems, the computer can check the telephone numbers before it releases information to the requesting party to be sure that only authorized people have access to the requested information.

Electronic transmission and distribution of records require special security precautions. Transmitting confidential information by fax is equivalent to posting the document on a bulletin board because fax machines commonly have multiple users. Calling ahead to alert the message receiver to watch for the fax or dedicating a fax machine for confidential material only would address this security problem. Electronic mail brings a new slant on records security and legal issues for records.

Approximately 23 million people nationwide now use E-mail, and E-mail messages may be obtained as evidence in lawsuits. Damaging evidence can often be found in messages that the sender or receiver thought were deleted. Because the main computer makes daily backups of all files, including electronic mail, copies of messages sent and deleted may still be in the backup file. In addition, software programs often make several copies of files and place them in different addresses. These files may be recovered by computer experts. Security issues stemming from unsuspected file copies call for the following measures:

1. Regularly purge old data—files that are no longer active nor needed for future operations or historical records.

2. Do not put anything on E-mail that you would not want repeated or to end up in court.

3. Protect your password, and always log off (sign off) the system properly.

What are security measures for E-mail?

Records Management Software

The control of records through automation increases rapid access to records and reduces the number of misplaced records. Records management software packages or customized software developed for a company can be used to maintain records location files, charge-out files, and retention records. Software programs may be single-function programs that manage only one aspect of the records management area—for example, archival records storage. Other software options include integrated packages that address the total records management of the business or organization and modular programs that have separate modules for each special records system function. Selection of appropriate software should be determined by several factors:

1. Complexity of the system and amount of training required for employee proficiency.

2. Well-written training manuals that accompany the software.

3. Reliability and experience of the vendor.

4. Initial cost and future costs of the software and installation.

5. Maintenance, backup, and support services offered.

Summary

Computer technology facilitates creation of records and management of records systems. A records management system consists of subsystems that interact to perform the task of controlling records. A records control system extends from records creation or receipt through distribution, use, maintenance, and disposition. Computer technology assists with each of these records management subsystems and helps records managers gain a company-wide perspective of records management. Advances in computer hardware and software simplify records creation and distribution, enable processing information into multimedia formats and reports, reduce storage space requirements, provide for efficient tracking of records, and make records retrieval accurate and rapid. With today's increase in volume and complexity of records, computer hardware and software are essential tools for records management.

A variety of computer hardware and software is available for input, output, processing, control, and feedback for records management. Computer technology is rapidly becoming more portable, multifunctional, and capable of high memory processing and storage. Image technology that scans paper documents for computer storage and retrieval, electronic coding of records for inventory and tracking, and off-the-shelf software for indexing and flagging records for retention improve the efficiency and effectiveness of records systems.

Automated records systems are moving rapidly from independent stand-alone computer systems to networks of computers. These networks support the teamwork emphasis in the workplace with shared access to software, hardware, and centralized databases. Local area networks connect microcomputers in an organization, and wide area networks link computers scattered over great distances.

Rapid transmission of information through local and wide area networks, the fax machine, electronic mail, commercial information services, and the Internet make consistent application of records system procedures critical for both paper and electronic records. Procedures for indexing, coding, organizing, storing, maintaining, retrieving, and disposing of records must be in place and rigorously followed. These procedures protect record safety and security and control the growth and disposition of nonessential records.

Important Terms

automated records system
automation
bar code
bar code reader
bubble memory
call-back system
cartridge tape unit
central processing unit (CPU)
client-server LAN
compact disk read only memory
  (CD-ROM)
compression
computer virus
control
data
decompression
digital signature
digital video cassette recorder (VCR)
digitizing
encryption system
erasable optical disk
external hard drive
facsimile (fax) machine
feedback
file server
fixed-disk drive
flash-memory card
floppy disk
hard disk
hardcopy
hard-disk cartridge
hardware
information
input
laser videodisk
light pen
local area network (LAN)

magneto-optical disk
mainframe computer
microcomputer
minicomputer
modem
mouse
multimedia
network
optical disk
output
password
peer-to-peer LAN
peripheral device
personal digital assistant (PDA)
primary (working) memory
process
random access memory (RAM)
read only memory (ROM)
records protection
redundant array of
  inexpensive disks (RAID)
scanner
secondary data storage
SecureRead field
sequential storage
server
software
subsystem
system
system components
systems approach
systems environment
touch screen
trackball
voice mail
wide area network (WAN)
write once read many (WORM) disk

Review and Discussion

1. What is meant by a *systems approach*, and how did the term originate? (Obj. 1)

2. How does computer technology support a systems approach for records management? (Obj. 1)

3. Give examples of three input and three output components of a computer system. (Obj. 2)

4. Explain how computers use primary memory and secondary data storage in processing records. (Obj. 2)

5. Give an example of control and feedback for a computer system. (Obj. 2)

6. How can installation of local area networks (LANs) improve communication within a business and contribute to the philosophy of teamwork? (Obj. 3)

7. How can wide area networks (WANs) be used in the creation and distribution of records? (Obj. 3)

8. Describe four methods of providing records safety and four methods of providing records security. (Obj. 4)

9. Explain why standard records procedures are essential to the management of electronic records. (Obj. 4)

Applications (APP)

APP 10-1. *Recommendations for Records System Automation (Objs. 1-4)*

You are an employee in a business that is just beginning to automate the records management program. You are asked to list five considerations for implementing computer technology for the records system. These recommendations should relate to one or more of the following: hardware, software, and/or procedures for records management. Team with a partner in your class to prepare this list.

APP 10–2. *International Communication with the Internet (Obj. 3)*

Intermezzo Corp., Inc., does business worldwide. A gateway to the Internet allows electronic mail with other companies throughout the world that are also linked with the Internet. You have recently been employed by Intermezzo Corp., Inc. Send an E-mail message to Monterey Manufacturers in Australia notifying the company that Order No. 8425 was shipped two days ago. The message should also convey goodwill and let Monterey Manufacturers know that its business is appreciated. A simulated E-mail message form is on the template. Follow the directions on the template to prepare the E-mail message. Save your work using the filename CH10.AP2, and print a copy. Also, determine the time difference between your location and Australia. If you sent the message within the next 30 minutes, what time would it be in Australia? Does time difference matter when sending an E-mail message? Why or why not?

Chapter 11
Image Records

Learning Objectives

1. Compare a microfilm system with a computer optical disk imaging system.
2. Describe and compare four types of microforms: roll film, microfiche, microfilm jacket, and aperture card.
3. Describe methods of improving microfilm quality and safeguarding the storage environment.
4. Discuss the benefits of using an integrated imaging system.
5. Identify advantages of using a hybrid imaging system.
6. Discuss three major stages of an image system.
7. Discuss two primary purposes of image system evaluation and give examples of information needed for each purpose.
8. Describe how businesses or organizations can benefit from imaging applications.

Image Record Usage

What is an image record?

Efficient records storage and retrieval gives organizations a competitive edge in customer service. For example, an insurance company that can quickly retrieve a record and mail it to a customer in four hours has a strategic advantage over an organization that takes up to a week. Electronic and photographic storage of image records combined with computer technology for rapid record retrieval enables organizations to improve the efficiency of records management. An **image record** is a photographic or electronic representation of a record that has been transferred to microfilm or optical disk.

Electronic records are created when information is transferred to digital form for computer processing or retrieval. Optical disk storage, as described in Chapter 10, is the most commonly used computer storage medium for long-term storage of records. The high-capacity storage and durability of optical disks allow the capture of text as well as graphic, photographic, and animation images for viewing on a computer screen. A scanner, along with special software, converts paper records to digital form for computer usage. Technology for scanning records, creating electronic forms, and digitizing handwritten forms has encouraged the conversion of paper records to electronic or microfilm records.

Microfilm records are created by photographing records to reduce their size to miniature images on film. **Microform** is a generic term for any medium containing miniaturized or microimages. This chapter describes the creation and use of microform records, as well as records systems that integrate microfilm-based images and electronic image technologies.

Savings in storage space result from storing records on microforms or optical disks. Figure 11-1 compares storage capacity and estimated cost savings for different storage media. Microfilming large, bulky materials such as engineering or architectural drawings eliminates serious storage and mailing problems. Greater use of the computer, combined with optical disk storage and microfilming, makes retrieval of these records faster, more efficient, and cost effective.

How are microfilm records created?

How do microrecords and optical disk storage save space?

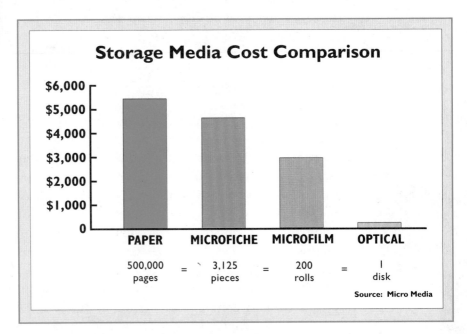

Figure 11-1   Storage Media Cost Comparison

Source: Reprinted with permission from *Imaging World,* © 1995, Volume 4, Issue 10, October. The Imaging Group, Cardinal Business Media, P.O. Box 1358, Camden, ME 04843 (207) 236-8524.

Records managers must ask critical questions when considering use of microforms, optical disk systems, or other long-term storage media:

1. What is the estimated life span of microfilm, optical disk storage, or other image media?
2. What records should be converted to these media?
3. Who uses these records, and how are they used?
4. How long must these records be retained?
5. What special equipment is required for the image media?

The life span of microfilm is as long as the life span of paper records. In a carefully controlled environment, microfilm records can be protected and preserved for decades with estimates extending to hundreds of years. This durability strengthens the practicality of microfilm storage. Optical disk storage maintains its quality for at least ten years, and improvements in laser disk technology may extend this life span. However, to ensure protection of microfilm or electronic records, records managers do not circulate the master copy of electronic, microfilm, or microform records. A *master* is the original microfilm, microform, or optical disk. Copies made for everyday use or for loan are duplicates of the master. Many records managers establish a policy of transferring optical disk records to new disks every ten years. The process of making new copies of the master record is called *remastering* and is one means of extending the life span of electronic records.

Records kept for 3 or fewer years may be kept as paper records or on magnetic or optical disk storage. Records kept from 7 to 15 years should be considered for optical disk storage or microfilming. These records can be kept accessible and stored in less space. Figure 11-2a shows a centralized storage system for microform records. Figure 11-2b shows centralized microform files.

Vital and archival records are often kept on microfilm because of its established durability. Microfilm records remain in original text format, just reduced in size; reading the text requires only projection and magnification. This standardized format of microfilm protects records from technological obsolescence that could occur over long time periods with electronic records. In addition, long-standing federal law permits acceptance of microfilmed records as legal documents, admissible as evidence in a court of law.

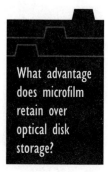

What advantage does microfilm retain over optical disk storage?

Courtesy of Eastman Kodak Co.

Figure 11-2a   **Centralized Microform Storage System**

Courtesy of IBM Corporation

Figure 11-2b   **Centralized Microform Files**

Equipment costs to produce microform records or optical disk records represent the major implementation costs for these records systems. For long-term records, the equipment cost may be off-set by savings in storage cost and in retrieval efficiency. With technological advances, new equipment costs less but produces better images and permits speedy computerized storage and retrieval.

Instead of purchasing specialized equipment for microfilming or scanning records to electronic format, organizations may use commercial services. Commercial records storage centers often are used to store the master copies of vital records. Rental costs for storing records on microfilm, microform, or optical disks are minimized because use of these media reduces required storage space.

Microfilm Records

What is the difference between microrecords and micrographics?

Microfilm is a fine-grained, high-resolution film used to record micro-images. A **microimage** is an image too small to be read without magnification. The miniaturized image of a document is called a **microrecord**. **Microfilming** is the process of photographing documents to reduce their size. The technology and processes used to record information in microform are known as **micrographics**.

294

Types of Microrecords

Microrecords may be formatted in various convenient and easy-to-use microforms. The most common microforms are roll film (open reels, cartridges, or cassettes) and unitized microforms (microfiche, microfilm jackets, and aperture cards). All microforms, however, originate from roll film.

Roll Film. The most inexpensive and most widely used microform is *roll film*. A typical 100-foot roll of microfilm can hold more than 2,000 images. These images may be either positive (black characters on a clear background) or negative (white characters on a black background). Positive images on a roll film could be compared to black images on a clear transparency for overhead projection. Negative images resemble negatives returned with your photographs when you send film for processing. Roll film holds long-term, sequentially arranged records or active, randomly arranged records for automated systems.

Large volumes of information can be stored on film in little space at low cost. Typically, roll film is used to photograph records used infrequently. Records are usually photographed and captured on film in a sequential order and must be located sequentially for retrieval, thus slowing the retrieval process. An example of sequential retrieval is a video cassette tape. To locate a particular segment of a television program recorded on a video cassette recorder (VCR), you must fast forward through the tape to the segment you are seeking. The only way that records can be stored effectively in a random sequence on roll film is to have an automated index system that uses computer technology to locate the correct roll and film.

What kinds of records are microfilmed on roll film?

Records requiring frequent changes usually are not stored on roll film. Changes can be made by cutting out the old information and splicing in new film. However, such changes in the film are expensive, may weaken the film, and may make it inadmissible as legal evidence in a court of law.

Roll microforms may be purchased as open reel, cassette, and cartridge (also called *magazine*). Figure 11-3 shows types of roll film. Open-reel film uses a separate takeup reel in a reader; a cassette includes both a supply and a takeup reel. The cartridge is an enclosed reel and also requires a separate takeup reel in a reader. The cassette or cartridge construction permits automatic film threading in a reader and also protects the film.

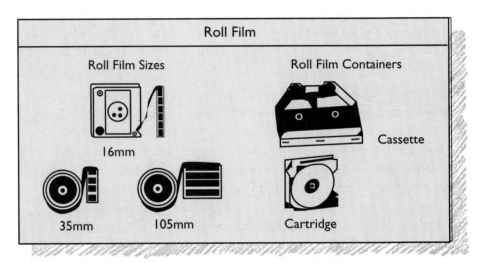

Figure 11-3 Types of Roll Film

Microfiche. **Microfiche**, usually shortened to *fiche* and pronounced "feesh," is a transparent sheet of microfilm, usually 6" by 4" in size, containing a series of microimages arranged in rows and columns with an identifying strip readable without magnification (see Figure 11-4a). The identifying strip is a *header*. Fiche is a *unitized microform* because it contains *one unit* of information such as one student's academic records.

Fiche permits direct access to any record without having to advance a roll of film to the appropriate location. As an aid to indexing and speeding retrieval of microrecords on the microfiche, images are arranged in a grid of uniform rows and columns. Letters of the alphabet identify rows, and numbers identify columns. A particular frame or microimage can be identified by the grid coordinates such as G-3, meaning Row G, Column 3. This location system is similar to a computer software spreadsheet that identifies cell addresses or locations by row number and column letter.

The maximum number of images that can be contained on a fiche depends on the amount of reduction. At a typical 24X reduction, 98 original images can be stored on one microfiche, arranged in a grid of 7 rows and 14 columns. A common method of arranging records on microfiche is to film documents in a continuous series by rows. Because the user can read the title (header) at its top without magnification, fiche can easily be stored and retrieved manually, similar to index cards.

Fiche can be mailed as easily and economically as 6" by 4" cards. With developments in color photography, fiche can be produced in colors closely resembling the colors on the original records. Color fiche can be viewed longer without eyestrain than can black-and-white pictures.

How many images can be stored on a 24X microfiche?

Figure 11-4a **Microfiche**

Microfilm Jackets. A **microfilm jacket** is a transparent plastic carrier with single or multiple horizontal channels for inserting strips of 16mm or 35mm microfilm—cut from roll film (see Figure 11-4b). The most commonly used format is 6" by 4" with 4 channels holding 12 images each. Strips of film in a jacket are protected and are easily organized into units of information similar to microfiche. The jacketed film may be duplicated without removing it from the jacket. In addition, new microfilm may be inserted into the jacket for a quick update of information. A header identifying the jacketed strips can easily be affixed at the top of the microform for storage and retrieval similar to microfiche. Jackets are useful for keeping together related records such as personnel and medical records; correspondence; legal, customer, and policyholder files.

What is the purpose of microfilm jackets?

Card jackets are also used for storing related records. Within the space of a regular index card, several document images with identifying information can be stored, representing a great savings in document storage space.

Aperture Cards.   An **aperture card** is a standard data processing card (7 3/8" by 3 1/4") with a rectangular opening (aperture) specifically designed as a carrier for a film image or images (see Figure 11-4c). Aperture cards are used primarily for holding 35mm engineering drawings or blueprints.

Figure 11-4b   Microfilm Jacket

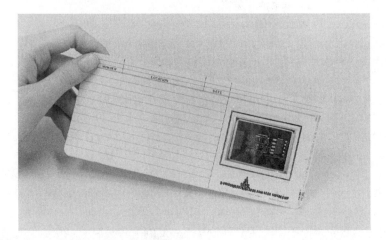

Figure 11-4c   Aperture Card

Aperture cards for storing 16mm film hold up to 8 images. Four letter-size (8 1/2" by 11") pages can be included within the aperture at a reduction ratio of 16X; and up to 400 pages can be contained in an aperture at a reduction ratio of 160X on 16mm film. Identifying information is printed along the top edge of an aperture card as a heading for indexed storage and retrieval. In addition, this and other identifying information can be keypunched for large-volume automatic sorting and retrieval. A record can be updated easily by removing an obsolete card and inserting a new one. Interfiling new cards or replacing cards within a file of cards can be accomplished quickly.

Large businesses and governmental agencies use aperture cards to store maps and other drawings, X-rays, and business records. The principal disadvantage of using aperture cards is cost. The expense of purchasing card supplies, mounting the images, and storing fewer images on each aperture card makes the cost of aperture cards higher than for other microforms. Filing space requirements for aperture cards may be at least five times greater than they are for records maintained on roll film.

What kinds of records are placed on aperture cards?

Microfilm Size

Microfilm width is measured in millimeters (mm). The three most commonly used widths are 16mm, 35mm, and 105mm. The narrowest film (16mm) is most frequently used for filming small documents, such as checks, and standard- and legal-size records. Larger records such as newspapers, maps, and engineering drawings require 35mm microfilm. Microfiche generally is filmed using 105mm microfilm.

What microfilm size is generally used for microfiche?

Microfilm length varies from 100 feet to over 200 feet. The thickness varies from 2.5 mils (.0025 inch) to 7 mils. Microfilm of 5 mils is commonly used; however, the 2.5 mils is gaining use because more processed film can be stored in less space. For example, a standard reel of processed microfilm holds 100 feet of 5-mil film but twice as much (200 feet) of 2.5-mil film. However, thinner film is less durable and not recommended for frequent usage.

Microfilm Quality

A microfilm copy of a record is no better than the original document. Blurred copies do not microfilm well, and colors on original documents may not microfilm. Defects on an original document may be magnified on the microrecord. Special procedures, equipment, and specific types of film are required to maintain a high level of microrecord quality. Four factors relate to quality in the microfilming process: (1) resolution, (2) density, (3) reduction ratio, and (4) magnification ratio. After inspecting the quality of the microimage using these factors with established standards of acceptability, the original record is usually destroyed. The intent of using microforms is to convert paper documents to a dependable media that can be stored for long time periods in a small amount of space—not to create a long-term duplicate record system.

Resolution.   **Resolution** is a measure of the sharpness of lines or fine detail in an image. Good resolution requires a high-quality film and a camera with a good lens. High resolution means that a microrecord is clear and easily readable when magnified on a reader with a viewing screen and light source.

What must be done to assure good resolution?

Density.   **Density** is the degree of opacity of microfilm which determines the amount of light that will pass through it or reflect from it. A **densitometer** is a device used to measure the contrast between the dark and light areas of the film. A high-quality microrecord has a wide variation in the dark and light areas of the film. The higher the contrast, the easier the images are to read. The reading density standard falls in the range of 1.0 to 1.2 with overexposure giving a higher reading. Contrast sharpness depends on the quality of the source document as well as on the proper lighting factors during filming.

Reduction Ratio.   The **reduction ratio** is the relationship between the dimensions of the original record and the corresponding dimensions of the microimage. The ratio is also a measure of the number of times a document's dimension is reduced when photographed. A 1:24 ratio (usually expressed as 24X) means that the film image is 1/24th the original record's size, both horizontally and vertically. (A document microfilmed at 24X is 1/24 times 1/24, or 1/576th its original size.) Reduction ratios range from 5X to 2400X; however, the most common reduction is 24X. The higher the reduction ratio, the smaller the images, and the greater the number of images that can be photographed on one square inch of film. For example, 8,100 regular-size bank checks can be photographed on 100 feet of microfilm at 24X reduction; 16,600 such

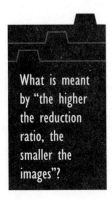

What is meant by "the higher the reduction ratio, the smaller the images"?

checks, at 50X. Banks use a microfilm that is 2,000 feet long to capture the high volume of checks that go through a special sorter. For easy retrieval, however, the film is cut down to 100-foot or 215-foot rolls after developing.

Magnification Ratio. For a user to read it, a microrecord must be enlarged or magnified. The **magnification ratio**, also called the *enlargement ratio*, describes the relationship between the sizes of an image and the original record when viewed on a microfilm reader screen. For example, a 1-inch square microrecord that is magnified 10 times (a magnification of 10X) appears in its enlarged form as 10 square inches. An image filmed at 24X reduction must be magnified at 24X to generate an original-size copy.

Microfilm Storage Environment

With constant handling, microrecords are subject to dirt, abrasion, oily fingerprints, contamination by foreign materials, and exposure to excessive light and temperatures. These elements can cause the microimage to fade and deteriorate over time. Records managers must ensure that established procedures are followed for the protection of microfilm records:

1. *Because of the film's unique chemical properties, special precautions must be taken to control the storage environment, especially temperature and humidity.* Microrecords that have a permanent retention period should be stored under controlled conditions that include a maximum temperature of 70 degrees and relative humidity that stays within a range of 30 to 40 percent. Maintaining a constant temperature and humidity is important; the change in a 24-hour period should never be greater than 10 degrees in temperature or 10 percent in humidity.

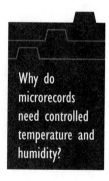

Why do microrecords need controlled temperature and humidity?

2. *Microfilm reels and cassettes require boxes for shelf or drawer storage.* If possible, film should be stored in sealed containers. If sealed containers are not available, the air in the storage room should be carefully controlled by an air-filtration system that will remove abrasive particles and gaseous impurities that can harm the film.

3. *Film reels, storage boxes, and paper enclosures or attachments to microfilm should be acid-free.* Acids and other contaminants can cause destructive chemical reactions on film.

Microfilm records require the same kinds of safety and security protection as other types of records. In addition to other records protection measures, a master (the original microform) should be kept in a safe, protected storage area. Procedures must be in place to safeguard these master records against damage or loss.

Integrated Imaging System

What are the advantages of using integrated imaging systems?

Combining computer hardware and software with imaging technology increases efficiency in the creation and retrieval of microrecords while maintaining their long-term storage benefit. Modern computer technology has not replaced micrographics. Instead, integration of microfilm with electronic imaging and computer indexing and retrieval provides stable, archival storage media with rapid access to records.

Computer-Assisted Retrieval (CAR)

The computer may be used to retrieve microrecords. **Computer-assisted retrieval (CAR)** is the use of a computer to identify the location of information not contained within that computer's database. The computer stores an index of all microform records. Using CAR, an operator may microfilm incoming paper records in random sequence because they may be stored and retrieved randomly by the computer through an index. During filming, an operator assigns each paper record a sequential location number (address) that corresponds to the location of the microfilmed image. Next, an operator enters into the computer the microrecord address and keyword descriptors such as record title or subject, dates, amounts, and document numbers. This information becomes the computer index to the microfilmed records. For a typical record request such as *Find all records relating to the Browning merger for November 19--,* the computer operator enters the keywords *Browning merger* along with numbers representing dates. To find the desired records, the computer compares the keywords/numbers entered on the terminal screen with the corresponding record keywords and numbers in the file index. When it makes a match of such identifiers, the computer lists the records found on the screen. The operator can then decide which, if any, microimages to access.

CAR systems may be offline or online. In an *offline CAR system*, microrecords are stored in standard storage equipment according to the location code index stored in a computer. To retrieve a microrecord, the user enters the appropriate record identification information into the computer. Next, the computer searches its memory for the microrecord's location code. When it locates the record, the computer displays on screen the microfilm record's location number (page and frame numbers of microfiche, for example) or its frame number and cartridge or roll number. With this information, the user manually retrieves the micro-form containing the desired record from the file for use in a reader.

In an *online CAR system*, microrecords retrieval is connected directly to a computer. To retrieve a requested record, the operator keys record identification information into the computer. The computer searches its online index and directs its micrographic retrieval device to locate and display the internally stored microimage on the screen or, if desired, to print the record.

What is an online CAR system?

Computer-Output Microfilm/Microform (COM)

Computer-output microfilm/microform (COM) is computer output converted directly into microfilm/microform without paper printout as an intermediary. The term also refers to the equipment that produces the microform or to the entire process of transferring data. Computer-created microforms can be processed faster and more economically than microforms created by the traditional microfilming process. With the use of a tape-to-film photographic device called a *recorder*, computer records on magnetic tape are converted to a microimage on roll film or on microfiche. Fewer than four ounces of microfiche can store the equivalent of 60 pounds of hardcopy. By eliminating the need for hardcopy output, COM reduces cost and space storage requirements.

How does COM reduce computer hard-copy output?

COM may be *online*; that is, a COM recorder photographs records directly from a computer. With online COM systems, a computer interacts with a COM recorder just as it would with a printer. Micro-filming with a COM recorder not directly connected to a computer is an *offline* operation. The computer generates a magnetic tape that contains all the data to be put on microfilm. This tape serves as input to a COM recorder that creates microfilm.

Computer-Input Microfilm/Microform (CIM)

The computer can be used with records already on microfilm. **Computer-input microfilm/microform (CIM)** is computer input taken directly from microfilm/microform by scanning and character recognition. CIM also refers to the system of software and hardware that makes possible this method of transferring data to disk. COM and CIM may be combined into one system to exchange both input and output between the computer and the microimage system.

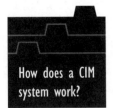

How does a CIM system work?

Computer-based document imaging has emerged as a means of managing paper-based information such as billing records, policy files, customer correspondence, legal contracts, and vital records not readily converted to database storage. Paper documents are captured on microfilm, and the locations of these film images are maintained in a database. Digitized images created from microfilm may be viewed at special workstations or on networked microcomputers using image display software. During the microfilming process, bar code or optical character recognition (OCR) can provide automatic image indexing.

Computer Output to Laser Disk (COLD)

Another form of long-term computer storage that integrates the imaging of paper documents with electronic records is **computer output to laser disk (COLD)**. COLD combines the capabilities of scanning paper documents created on another system and linking them to COLD documents (computer-created records saved by laser to optical disks). This combination of digital image scanning of paper documents, optical disk storage, and search capabilities of database software facilitates development of a computerized records storage and retrieval system for both active and long-term records.

What are COLD documents?

COLD technology uses an optical disk jukebox with a controller and server. Each disk can store more than 200,000 pages. Optical storage media range from 1.36GB [one gigabyte (GB) = one billion characters] on a 5.25-inch optical disk to a high-capacity 12-inch, 15GB write-once drive and a 2.3TB capacity jukebox [one terabyte (TB) = one trillion characters]. Software management of optical drives and jukeboxes is available for microcomputer and minicomputer environments. Figure 11-5 shows the projected increase in use of optical record storage.

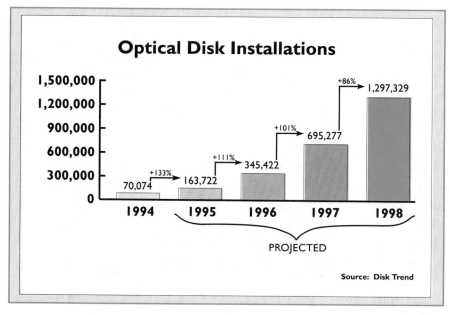

Figure 11-5   Projected Optical Disk Installations

Source: Reprinted with permission from *Imaging World,* © 1995, Volume 4, Issue 10, October. The Imaging Group, Cardinal Business Media, P.O. Box 1358, Camden, ME 04843 (207) 236-8524.

COLD technology includes fully automated search and retrieval capability with selected records displayed on a screen or printed to paper copy. Distribution of COLD records through networks permits shared access to the database with rapid retrieval from various work sites.

What are the benefits of using a COLD system?

Hybrid Imaging Systems

A **hybrid imaging system** is the integration of microfilm-based images with electronic image processing technologies. A hybrid system includes devices that can scan microfilm; computers that can display the scanned images; and software or hardware that can process the images, compress them, and manipulate them to allow users to move them around an information highway efficiently. Optional components include fax capabilities, laser printers, and networks that can transmit images across local or wide area networks or to mass storage devices—magnetic or optical.

A hybrid system operates in the same manner as a microfilm-retrievable system up to the point at which a scan is complete. When a record request is received, the system operator locates the image or images on microfilm, retrieves the film image, and projects the image on a device. However, instead of printing a paper copy of the image, the image is digitized and transmitted to a microcomputer for further processing.

After an image is transmitted to a microcomputer, it can be manipulated and printed on a local or network laser printer. The image can be sent through an E-mail system or faxed to the user. Additionally, the image can be routed to a character recognition device for conversion to textual data or to a magnetic or optical storage device. With digital imaging, a computer can deliver information where it is needed, when it is needed, and in the form in which it is needed. A digital image can also be incorporated into word processing software for editing and for removing confidential information before it is delivered to a user.

A primary advantage of using a hybrid system is that stored images can be delivered using an already existing system in many organizations—E-mail. For example, a user can E-mail a request for a certain document from the microfilm storage center. Personnel in the center can retrieve the document image, scan it, compress it (remove redundant spaces), attach it to the E-mail reply message, and transmit it across the system. All the user needs is software to decompress (restore to original format) the image for viewing, printing, or faxing. The ability to distribute information, to incorporate it into other processes, and to integrate it with software provides the cost justification for hybrid systems.[1]

An example of a hybrid imaging system, the KODAK IMAGELINK™ is shown in Figure 11-6. This system retains both the long-term storage feature of microfilm and the ready access of optical disk records. Combination scanner and microimage systems such as KODAK IMAGELINK offer one-step data capture and output of both microfilm and electronic images. Archival images are immediately deliverable to computer users. One pass-through in the scanner delivers either front-side or duplex (front and backside images) microfilm. An index of image locations can be displayed on a screen, and the user can make selections for retrieval. Image delivery can be handled four ways:

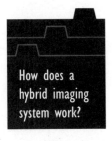

How does a hybrid imaging system work?

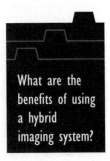

What are the benefits of using a hybrid imaging system?

[1]Dan Kehoe, "Hybrid Imaging Systems: The Reincarnation of Microfilm," *Proceedings of the ARMA International 40th Annual Conference,* (Prairie Village, KS: ARMA International, 1995), pp. 149-160.

Courtesy of Eastman Kodak

Figure 11-6   KODAK IMAGELINK™

(1) a special computer workstation, (2) networked microcomputers with image display software, (3) hardcopies produced by printer, and (4) delivery by fax to another location.

Imaging Procedures and Equipment

An **image system** refers to a combination of procedures and equipment that forms an efficient unit for creating and using records in microform or electronic images. Figure 11-7 identifies records procedures used in the three stages of an image records system: preparation, processing, and use of records. The procedures and equipment used in an image system are described in the next section.

Document Preparation

Documents must be checked carefully before either microfilming or scanning to ensure that the camera or the scanner will work correctly. All paper clips and staples must be removed and records that are torn should be mended. Attachments to records such as envelopes, routing slips, and notes should be removed. For some microfilming systems,

How are documents prepared for imaging?

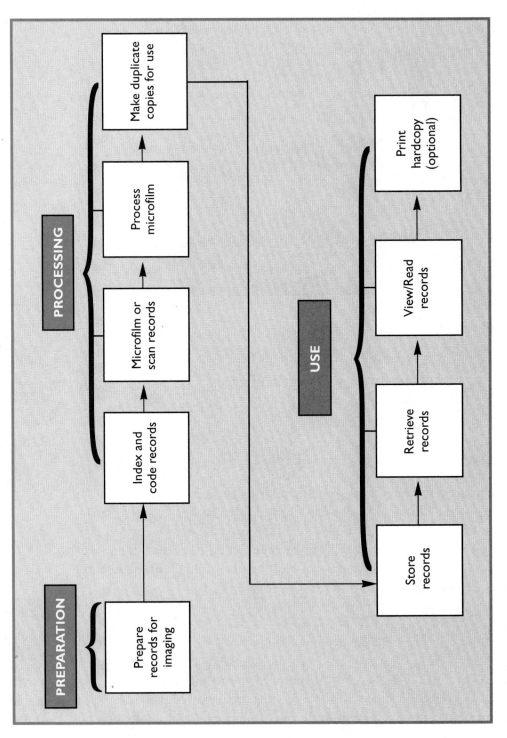

Figure 11-7   An Image System

records should also be batched and placed in sequential order before filming. Documents captured on optical disk do not require sequential arrangement and may be entered randomly. Computer storage enables random access for rapid retrieval.

Indexing Procedures

Recording information to serve as a location directory for microforms or electronic records is referred to as *indexing*. An index attaches identification data referred to as an *address* to microrecords or electronic records. The term *index* refers to a list of microrecords on roll film, microfiche, aperture cards, or electronic records.

What is the purpose of indexing?

Automatic indexing of document images while scanning or microfilming can take place with data capture options available on microimaging and scanning systems. Microrecord indexing may be accomplished manually either at the time of filming or after the filming. To index manually during filming, a computer operator stationed adjacent to the microfilm camera assigns identifiers. To index microrecords after filming, an operator places a roll of microfilm into a retrieval terminal, views each image, and assigns an identifier by keying the identifier and sequential number of the microimage into the computer. Five common methods of indexing are shown in Figure 11-8 and discussed in the following paragraphs.

Flash Indexing. Flash indexing is one means of indexing records on roll film. Each 100-foot length of film is divided into sections or groups of records similar to the way guides separate sections in a file drawer. Before filming, an operator groups records into sections (usually the same order as these paper records were in a file drawer). The operator then prepares *flash cards* with identifying information for each section and places them in front of each group of records before filming. After filming, the operator places the film in a container that should be marked to show the section position and contents of each section. When flash targets are used in preparing computer output microfiche, an index of contents may be placed in the last frame.

How does flash indexing help locate records?

Sequential Numbering. Rotary cameras may include a device that imprints sequential numbers on documents as they are filmed. After filming, an operator keys the document description, sequential number,

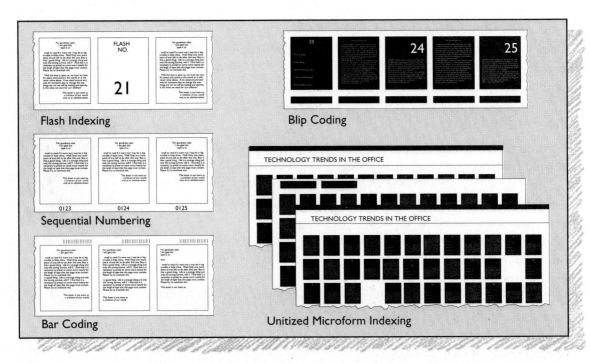

Figure 11-8 **Methods of Indexing Microrecords**

and roll number into a computer database as a document index. To locate and retrieve a document, the operator consults the index for the roll and frame number to locate the microform. Then, the operator inserts the correct roll into the reader–printer, and the film is advanced to the document frame number.

Blip Coding. Blip coding is another automated system for indexing and retrieving microrecords from roll film. A *blip* or rectangular mark is placed below or above each microimage, and each blip is assigned a sequential number. To retrieve a document, the operator consults an external index to find the roll and image number and keys this information into the retrieval device. This device counts the blips at high speed until it finds the requested record number.

Bar Coding. Bar codes help automate the indexing for scanned or filmed documents. Bar codes, as described in Chapter 10, may be preprinted on documents signifying an identifier such as a purchase order number. If the identifiers are sequential numbers, bar code labels can be generated in order and printed on adhesive tape with a bar code printer.

These tapes are placed on the records before microfilming or scanning to optical disk. Bar codes are also used to identify storage areas for archived records and to index optical disk images.

How are bar codes used?

Unitized Microform Indexing.   Unitized microforms may be indexed in various ways. Microfiche, microfilm jackets, and aperture cards can be indexed by adding a title (header) at the top of the micro-form. The camera may create this header, or the operator can add it manually. The header usually includes the name of the document and microrecord sequence number. Also, a bar code may be affixed to the header. Microfiche and microfilm jackets may have a color band on the header for color coding. A color code represents a batch of records or an entire file and identifies a particular type of record. Color coding helps filers locate misfiled records quickly.

Imaging Equipment

Records may be captured on microfilm or optical disk through use of special equipment. Both manual filming equipment and computerized equipment for imaging are described in this section.

Rotary Camera.   For filming large-volume records such as checks and invoices, a rotary camera may be used. It is the least expensive record filming method. A **rotary camera** is a microfilm camera that uses rotating belts to carry documents through the camera and makes images on 16mm film at a speed of over 500 documents a minute.

Planetary Camera.   A **planetary camera** is a microfilm camera that uses 35mm film to film large engineering drawings, hardbound books, and other large documents. These documents are placed on a plane (flat) surface for filming. This camera is slower than the rotary camera because documents remain stationary during filming and are photographed one by one. Because of the greater time involvement, filming with a plan-etary camera is more expensive but produces higher quality than the rotary camera.

What documents are filmed with a planetary camera?

Step-and-Repeat Camera.   The **step-and-repeat camera** is a microfilm camera that produces a series of separate images, usually in orderly rows and columns. It is used to film microfiche. This camera films images directly onto a 4-inch film width, which when cut into 6-inch lengths, produces a standard 6" by 4" master microfiche. In systems requiring frequent changes in the records—as in maintaining inventory records—an *updatable microfiche camera* (a modification of the step-and-repeat camera) is available. With such a camera, additional images can be added to a microfiche at any time if unexposed space exists on the fiche. Also, the camera can alter existing images by overprinting such words as VOID and PAID.

Digital Imaging. Instead of using camera equipment for manual capture of documents on microfilm, a computer and scanner with software may be used for document imaging to either microform or electronic media. As described in earlier sections in this chapter, computer-output microform (COM) or computer output to laser disk (COLD) requires specialized equipment. Computerization of the microfilming process with a COM recorder replaces manual photographing with a rotary, planetary, or step-and-repeat camera. COLD systems require computer equipment with an optical disk drive and jukebox. Imaging of paper records for computer processing requires a scanner, which translates a document to digitized format for computer entry and display. A document is placed on the flat surface of a flatbed scanner for imaging. Hand-held scanners may be used for capturing portions of a document. High-volume scanning requires more sophisticated scanners with automatic document feeders. A combination of scanner and computer microimaging equipment can be used to produce both microfilm and electronic images.

Processing Equipment

After records are microfilmed, the film is processed. A machine used to develop microfilm is called a **processor**. An organization may purchase processing equipment or use commercial services for microfilm processing. Most processors do not require a darkroom and can operate in daylight; the exposed film is protected by a cover on the processor in which the film is placed or by a canister placed over the exposed film outside the processor.

Duplicating Equipment

The *microform master* (original) is not circulated for use. Instead, duplicates are used as working copies. A duplicate may be made by simultaneously exposing two rolls of film in the film unit of the camera. **Contact printing**, the most frequent method of making multiple copies, is a process that makes a duplicate copy of microfilm by placing the emulsion side of the developed original film in contact with the emulsion side of the copy film and directing a light beam through the original image to the copy. Developing the copy film then produces a duplicate.

What is a microform master?

Storage Equipment

Special storage equipment is available for each type of microform. Microform reels (16mm or 35mm film) are stored in boxes on shelves or in cabinets partitioned to fit the boxes. Carousels with partitioned shelves or small workstation storage units may be used to store microfilm cartridges and cassettes. Figures 11-9a and 11-9b show an example of a roll film storage box and a roll film storage cabinet.

Figures 11-10a and 11-10b show a workstation tray and a cabinet for storing microfiche records. Fiche may also be stored in three-ring binders and in drawer cabinets. Plastic microfilm jackets and microfilm card jackets can be stored in the same type of equipment as microfiche. Aperture cards are stored in drawers.

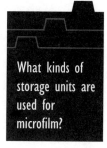

What kinds of storage units are used for microfilm?

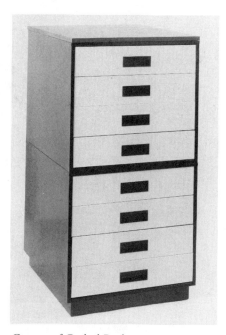

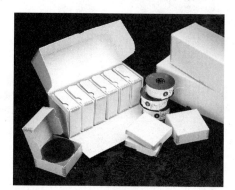

Courtesy of Gaylord Brothers

Figure 11-9a **Roll Film Storage Box**

Courtesy of Gaylord Brothers

Figure 11-9b **Roll Film Storage Cabinet**

Fellowes Manufacturing Co.

Figure 11-10a   **Microfiche Storage Tray**

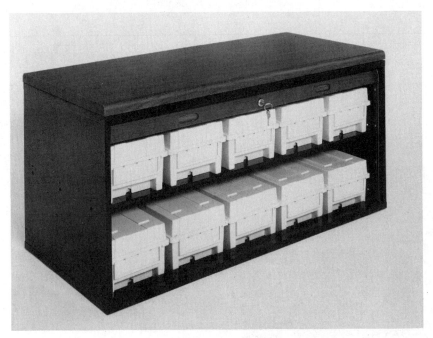

Fellowes Manufacturing Co.

Figure 11-10b   **Microfiche Storage Cabinet**

Computer tapes, cassettes, cartridges, and floppy disks may be stored in special cabinets or in workstation storage units. Small businesses or organizations may use floppy disk storage boxes. CD-ROM disks are placed in a plastic case before storage in cabinets or on carousels, shelves, or display racks. Figures 11-11a and 11-11b show a workstation CD storage case and a CD storage carousel. Optical disk storage equipment for large organizations that use multimedia database imaging includes optical disk libraries (jukeboxes). An **optical disk library** or **jukebox** is a device that contains multiple optical disk platters, from one to five optical disk drives, and a robotic mechanism (picker) used to move platters to and from the drives.

Commercial Imaging Services

Commercial service bureaus provide an alternative to in-house microfilming, microform duplicating, and microform storing. Service bureaus may perform scanning, storing, indexing, and retrieving operations as well. Small- and mid-size companies may use these services as part of their records system without purchasing expensive equipment. Limited physical facilities and/or lack of specialized staff

Courtesy of Highsmith Co.

Figure 11-11a **CD-ROM Storage Case**

Courtesy of Highsmith Co.

Figure 11-11b **CD-ROM Storage Carousel**

sometimes make outside commercial services the best choice for producing microfilm or for capturing images to optical disks. Commercial services may be selected for their reputation for good service, short turnaround time, safety (security) of storage facilities, efficiency in records retrieval, and reasonable cost of their services.

Retrieval and Viewing Equipment

What equipment is needed for manual microform retrieval and use?

For manual location of microforms on reels, cartridges, or cassettes, extra equipment is not required. Nor is any special equipment required for manual retrieval of microfiche or microfilm jackets. Aperture cards, however, may be retrieved manually or more quickly by a sorter that decodes records storage information on the cards.

Computer hardware and software may be used to locate and/or retrieve microforms, as well as electronic records. Computer-assisted retrieval in some form is widely used.

Reading information on a microrecord uses special equipment called a *reader* or *viewer*. A **reader-viewer** is a device that displays an enlarged microimage on a screen for reading the record. Stationary (or workstation) and portable readers and reader-printers may be used to view image records.

A **stationary reader** is a magnification device that provides a large screen for viewing and a wide choice of optional features such as a hood to reduce glare. A typical stationary reader-printer is shown in Figure 11-12.

A **portable reader** is a magnification device that is small enough to be moved easily to various locations. It usually weighs less than 10 pounds. A portable **lap reader** is often used when traveling. These readers can be powered by dry cells, by automobile battery, or operated from a vehicle cigarette lighter. Small hand-held viewers may be used for browsing microfiche but not for intensive reading.

What equipment is used to make hardcopies of microforms?

A **reader-printer** is a microform reader with the added capability of reproducing an enlarged microimage in hardcopy. Hardcopies generally range in size from 8 1/2" by 11" to as large as 18" by 24". When larger sizes are desired, an *enlarger-printer* must be used.

Figure 11-12   A Microform Reader-Printer

Image System Evaluation

To determine the best image system for implementation, organizations planning to implement microform, optical disk, CAR, CIM, COM, or COLD systems should consider answers to the following:

1. What will be the effects of the new system on the organization's efficiency and effectiveness?

2. What additional equipment and supplies will be needed?

3. What kinds of personnel training will be required?

4. What types and quantity of records will become a part of the new system?

5. What will be the implementation cost?

The records manager must continuously evaluate the new system after implementation. This evaluation requires a look at the following areas:

1. Volume of records created, maintained, and destroyed.

2. Frequency of use of records created, maintained, and destroyed.

3. Consistent application of records procedures.

4. Efficiency of microform or computer storage.

5. Equipment adequacy in meeting organization needs.

6. Records storage and operations efficiency.

What are two purposes of image system evaluation?

Evaluation serves a valuable purpose. Organizations need to know how well they are doing what they are designed to do and how they can do it better. This same axiom holds true for records systems. Records system evaluation provides a basis for continual improvement in equipment and processes.

Imaging Applications

Numerous examples of records system applications of imaging may be found in both governmental agencies and private businesses and organizations. Scanning paper records to convert them for computer access and storage and implementing COLD systems are two major changes taking place in records systems.

Why is Library of Congress material being digitized?

One major project to convert paper records to digital images is the Library of Congress National Digital Library Program.[2] The goal of this program is to digitize five million original documents dealing with American history and culture. Schools, libraries, homes, and offices in the United States and abroad can then access these documents. Books deteriorate and much of the vast Library of Congress collection is too fragile to touch. In addition, some documents are lost to theft or have been damaged through misuse. Digitization is the only hope for availability of these books and documents to the public. The collection to be electronically imaged includes one of the few surviving copies of the first printing of the Declaration of Independence.

A retail mail-order company estimated a 41 percent return on its investment in an imaging system.[3] The company was looking for a way to minimize cost of offsite storage of records and to streamline accounts payable. The business was paper-intensive and generated millions of charge slips and checks annually. Therefore, an imaging system was

[2]"Kodak Gives $1 Million to Library of Congress," *Imaging World,* Vol. 4, No. 12, December 1995, p. 1.
[3]"Imaging Dresses Up Eddie Bauer's Customer Service," *Imaging World,* Vol. 4, No. 10, November 1995, pp. 23, 55.

implemented to handle accounts payable. This system included a LAN with a file server, print server, 20-platter jukebox, five-inch optical disk drive, four indexing stations, and a scanning station. Images of checks and charge card slips were placed on the imaging system, thus, eliminating work time to locate and pull the paper file. Refiling was also eliminated with the switch to electronic storage.

In the future, more large and small organizations will apply new technologies in their workplaces. As prices decrease, the integration of image and electronic media will increase.

Summary

Microfilm and optical disks are used extensively for storage of long-term records. Integrating systems of computer technology with microfilm systems has enhanced the efficiency of creating and retrieving microfilm records. Optical disk storage, with a predicted long-term life and high-capacity storage, has enabled organizations to computerize both long-term and active records for rapid creation, retrieval, and transmission to multiple workstations. Both microfilm and optical disk storage represent considerable space savings for record storage as well as for durable, dependable records systems.

Miniaturized images of documents on roll film, microfiche, microfilm jackets, or aperture cards are called microforms. Records managers need an understanding of equipment and processes for creating high-quality microfilm images and for storing microforms in a safe and secure environment.

A microfilm records system combined with computer hardware and software is an integrated imaging system. Automated records systems have not replaced micrographics; however, the use of computer-assisted retrieval (CAR), computer-output microform (COM), and computer-input microform (CIM) systems have resulted in records management systems more responsive to organizational needs.

COLD technology (computer output to laser disk) has recently emerged as a dependable alternative to microforms. Optical disk storage is likely to double in use for the next few years. With predicted long-term storage durability, laser-created optical disks are replacing microforms in many businesses. However, microfilm records will not likely disappear. Enlarging and viewing microforms are less dependent on specific technology and, therefore, less subject to technical obsolescence. However, large organizations that need rapid creation, storage, retrieval, and transmission of records are moving to COLD installation. COLD systems capture paper documents on optical disks and permit distribution of records in electronic format through networks to various work sites.

Hybrid imaging systems combine microfilm and scanning technology with computerized records systems. Records are kept on microfilm, retrieved, digitized, and transmitted to a microcomputer for processing, printing, or sending to another site through E-mail or fax.

Imaging involves various steps throughout document preparation, processing, and use. Special equipment and procedures must be in place to ensure that documents are properly prepared for processing, appropriate camera equipment or scanners are used, records are stored in protected environments, and the documents can be rapidly retrieved and viewed.

Evaluation of image systems takes place to select an appropriate system for implementation and to improve systems that are already in operation. Collecting data on how the system will be used, capabilities of the system, expected results, and training requirements provides essential information for system selection. Determining how well the system is functioning after implementation is an ongoing evaluation and improvement process.

More and more organizations are using imaging as a means of records efficiency and improved customer service. The Library of Congress is an example of an organization undergoing a major transition of paper records to electronic imaging. Digitization of historical documents not only protects these records for future generations, but also increases their availability to the public.

Important Terms

aperture card

computer-assisted retrieval (CAR)

computer-input microfilm/
    microform (CIM)

computer-output microfilm/
    microform (COM)

computer output to laser
    disk (COLD)

contact printing

densitometer

density

hybrid imaging system

image record

image system

jukebox

lap reader

magnification ratio

microfiche

microfilm

microfilm jacket

microfilming

microform

micrographics

microimage

microrecord

optical disk library

planetary camera

portable reader

processor

reader-printer

reader-viewer

reduction ratio

resolution

rotary camera

stationary reader

step-and-repeat camera

Review and Discussion

1. Compare a microfilm system with a computer optical disk imaging system.   (Obj. 1)

2. Describe and compare four types of microforms: roll film, microfiche, microfilm jacket, and aperture card. (Obj. 2)

3. Describe four factors related to processing that affect microfilm quality.   (Obj. 3)

4. List three considerations for protecting the microfilm storage environment.   (Obj. 3)

5. Discuss the benefits of using an integrated imaging system. (Obj. 4)

6. Identify advantages of using a hybrid imaging system. (Obj. 5)

7. Discuss three major stages of an image system. (Obj. 6)

8. Discuss two primary purposes of image system evaluation and give two examples of information needed for each purpose.   (Obj. 7)

9. Describe one example of implementation of imaging applications by a business or organization and the benefits derived from this application.   (Obj. 8)

Applications (APP)

APP 11-1.   Microform Questionnaire (Objs. 2, 3, and 8)

Relate what you have studied about image records systems to their actual use by surveying businesses in your community. Determine how the various businesses and organizations use microfilm, microfiche, and aperture cards. To complete this survey:

1. Use the telephone directory and/or your knowledge of the community to compile a list of businesses, organizations, or governmental agencies that are likely users of microrecords.

2. Compile a questionnaire to identify: how microforms are used; how the microforms are produced; how these records are stored; how these records are retrieved; and the types of equipment used for preparation, storage, and retrieval.

3. Prepare a cover letter to send with the questionnaire explaining this class project and its relevance to the study in your class.

4. Develop a database plan for entering the results of the questionnaire into the computer, and design a report format for summarizing the survey results.

Critical Thinking

APP 11-2. Determine the Image System—COM or COLD (Obj. 4)

Read the following scenario and make a recommendation for adoption of a COM or COLD system for storage and retrieval of long-term records (inactive and archival records). Describe the features that you would recommend for the system selected. Write a report giving your recommendations, the analysis you made of the organization's records needs, and the rationale for your selection of records system. In developing this report, use a problem-solving approach: (1) Define the problem; (2) Gather data (outline pertinent data from the scenario); (3) Examine alternative solutions; (4) Evaluate advantages and disadvantages of each system; (5) Select the system for implementation.

Scenario

A multistate trucking company, MIT Tuff Transport, needs to provide more efficient operations and better customer service. With headquarters in Chicago and branch offices in Wichita and Miami, MIT Tuff has computer-network capability to transmit electronic mail among all three work sites. Driver trip packages are currently captured on microfilm with a rotary camera. These trip packages include delivery receipts, bills of lading, weigh tickets, and the trip envelopes. From 500 to 1,500 documents are generated daily. Matching order forms and freight bills with the trip package documents currently requires manual location on microfilm readers, although a computer-indexing system provides location codes for these documents. This company is looking for a computerized system with rapid storage and retrieval, as well as long-term records storage.

Part 5

Records Control

12 *Controlling the Records Management Program*

Part 5 provides a review of a complete records management program and a comprehensive picture of the most essential records management function—control. The coverage includes standards, control tools, and the types of controls used to evaluate a records system. Part 5 also gives practical procedures for controlling records creation related to business forms, correspondence, and copymaking.

Chapter 12

Controlling the Records Management Program

What is a standard?

The Essentials of Records Control

Control literally means to check or verify by comparison with a *standard*. A **standard** is a measure or yardstick by which the performance of a system or program is rated. In records management, controlling is an important management function in which managers measure how well their program objectives have been met and proceed to make any necessary adjustments. This chapter is about measuring—or evaluating—a records management program.

The Records Management Program

The essentials of a records management program outlined in the following list are comprehensive. In reality, a records manager's responsibilities may not include all of them. For example, some records managers' responsibilities begin with the *storage* phase of a record rather than the *creation* stage of a record's cycle. Nonetheless, a complete records management program should provide the following essentials:

What does a complete records program provide?

1. *Systematic control* over creating, handling, processing, filing, storing, retrieving, and disposing of *all media* containing business information—i.e., paper records, magnetic media, optical disks, microforms, slides, audio tapes, and videos.

2. *Adequate evidence (records) of all business activity* needed to document accurately and to protect legally the interests of the organization including its shareholders, its employees, and its clients.

3. *Uniform policies and procedures* for identifying, storing, and retaining every type of records medium used. Records need to be classified and indexed so that they can be identified and retrieved quickly and accurately.

4. *Systematic and accurate distribution of and access to* records used in day-to-day operations, while still controlling access to confidential information.

5. *Protection for all records* from accidental loss and disaster; a disaster prevention and recovery plan, which protects vital and historical records and those records needed for business continuity if such a plan becomes necessary.

6. *A records appraisal process* that results in a retention and destruction program developed after consulting program users, corporate attorneys, and auditors to ensure that user needs and legal requirements are met.

7. *Cost, efficiency, and performance controls* to evaluate *personnel, space use, equipment needs, and procedures.* Such controls result in reduced labor costs, space requirements, and number of lost and misfiled records, while they increase response time to requested information.

8. *Training and education* to assure that all users are familiar with the program and are made aware of any program changes.

Tools for Control

In effective records systems, controls are used widely. At the outset, records managers develop policies and standards for operating their programs—the management functions of planning and organizing. From that point, all the main elements in the records system are involved with control.

To achieve control in a records program, records managers use tools that include the records inventory, records retention schedule, records audit, disaster prevention and recovery plan, and the records management manual.

What are some records control tools?

Records Inventory. Before a records manager can decide what records to retain, a records inventory must be taken. A records inventory is a survey that provides a detailed listing of an organization's records. The inventory includes quantity, type, function, location, and frequency of use of the records surveyed. Chapter 6 explains the records inventory and the benefits that can be achieved from such a survey.

Records Retention Schedule. A basic records control tool is the records retention schedule, a listing of an organization's records along with the stated length of time the records must be kept. The records retention schedule is illustrated and discussed in Chapter 6.

To better manage the records retention schedule as a control tool, records managers can choose among several types of available computer application software. Some software programs focus only on maintaining and distributing the contents of the schedule; other programs are more comprehensive and help manage active and inactive records systems according to the organization's retention schedule. PC software is available for automating many functions of a records program. Vendors such as Automated Records Management Systems, Smead®, and Tab Products, Inc., offer PC-based software designed to automate functions of a corporate or commercial records center. Separate packages are available specifically for automating retention schedules. *Criteria for Developing/ Evaluating Records Management Software*, an ARMA International publication, provides basic information on the selection of software intended to automate records management functions. (The discussion on electronic document management systems [EDMS] in "Current Trends in Records Management" includes a checklist for selecting an integrated document management system.)

Records Audit. A **records audit** is a regular examination of the records management program to determine how well it is functioning. From the audit, managers hope to find ways of improving the program's performance. Large organizations may use their own technically trained staff to undertake such an audit, or they may hire outside consultants (usually having more objectivity and expertise) for this purpose. Because they usually have no qualified records auditor on staff, small firms commonly use the services of outside auditors.

What does a records audit provide?

The records audit provides three kinds of information about the records management program:

1. *Information about the present operations.* This information includes how well the program's objectives are being achieved; whether written policies and procedures are available and followed by all personnel; whether policies and procedures actually reflect the way documents are processed; and the scope of records management activities and any problems associated with them.

2. *Analysis of the present system and its needs.* This analysis includes the layout of the files; the effectiveness and validity of policies and procedures; the qualifications of the staff; the uses of the available equipment; active and inactive storage systems; costs of operating the system versus projected costs; and security measures taken for preserving and protecting records.

3. *Recommended solutions for improving the program.* These solutions also include cost estimates for putting the recommendations into practice.

Disaster Prevention and Recovery Plan. Also referred to as *contingency planning*, a **disaster prevention and recovery plan** is a written and approved plan detailing how records will be handled in a disaster prior to, during, and after in the recovery stage. The plan also establishes *procedures* for the immediate resumption of business operations after a disaster. How an organization prepares for a disruption to its

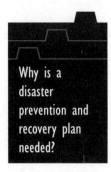

Why is a disaster prevention and recovery plan needed?

business determines how well, or if, it survives. As a result of the 1992 Chicago River tunnel flood, 150 companies based in downtown Chicago went out of business. Flooding is the most common cause of business interruptions, followed by equipment outage, power outage, fire or explosion, earthquake, hurricane, and building outage resulting from construction or from environmental problems.

Florida's Hurricane Andrew, the California earthquakes, the World Trade Center bombing in New York City, and the Federal Office Building bombing in Oklahoma City have alerted all businesses to the critical importance of a disaster prevention and recovery plan. A business continuity plan should consider all steps necessary to keep a company operational in the event of a disaster. These steps include the following:

1. Form a crisis management team with each member given specific responsibilities in the event of a disaster.

2. Identify vital, mission-critical information and identify salvage techniques or other means of recovering critical information.

3. Estimate the cost of various types and lengths of disruptions.

4. Provide for offsite storage for vital records and backup computer data storage.

5. Designate alternative sites for critical tasks, including computer and computer-related operations.

6. Establish procedures for communicating the plan throughout the organization.

7. Periodically test the plan through mock disasters and make appropriate changes.

Natural disasters do not cause all losses of records. Records can be lost and/or damaged simply when necessary precautions are not taken to protect them. Small precautions are taken routinely to protect electronic data such as controlling extremes in temperature and humidity, backing up high-value data, installing antivirus programs that detect and remove computer viruses, installing surge protectors to minimize damage caused by electrical variances, and removing magnetic items from around hard drives and floppy disks. Records protection, records safety, and records security are covered in Chapters 10 and 11. The discussions in Chapters

10 and 11 include procedures for (1) controlling and protecting all records from physical hazards existing in an office environment, (2) controlling the physical environmental office conditions necessary to ensure safe storage of all records, and (3) protecting records from unauthorized access.

The test of a sound disaster prevention and recovery plan—and any other precautionary procedures and safety measures taken to protect records and business operations—is one that allows business activity to resume within a few days after a disaster. Such a plan includes *not only* a recovery of records, *but also* a recovery of the work site, essential equipment, and the work force.[1]

Records Management Manual. The most important control reference for a records management staff is the **records management manual**. Especially useful in conducting the records audit, this manual is the official handbook of approved policies and procedures for operating the records management program. Such a manual also establishes responsibility for the various phases of the program, standardizes operating procedures, and aids in training employees.[2] The contents of a typical records management manual established by a large firm are listed as follows:

What is a records management manual?

Main Sections	Section Contents
1. The records program	Definition, goals, policies, and personnel responsibilities
2. Main phases of the records program	Records classifications, alphabetic index, records retention schedules
3. Records codes	Records classification codes, retention and disposition codes
4. Types of files in the records system	Subject files, case/project files, special files
5. Retention schedule	Permanent records, semipermanent records, and short-term storage records

---

[1]Susan L. Bulgawicz and Dr. Charles E. Nolan, *Disaster Prevention and Recovery: A Planned Approach* (Prairie Village, KS: ARMA International, 1988).

[2]For excellent, detailed coverage of manuals, see Betty R. Ricks, Ann J. Swafford, and Kay F. Gow, *Information and Image Management: A Records Systems Approach*, 3d ed. (Cincinnati: South-Western Publishing Co., 1992), Chapter 19.

6. Records storage	Department sites, central sites, offsite locations
7. Annual program evaluation	Purposes and requirements of each program evaluation

8. Creation criteria and storage procedures for
  a. Paper records
  b. Microimage records
  c. Electronic records
	What to store and when, preparing records for storage, classifying and coding, preparing cross-references, sorting records, placing records in storage, restricting access to records, retrieval suggestions, charge-out system, and folders and storage container maintenance

9. Records disposition	Disposition functions, implementing retention schedules, packing records and labeling boxes, retrieving inactive records from storage, destroying records in inactive storage
10. Records manual: distribution, maintenance, and use	General policies and procedures, records classifications, records schedules, and administrative responsibilities

Types of Control

Three specific types of ongoing controls are efficiency controls, cost controls, and performance controls. When these controls are applied to *people, storage space, filing equipment, and routine procedures*, they become key elements that make a records management program function effectively. Inherent in all controls is the **benefit/cost ratio**, a comparison to determine that *every cost originated (input) results in an equal or greater benefit (output)*. When applied, the benefit/cost ratio gives guidance and purpose to the process of efficiency, cost, and performance controls.

Efficiency Control. An **efficiency control** evaluates the ability to produce a desired effect with a minimum of time, energy, and space. When efficiency controls are applied to filing and electronic equipment, many possibilities surface for delivering faster output of data, documents, and paper records while conserving time, energy, and space. For example, the laptop computer today stores more data and manipulates data faster than earlier computers that once filled entire rooms. The multifunctional products described in "Current Trends in Records Management" demonstrate a current craze for doing more with less—efficiency control!

Efficiency controls also include measuring filers' speed and accuracy and developing standards from such measurements. Practical standards for storing and retrieving records are developed by answering three important questions: (1) How much time is required to store a record from the time such storage is authorized? (2) How much time is required to retrieve a record from storage? and (3) What is the expected **turnaround time** (the amount of time required to find and deliver a record to the requester after the request for the record has been made)? Time standards will depend on whether a task is performed manually or electronically. Also, times may vary among organizations because of types of records stored, storage facilities and equipment selected, and filers' skills. The three questions can be directly related to the published standards for manual storage and retrieval systems, such as those outlined in Figure 12-1, which large firms and standards associations have developed. Efficiency controls have value and include both *efficiency standards* and *efficiency ratios*.

What are two efficiency controls?

Efficiency Standards. Because providing needed information is the main function of any records program, the most important test of any records system is the speed with which stored information can be located. Efficiency standards that are used to measure the filers' ability to locate information include the following:

1. The number of misfiles, usually about 3 percent of the total records filed.

2. The number of "can't find" items, which one authority suggests is excessive at a 1 percent level.

3. The time required to find items, which should never exceed 2 to 3 minutes.

At least once a year an office or records manager should check the efficiency of a records program. In addition to the three efficiency

TASK	TIME UNIT (*h = hour; m = minute*)
Manual Systems	
Code typical one-page letter	200/h
Type folder labels	100/h
Sort 5" by 3" cards	300/h
Sort invoices into 3-digit numeric sequence	1,500/h
Sort coded letters	250/h
Place cards in alphabetic file	300/h
Place records in subject file	150/h
Place vouchers in numeric file	250/h
Retrieve record from color-coded file	2.5/m
Retrieve daily report	.5/m
Retrieve 5" by 3" cards	180/h
Retrieve correspondence and prepare charge-out records	70/h
Automated Systems	
Store and retrieve files: Depends on *access time* (the number of microseconds of time required of a specific computer to store and retrieve data).	

Figure 12-1   Records Storage and Retrieval Standards

standards mentioned above, other measures to check include: (1) the number of records retrieved compared to the total cubic feet of stored records, (2) the number of records received (in number of records or in cubic feet of space occupied), (3) the amount of space being used for records compared to the total square feet of floor space, (4) how much unused space is available, (5) how often records are requested from the files, (6) how much equipment is (or is not) being used, and (7) how many records have been destroyed or transferred from active to inactive storage.

Efficiency Ratios.   An **efficiency ratio** is a standard for measuring the efficiency of various aspects of records systems. Ratios provide records managers with a quantifiable means of measuring efficiency, progress or decline in efficiency, and the ability to either establish an efficiency or to compare their organization's efficiency against another's. The most useful ratios relate to: (1) the **activity ratio**, (2) the **accuracy ratio**, and (3) the **retrieval efficiency ratio**. These ratios are explained in Figure 12-2.

> **What are three efficiency ratios?**

TYPE OF RATIO	HOW RATIO IS COMPUTED
1. **Activity ratio** (measures the frequency of records use)	$$\frac{\text{Number of records requested}}{\text{Number of records filed}}$$ Example: 500 records requested; 5,000 records filed or a 10% activity ratio. (When the ratio is below 5%, all records in the file that fall below 5% should be transferred to inactive storage or destroyed.)
2. **Accuracy ratio** (measures the ability of filers to find requested records)	$$\frac{\text{Number of records found}}{\text{Number of records requested}}$$ Example: 5,950 records found, 6,000 records requested, or a 99.17% accuracy ratio. (When the ratio falls below 97%, the records system needs immediate attention.)
3. **Retrieval efficiency ratio** (measures the speed with which records are found and verifies how filers spend their time)	$$\frac{\text{Time to locate records}}{\text{Number of records retrieved}}$$ Example: A ratio of 75% (retrieving 80 records in 60 minutes) suggests an efficient records system and a productive filer, depending on the type of files and filing conditions.

Figure 12-2   **Efficiency Ratios for a Records System**

Cost Control.   The volume of paper records pointed out in Chapter 1 carries with it tremendous costs. These costs are illustrated in Figure 12-3 and are estimated as follows:[3]

80%   Salaries of managers, supervisors, and operating personnel working directly with records.

---

[3]*Shelf Filing Systems for Modern Records Management,* Smead® Manufacturing Company brochure, 1993, p. 2.

5% Space occupied by records systems, including personnel.
11% Equipment used in the records system.
4% Supplies.

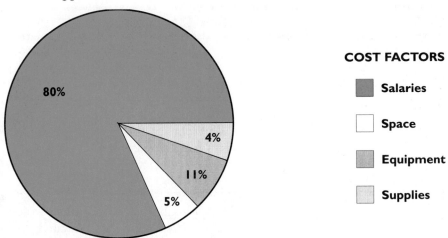

Figure 12-3 **Records Management Costs**

Because labor costs represent about three-fourths of total records management costs, the greatest potential for controlling costs is by controlling people costs. This cost factor includes managerial, supervisory, and operating personnel salaries, along with the employee benefits—retirement plans, social security contributions, and health insurance, to name a few. Reducing long-term labor costs by installing automated systems should not be overlooked. Converting from a manual to an automated records system may require a large, initial capital investment, but the benefits of automating a records program might significantly reduce labor costs in the long term (cost/benefit ratio!).

Records systems studies point out many opportunities for identifying and reducing costs. The steps commonly taken to reduce costs include the following:

How are records costs controlled?

1. *Identify all the elements in the four cost categories mentioned earlier.*

2. *Assign cost figures to the elements in the records system.* These elements include hourly rates for all records personnel and costs of the equipment and the space that it occupies. Thus, the costs of maintaining typical files (such as five-drawer vertical cabinet files) can be computed and used in many cost-reduction studies.

3. *Compare the labor costs of storing and retrieving records in the organization with estimated costs of alternative systems.* For example, apply the cost/benefit ratio to filing equipment that requires less floor space cost or to automated equipment that reduces storage and retrieval time and requires fewer filers.

Costs of equipment, space, and supplies can be controlled by (1) eliminating unnecessary records, (2) carefully supervising the use of equipment and supplies, and (3) selecting equipment and media that require smaller amounts of space and less time to operate (see multifunctional equipment mentioned later under "Current Trends in Records Management"). Another opportunity for reducing labor costs can be realized by implementing performance standards. The performance of employees can then be measured against these standards.

Performance Control.   The attitudes that each records employee brings to the job affect performance standards. In addition to the efficiency and cost controls discussed earlier, each of the following aspects of human behavior needs to be controlled in the records system:

Why control performance?

1. Poor attendance records of workers (frequent tardiness and absences).

2. Excessive need for overtime work.

3. Numbers and patterns of errors in each employee's work.

4. Slow response to work assignments.

5. Low morale and lack of interest in the work assigned.

6. Lack of concern for, or inability to follow, budget limits.

7. Repeated failure to meet performance standards.

Supervisors should discuss these performance problems with their employees. By working together in this way, they can develop solutions for increasing productivity in the records system.

Controlling Records Creation

From your study of records management up to this time, one point should stand out: *All work in the office centers around information and records.*

Because most records are paper records, records control systems deal largely with methods of controlling records creation.

Ideally, the records manager is involved with records from their creation to their destruction. Unfortunately, this is not always true. For if it were, the records manager's involvement with records creation would begin by controlling paper *selection*. The cost-conscious records manager realizes that various documents require different paper qualities. Whether the document is one- or two-sided, whether the document is for internal or external use, or whether the document contains graphics and requires sharp details—all these requirements affect paper selection and ultimately the total cost of operating a records management program.

How does paper selection affect cost?

To control records creation beyond paper selection, the records manager must influence those who are responsible for creating and using the records; namely, the records originators, records receivers, and the administrative support staff who distributes and manages the records. Records originators need to be reminded that the most expensive cost in a record's cycle is incurred at its creation stage and need to be urged to exercise restraint at this time. Also, records receivers and the administrative staff need to distinguish records that are required for documentation from those that can be destroyed. The easiest way to control records costs is to reduce the number of records that enter the system in the first place by destroying those records that are *not* needed and by controlling only those that are needed. The importance of controlling business forms, correspondence, and extra copies is addressed in this section.

Controlling Business Forms

The **business form**, a standardized record used to collect and transmit information in a uniform manner, is used within or among departments or between organizations. The records manager's responsibilities include controlling business forms. In large organizations that use many forms, this responsibility may be delegated to a forms manager and staff who are part of the records management program. See Appendix A for more about forms management positions.

A form contains two types of data: (1) **constant data** that are printed on a form and, therefore, do not require rewriting each time the form is filled in (such as the word "date" and the phrase "Pay to the order of" on a bank check); and (2) **variable data** that change each time a form is filled in. Examples of variable data on a bank check are the filled-in date, the payee's name, the amount of money, and the signature.

Goals of Forms Control Programs.   Large firms use thousands of forms for recording information. To ensure that these forms are efficiently and economically used, company-wide programs to control all phases of forms work are developed. Typical goals of forms control programs are to:

Why control
business forms?

1. *Determine the number and use of forms.* This step occurs as a part of the records inventory.

2. *Eliminate unnecessary forms.* This goal includes: (a) eliminating forms that overlap or duplicate each other by combining them, (b) eliminating forms that collect unused information, and (c) eliminating forms that are no longer needed.

3. *Standardize form size, paper quality, and design features such as logos and form numbers.* Standardization results in lower form costs.

4. *Ensure efficient forms design.* Sound design principles must be applied.

5. *Establish efficient, economical procedures for printing, storing, and distributing forms.* These procedures should include an inventory control program to allow sufficient time to renew forms before reordering them.

Types of Forms.   Forms are produced in several types of construction and are used for many different purposes. *Single-copy forms*, called "cut sheets," such as telephone message forms are used within one department for its own needs. *Multiple-copy forms*, called "unit sets" or "snap sets," such as a four-copy purchase order are used to transmit information outside the "creating" department. These preassembled sets of forms are perforated for easy removal of each copy. *Continuous forms* with punched holes in the left and right margins are used in computer printers for high-volume usage. In automated records systems, *electronic forms*, created by special forms design software, appear on terminal screens for the input of data from the keyboard. Unlike paper forms, electronic forms are not printed and stocked. Instead, they are designed, filled in, and either transmitted to another workstation or printed out.

Design of Forms.   Efficiency in the design of forms requires that well-tested guidelines be applied to the design. In the case of a business form, the designer must understand (1) how the form will be used; (2) the types of items to be filled in and their sequence; (3) the size, color, and weight of paper stock to be used; and (4) the amount of space needed for each "fill-in."

The main objectives in forms design are to make the form efficient to fill in (whether manually or electronically), efficient to read and under-stand, and *efficient to store and retrieve.* These objectives can be met by applying the design guidelines shown in Figure 12-4. Study carefully the application of each guideline that appears in the right column.

Although forms design should be left to the experts, forms design books and computer application software have turned computer opera-tors into "overnight" forms designers.[4] Computer forms software is available from many vendors. For example, WordPerfect 6.1 includes templates for over 30 commonly used forms. The forms (or templates) include a purchase order, invoice, cost estimate, invoice, job application, five different memo styles, etc. Figure 12-5 shows forms that can be individualized to meet specific needs. WordPerfect also has a specialized forms design software program called *Informs.* Specialized software programs for forms design such as this one have features that make designing forms more convenient. Features include grids to help with form layout and a variety of typefaces. Drawing horizontal and vertical lines, shading, creating rounded corners, and other graphic features make these programs useful to forms designers and are especially beneficial when applied to forms that require frequent updating.

Cost of Forms.   Because the cost of the paper and ink to print forms are tangible (physical) items, they often attract the most attention in trying to control the cost of business forms. Actually, the cost of *using* forms, estimated to be as high as 40 times the physical cost, is the place to look for cost savings. Such costs include users' fill-in time, processing costs, and costs of acquiring, storing, retrieving, and distributing the forms. Each of these costs is mainly related to various types of labor.

Purchase of Forms. When new forms are needed, they may be purchased from office supply stores. Examples of such forms are

What determines a well-designed form?

How are forms costs controlled?

---

[4]Marvin Jacobs and Linda I. Studer, *Forms Design II: The Course for Paper and Electronic Forms* (Prairie Village, KS: ARMA International, 1991). This text provides step-by-step instructions for designing professional, efficient paper and electronic forms.

GUIDELINES		APPLICATIONS	
GUIDELINE 1:	Design the form with the user in mind.	1.1	Use a different color for each department receiving its own copy of the form.
		1.2	Use heavy card stock for forms to be used out-of-doors or subject to large-volume indoor use.
GUIDELINE 2:	Keep the design simple by eliminating excessive graphic features such as borders and drawings and unnecessary or unlawful information.	2.1	Don't ask for age and date of birth even when this information must be obtained.
		2.2	Place instructions for filling in the form at the top and instructions for its distribution at the bottom.
		2.3	Don't request information that may be personal or used for illegal purposes (religion, ethnic background, etc.).
		2.4	Don't use horizontal ruled lines when the fill-in is to be typewritten or printed by computer.
GUIDELINE 3:	For proper identification, give each form a name that designates its function and a number that shows its sequence within the creating department. The date of the form's revision should also be included in the number.	3.1	Name: Sales Invoice (*not* Sales Invoice Form).
		3.2	Number: S-15(11/96)—to identify the 15th form in the Sales Department last printed 11/96.
GUIDELINE 4:	Use standard paper stock size and standard typefaces.	4.1	Use card/paper sizes that may be cut from standard 17" by 22" mill-size stock without waste. Standard paper sizes such as 5" by 3", 6" by 4", 8" by 5", and 8 1/2" by 11" are economical to buy, use, and store.
		4.2	Use sans serif typeface for captions and serif for text.
GUIDELINE 5:	Arrange items on the form in the same order in which data will be filled in or extracted from the form.	5.1	Information on purchase orders is usually copied directly from approved purchase requisitions. In designing purchase order forms, use the same order of data as that shown on the purchase requisition.
		5.2	Use the normal reading pattern of left to right and top to bottom to sequence items.
GUIDELINE 6:	Preprint constant data to keep fill-in (variable data) to a minimum and to allow fill-in to stand out clearly.	6.1	Use black printing on form for scanning (optical) and microfilm processing.
		6.2	Use print size smaller than elite spacing on a standard typewriter or printer, which draws the reader's attention to the fill-in.
GUIDELINE 7:	Adapt spacing to the method of fill-in (handwritten or machine) allowing sufficient space. (Computer software controls the spacing on computer forms.)	7.1	For handwriting, use a minimum of one inch for every five characters.
		7.2	For typewriting or machine fill-in, allow double vertical spacing (1/3").
GUIDELINE 8:	Use check boxes to minimize fill-ins and to save time.	8.1	Poor design: Married? ___yes___ Gender? ___male___
		8.2	Good design: Marital Status ❑ single ☑ married ❑ widowed ❑ divorced / Gender ❑ female ☑ male
GUIDELINE 9:	Locate filing or routing information properly to speed retrieval of the form.	9.1	Place filing information on the bottom of the form.
GUIDELINE 10:	Use the box design style rather than caption-on-the-line or caption-under-the-line for constant data.	10.1	Poor design: Name _____ Address _____ Good design: Name / Address
GUIDELINE 11:	Key captions in uppercase; key text in upper- and lowercase.	11.1	Instructions that appear in several lines or paragraphs are more easily read in lowercase and initial caps.

Figure 12-4 **Forms Design Guidelines**

Invoice

Invoice Number: [Invoice Number]
Date: February 7, 19 --

<Organization>
<Address>
<City, State Zip>
<Telephone>
Fax: <Fax>

To:

Ship to (if different address):

SALESPERSON	ORDER NO.	DATE SHIPPED	SHIPPED VIA	F.O.B.	TERMS
[Salesperson]	[Purchase Order Number]	[Date Shipped]	[Shipped Via]	[F.O.B.]	[Terms]

QTY.	DESCRIPTION	UNIT PRICE	TOTAL
			0.00
			0.00
			0.00
			0.00
			0.00
			0.00
			0.00

SUBTOTAL	0.00
SALES TAX RATE %	
SALES TAX	0.00
SHIPPING & HANDLING	
TOTAL DUE	$0.00

THANK YOU FOR YOUR ORDER!

Purchase Order

P. O. Number: [Purchase Order Number]

<Organization>
<Address>
<City, State Zip>
<Telephone>
Fax: <Fax>

To:

Ship to (if different address):

P.O. DATE	PLACED BY	DATE EXPECTED	SHIP VIA	F.O.B.	TERMS
Feb 7, 19 - -	[Order Placed By]	[Date Expected]	[Ship Via]	[F.O.B.]	[Terms]

QTY.	DESCRIPTION	UNIT PRICE	TOTAL
			0.00
			0.00
			0.00
			0.00
			0.00
			0.00
			0.00

SHIPPING & HANDLING	
SUBTOTAL	0.00
SALES TAX RATE %	
SALES TAX	0.00
TOTAL DUE	$0.00

Authorized Signature

Figure 12-5   Computer Forms Samples

statements or invoices, telephone message forms, purchase requisitions, and sales receipts. Buying standard forms is less expensive than custom-designed forms so long as a standard form meets the needs of the office. As you have already seen, some word processing programs and special forms software provide the necessary tools for producing professional-looking forms that can be tailored to individual needs.

Standardized forms will continue to be used in large numbers because they are capable of handling large quantities of information in the least amount of time, effort, and space. As forms continue to be an efficient way of gathering and transmitting information, their design, use, cost, and storage shall require managerial approval and periodic evaluation. Forms management software is available to help in this regard, and organizations that make use of these software packages have a more efficient and productive forms management program.

Controlling Correspondence

Correspondence usually refers to two types of records—external messages written to and from people or organizations outside the organization and internal messages or memos that convey written messages among the firm's departments. Fax messages and Internet messages sent and received may be either internal or external messages. For example, E-mail and fax messages may be sent to a branch office or to an outside company. The total system of producing correspondence includes composing the message (dictating, handwriting, or composing at the keyboard), transcribing or formatting into final copy, and transmitting or mailing the correspondence.

Labor costs of dictating and transcribing correspondence comprise a major portion of correspondence costs. Yet, computer online costs and electronic equipment costs for E-mail and fax communications also need to be considered as more businesses invest in high-tech networking systems to move information more rapidly.

Dartnell Corporation of Chicago provides annual reports of business-letter costs. Over the years, its reports have shown a steady increase in the cost of producing a letter dictated face to face. In 1960, the cost was $1.83. By 1970, this cost had risen to $3.05; in 1990, $10.85; in 1994, $19.15; and in 1995, $19.87.[5]

---

[5]*Dartnell Target Survey, 1995,* The Dartnell Institute of Business Research, Chicago, IL.

For this study, the cost of producing a one-page, 185-word business letter is based on (1) dictation time and method and (2) transcription time and method. Labor costs represent over 60 percent of total cost. When the same letter is dictated to a machine or when a personal computer rather than an electric typewriter is used, the total cost of the letter is reduced over 25 percent.[6]

In correspondence systems, specific costs related to the production of letters and reports include salary and time of dictator, salary and time of assistant taking dictation and transcribing the correspondence, nonproductive labor (waiting time, interruptions, etc.), fixed costs (rent, taxes, overhead including supervision, and fringe benefits), materials costs (stationery, etc.), and mailing costs (postage, gathering, sealing, stamping, and sorting). Labor time accounts for the greatest percentage of total costs. Because correspondence accounts for such a large portion of all stored documents, their creation, distribution, use, and storage require close examination and evaluation. Originators can exercise restraint in their use of correspondence by seeking alternative, less expensive means of communicating such as a telephone call. The only alternative to controlling correspondence is to ensure that such documents are being produced, distributed, and stored by the most economical and efficient means.

How are correspondence costs controlled?

Many of the automatic features of word processing software save valuable time for the office staff. Some of the most used features include automatic centering, decimal alignment, indentation, detection and correction of spelling errors, and substitution of one word for another throughout an entire stored message. Automated equipment saves the time of dictators, or word originators, by storing form letters. Commonly used paragraphs, letterheads, special letter parts, special forms, and a variety of text data and graphics can be indexed and electronically stored and retrieved as needed. These stored data not only control the content of office correspondence, but they also reduce the time required to create the documents.

Controlling correspondence includes evaluating the tasks of creating, distributing, using, storing, and eventually disposing of correspondence and then looking for the most economical ways of accomplishing these tasks. However, the ultimate goal of controlling correspondence is to reduce the number of records that must be stored and maintained.

[6]*Ibid.*

Controlling Copying of Records

Computers and photocopiers turn out records by the millions, many of which are unnecessary and add to office expenses. To control copymaking costs, records managers are conscious of this overriding point: *Every cost originated should result in an equal or greater benefit*—the benefit/cost ratio mentioned earlier. In other words, when the benefits realized are divided by the cost, the result should be 1 or greater. Records employees, therefore, need to identify all costs of creating and copying records (personnel, equipment, supplies, space, and so on) already mentioned. In addition, they should uncover hidden costs, including the costs of ordering supplies, filing equipment for records storage, and mailing.

Why control copymaking costs?

Many simple ideas have been developed to control copymaking costs. Examples include: (1) selecting the most suitable—and least expensive—methods and supplies; (2) eliminating an unnecessary variety of copier models, which may add to maintenance costs; (3) computing per-copy costs regularly; and (4) charging all copymaking costs to the department involved (called *chargeback*). Even tighter controls over copiers are possible by securing the approval of a supervisor before making copies and by installing copiers that require the use of a key or access card to unlock and use the machine. Such a machine may also record the job number, the number of copies made, and a reference for charging the copy costs to the using department. The computer can then regularly process usage reports.

No one piece of equipment creates more copies (and often unnecessary copies) with greater speed than the photocopier. Because producing extra copies of documents and reports can easily become standard practice in an office, photocopying is an important part of the total control process.

Current Trends in Records Management

Two exciting trends to track in the years ahead are multifunctional products and integrated document management systems. Both technologies show a trend toward the functions of borrowing and merging.

Multifunctional Products

A **multifunctional product** combines two or more functions into one piece of equipment. In reality, however, multifunctional equipment generally integrates three or four functions but can combine six or more—i.e., the computer printer that is also capable of faxing, copying, and scanning. Added features might include a telephone and a PC-based faxing feature—the ability to fax directly from a personal computer. The ability to perform all tasks from one piece of equipment certainly saves time and space. However, congestion around one piece of equipment may result in large offices where many workers are performing different tasks, and the equipment may not be cost-effective at all.

Scanning or copying a conventional faxed document is not new. However, when information can be converted into a single, high-quality digital file without the need for rekeying, the quality of faxing and copying outputs is enhanced. Xerox offers the Document WorkCenter™ Pro 250, which is available in a number of combinations, depending on the quality desired, so that printing, faxing, scanning, copying and PC faxing result in very high-quality laser printing (see Figure 12-6).

> **What are multifunctional products?**

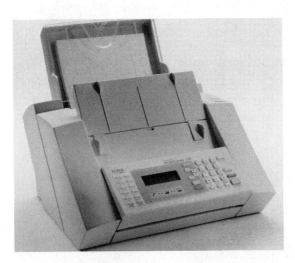

Courtesy of Xerox Corporation

Figure 12-6   Xerox Document WorkCenter™ Pro 250

Integrated Document Management Systems

Large paper filing systems can be costly and inefficient. As paper systems slowly migrate to computer systems, records managers will search ways to automate their information storage and retrieval systems. Referred to as **integrated document management systems (IDMS)**, these computer systems link paper, imaged, and electronic documents into one flexible and expandable document management system. These systems allow for a gradual conversion from paper to electronic and image records storage while promising to integrate all information media. Digital images, raw data, facsimile transmission, E-mail, sound or video clips, and paper records can be linked through a single indexing and retrieval application. Color-coded labels are prepared with filenames, bar codes, and color codes on adhesive labels as needed. Bar code technology used on both paper and imaged documents allows all records to be indexed, tracked, and retrieved through a single-user application.

What is IDMS?

Simultaneous, remote access to scanned documents by multiple users is possible through the scanning and network features of some systems. All authorized users on the network can index, store, retrieve, print, or fax records. Fax messages are captured, stored, routed, or refaxed, eliminating the need for hardcopies. Once retention and destruction parameters are defined, users can maintain electronic and hardcopy records in compliance with retention schedules. The use of bar code technology and remote scanners provides automatic charge-out and follow-up of all hardcopy records. Electronic documents can be stored on optical as well as on electronic media, and raw data can be automatically and instantly located via searches on computer output to laser disk (COLD).

Document management software can do as much as you want it to do and can cost from hundreds of dollars to hundreds of thousands of dollars. Therefore, when selecting software, compare and evaluate carefully the needs of your records program with a checklist of software features. The checklist in Figure 12-7 not only serves as a comprehensive checklist when selecting software, but it also demonstrates the power of integrated document management systems.[7]

[7]"Document Management Software: Make Sure What You Get Is What You Need," *Modern Office Technology*, 1992, p. 38.

❑ Log in new files or documents
❑ Index files or documents
❑ Print file folder labels
❑ Print bar codes
❑ Scan/log documents out and in
❑ Find files/documents along the paper-work route
❑ Track active files, inactive files, historical and vital records, offsite storage
❑ Produce transfer notices
❑ Track nonpaper documents such as tapes, PC disks, hard disks, microforms, optical media, a/v material, drawings, etc.
❑ Perform searches such as key word or full text index, multiple field, boolean, etc.
❑ Ability to add new index fields or to redefine existing ones
❑ Wait lists/flags for files or documents
❑ Generate file activity reports by location, department, and/or user, and of delin-quent, overdue files/documents

❑ Generate inventory reports (by user, department, project number, contract number, etc.)
❑ Audit trail of activity
❑ Chargeback billing data
❑ Records retention and disposal guidelines
❑ Generate destruction procedures (authorizations, destruction certifications, etc.)
❑ Help screens
❑ Security and password provisions for both stand-alone and network systems
❑ Interface to COM, CAR, COLD, and document imaging systems
❑ Operator's manual and documentation; tutorial disk
❑ Installation support
❑ Service support
❑ Online or hotline help
❑ Training

Figure 12-7 Checklist for Selecting an Integrated Document Management System

Summary

To control a records management program, you must understand the essential aspects of a records program and the management function of controlling. Tools for controlling a records management program include a records inventory, records retention schedule, records audit, disaster prevention and recovery plan, and a records management manual. To provide information quickly and at the lowest possible cost, apply efficiency, cost, and performance controls to records management personnel, space requirements, equipment, and procedures.

Controlling records creation is an important part of the overall control process because more records are stored on paper than on any other storage medium. Give careful attention in the control process to business forms and correspondence because they comprise a large part of paper records storage. Seek ways to minimize the costs of creating, distributing, and storing these kinds of records. Copies not only produce excessive records, but they also sometimes contribute unnecessar-

ily to a paper storage problem and, therefore, need control as well. Multifunctional equipment and electronic document management systems are technology trends that require benefit/cost evaluations in support of them.

The guidelines discussed in this chapter are intended to acquaint you with the many aspects involved in controlling a records management program and are offered as a basis from which to grow. Your success as an office worker into the next century will depend on your ability to manage records better. To contribute in this regard, you need to know all you can about filing methods and filing procedures. Study the chapters in this text on the technology that has eased the burden of paper records storage and retrieval. Know as much as you can about new storage equipment, supplies, and technology so that you can make a difference in the office where you will work. Ways and means to improve productivity, to cut personnel requirements, to save space, to reduce equipment and supply costs, and to reduce or eliminate lost or misfiled documents will be important objectives for all office workers in the years ahead.

Important Terms

accuracy ratio

activity ratio

benefit/cost ratio

business form

constant data

control

disaster prevention and recovery plan

efficiency control

efficiency ratio

integrated document management
   systems (IDMS)

multifunctional product

records audit

records management manual

retrieval efficiency ratio

standard

turnaround time

variable data

Review and Discussion

1. Define *control* as a management function. (Obj. 1)
2. List three essentials of a well-developed records management program. (Obj. 2)
3. List the five control tools commonly used in a records management program. Explain how they function as tools in controlling a records program. (Obj. 3)
4. Describe efficiency, cost, and performance controls and explain how each assists in the control of a records management program. (Obj. 4)

5. What do the three efficiency ratios (activity, accuracy, and records retrieval) measure? How is each ratio computed? (Obj. 4)

6. What are the major costs involved in records management programs? How does each cost compare with the other costs in terms of its proportionate share of total costs? (Obj. 5)

7. Identify the major costs of records management programs and explain how these costs can be controlled. (Obj. 5)

8. Name three objectives of a forms control program. (Obj. 6)

9. Why is forms design so important in achieving control in a records system? How have computers affected forms design? (Obj. 6)

10. List at least three guidelines to follow when constructing a well-designed form. (Obj. 7)

11. Identify the major costs involved in producing correspondence. How can such costs be reduced? (Obj. 8)

12. What suggestions do you have for controlling copymaking costs? (Obj. 9)

13. How can the use of multifunctional equipment reduce costs? (Obj. 10)

14. How can the use of integrated document management systems reduce costs? (Obj. 10)

Applications (APP)

Critical Thinking

APP 12-1. *Designing a New Video Rental Application Form (Objs. 8 and 9)*

You work part-time for EVC (Electric Video Center), a local video rental store. A form is needed to gather information from customers who rent movie and music videos. The information gathered will be keyed into a computer database *in the following order*:

(1) account no.; (2) customer name, address, and telephone number; (3) how long at present address; (4) name of friend or close relative, address, and telephone number; (5) date of the application; (6) movie video preference—i.e., science fiction, romance, western, classic, drama, psychodrama, adventure; (7) a signature line preceded by "I agree to all EVC video rental terms and conditions."; and (8) a short application approval line for the manager's initials (Approved _____).

Your employer designed the following form and asks you to improve it if you can.

Customer Name _____ Acct. No._____

Customer Address _____

How Long at Present Address? _____ Telephone No. _____

_____

Name of Close Friend or Relative

_____

Address of Close Friend or Relative

List your movie video preferences: science fiction, romance, western, classic, drama, adventure, psychodrama.

_____

I agree to all EVC video rental terms and conditions.

            _____
            Signature

                        Approved _____

Apply the forms design guidelines presented in this chapter to design a better form that will meet the video store's needs. Be sure to include in your form all needed data for input into the store's computer database. Be prepared to defend any changes you make to the old form.

APP 12-2. *Improving Control in a Records System (Objs. 1-10)*

You are the assistant office manager in a law office involving the legal practice of three attorneys. During the past month, you have carefully observed your records operations, noting especially the following typical conditions:

1. Each of three keyboarding specialists uses a different style of letter when keying correspondence.

2. Re-sorting an alphabetized client file of 500 cards into numeric order by ZIP Code required five hours of clerical time.

3. Over a one-week period, 20 of the last 75 records requested could not be found quickly or were not found at all.

4. Two of the 25 four-drawer file cabinets have not been "consulted" for retrieval purposes during the past two weeks.

5. The hard drive of one of the three office PCs crashed, and no data could be accessed for five days.

6. Each of the six office employees designs his or her own forms and orders them from outside firms on an individual basis.

7. Each employee has free access to the office copier at all times.

8. The most common problems found in examining the files were these:
   a. Few guides were used in the file drawers.
   b. Different folder cuts in a variety of positions were used with some handwritten captions.
   c. Some label captions were handwritten; the position of captions on labels varied with each person who prepared them.
   d. Many folders were overcrowded (some contained five inches of filed records) and many label captions were hidden.

Analyze these problem areas cited. What specific control problems do you see? What can be done in this office to eliminate or, at least, to improve these conditions? Key a report answering these questions. Store the report on the template disk as filename CH12.AP2.

Appendices

Appendix A -
*Records Management
Career Opportunities and
Job Descriptions*

Appendix B -
Card and Special Records

Appendix A
Records Management Career Opportunities and Job Descriptions

When you were introduced to the field of records management in Chapter 1, you were briefly exposed to the three job levels and job titles in the records management field. At this point, whether it be for supplemental reading following Chapter 1 or for additional information as you complete the last chapter, a more in-depth look at career opportunities in records management and related areas is in order.

Appendix A offers: (1) a concise overview of the growth of the information profession of which records management is a part, (2) a discussion of career opportunities and job descriptions at the various job levels in records management, and (3) a look at professional development programs to enhance advancement in the records management field. Special attention is given to jobs and related career opportunities that will allow students who are entering the world of office work to advance in their profession.

The Growth of Information Professions

By following the daily news reports on the world economy, you find that one point among all others stands out: *The United States is rapidly moving from a production-based economy to a service-based economy.* As such, businesses and industries are, for example, becoming less involved with producing steel and its many by-products and more involved with computers and related information services that computers make possible.

With this new focus in mind, you should ask yourself several questions about the career you are considering. They are:

1. What effects are the rapid changes in the United States and world economies and information technology having on the records management field?

2. What specific jobs in records management and allied fields are being created (or maintained) in the new service- and information-oriented economy?

3. Which jobs are changing significantly or being eliminated?

4. How can you keep up-to-date on career opportunities in records management to take advantage of opportunities as they occur?

As you seek answers to such questions, keep in mind that in a service-oriented world, *information is a* (and in most cases, *the*) *key resource.* To be successful, all organizations, workers, and citizens in general must accept this viewpoint. Further, they recognize that for information to be used repeatedly, it must be recorded. Time and time again as you worked your way through this textbook, you were reminded of the vital role that records play in operating business organizations.

Records and their relationship to information systems are briefly discussed next. (Even though some of these concepts have been discussed in one or more of the 12 chapters in this textbook, they are discussed here in the context of careers so that you can understand the relationship of such careers to the business firm and to the world economy of which it is a part.)

Records and Information Management

As Chapters 1, 4, 5, 10, and 11 point out, many new information technologies are rapidly being employed in the operation of businesses. Consider how important computers, microimage systems, telecommunications, and many other hardware and software systems are to the operation of a business. These technologies impact not only your access to vast amounts of information, but they also affect the speed and accuracy with which you can retrieve that information. (Notice, for example, the almost universal presence of computers, computer terminals, and printers in offices of all sizes.)

Because information is important to large and small firms, a new concept of information management has emerged. **Records and information management (RIM)** is dedicated to establishing company-wide controls over the staff, equipment, and services that generate and maintain information. These controls include the traditional records management responsibilities for creating, processing, storing, retrieving, and using information. Because technology is interwoven into all aspects of businesses today, RIM must be concerned not only with the necessary paper records systems, but also with the growing number of technological developments being applied to handle a firm's information needs. Information is an expensive and vital resource that must be represented at the top levels of management. For this reason, many forward-looking firms have created the position of **chief information officer (CIO)** as the top-level manager in charge of all information management services. Such an approach recognizes information as a vital resource that will help support and achieve organizational goals. With the expanded processing and use of information, many new jobs in information-related fields have been created. Thus, records management as a part of RIM continues its rapid growth as the need for information increases.

Records Management—A Growing Area

A few years ago records management was known as the efficient storage and retrieval of paper records. With the passage of time, the increase in the amount of information, and the advancements in technology, however, organizations are growing larger and more complex. As a result, the records management field has expanded to include many diversified areas dealing with information resource management. Examples of such areas include:

- Forms and reports management (electronic and paper forms).

- Correspondence management.

- Records center operations.

- Records and information retention.

- Vital records.

- Archival records preservation.

- Integrated technology records applications as discussed in Chapters 10 and 11.

- Understanding of the business world's dependence on timely and accurate information in the global community.

When more records are produced, more jobs are opened to qualified people. As discussed in this section, job opportunities in records management exist in many new, as well as in many long-term, work environments.

The Small Business Environment.   Small businesses require generalists—employees who can handle a variety of office tasks. Take the administrative assistant as an example. The typical administrative assistant in a small firm composes responses to routine correspondence, screens telephone calls, makes appointments, handles travel arrangements, and *maintains filing and information systems*. Therefore, if you expect to work for a small business, you will be the "files specialist" responsible for paper and automated records along with your other duties.   For example, additional duties may include making computer backups and setting up and maintaining electronic indexes and databases.

The Large Business Environment.   In large firms, much more specialization will be found. Within departments, administrative assistants and general support personnel such as records clerks may be responsible for all records activities. If a firm has a formal records management program, these responsibilities may be centralized under a records manager with a specialized staff.   In addition to supervisory duties, a records manager will, among other things, establish procedures, initiate long-range planning, and develop budgets. The nature of such specialized staff positions is discussed later.

The Professional Office Environment.   In an increasingly specialized economy, many professional offices require management of their specialized records (see Figure A-1).   Brief examples of such office settings are discussed next.

Law Office Jobs.   Large law firms—some with hundreds of attorneys on their staff—employ records personnel at the three levels (managerial, supervisory, and operating). All three levels require an understanding of general records management principles and practices. Further, such staff members must have specialized knowledge of how attorneys think and work and of the unique characteristics of classifying and storing legal records.

Medical Office Jobs.   One- and two-physician offices still dominate the medical field although the number of multiple-physician clinics is increas-

Figure A-1   Staff Members Generating Specialized Records at a Meeting

ing. With an increasing number of medical facilities consolidating, recordkeeping requirements have multiplied. The relationship of records to the health insurance field also creates many new records jobs. Note, for example, these common medical records. Patient charts are used not only for histories, diagnoses, treatment, and research, but also as information needed for insurance claims and bill collections. Other typical records include discharge summaries, operative and pathology reports, X-rays, and health-insurance correspondence. A knowledge of medical terminology and records functions is especially important to the individual handling records in the health field.

Other Professional Office Jobs.   In other professional offices such as the government offices at the city, county, state, and federal levels and in offices primarily responsible for technical computer processing, special records job opportunities exist. Records personnel in city and county government offices keep track of registrations, licenses, social services cases, taxes, and citizen protection. At the federal and state levels, these same types of records are maintained with additional information—and additional records—required at each succeeding level. In all four levels of government, more and more records are computerized and many are microfilmed. Centralized records management positions are available in most state and federal offices, which provide a longer career path for the student to consider. Information on such career opportunities is available from the administrative services or archives division in each state capital and from each main office responsible for administering federal agencies.

Regardless of the type of business or industry, the information worker needs to learn and understand all aspects of the business and how the information flows through the organization. Just as important is the ability to recognize how the management of information impacts or impedes the organization's effectiveness.

Students with career interests that combine the computer and records management must understand basic computer concepts, especially how automated records are created, stored, and retrieved. At the same time, they should know the fundamentals of records control as outlined in this textbook. Armed with such information, students can gain entry-level positions in large organizations in which the computer tracks records through the record life cycle and provides appropriate reports about the records' uses as needed. Similar information on careers in the library records field can be obtained from the American Library Association (ALA), 50 East Huron Street, Chicago, IL 60611.

Records Management Career Opportunities and Job Descriptions

The three job levels and position titles typically found in records management are shown in Figure A-2. By advancing from the operating level to the supervisory level and finally to the managerial level over a period of time, a career path for the employee is provided. Thus, a **career path** outlines a typical route of advancement for workers on the job. Knowing that opportunity for advancement is available motivates workers toward more effective performance. At the same time, a career path stimulates the interest of students seeking opportunities for professional growth and advancement.

In this section, job descriptions for common records positions shown in Figure A-2 are discussed, and job opportunities including career paths for each job level are explored. However, primary attention is given to the operating level because this level is where you will likely enter the work force. If you choose not to pursue a higher educational level, you may find that advancement opportunities are limited.

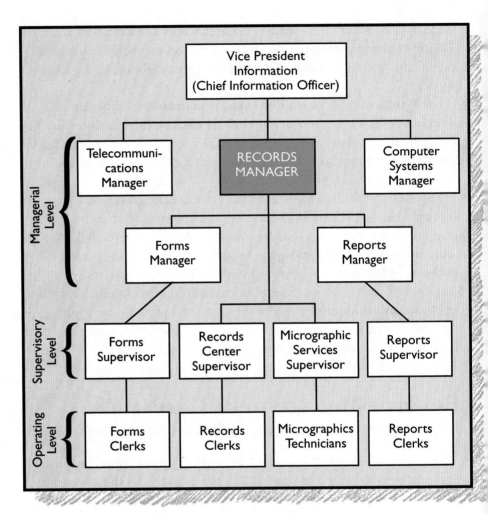

Figure A-2   Records Management Organization Chart

Operating Level

At the *operating level*, as shown in Figure A-2, workers are generally responsible for routine filing and retrieving tasks and for assisting with vital records, records retention, and occasional special projects. In large organizations, however, other more specialized jobs are found as described on the following pages.

Job Opportunities.   Figure A-3 illustrates a job description for the *records clerk* (sometimes called a *records and information clerk*), the most common operating-level position. (A **job description** summarizes the content and essential requirements of a specific job. Similar job descriptions would be available for all positions in the records department.) A *records center clerk* is another typical operating-level position in a centralized records management program. Generally, operating level personnel must be able to communicate well orally and in writing, to handle details (such as working frequently with names, numbers, and titles of documents), to handle and process records, to index records, to keyboard, and to perform general administrative duties.

Other operating duties assigned will depend on the specific nature of the work to be done, the worker's education and work experience background, and the records needs of the organization. For example, some organizations provide *forms clerks*, *reports clerks*, and *micrographic technicians* at this level to handle technical duties of an elementary nature. Each of these employees works closely with supervisors having the same special work interests. Figure A-4 provides detailed information on the key duties and job qualifications for each of these common operating-level positions.

Career Path.   Employees at this work level have the opportunity for advancement as shown in Figure A-2. Keep in mind that the lowest rung on the career ladder is especially important, for it provides the most basic job information needed to understand the total records system. Workers with the motivation to advance up the ranks usually appreciate most their operating-level experience after their promotion to higher levels of work. Workers with the highest levels of education but without work experience at the operating level may, therefore, possess certain limitations that restrict their full understanding of records management programs.

Supervisory Level

Supervisory-level personnel oversee the work of operating-level workers and are also responsible for other administrative duties. Supervisors must work with budgets; select, motivate, train, and evaluate workers; establish and meet deadlines; and delegate responsibilities. These duties require the ability to write instructional materials and procedures, to give and follow up on instructions, and to plan and organize work efficiently.

JOB TITLE: Records Clerk   Job Code: 482.10

Date: March 1, 19--

Duties

1. Sort and classify documents and other material for filing.

2. File materials.

3. Retrieve material from files.

4. Maintain charge-out system for records removed from files.

5. Assist in accession, reference, and disposal activities of the department/records center.

6. Assist with vital records.

7. Maintain logs and indexes to provide status of information.

8. Follow up on materials charged out to users.

9. Set up new file categories.

10. Perform other administrative duties as assigned by supervisor.

Job Requirements

1. Ability to maintain pleasant working relationships with all levels of personnel.

2. Strong oral and written communication skills.

3. Ability to analyze data for answers to questions concerning stored information.

4. Mechanical aptitude that allows efficient and effective operation of office equipment, including keyboard data-entry equipment (computer and typewriter).

5. Ability to handle confidential information.

Education/Work Experience

This is an entry-level position requiring:

1. High school diploma or equivalent; or demonstrated skill to perform the job.

   or

2. Work experience as records clerk, office trainee, or clerk-typist in lieu of high school graduation.

Career Path

Advancement to Records Center Supervisor

Figure A-3   Job Description for Records Clerk

Job Title	Duties	Personal Characteristics	Education/Work Experience	Advance to
Forms Clerk	Analyze forms requirements; design forms; revise existing forms; maintain forms; control records	Ability to analyze data; provide answers to questions; work well with all levels of personnel; be accurate in working with detailed information	High school diploma; some experience in working with records preferred	Forms Analysis (if job is available); Forms Supervisor
Micrographics Technician/ Clerk	Prepare documents for microfilming; operate microfilming equipment; develop and maintain index and retrieval aids	Ability to work well with people; have mechanical aptitude; understand office procedures	High school diploma or equivalent; technical training in microfilming; two years' business experience required; records experience preferred	Micrographic Services Supervisor
Reports Clerk	Review firm's reports; design report formats; assist forms and records clerks	Ability to work well with people; good writing skills; creativity; self-motivation	High school diploma; some experience in working with records and reports	Reports Analyst (if job is available); Reports Supervisor

Figure A-4 Job Duties, Personal Characteristics, and Education/Work Experience Required of Three Common Operating-Level Records Personnel

Job Opportunities. Supervisory positions in records management will only be found in large organizations with records management programs because such organizations can afford work specialization. As shown in Figure A-2, supervisory positions include *records center supervisor, forms supervisor, reports supervisor*, and *micrographic services supervisor*. In a small business organization, one person fulfills all these duties. Figure A-5 shows a job description for records center supervisor, the most common position at this work level. Figure A-6 outlines key duties and job qualifications for other common supervisory personnel in records management programs. Note that the work of such supervisors requires some college-level education or from three to five years of closely related work experience. Many times this work experience is obtained as the worker advances from operating levels to supervisory levels of work within a business. By the time of promotion, such workers know their organizations well and can usually become more productive much sooner than people hired from outside the organization.

Career Path. The typical promotion route for supervisors in business, industry, and government is to advance to manager. This same principle applies to supervisors in records management programs. In Figure A-2, the career path for each supervisor discussed earlier is identified by those positions appearing immediately above on the organization chart.

Managerial Level

A *records manager* (sometimes called a *records administrator*), a middle management position, directs the records management program. As a rule, both a college degree and considerable work experience with records systems are required for this top position; however, motivated people can occasionally move up through the "experience" ranks to such a position without a degree. A job description for a records manager is provided in Figure A-7. It shows responsibilities for (1) many administrative duties (organizing resources; recruiting and hiring staff; motivating and evaluating staff; and establishing effective systems), (2) many technical areas (microimage systems, forms control,

---

JOB TITLE: Records Center Supervisor   Job Code: 1482.00

Date: March 1, 19--

Duties

1. Supervise the work of the other supervisory personnel and of the operating-level staff.

2. Arrange for pickup and transportation of records.

3. Coordinate the creation, receipt, storage, retrieval, and disposition of records.

4. Develop procedures for controlling all aspects of the record life cycle (from creation through disposition).

5. Coordinate the transfer of records from active to inactive storage.

6. Select, train, supervise, and evaluate staff.

7. Make salary recommendations for records personnel.

8. Plan, schedule, and assign work tasks.

9. Recommend budget for the areas of assigned responsibility.

10. Perform other supervisory-level duties as requested by the records manager.

Job Requirements

1. Strong oral and written communication skills.

2. Ability to supervise effectively and coordinate the use of resources assigned to the program.

3. Ability to plan and organize work, to motivate personnel, and to make sound decisions regarding work assignments.

4. Ability to recognize, analyze, and solve problems.

5. Thorough knowledge of records management principles and practices.

Education/Work Experience

1. Minimum of two years of college, or equivalent level of related work experience.

2. Knowledge of automated records systems principles and practices.

Career Path

1. Records Manager or Records Administrator

2. Other staff positions

Figure A-5   Job Description for Records Center Supervisor

Job Title	Duties	Personal Characteristics	Education/Work Experience	Advance to
Forms Supervisor	Supervise work of forms clerks; analyze forms and coordinate forms control program; provide forms assistance to departments; select, train, and evaluate forms clerks	Ability to work well with and motivate people; good communication skills; broad background in manual and automated forms control practices	Minimum of two years of college; at least five years' experience in business and in records systems work	Forms Manager or Assistant Records Manager
Micrographics Services Supervisor	Plan, organize, and coordinate microimage systems program; select, train, and evaluate staff; work closely with department heads and other records supervisors	Ability to work well with and motivate people; good communication skills; organizational and analytical skills; mechanical aptitude to maintain equipment	High school diploma plus two years' micrographics work experience and four years of related work experience	Records Analyst (if available) or Assistant Records Manager
Reports Supervisor	Supervise work of reports clerks; analyze reports and coordinate reports control program; select, train, and evaluate reports clerks	Ability to work well with and motivate people; maintain confidentiality of data; good writer, planner, and creative reports organizer	Minimum of two years of college; at least five years' experience in business and in records systems work	Reports Manager or Assistant Records Manager

Figure A-6   Job Duties, Personal Characteristics, and Education/Work Experience Required of Three Common Supervisory-Level Records Personnel

JOB TITLE: Records Manager
Job Code: 2482.01

Date: March 1, 19--

Duties
1. Report, as instructed, to Vice President, Information (Chief Information Officer).
2. Establish company-wide policies and procedures for creating, classifying, storing, retrieving, and disposing of company records.
3. Assist department to plan, develop, improve, and modernize records availability and to maximize service to records users.
4. Coordinate the preparation of records management manuals.
5. Make effective use of automated storage and retrieval systems to the extent possible.
6. Coordinate the use of microimage systems throughout the organization.
7. Select methods for safeguarding records.
8. Coordinate the supervision and evaluation of all records, personnel, equipment, and procedures with supervisors.
9. Report regularly to top management to justify, publicize, and support the records management program.
10. Plan and develop a budget and cost control system for the records management program.

Job Requirements
1. Excellent oral and written communication skills.
2. Strong organizational, planning, and evaluation skills.
3. Ability to lead and motivate people and to work effectively with all levels of personnel in the organization.
4. Professional appearance as evidenced by active participation in professional organizations and up-to-date knowledge of information technology.
5. Excellent overall knowledge of records management and its relationship to information resource management.

Education/Work Experience
1. College degree, with MBA degree and five years' experience in records management preferred. Must demonstrate that coursework has been completed in computer systems, business law, and human relations and must have a working knowledge of automated records systems.
2. Work experience may, in some cases, be substituted for college coursework.

Career Path
1. Vice President, Information Services (Administrative Services)
2. Vice President, Information Resources

Figure A-7   **Job Description for a Records Manager**

and records protection), and (3) a growing body of knowledge of computers and other information technology.

Very large firms may also have other managerial-level personnel reporting to the records manager. These positions include *reports manager* and *forms manager.* Candidates for such positions may "come up through the ranks." That is, they advance from one or more lower levels in the program; or they may be hired from outside the organization. Typical duties and job qualifications for these managers are shown in Figure A-8. (In some progressive firms with strong information services orientation, records and information analysts, as well as an assistant records manager, may also be provided at this same work level.) Depending on the breadth of experience and education, a successful records manager may advance to a higher level in information systems such as director of administrative services or chief information officer.

Students interested in learning more about such positions should complete more advanced courses in records management and should correspond with ARMA, 4200 Somerset Drive, Suite 215, Prairie Village, KS 66208.

Professional Development in Records Management

A wise business executive once told a college student, "Once you graduate from school, your real education begins." What this statement means is simply this: Each new "hire" must learn all phases of the new job; and once experience on that job is gained, the worker must maintain a continuous program of learning through self-development courses as well as participation in the programs offered—some voluntary, some required—by the employer. Further, this self-development should continue throughout the employee's career. Several types of professional development approaches are available.

Taking Professional Development Courses

At the operating level, the records manager or supervisor or the organization's human resources or training department may teach

Job Title	Duties	Personal Characteristics	Education/Work Experience	Advance to
Forms Manager	Plan, organize, and implement a forms control program throughout the firm; evaluate the work of forms supervisor; select forms staff	Ability to work well with and motivate people; excellent communication skills; understanding of manual and automated forms system; good problem solver	College degree and five years' experience in forms work	Assistant Records Manager (if available); Records Manager
Reports Manager	Plan, organize, and implement a reports control program throughout the firm; evaluate the work of reports supervisor; select reports staff	Excellent communication skills; high level of creativity in designing and analyzing reports in the organization; ability to work well with people	College degree and five years' experience in reports work	Assistant Records Manager (if available); Records Manager

Figure A-8   Job Duties, Personal Characteristics, and Education/Work Experience Required of Two Common Managerial-Level Records Personnel

in-house courses focused on information systems. Courses in forms design, reports management, and records automation may be offered free to an employee on the job as a means of increasing the employee's skills level. With such skills, the employee will find the doors to better work performance and more advancement opportunities open. Outside professional groups such as ARMA, the American Management Association (AMA), or consultants with expertise in areas related to the firm's records program offer similar programs. Educational institutions such as a local university or community college offer credit and non-credit courses, often at night, that not only add to the employee's skills level, but also help the employee accumulate college credit toward a college degree. With a degree, a records management employee may be eligible for positions in management sooner than without a degree.

Participating in Professional Organizations

Many forward-looking employees seeking to advance in the business world belong to professional organizations in their fields. These professional organizations are a network of peers with similar business concerns and solutions and can provide educational opportunities as well.

However, membership alone is not enough. You must take an active part; that is, participate on a continuing basis in such organizations to get the maximum benefit from them. Such organizations provide you with the opportunity:

- To meet professional-minded people in positions similar to yours.

- To exchange ideas on making your records system more efficient.

- To become acquainted with performance standards that the organization recommends.

- To become aware of, and participate in, the research conducted to improve your records systems operations.

- To keep up-to-date on management thinking and technology affecting the records management field.

Professional organizations of special interest to records personnel include: (1) the *Association of Records Managers and Administrators, Inc.*

(ARMA), for general records management coverage; (2) the *Association for Information and Image Management* (AIIM), which specializes in microimage and optical disk technology; and (3) the *National Association of Government Archives and Records Administrators* (NAGARA), for records personnel in the government. Organizations having closely related interests are the *Association for Systems Management* (ASM), the *Society of American Archivists* (SAA), the *American Library Association* (ALA), the *American Health Information Management Association* (AHIMA), and the *National Business Forms Association* (NBFA). Information on these professional organizations is available in city, college, and university libraries.

Of all these organizations, ARMA is the most active and most relevant to business records management. Its membership continues to grow in numbers, and its importance to the records management profession continues to increase. Typical of ARMA's professional developments are the guidelines for various filing methods discussed in this textbook, the job description guidelines for various records management positions, and the certification program discussed next. ARMA also sponsors technical publications, a series of seminars, and an annual conference. Locate the ARMA chapter nearest you and attend one or more of its meetings. Guests—as prospective members—are always welcome! And, as a student, you are eligible to join ARMA at a special student membership rate.

Becoming Professionally Certified

Certification programs are designed to test and to verify that candidates successfully meeting the program's requirements have the qualifications for managerial work in the area. Having a certification also demonstrates to potential employers that a candidate has specialized expertise that other candidates do not possess. Typically, such certification is attained when a member passes qualifying examinations that test the knowledge, skill, and other relevant information pertaining to the professional field.

The Institute of Certified Records Managers (ICRM) administers the certification program in records management. The CRM examination consists of the following six parts:

1. Management principles and the records management program.

2. Records creation and use.

3. Filing systems, storage, and retrieval.

4. Records appraisal, retention, protection, and disposition.

5. Equipment, supplies, and technology.

6. Case studies.

Parts 1-5 of the CRM exam can be taken in any order, but all five parts must be successfully passed before the candidate is able to sit for Part 6. These five parts can be taken in any sequence; each part can be retaken separately, but all must be passed within five years for the individual to be CRM-certified. Candidates for certification must have a minimum of three years' full-time or equivalent professional experience in records management in at least three of the areas covered in the CRM examination. In addition, the candidate must have been awarded a bachelor's degree from an accredited institution before certification can be achieved. In some cases, the ICRM permits the substitution of additional qualifying experience for some of the required education. By meeting these educational, experience, and test requirements, the candidate is given the designation Certified Records Manager, which indicates a high degree of professionalism and competence in records management.

To promote a similar degree of competence in the medical records profession, the American Health Information Management Association (AHIMA) conducts annual qualification examinations to credential medical personnel as Registered Records Administrators (RRA) and Accredited Records Technicians (ART). Information on education programs, certification examinations, and career opportunities in the medical records field is available from AHIMA, 919 North Michigan Avenue, Suite 1400, Chicago, IL 60611-1683.

Other records-related associations also offer certification programs. ASM, mentioned earlier, sponsors the *Certified Systems Profession (CSP)* program covering systems environments, project management, systems analysis, systems design and implementation, and systems tools and technology. The NBFA sponsors the *Certified Forms Consultant (CFC)* program, which covers such topics as business forms production and materials, forms design, construction and control, business systems and procedures, products, and processing and handling equipment. Several computer-based certification programs such as the *Certified Data Processor (CDP)* program that the *Data Processing Management Association (DPMA)* developed are also available.

Professional-minded people proudly display their certification, which sends a strong message to the business public. CRMs, for example, have met high professional standards and are recognized internationally by their profession. Such attainment leads not only to professional advancement, but also to respect from their subordinates, peers, and superiors on the job.

Some Final Thoughts About a Career in Records Management

Career choices that affect your future involve one of the most important decisions you will ever make. Make your decision carefully after considerable study and thought; but in the process, avoid letting the growing number of professional associations and detailed information about careers confuse you!

As you prepare for full-time employment (or if you are now employed full-time or part-time and are seeking other employment), keep in mind these final thoughts about a career in records management:

1. *Information processing is now our biggest industry nationally*, and records—in whatever form—are storehouses of information.

2. *The people in control of records are actually controllers of information*; and that means power, for using information leads to knowledge, and knowledge leads to power in society as well as in the workplace. More important, however, is that your career should lead to personal satisfaction. Visit one or more records installations in your area and talk to people with experience in the field before making your career decision.

3. *The days of full-time, often monotonous, manual filing operations are numbered.* In their place will be greater numbers of automated records systems that are integrated with the information systems by which the organization is managed. The "bottom line," then, is that in records management you can become a member of the informa-

tion systems team and, along with it, enjoy a rewarding and even exciting career. Students with majors in liberal arts, library science, and other nonbusiness fields can find satisfying positions in records management.

4. *Keep up-to-date.* Information on career opportunities, as well as on new developments in the field, can be found in ARMA's publication, *Records Management Quarterly*, in the *Dictionary of Occupational Titles*, and in the *Occupational Outlook Handbook*. The other professional associations cited earlier also publish valuable periodicals that contain similar information about the field of records management. Copies of such publications are commonly found in college, university, and city libraries.

As always, the final decision is up to you, keeping in mind your interests and your aspirations. Regardless of whether you are employed full-time in records management, you will still be using records to a significant degree in whatever field you enter. Good luck to you in making your career decision.

Important Terms

career path
chief information officer (CIO)
job description

records and information
   management (RIM)

Appendix B
Card and Special Records

T wo types of records are emphasized in this textbook: (1) *paper records* and (2) *nonpaper records* such as image records and electronic records. You will learn also that businesses frequently use a large number of other records. In Appendix B, card and special records that you will use in your personal and professional lives are discussed.

Card Records

If you were to look behind the records environment in today's businesses, you would find that although computers are becoming commonplace in the work environment, companies continue to store information on cards for internal and external uses. (The definition of card record and a discussion of its advantages and disadvantages are presented in Chapter 2.) Because card records are smaller in size than correspondence, they are usually stored in special noncorrespondence filing equipment.

In this section, card records are described in three ways: (1) by physical characteristics, (2) by use, and (3) by the filing equipment in which they are stored.

Physical Characteristics

Paper companies manufacture card records in standard sizes to fit commonly used storage equipment. The most common card sizes are 5" by 3", 6" by 4", 8" by 5", and 9" by 6", with the horizontal measurement of the card listed first.

Cards may be blank or may have horizontal and/or vertical rulings such as those used in accounting journals, sales department quotation forms, and patient medical histories. Cards may also be single thickness, folded, or hinged to provide additional sides for recording information. Other cards are designed as special records and discussed later in this appendix.

Use

A card that contains information used for reference only is called an **index record.** Index records are found in most offices and contain the following kinds of information:

1. Names and addresses of customers, clients, patients, or students.

2. Names and addresses of suppliers or vendors.

3. Employee or membership lists.

4. Most frequently used telephone numbers.

5. Inventory of locations of furniture and equipment within an organization.

6. Prospective customer lists.

7. Subscription lists.

For example, you could consult an alphabetic card file of customer names and addresses to answer such questions as: What is the mailing address of Knutson Insurance Company? What is the telephone number of the O'Keefe and Jameson accounting firm? and What is the customer number of Krenlot Temporary Services?

A second type of record classified by use is the posted record. A **posted record**, sometimes called a *secondary record*, contains information that is continually updated. Information on the record is added to, deleted, or changed in some other way to reflect the current status. New information is posted on the card record either by hand or by machine. Examples of posted records are:

- Inventory and stock control cards

- Medical and dental record cards

- Department ledger cards

- Payroll cards

- Membership files

- Credit and collection cards

Filing Equipment

The type of filing equipment used determines how card records are filed. Many card records are filed *vertically*; that is, on edge or in an upright position. A collection of such records is called a **vertical card file**, or a *vertical file*. (See Figure B-1 for an example of a vertical card file.) A second way to file cards is to store such records *horizontally* in an overlapping arrangement. When the cards overlap, one important line of information for each record—usually the bottom margin—is visible when the tray in which the card is held is pulled out from the file cabinet. For this reason, a collection of these records is called a **visible card file**, or a *visible file*. Figure B-2 shows a visible card file with one record tray pulled out. Users can retrieve information or make an entry without removing a card. Many visible record systems also use one-line strips of card stock. The information on the strips may identify a customer/student name, address, telephone number, or some other readily used item of information.

Figure B-1 **Vertical Card File**

Information on the visible margin of a card summarizes the detailed information entered on the other areas of the card. In an office equipment inventory file, for example, the visible margin of a card may show "ergo-body-fit chairs," while the remaining areas of the card show a history of the receipts and withdrawals of such chairs from inventory over a period of time.

A third type of equipment used to store card records is **rotary (wheel) equipment**. In rotary equipment, card records are attached to a frame that rotates on an axis similar to a wheel. (Figure B-3 illustrates a small, compact workstation unit.) Larger rotary card files are available, as discussed later in this appendix.

Equipment and Supplies for Card Files

The equipment and supplies required for card record files depend solely on the type of filing equipment—vertical, visible, or rotary—used. The equipment and supplies used in each type of card record file are discussed in this section.

Vertical Card Files

Remember that records are stored *on end* in vertical card files, as compared with the type of storage used in visible systems. Card records stored in rotary wheel files appear in a modified version of both vertical and horizontal files. The most important special equipment and supplies for vertical card files are explained here.

Equipment.   Cards may be filed vertically in two types of filing equipment: (1) manual equipment that includes drawers housed in cabinets, boxes, trays, and rotating wheel equipment; and (2) motorized or power-driven equipment.

Drawer Cabinets.   Perhaps the most widely used housing for vertical card records is the *drawer cabinet*, which has drawers similar to, but smaller than, correspondence file cabinet drawers. Filed records rest on their longest edge in these files; that is, the 8" edge of an 8" by 5" card rests on the bottom of the drawer. When card records are used in conjunction with other types of records such as correspondence, a file cabinet that provides drawers for vertical card record storage and other drawers that accommodate business forms or correspondence

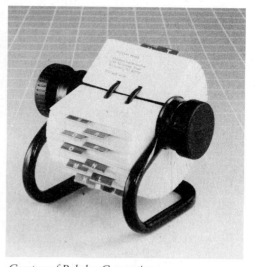

Courtesy of Rolodex Corporation

Figure B-3   **Rotary Card File**

Acme Visible Records

Figure B-2   **Visible Card File**

may be used. Such cabinets may contain from two to six or more drawers.

Boxes.   Boxes of heavy cardboard or high–impact, durable plastic are sometimes used to store card records, which are most often found in 5" by 3", 6" by 4", and 8" by 5" card sizes. Box files are commonly used for home and small–office record storage (see Figure B-4).

Trays.   Card records may be stored on portable trays. Individual trays or a set of multiple trays may be placed side by side on shelves. Individual portable trays may be removed from the multiple group of trays for use at the workstation, for storage in a desk drawer, or for distribution of trays to various departments in the firm. By mixing card and tray sizes, a variety of card records may be stored in a mechanized unit.

Photo by Erik Von Fischer/Photonics Graphics

Figure B-4   **Box File**

Supplies.   Folders are not required in vertical card files. Cards are filed upright and separated by guides into the desired sections. Guides and signals are the main supplies used in vertical card files.

Guides.   Guides used in vertical card files are much the same as those used in correspondence files, varying only in size. Guides are available for cards filed in drawer cabinets, boxes, trays, and rotary files. In vertical card files, the guide tabs are visible, protruding above the cards to help the filer store and retrieve cards quickly and efficiently. The most important consideration in selecting guides is durability, which in turn depends on the type and weight of the guide material. Although guides are made from various materials, bristol board or pressboard is usually used for guides in vertical card record files. The thickness of the guide stock is referred to in terms of points, a point being 1/1000 of an inch. The greater the number of points, the thicker and more durable the paper or guide.

Vinyl guides in bright colors are also available for vertical and rotary files. Vinyl guides are washable and will not warp, crack, or become dogeared from extensive use—problems that may develop if paper-based guides such as bristol board or pressboard products are used.

Signals. A **signal** is a special marker used for drawing immediate attention to a specific record. Two types of signals are used in vertical card files to convey to the filer special information about the cards. Special add-on or clip-on markers of movable transparent or opaque materials may be attached to the top of selected cards. In other cases, a distinctive color is placed on the signal, on the tab, or on the cards themselves. Different colors may be used to show different types of information on the marked cards.

Visible Record Files

The kinds of equipment and supplies used for visible records depend on the following factors: (1) the organization's requirements as reflected by the number of cards or strips to be filed, (2) the importance of their location to their use, (3) whether the files must be portable, (4) the frequency of use, and (5) whether the visible records are to be used for reference or for posting purposes.

Equipment. The main types of visible card equipment are (1) card visible files and (2) reference visible files. Each type of equipment is discussed in this section.

Visible Card Files. A number of different forms of visible card files, often called *posting visible files*, are available. The most frequently used visible equipment is the cabinet with shallow drawers or trays, each one labeled to show the contents. Each drawer contains a number of overlapping cards held horizontally by hangers or hinges or in slots called *pocket holders*. Figure B-5a, page 382, shows such equipment with drawers that can be pulled out and down but that remain attached to the cabinet by a hinge. Both sides of most visible record cards may be used.

Courtesy of Kardex Systems

Figure B-5a   **Visible Record Cabinet**

By raising the set of cards preceding a card that requires posting, the filer can quickly post the desired information on the card without removing it from the storage container. Note that Figure B-5b shows an example of the contents of the visible margin on such a card. In this case, the name identifies a piece of office equipment and its stock number.

Cards are inserted into the holders so that one or two lines of each card are visible. Pocket holders are slotted to accommodate cards of various sizes. Some holders have transparent edge protectors, and others have the complete pocket made of transparent material. This see-through covering protects the edge or the entire card from wear, tear, moisture, and dirt.

When portability of cards is a necessity, when the volume of cards to be filed is small, or when many employees need to post simultaneously, hinged pocket books may be used instead of other storage methods. These card books may have fastenings at the top of the cards for ease in posting, or the cards may be snapped in and out at any point. Loose-leaf books with removable panels of cards provide portability and contain much data in a small space. Contents of the book are labeled on the back binding or spine.

INVENTORY RECORD					
Amount Received	**Date Received**	**Location**	**Amount Used/Requested**	**Date Used/Requested**	**Balance on Hand**
25	11-18-95	Aisle 10	10	12-10-95	15
10	1-15-96	Aisle 10	0		25
H1770 Ergo-Body-Fit Chairs					Location: SH203 Aisle 2

Figure B-5b   Contents of a Visible Margin on a Card

Racks and cabinets are used to house card books in an upright position. A cabinet may revolve so that several people can reference information.

Reference Visible Files.   If only one line or a few lines of information are needed for reference purposes, *reference visible files* are used. Information is placed on narrow strips of card stock that are inserted into holders attached to panels, trays, or frames. Figure B-6 shows one-line strips of information on panels attached to a revolving center post.

Kardex Systems, Inc.

Figure B-6 **Visible Strip File Desk Stand**

Supplies. Visible records housed in horizontal trays do not need guides. When the trays are pushed into their cabinets, labels on the front of the trays indicate the range of the tray contents. Thus, the only guides used for visible records are those found on strip file panels in vertical equipment such as that shown in Figure B-7. Guide tabs at the sides of the panel are the primary dividers that indicate the range of the names on each panel.

Visible card files also use signals or markers that call attention to some specific condition or content of a card. Signals (also called *flags*) that may be used with visible equipment include colored card stock, special printed edges that may be cut in various ways, and removable metal or plastic tabs of various colors and shapes (see Figures B-2 and B-7).

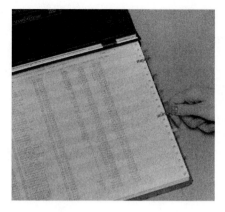
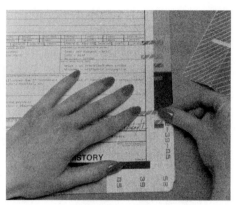

Ames Color File

Figure B-7   **Signals for Visible Card Systems**

Rotary (Wheel) Files

Two types of rotary files are used for storing card records: (1) manual rotary files and (2) motorized rotary files. Each is discussed in this section.

Manual Rotary Files.   *Manual rotary files* provide an arrangement in which card records are attached directly to the equipment frame. Guides are snapped into place over a center rod, and the cards are kept within bounds by the outer rims of the wheel. Wheel files may contain one or more rows of card records side by side. The entire file is rotated by hand to locate the desired record.

Larger versions of manual rotary files, called *rotary file cabinets*, rotate horizontally around a hub as shown in Figure B-8, page 386. Several people can access records at the same time when a rotary cabinet is placed between workstations. Fewer misfilings occur because fatigue, discomfort, and poor visibility (often found when using drawer cabinets) are reduced. Also, records need not be duplicated because one set of records can serve several departments; and sliding covers with locks are available on some models to provide security. Rotary files use the same kinds of vertical file supplies (cards, guides, signals) that have been specially designed for the equipment in which they will be stored. Additionally, records kept in such files require less floor space than would be needed to house the same number of records in drawer cabinets.

Courtesy of Datum Filing Systems, Inc.

Figure B-8   Multitiered Rotary File with Shelf for Cards

Motorized Rotary Files.   *Motorized* or *power-driven rotary files* provide shallow trays on movable shelves for storing card records. Because an electric motor powers the shelves, any shelf can be brought to the front of the machine by pressing one or more of a series of buttons mounted on a control panel. Figure B-9, page 387, illustrates such a motorized unit with trays of cards appearing in a horizontal side-by-side arrangement. The trays can be removed from the shelves, or the operator may reference the card records without removing any trays from the unit.

Special Records

Special records are records of unconventional size, shape, or weight commonly used in business and professional offices. Such records

Kardex Systems, Inc.

Figure B-9   **Motorized Card Record Storage Unit**

often cause difficulty for the filer who does not have an effective procedure for storing these items so that they can be found quickly and also preserved for later use. Therefore, efficient storage procedures for each type of special record are needed and are discussed in the first part of this section. The second part briefly reviews storage and retrieval procedures for special records.

Methods of Storing Special Records

Many of the special records discussed in this section are created because of the advances made in office technology. Automated offices produce large volumes of computer output that require special types of files, and imaging technology has created its own types of special records. Electronic and image records are discussed in Chapters 10 and 11, respectively.

Some records are considered *special* because they differ in size, shape, and construction from the regular office records and are stored in specialized equipment. The nature of the information, especially the manner by which it is retrieved, determines how these records are stored.

Accounting Records

Noncomputerized offices in small firms continue to use large numbers of records that are prepared by hand or by relatively simple machines. Records such as cash receipts journals and ledgers that store administrative information about the accounting system are vital to the survival of a small organization.

A **voucher** is an accounting record used to confirm that a business transaction has occurred. Vouchers are usually larger than checks but smaller than correspondence and are stored alphabetically or numerically in equipment the size of the vouchers. For example, 8" by 5" vouchers would be stored in drawers of a corresponding size near the user's workstation.

Drawings

Highly specialized departments in large organizations create and use a wide variety of nonstandard records. For example, art and advertising departments store posters, art prints, tracings, and other types of graphic art. Also, engineering departments commonly use blueprints, charts, maps, and other types of drawings, some of which are very large and bulky. Maps and engineering drawings are often rolled and stored in pigeonholes for convenience. However, this practice is not recommended because rolled records are difficult to use after they have been rolled for any length of time.

For storing large flat items, two alternatives are recommended: (1) placing the records in flat, shallow drawers in cabinets made for this purpose, or (2) hanging the items vertically using hooks or clamps. Figure B-10, top of page 388, shows a type of flat-file cabinet commonly used for storing bulky records. The labels on the drawers show the range of the contents, arranged either by alphabet or number.

Legal Documents

Some records maintained in legal offices are on 8 1/2" by 14" paper. Legal-size paper is widely used for abstracts, affidavits, certificates of incorporation, contracts, insurance policies, leases, and mortgages. In addition to the use of legal-size vertical file cabinets, legal-size records

Figure B-10   Large Records Flat-File Cabinet

may be stored in document boxes on open shelves. Numbers are assigned to the boxes, and an alphabetic index and an accession log are required as discussed in Chapter 8. These boxes are labeled appropriately to show their contents.

Magnetic Records

Many offices store information on a variety of magnetic media such as computer disks, CD-ROMs, laser disks, optical disks, data cartridges, data cassettes, videotape cassettes, and audio cassettes. Thorough coverage of these electronic records is presented in Chapter 10.

Magnetic media may be labeled by subject, by originator, or by date. The contents of computer disks are usually identified by a label affixed to the flat plastic casing around the disk. Audio cassettes are usually labeled on their flat, broad surface as well as on the spine of the plastic containers in which the cassette is stored. Videotape cassettes, data cartridges, and data cassettes usually have a label affixed to the spine of the outer casing of the media. CD-ROMs, laser disks, and optical disks are typically labeled on the spine of the container in which the media is placed in preparation for storage.

Storage equipment for magnetic media consists of drawers or files made of durable plastic or metal that protects the records from dust and moisture. Sturdy dividers or guides (usually plastic) hold the media in a position for reading the identifying content labels easily. A label attached to an outer surface of a container identifies the content of the magnetic media within the container (see Figures B-11a and B-11b for examples).

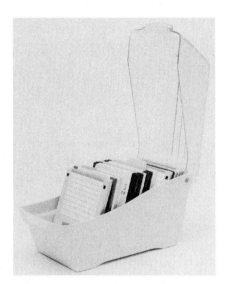

Alan Brown/Photonics Graphics

Figure B-11a   **3.5" Computer Disk Storage Unit**

Figure B-11b   Multimedia Storage Unit

Photographic Records

Cameras are used to photograph many types of records, some of which are highly specialized. However, only the most common photographic records are discussed here.

Films and Filmstrips.   Motion-picture films are commonly placed in canisters that are stored vertically in open wire racks. The canisters may be stored alphabetically by subject or film title or numerically by film number. When a numeric storage system is used, an alphabetic index is required for reference to titles or subjects; and an accession log is necessary for assigning numbers.

Usually, filmstrips are placed in canisters and kept in cabinets with shallow drawers that have compartments formed by adjustable or fixed dividers. The top of a filmstrip container is labeled by subject, alphabetic title, or filmstrip number. Each drawer is labeled to show the range of its contents.

Slides. Slides are usually stored in boxes with compartments or in ring binders. Rotary slide trays that fit on a projector may store in sequence all slides relating to one subject, with the tray being labeled to indicate the subject. Numbered slots in drawers in which slides may be stored correspond to numbers written on the slides.

Published Materials

The most common methods of storing published materials such as books, catalogs, periodicals, and pamphlets are discussed briefly in this section.

Books. To save office space and to still provide convenient access, books should be stored in bookcases or on other types of shelves. Books may be arranged alphabetically by book titles, alphabetically by authors' names, or numerically by the decimal method. As a rule, books are labeled on the back binding or spine. Frequently used reference books such as dictionaries and reference manuals are kept at the workstations where they are used. Charge-out procedures, similar to the procedures used for other types of records discussed in Chapter 6, should be developed to ensure proper control over these important and expensive records.

Catalogs. Catalogs are best housed on shelves or in bookcases. A procedure that has proved effective for storing a large number of catalogs is to place the catalogs in alphabetic order by the names of the firms issuing the catalogs. Then prepare a separate subject index listing the names of all firms issuing catalogs on each specific subject. A small number of catalogs may be stored in folders by subject as shown in Figure 7-2a, page 181.

Due to high mailing and printing costs, catalog supplements rather than entirely new catalogs may be sent to users. These supplements often contain only a few pages and are, therefore, quite flimsy; file folders are used for storage to provide the needed rigidity. When this practice is used, the folders are labeled according to the storage system used and are stored next to the respective catalogs. When a new catalog is received, the old catalog is destroyed.

Periodicals.   Periodicals are magazines or other publications that are issued at regular recurring intervals. Current issues of magazines are usually kept in stacks and arranged in chronologic order by date of publication, with the most recent issue on top. The stacks on the shelves are usually in alphabetic order by magazine name. Sturdy fiberboard or durable plastic boxes with open backs may also be used to house current issues to keep them from becoming worn and dusty (see Figure B-12). Some publishers sell boxes with the names of their magazines already printed on them, in which case only date information needs to be added to the label on the back of the box. These boxes are stored chronologically by date of publication.

Alan Brown / Photonics Graphics

Figure B-12   **Periodical File**

Pamphlets. Because they lack rigidity, pamphlets are stored in folders according to subject. The pamphlet folders are stored in alphabetic order by subject as well.

Procedures for Storing and Retrieving Card and Special Records

Steps required to store and retrieve special records are the same steps needed to store and retrieve other manually processed records. However, special records have certain unusual features that more traditional records do not possess. These special features affect the procedures for storage and retrieval. In this section, an abbreviated discussion of storage and retrieval procedures is presented.

Inspecting

Inspecting special records requires much more time than does the inspection of paper records because the filer must check to see whether the record is in good condition and complete. Also, such a record should be inspected to be sure that it is clean, that it is properly encased (if a protective cover is required), and that the record bears a cross-reference to its source if it is a partial copy or excerpt of an original.

Indexing

The indexing step requires carrying out the same procedures that are used to index and classify paper records. The filer analyzes the contents of the record to determine the filing segment for coding and storing.

Coding

Because of the wide variety of special records, coding procedures will vary. For example, coding could involve affixing a number on a film canister or affixing a label to the back of a book. The purpose of coding, however, is always the same—to facilitate accurate and efficient storage and retrieval.

Cross-Referencing

In some cases, special records do not require cross-references. Such records are unique and can be stored in only one place. If, however, a record is requested by an alternate name, by a subject, or by a number, a cross-reference should be prepared and inserted in the alphabetic index or a subject listing in the usual manner. Chapters 2 and 3 contain detailed information on cross-referencing procedures.

Sorting

If a number of special records of the same type must be stored, a separate sorting procedure will save time when the filer takes the records to the equipment to be stored. For instance, if 15 numbered filmstrip boxes need to be stored, arranging such boxes in their appropriate order on a carrying tray would save the filer time at the storage cabinet.

Storing

Special records should be stored as soon as possible after they are approved for storage. Because they are unusual and often bulky, special records may be unsightly and give a cluttered, inefficient appearance to an office if they are allowed to accumulate over long periods of time. Care must be taken to turn all special records of the same type in the same direction (covers of books facing forward and spines of magazines readable from the same directions, and so on). Because of the varying sizes of special records, as discussed earlier, large records frequently must be stored alongside small records. Thus, the filer needs to be alert to see that the smaller records do not get crushed among the larger ones.

Retrieving

The efficient retrieval of special records requires a charge-out and follow-up system that includes these steps:

1. Require a requisition form to be presented whenever a special record is removed from storage to be used by someone other than the filer.

2. Insert an OUT or IN USE indicator in place of a record removed from storage.

With this information on hand, the office manager or records manager knows where every record can be located, when it was taken from storage, and when it is due to be returned.

Selecting Equipment and Supplies for Card and Special Record Files

Before equipment and supplies can be properly selected for *any* record file, the system in which the records are used, stored, and retrieved must be studied carefully. In such a study, the records manager must ask questions such as the following to obtain information needed in decision making:

1. What kind of information is needed, and why is this information stored on cards (or special records)? Is a better type of record form available?

2. Who uses these records and how frequently?

3. How are the records used, stored, and retrieved?

4. What volume of records is used presently and how much do you anticipate will be used in the future?

5. How many hours a day/month will the equipment be used and how many supplies will be used?

6. What type of records protection and security is required?

7. How much space is available for the equipment and supplies?

The same sources of information used for selecting equipment and supplies, in general, can be used for selecting card and special record files.

Current Trends in Records and Information Management

In many offices, records that were once kept on cards are now stored on electronic or image media. For example, records such as customer, employee, or membership lists frequently are stored on electronic media such as computer disks because of the ease with which office workers can update and manipulate the record information. As mentioned in Chapter 8, the need to key data into the computer more than once has been eliminated through the use of electronic and image media. Several different indexes, as well as mailing labels, can be created using the same inputted data by retrieving and manipulating the data into a useful format that is appropriate for the situation in which it will be used.

Organizations often keep track of their inventory on computer. In a manufacturing company, computers may be strategically placed in the plant or warehouse so workers can easily access inventory records to determine the availability of a product and where that product is located. Some retail businesses are now using computers at checkout lanes, which allows inventory to be adjusted automatically as stock numbers are entered as part of a sales transaction.

Parts departments of auto dealerships and appliance stores now receive parts catalogs on microfiche or CD-ROM rather than the bulky catalogs they once received.

Card records that contain frequently called numbers such as those in a desk rotary file continue to be used because of their ease of use and portability. (They can be used at various workstations without the aid of expensive or cumbersome equipment.) However, electronic and image media will gradually replace many card records.

Important Terms

index record

posted record

rotary (wheel) equipment

signal

special records

vertical card file

visible card file

voucher

Glossary

A

accession log – A serial list of numbers assigned to records in a numeric storage system; also called an *accession book* or *numeric file list*.

accuracy ratio – A measure of the ability of filers to find requested records.

active record – A record needed to carry out an organization's day-to-day business; used three or more times a month.

activity ratio – A measure of the frequency of records use.

alphabetic index – An alphabetic list of and cross-references for correspondents' names or any subjects used in a numeric file with their assigned file codes.

alphabetic records storage method – A method of storing records arranged according to the letters of the alphabet.

alphanumeric coding – A coding system that combines alphabetic and numeric characters. Main subjects are arranged alphabetically, and their subdivisions are assigned a number.

aperture card – A standard data processing card (7 3/8" by 3 1/4") with a rectangular opening (aperture) specifically designed as a carrier for a film image or images.

archive record – A record that has continuing or historical value and is preserved permanently by an organization.

archives – The facilities where records of an organization are preserved because of their continuing or historical value.

ASCII – An acronym for the American Standard Code for Information Interchange. The code assigns specific numeric values to the first 128 characters of the 256 possible character combinations.

Association of Records Managers and Administrators, Inc. (ARMA) – The professional organization for the records management field.

automated records system – A records system in which the computer or computer-related equipment controls all or most of the records functions.

automation – The self-operation, regulation, or control of a process, machine, equipment, or system.

B

bar code – A coding system consisting of vertical lines or bars that, when read by an optical scanner, can be converted to machine-readable language.

bar code reader – A photoelectric scanner that translates bar code symbols into digital forms so that a computer can read them.

bellows (expansion) folder – A folder that is made with creases along its bottom and sides so that it can expand like an accordion.

benefit/cost ratio – A comparison between cost and benefit to determine that every cost originated results in an equal or greater benefit.

block numeric coding – A coding system based on the assignment of groups of numbers to represent primary and secondary subjects.

bubble memory – A type of computer memory consisting of small electromagnetic bubbles.

business form – A standardized record used to collect and transmit information in a standardized manner; it is used within or among departments or between organizations.

C

call-back system – A records protection procedure requiring the individual requesting data from a computer system to hang up after a telephone request and to wait for the computer to call back.

caption – The content identifying information on a label.

card record – A piece of card stock used for storing information that is referenced often.

career path – A typical route of advancement for workers on the job.

cartridge tape unit – An external magnetic tape unit connected to a computer or a quarter-inch cassette that fits into a standard hard-disk drive bay of a microcomputer.

central processing unit (CPU) – The computer microprocessor.

charge out – A control procedure to establish the current location of a record when it is not in the records center, by manual or automated system.

charge-out and follow-up file – A tickler file that contains the requisition forms filed by dates that records are due back in the inactive records center.

charge-out log – A written or electronic form for recording what record was taken, when it was taken, who took it, the due date, the date actually returned, the date an overdue notice was sent, and the extended date due if necessary.

chief information officer (CIO) – The top-level manager in charge of all information management services.

chronologic storage – A method of storing records by calendar date with the most recent date always on top.

client-server LAN – A network that links microcomputers, referred to as *clients*, to supplying devices called *servers*.

coding – The physical marking of a record to indicate the name, number, or subject by which it is to be stored. Place a diagonal between the units, underline the key unit, and number each succeeding unit when coding.

color accenting – A method by which different colors are used for the different supplies in the storage system—one color for guides, various colors for folders, another color for OUT indicators, and specific colors of labels or stripes on labels.

color coding – A method by which different colors are used to divide the alphabetic sections in the storage system.

compact disk read only memory (CD-ROM) – An optical disk that can be read only; it cannot be written on.

compression – A process that removes blank spaces between words, in margins, in boxed material, and in graphical material to conserve disk space.

computer output to laser disk (COLD) – Computer storage that integrates the imaging of paper documents with electronic records.

computer record – The total collection of fields or specific pieces of information about one person or one item within a file.

computer virus – A special computer program created for illicit reasons and used to distort or to erase electronic records.

computer-assisted retrieval (CAR) – The use of a computer to identify the location of information not contained within that computer's database.

computer-input microfilm/microform (CIM) – Computer input taken directly from microfilm/microform by scanning and character recognition. CIM also refers to the system of software and hardware that makes possible this method of transferring data to disk.

computer-output microfilm/microform (COM) – Computer output converted directly into microfilm/microform without paper printout as an intermediary. COM also refers to the equipment that produces the microform or to the entire process of transferring data.

consecutive numbering method – A storage method in which consecutively numbered records are arranged in ascending number order—from lowest to highest numbers.

constant data – Data that are preprinted on a form and, therefore, do not require rewriting each time the form is filled in.

contact printing – A process that makes a duplicate copy of microfilm by placing the emulsion side of the developed original film in contact with the emulsion side of the copy film and directing a light beam through the original image to the copy.

control – A means of checking or verifying by comparison with a standard; the standards for processing that a system uses to improve its output.

cross-reference – An aid used to find a record stored by a filing segment other than the one selected for storing.

D

data – Factual or statistical items.

database – A collection of facts or information organized especially for rapid search and retrieval of specific facts or information.

decimal-numeric coding – A system for coding records numerically in units of 10. An unlimited number of subdivisions is permitted through the use of digits to the right of the decimal point.

decompression – The process of restoring compressed data to usable form for viewing or processing.

densitometer – A device used to measure the contrast between the dark and light areas of the film.

density – The degree of opacity of microfilm, which determines the amount of light that will pass through it or reflect from it.

destruction date file – A tickler file containing copies of forms completed when records are received in the records center.

destruction file – A file that contains information on the actual destruction of inactive records.

dictionary arrangement – A subject filing arrangement of subject folders behind A-to-Z primary guides in their correct alphabetic order by subject title. An arrangement of geographic records in alphabetic order (A–Z).

digital signature – A string of characters and numbers added as a code on electronic documents that a computer is transmitting.

digital video cassette recorder (VCR) – A device that stores video pictures, television pictures, and vast amounts of computer data.

digitizing – Translating communication signals into a two-state form for computer input.

direct access – A method of accessing records without prior use of an index or a list of names in the files.

directory – A subdivision of a disk that the computer's operating system creates.

disaster prevention and recovery plan – A written and approved plan detailing how records will be handled in a disaster prior to, during, and after in the recovery stage.

document imaging – An automated system for scanning, storing, retrieving, and managing paper records in an electronic format.

duplex-numeric coding – A coding system using numbers (or sometimes letters) with two or more parts separated by a dash, space, or comma.

E

efficiency control – An evaluation of the ability to produce a desired effect with a minimum of time, energy, and space.

efficiency ratio – A standard for measuring the efficiency of various aspects of records systems.

electronic data interchange (EDI) – A communication procedure between two companies that allows the exchange of standardized documents (most commonly invoices or purchase orders) through computers.

electronic file management – The management of records using a computer.

electronic mail (E-mail) – A means of transmitting correspondence over telephone lines and/or computer networks or of relaying messages via satellite networks.

electronic record – A record created by an electronic device such as a computer and is stored on electronic media.

encryption system – A method of scrambling data in a predetermined manner at the sending point to protect confidential records.

encyclopedic arrangement – A subject filing arrangement in which broad main subject titles are arranged in alphabetic order with subdivisions arranged alphabetically under the title to which they relate; an alphabetic arrangement of major geographic divisions *plus* one or more geographic *subdivisions* also arranged in alphabetic order.

erasable optical disk – An optical disk that allows data to be erased and, therefore, provides for repeated use.

external hard drive – A disk drive unit that sits on the desk beside the microprocessor and connects to it.

external record – A record created for use outside a firm.

F

facsimile (fax) machine – A device that transmits an exact reproduction of an image to another location electronically.

feedback – Communication based on evaluation of output against quality and quantity standards.

field – A combination of characters to form words, numbers, or a meaningful code.

file – A collection of related records.

file server – A high-speed computer in a LAN that stores the programs and files that users share.

filename – A unique name given to a file stored for computer use that must follow the computer's operating system rules.

filing segment – The name by which a record is stored and requested.

fine sorting – Arranging records in exact sequence prior to storing.

fixed-disk drive – A high-speed, high-capacity disk drive housed in a cabinet and used with a mainframe or a minicomputer.

flash-memory card – A credit-card size variation of memory chips that can be placed inside a computer case in slots connecting to the system board.

floppy disk – A piece of round plastic that stores data and records by electromagnetic charges.

folder – A container used to hold and to protect stored records in an orderly manner.

follower block (compressor) – A device placed at the back of container that may be moved to allow for contraction or expansion of its contents.

follow-up – Checking on the return of borrowed records within a reasonable (or specified) time.

G

general folder – A folder that contains records to and from correspondents with a small volume so that an individual folder or folders are not necessary.

geographic records storage method – A method of storing and retrieving records in alphabetic order by location of an individual, an organization, or a project.

guide – A rigid divider with a projecting tab used to identify a section of a file and to facilitate reference.

H

hard disk – A thin, rigid metal platter covered with a substance that holds data in the form of magnetized spots.

hard space – A computer character code used to keep two or more parts of a name, phrase, date, or number together.

hard-disk cartridge – A hard plastic case enclosing one or two storage platters that have read/write heads.

hardcopy – A paper copy of an electronic record.

hardware – A computer and other equipment used with it.

hybrid imaging system – A system that integrates microfilm-based images with electronic image processing technologies.

I

image record – A photographic or electronic representation of a record that has been transferred to microfilm or optical disk.

image system – A combination of procedures and equipment that forms an efficient unit for creating and using records in microform or electronic images.

important record – A record that assists in performing a firm's business operations and, if destroyed, is replaceable only at great cost.

inactive record – A record that does not have to be readily available but must be kept for legal, fiscal, or historical purposes; referred to fewer than 15 times a year.

inactive records index – An index of all records in the inactive records storage center.

index – A systematic guide that allows access to specific items contained within a larger body of information.

index record – A card record that contains information used for reference only.

indexing – The mental process of determining the filing segment (or name) by which a record is to be stored.

indexing order – The order in which units of the filing segment are considered when a record is stored.

indexing rules – Written procedures that describe how the filing segments are ordered.

indexing units – The various words that make up the filing segment.

indirect access – A method of locating records requiring prior use of an index.

individual folder – A folder containing records of an individual correspondent.

information – Data that have been processed to communicate knowledge in meaningful ways for decision making.

input – Resources entered into a system.

inspecting – Checking a record for its readiness to be filed.

integrated document management systems (IDMS) – Computer systems that link paper, imaged, and electronic documents into one flexible and expandable document management system.

internal record – A record that contains information needed to operate a firm.

Internet – A series of connected supercomputers that allow communication among the connections.

J

job description – A summary of the content and essential requirements of a specific job.

jukebox – A device that contains multiple optical disk platters, from one to five optical disk drives, and a robotic mechanism (picker) used to move platters to and from the drives. Also called an *optical disk library*.

K

key unit – The first unit of the filing segment.

L

label – A device by which the contents of a drawer, shelf, folder, or a section of records is identified.

lap reader – A portable microform reader that is often used when traveling.

laser videodisk – A device that stores sound and visual images by using a laser to burn small holes into a disk to expose a reflective surface.

lateral file cabinet – Storage equipment that is wider than it is deep. A cabinet with drawers that open from the long side and looks like a chest of drawers or a book-shelf with doors.

leading zero – A zero added to the front of a number so that all numbers align on the right for computer sorting in numeric order.

lettered guide plan – An arrangement of geographic records in which primary guides are labeled with alphabetic letters.

light pen – A computer input device used for writing or sketching on a display screen.

local area network (LAN) – A group of micro-computers or workstations within the same building or within one mile of each other that are connected to enable transmission of information to one another and to share hardware and software.

location name guide plan – An arrangement of geographic records in which primary guides are labeled with location names.

M

magneto-optical disk – A rewritable optical disk.

magnification ratio – The relationship between the sizes of an image and the original record when viewed on a microfilm reader screen.

mainframe computer – A fast, large-capacity computer that organizations use to handle millions of transactions and data items.

management – The process of using an organization's resources to achieve specific goals through the functions of planning, organizing, leading, and controlling.

master index – A printed alphabetic listing in file order of all subjects (filing segments) used as subject titles in the filing system.

microcomputer – A desktop or notebook (por-table) computer that is widely used in offices, schools, and homes.

microfiche – A transparent sheet of microfilm, usually 6" by 4" in size, containing a series of microimages arranged in rows and columns with an identifying strip readable without magnification.

microfilm – A fine-grained, high-resolution film used to record microimages.

microfilm jacket – A transparent plastic carrier with single or multiple horizontal channels for inserting strips of 16mm or 35mm microfilm—cut from roll film.

microfilming – The process of photographing documents to reduce their size.

microform – A generic term for any medium containing miniaturized or microimages.

micrographics – The technology and processes used to record information in microform.

microimage – An image too small to be read without magnification.

microrecord – The minia-turized image of a document.

middle-digit storage – A numeric storage method in which the middle two or three digits of each number are used as the primary division under which a record is filed. Groups of numbers are read from the middle to left to right.

minicomputer – A scaled-down version of a mainframe computer; it has less data storage capacity and operates at a slower speed.

mobile aisle system – Mobile shelving that is electrically powered so that shelves can be moved to create an aisle between any two shelving units.

mobile shelving – Records storage shelves that move on tracks attached to the floor.

modem – An electronic device that transfers data from one computer to another computer using telephone lines.

motorized rotary stor-age – A motorized file unit that rotates horizontally around a central hub.

mouse – A device used to move a cursor on a display screen or to point and select specific operations that a computer is to perform.

multifunctional product – Equipment capable of performing two or more functions such as printing, faxing, copying, and scanning.

multimedia – Information that includes two or more data types: text, graphics, animation, video, or sound.

N

name index – A listing of correspondents' names stored in a subject file.

network – A linkage of computers that allows computer users to share peripheral devices, programs, and data.

nonconsecutive numbering – A numbering system that either has no logical sequence or has a logical sequence from which blocks of numbers have been omitted.

nonessential record – The least valuable record that should be destroyed after use.

numeric index – A current list of all files by the file numbers.

numeric records storage method – A storage method in which records are assigned numbers and then arranged in one of various numeric sequences.

O

official record – A document that is legally recognized as establishing some fact.

on-call (wanted) form – A written request for a record that is *out* of the file.

one-period transfer method – A method of transferring records from active storage at the end of one time period, usually once or twice a year, to inactive storage.

operating system – The computer's link between the computer hardware, the user, and the application software.

optical disk – A storage medium for digitally encoded information that is written and read by means of a laser.

optical disk library – A device that contains multiple optical disk platters, from one to five optical disk drives, and a robotic mechanism (picker) used to move platters to and from the drives. Also called a *jukebox*.

OUT folder – A special folder that replaces a folder that has been removed from storage.

OUT guide – A special guide that replaces any record that has been removed from storage and indicates what was taken and by whom.

OUT sheet – A form that is inserted in place of a record or records removed from a folder.

output – The desired product or service that a system produces.

P

password – A special word, code, or symbol that is required to access a computer system.

peer-to-peer LAN – A connection of microcomputers in a network to enable direct communication with one another without using a server.

periodic transfer method – A method of transferring active records at the end of a stated time period, usually one year, to inactive storage.

peripheral device – Hardware connected to a computer processing unit.

permanent cross-reference – A guide that replaces an individual folder to direct the filer to the correct storage place.

perpetual transfer method – A method of transferring records continuously from active to inactive storage areas whenever they are no longer needed for reference.

personal digital assistant (PDA) – A hand-held computer controlled by a pen similar to a stylus that processes handwritten commands and messages.

planetary camera – A microfilm camera that uses 35mm film to film large engineering drawings, hardbound books, and other large documents.

pocket folder – A folder with more expansion at the bottom edge than that of an ordinary folder.

portable reader – A magnification device that is small enough to be moved easily to various locations.

position – The location of a tab on a guide or folder.

posted record – A record containing information that is continually updated; also known as a *secondary record*

primary guide – A divider that identifies a main division of a file and always precedes all other material in a section.

primary (working) memory – Temporary internal computer storage that holds data being processed by a computer.

process – The operation of a system that changes its input.

processor – A machine used to develop microfilm.

R

random access memory (RAM) – A computer's working memory that serves as a temporary storage location for the software and data used at any one time during processing.

read only memory (ROM) – A permanent storage location for instructions a computer needs each time it is turned on.

reader-printer – A microform reader with the added capability of reproducing an enlarged microimage in hardcopy.

reader-viewer – A device that displays an enlarged microimage on a screen for reading the record.

record – Recorded information, regardless of media or characteristics, created or received, and used in the operation of an organization.

record copy – The official copy (usually the original) of a record that is retained for legal, operational, or historical purposes.

record life cycle – The life span of a record that includes five functional phases that occur from the creation of a record to its final disposition.

records and information management (RIM) – The company-wide controls over staff, equipment, and services that generate and maintain information.

records audit – A regular examination of the records management program to determine how well it is functioning.

records center – A centralized area usually in a lower cost facility for housing and servicing inactive records whose reference rate does not warrant their retention in the prime office area.

records inventory – A detailed listing of the volume of an organization's records. It includes quantity, type, function, location, frequency of use, and organization of the records obtained from a records survey.

records management – The systematic control of all records from their creation or receipt through their processing, distribution, organization, storage, and retrieval, and to their ultimate disposition.

records management manual – An official handbook of approved policies and procedures for operating the records management program.

records protection – Safeguarding records against intentional or unintentional destruction or damage and protecting record confidentiality.

records retention – Established policies and procedures relating to what documents to keep, where the documents are kept, and how long these documents are to be kept.

records retention schedule – A listing of an organization's records along with the stated length of time the records must be kept.

records series – A group of related records that are normally used and filed as a unit and can be evaluated as a unit to determine the records retention period.

records system – A group of interrelated resources— people, equipment and supplies, space, procedures, and information—acting together according to a plan to accomplish the goals of the records management program.

records transfer – The physical movement of active records from the office to inactive or archive storage areas.

reduction ratio – The relationship between the dimensions of the original record and the corresponding dimensions of the microimage.

redundant array of inexpensive disks (RAID) – A computer storage system that consists of over 100 disk drives in a single cabinet and that sends data simultaneously to a computer over parallel paths.

reference document – A record that contains information an organization needs to carry on its operations over long periods of time.

relative index – A dictionary-type listing of *all* possible words and combinations of words by which records may be requested.

release mark – An agreed-upon mark placed on a record showing that it is ready for storage.

requisition – A written request for a record or for information from a record.

resolution – A measure of the sharpness of lines or fine detail in an image.

retention period – The length of time, usually based on an estimate of the frequency of use for current and anticipated business, that records should be retained in offices or records centers before they are transferred to an archives or otherwise disposed of.

retrieval – The process of searching for and finding records and/or information.

retrieval efficiency ratio – A measure of the speed with which records are found and a verification of how filers spend their time.

rotary camera – A microfilm camera that uses rotating belts to carry documents through the camera and makes images on 16mm film at a speed of over 500 documents a minute.

rotary (wheel) equipment – A piece of equipment on which cards are attached to a frame that rotates on an axis similar to a wheel.

rough sorting – Arranging records according to sections but in random order within the sections.

S

scanner – A device that converts an image (text, graphic, or photograph) to electronic form for processing and storage.

secondary data storage – An electronic medium (such as a floppy disk or hard disk drive) that a computer uses as a more permanent storage for records transferred (saved) from its temporary working memory.

SecureRead field – A shaded box that holds confidential information on a form.

sequential storage – A method of organizing and accessing stored records in alphabetic or numeric order.

server – A computer that manages shared devices in a network.

shelf file – Side open shelving equipment in which records are accessed horizontally.

signal – A special marker used for drawing immediate attention to a specific record.

software – A package of programmed instructions that direct a computer in machine language to perform specific tasks or procedures in an exact sequence.

sorter – A device used to hold records temporarily and which serves to separate them into alphabetic or numeric categories to be stored later.

sorting – The act of arranging records in the sequence in which they are to be filed or stored.

special folder – A folder that follows special or auxiliary guides in an alphabetic arrangement.

special (auxiliary) guide – A guide that leads the eye to a specific place in a file.

special records – Records of unconventional size, shape, or weight commonly used in business and professional offices.

standard – A measure or yardstick by which the performance of a system or program is rated.

stationary reader – A magnification device that provides a large screen for viewing and a wide choice of optional features such as a hood to reduce glare.

step-and-repeat camera – A microfilm camera that produces a series of separate images, usually in orderly rows and columns for microfiche.

storage – The actual placement of records into a folder, on a section of magnetic disk, or on a shelf according to a plan.

storage (filing) method – A systematic way of storing records according to an alphabetic, subject, numeric, geographic, or chronologic arrangement.

storage procedures – A series of steps for the orderly arrangement of records as required by a specific storage method. The steps are inspecting, indexing, coding, cross-referencing, sorting, and storing.

storing – The actual placement of records into containers.

subject records storage method – The storage and retrieval of records by subject matter or topic.

subsystem – A grouping of interrelated components within a system that accomplishes one phase of a task.

suspension (hanging) folder – A folder with built-in hooks that hang from parallel bars on the sides of the storage equipment.

system – Related components that interact to accomplish a task. System, as used in records storage, means any storage plan devised by a storage equipment manufacturer.

system components – Related elements or resources (i.e., people, space, equipment, forms, related records, work procedures, and data) necessary to accomplish the system task.

systems approach – Using a company-wide perspective to look at the interrelated parts when solving organizational problems.

systems environment – Circumstances, objects, or conditions surrounding a system.

T

---

tab – The portion of a folder or guide that extends above the regular height or beyond the regular width of a folder or guide upon which the caption appears.

tab cut – The length of the tab expressed as a proportion of the width or height of the folder or guide—i.e., one-third cut means a tab is one-third the width or height of the folder or guide.

terminal-digit storage – A numeric storage method in which the last two or three digits of each number are used as the primary division under which a record is filed. Groups of numbers are read from right to left.

tickler file – A chronologic arrangement of information that "tickles" the memory and serves as a reminder that specific action must be taken on a specific date.

touch screen – A sensitized computer display screen that receives input from the touch of a finger.

trackball – A device used to move a cursor on a display screen or to point and select specific operations that a computer is to perform.

transaction document – A record a firm uses in its day-to-day operations.

turnaround time – The amount of time required to find and deliver a record to the requester after the request for the record has been made.

U

unit record – A record that contains one main item or piece of information.

useful record – A record that is helpful in conducting business operations and may, if destroyed, be replaced at slight cost.

V

variable data – Data that change each time a form is filled in.

vertical card file – A collection of card records that are stored on edge or in an upright position; also known as a *vertical file*.

vertical file cabinet – Storage equipment that is deeper than it is wide. Conventional storage cabinets are in one- to five-drawer sizes.

visible card file – A collection of records that are stored horizontally in an overlapping arrangement in which the bottom margin of each card is visible when the card is held and pulled out from the file cabinet; also known as a *visible file*.

vital record – A record that must be kept permanently because it is needed for continuing the firm's operations and is usually not replaceable.

voice mail – A computer-based message system (CBMS) that sends and receives voice messages electronically.

voucher – An accounting record used to confirm that a business transaction has occurred.

W

wide area network (WAN) – A communication link with computers scattered in a wide geographic region—a state, a country, or the world.

write once read many (WORM) disk – A nonerasable, nonrewritable optical disk.

Index